Sacrificing
Commentary

Sacrificing Commentary

Reading the End of Literature

Sandor Goodhart

The Johns Hopkins University Press
Baltimore and London

© 1996 Sandor Goodhart
All rights reserved. Published 1996
Printed in the United States of America on acid-free paper
05 04 03 02 01 00 99 98 97 96   5 4 3 2 1

The Johns Hopkins University Press
2715 North Charles Street
Baltimore, Maryland 21218-4319
The Johns Hopkins Press Ltd., London

ISBN 0-8018-5084-3

Library of Congress Cataloging-in-Publication Data
will be found at the end of this book.

A catalog record for this book is available
from the British Library.

*For my parents, Abraham and Evelyn,
my brother, Ray, and my children,
Joshua, Noah, and Jonah*

> . . . blood, like sacrificing Abel's, cries
> Even from the tongueless caverns of the earth
> To me for justice . . .
>
> William Shakespeare, *Richard II*

> On another occasion it happened that a certain heathen came before Shammai and said to him, "Make me a proselyte, on condition that you teach me the whole Torah while I stand on one foot." Thereupon he repulsed him with the builder's cubit which was in his hand. When he went before Hillel, he said to him, "What is hateful to you, do not to your neighbor: that is the whole Torah, while the rest is the commentary thereof; go and learn it."
>
> *Tractate Shabbath,* 31a

Contents

Preface and Acknowledgments   xi

Introduction: Literature, Criticism, and Reading   1

I. Literary Reading

1. *Lēstas Ephaske:* Oedipus and Laius's Many Murderers   13

2. "Being Nothing": Kings, Mirrors, and Subjects in Shakespeare's *Richard II*   42

II. Biblical Reading

3. "I am Joseph": Judaism, Anti-idolatry, and the Prophetic Law   99

4. Reading the Ten Commandments: Torah, Interpretation, and the Name of God   122

5. "Out of the Fish's Belly": Prophecy, Sacrifice, and Repentance in the Book of Jonah   139

6. "The End from the Beginning": Evil and Accusation in the Book of Job   168

III. Modern Reading

7. "Writing on Fire": The Holocaust, Witness, and Responsibility   215

Conclusion: Reading after Auschwitz   245

Notes   289

Works Cited   319

Index   345

Preface and Acknowledgments

The idea for this volume was born when I realized—in the course of working in the four fields from which these essays were drawn—that I was repeatedly struck by the same few complementary observations. In the first place, the writing that we customarily call "literature," or more precisely "great literature," and that we offer to ourselves as the object of our aesthetic contemplation turns out in fact to be a form of critical reading or commentary, a critical staging or dramatization of the very structures of difference—the myths or stories—of which it is composed. In the second place, the writing that has grown up around and attached itself to this "literature"—which we have called, at least within the Arnoldian tradition, "criticism" or "literary study" and which we have convinced ourselves "represents" this writing—in fact systematically displaces it, emptying it of its critical content and rewriting it in favor of the more familiar structures of difference criticism has expected.

Finally—and here for me is the most interesting part—the subject matter of this "inner" literary criticism or commentary turns out to be an account of the very displacement process criticism enacts in reading these texts as literature in the first place. It is not, in other words, just any myth or story that literature examines but the very myth criticism comes along and uncannily repeats, a myth that criticism found in the sources from which this writing emerged and that it substitutes for the monstrous and unsettling display now before it.

How has such a situation come about? How has it happened that academic literary criticism as we have constituted it since the beginning of the nineteenth century so egregiously misunderstands the nature of both its own project and that of the "literature" it reads? If literature is not the sacralized body of writing criticism fashions it to be, but a reading of such sacrificial processing, how does a given set of texts come to assume such a dislocated status?

I recognized that in pursuing these questions notions like "accident" would be of little help. I began to ask myself whether such avoidance and symptomatic replaying by criticism of the very deconstructive activity under analysis was structural, whether, for example, criticism was not simply "blind" to what literature was doing but missed this internal mirroring of its projects systematically, less in spite of that literary activity than because of it, as the consequence of some deliberate, constitutional, segregational, critical procedure yet to be disclosed. But what procedure? What purpose could such a displacement process serve within a larger academic humanistic economy, a substitutive critical apparatus that, while not entirely excluding the texts to which it attaches itself, maintains them in such a transfigured, constrained, and transcendental fashion?

Such discoveries and questions turned my guiding assumptions about literature and literary study inside out. I quickly surmised that the inquiry I was developing was larger than any I could encompass within a single essay. As a first step toward exploring some of these problems, I decided to set some of the studies I had undertaken side by side, to see what insights might be gleaned from their unaccustomed proximity.[1] The result is the book that follows.

※　※　※

Four of the essays that follow appeared previously in earlier versions in *Diacritics, Stanford French Review, Semeia,* and *Philosophy and Literature*. Permission to reprint portions of this material in chapters 1, 3, 5, and 7 is gratefully acknowledged.

Several people have been kind enough to read and comment upon these studies in various stages of their development. Jonathan Bishop, Tony Brinkley, Tony Caputi, Rabbi Laurence Edwards, Sander Gilman, and Suzanne Stewart read substantial portions of the manuscript. Gordon Kirkwood introduced me to the subtleties of the ancient Greek language. Meyer Abrams, Cynthia Chase, Jonathan Culler, Neil Hertz, Phil Lewis, Piero Pucci, and Edgar Rosenberg read and encouraged my work on Sophocles in the 1970s. Ross Chambers, Mike Clark, Julie Ellison, Ellen Fine, Carolyn Forché, Lea Hamaoui, Geoffrey Hartman, Patrick Henry, Patty Joplin, Ira Konigsberg, Paisley Livingston, Andrew McKenna, Scott McMillin, Phil Mitsis, Richard Prystowsky, Herman Rappaport, Enrico Santí, Toby Siebers, and Steven Youra read and commented upon individual essays. I thank all of these individuals for their suggestions and kindnesses.

I thank Wallace Martin in particular who read the manuscript in its entirety for the Press and whose careful and thoughtful questionings were among the most probing and helpful responses I received. The book is better for them. I thank Eric Halpern, editor-in-chief of the Johns Hopkins University Press, who saw the value of this project from the first and saw it through to its completion. And I thank Barbara Lamb and Carol Zimmerman, who guided its progress from editing through production.

My children, Joshua, Noah, and Jonah, have waited patiently and lovingly for me to complete this project. They have my unceasing love, gratitude, and affection. I also thank my brother, Ray, and my parents, Abraham and Evelyn, for their continued love and support.

The influence of one individual in these pages is pervasive and more difficult to specify. My engagement with the work of my teacher and friend, René Girard, has been constant and active throughout my academic career. Girard's analyses of the structurative mechanism of the sacrificial in human communities and of the anti-sacrificial as a response to human violence (as revealed to us in our greatest literature and scripture) have seemed to me only increasingly powerful over the years.[2] It has been Girard's example—his boundless generosity, honesty, fortitude, and courage of spirit—that has compelled me to examine my own Judaic tradition and to discover there a richness and plenitude that as a child I did not dream possible.

If here or there in the course of these pages I appear to "catch him on the hip" in a sacrificial move of his own, I am reminded of Jacob's encounter just before his reconciliation with his brother Esau. Alone, and yet somehow wrestling all night with a divine stranger and at length extracting a blessing from him, he awakes only to find *himself* crippled and newly named, "Israel." Moreover, that name confers upon him (as it did upon his grandfather Abraham) the Adamic capability to bestow names in turn: upon the place where this face-to-face encounter occurred (Peniel, "face of God"), and upon the community that remembers the encounter in rituals that bear its traces (Israel, "one who struggles with God"). And that blessing (or wound) leads him in turn to bless his own grandchildren, Ephraim and Manasseh, the children of Joseph, in such a way that one should not come before or supplant the other, a movement that thus completes a history begun at the beginning of Torah with the murderous offspring of Adam and Eve, and that prepares the way for a greater revelation still to come, one that will be given to another shepherd who "turned aside to see."

In Judaism, at the altar, before the ark of the covenant, in the place where older cultures would identify a sacrificial victim, one discovers a text—a teaching, a *torah*—which speaks anti-sacrificially of that victimage from one end to the other. In place of sacrificing a victim, one intones or recites or reads this text, which is taken itself as the trace of an encounter with the infinitely Other and as such the foundation of ethical response.

In the shadow of Auschwitz, no reading, no encounter, and no response is more urgent. The Messiah will not come, the rabbis are fond of saying, until the tears of Esau will be exhausted.

Sacrificing Commentary

Introduction

Literature, Criticism, and Reading

Two passages drawn from the work of Paul de Man may help us to situate the studies that follow. The first, from the preface to *Blindness and Insight,* his earliest collection of critical essays, written at the outset of the phase of his career for which he was until recently the best known, takes up the relation of criticism to literature.[1] The second, from an essay published originally in *Yale French Studies* in 1982 entitled "The Resistance to Theory" and reprinted shortly after his death as the lead-off essay in a volume of the same name, offers a report on the success of some efforts on the contemporary theoretical scene to pursue the concern with reading he had earlier advocated, a scene that was itself, before its unexpected prominence, staunchly resisted.[2]

> Why then complicate matters further by choosing to write on critics when one could so easily find less ambivalent examples of literary texts among poets or novelists? The reason is that prior to theorizing about literary language, one has to become aware of the complexities of reading. And since critics are a specifically self-conscious and specialized kind of reader, these complexities are displayed with particular clarity in their work. They do not occur with the same clarity to a spontaneous non-critical reader who is bound to forget the mediations separating the text from the particular meaning that now captivates his attention. Neither are the complexities of reading easily apparent in a poem or a novel, where they are so deeply embedded in the language that it takes extensive interpretation to bring them to light. Because critics deal more or less openly with the problem of reading, it is a little easier to read a critical text *as text*—i.e. with an awareness of the reading process involved—than to read other literary works in this manner. The study of critical texts, however, can never be an end in itself and has value only as a preliminary to the understanding of literature in general. The problems involved in critical reading reflect the distinctive characteristics of literary language.[3]
>
> This conclusion allows for a somewhat more systematic description of the contemporary theoretical scene. This scene is dominated by an increased stress on reading as a theoretical problem. . . . And

since the models that are being used are no longer *simply* intentional and centered on an identifiable self, nor *simply* hermeneutic in the postulation of a single originary, pre-figural and absolute text, it would appear that this concentration on reading would lead to the rediscovery of the theoretical difficulties associated with rhetoric. This is indeed the case, to some extent; but not quite. Perhaps the most instructive aspect of contemporary theory is the refinement of the techniques by which the threat inherent in rhetorical analysis is being avoided at the very moment when the efficacy of these techniques has progressed so far that the rhetorical obstacles to understanding can no longer be mistranslated in thematic and phenomenal commonplaces. The resistance to theory which, as we saw, is a resistance to reading, appears in its most rigorous and theoretically elaborated form among the theoreticians of reading who dominate the contemporary theoretical scene.[4]

De Man's claim in these passages is bound to surprise readers more accustomed to remembering him as the theorist par excellence of secondary texts, as the doughty practitioner of a certain style of rhetorical criticism at Yale, or as a critic with considerably more ironic and distant approaches toward "literature in general." For here at both the outset and the conclusion of a phase of his career in which his work was beginning to assume major importance in this country, he articulates an allegiance that places him as much at odds with the increasingly vocal, admiring, and later dominant cadre of younger deconstructive critics as it does with older literary apologists who would find in great literature or literary language an enduring reservoir of humanistic value.

For his primary concern, he tells us in the first passage, is in fact with primary "literature" and what interests him in particular about this literature is that it is a form of critical reading. If he turns to secondary texts, and in particular to critical texts written by writers who are themselves also acclaimed literary artists, he does so because "the problems involved in critical reading" (which for him "reflect the distinctive characteristics of literary language") are "a little easier to read" in this slightly more "self-conscious" setting than they are in literary texts where such "complexities" are more often "so deeply embedded in the language" that it requires "extensive interpretation to bring them to light." It is easier to read critical texts "*as texts,*" he argues, "with an awareness of the reading process involved." But the first step of this reading lesson as it has come to be called, "can never be an end in itself and has value only as a preliminary to the understanding of literature in general," from which in fact these reading complexities or complications originate.[5]

And in the second passage, if he appears to deviate somewhat from his earlier concern, to immerse himself more specifically in rhetorical considerations, to inquire whether this new theoretical movement which advertised "an increased stress on reading" has indeed overcome the difficulties attendant upon earlier critics, the appearance may be misleading. Several years had passed since the publication of the earlier book. The abundant energy with which American new criticism after World War II promoted the Arnoldian project of close critical reading of literary works had begun to give way in the 1960s, in the name of "critical theory" coming largely (although not exclusively) from France, to a new concern with language and texts. Although in 1971, when de Man's first collection from Oxford appeared, "structuralism" or "poststructuralism" had still not gained a foothold within departments of language and literature, by the early 1980s that was no longer the case.[6] And the shift now inspired—especially among older humanistic readers—a massive resistance.[7]

What de Man wonders in the second passage is whether there is something instructive to be read in this new phenomenon, with regard to both the older approaches now doing the resisting and with regard to the newer approaches being resisted. In the first place, he notes, the current resistance to theory is in fact the *same* "resistance to reading" that had always been practiced by this group (and that he had earlier observed), a resistance, that is to say, to the problematizing of reading which these younger theoreticians were now simply enacting.[8] Is not this current humanist resistance to theory, he asks, a resistance, as before, to textualization, to "reading textually," with the difference that this time the object being resisted manifests itself as a concern with "the rhetorical or tropological dimension of language" localized and concretized in the figure of these younger and more linguistically minded critics. "The resistance to theory," de Man writes in the second essay just above the quoted passage, "is a resistance to the rhetorical or tropological dimension of language, a dimension which is perhaps more explicitly in the foreground in literature (broadly conceived) than in other verbal manifestations or—to be somewhat less vague—which can be revealed in any verbal event when it is read textually."[9]

On the other hand, this current resistance, by virtue of the defensive posture it assumes, may also reveal something interesting about the very theoreticians who would advocate such textual or linguistic reading, as if resistance were somehow less a historical by-product of the course these theoreticians chose to pursue than endemic to the critical activity itself, "built-in" perhaps to any theoretical undertaking. "It may well be . . . ," de Man writes, "that the development of literary theory is itself overdetermined by complications inherent in its very project and unsettling with regard to its status as a scientific discipline. Resistance may be a built-in constituent of its discourse" and "the polemical opposition . . . the displaced symptoms of a resistance inherent in the theoretical enterprise itself."[10]

How so? One of the consequences of such a "polemical opposition" of older critics to younger is that the presuppositions of each group suddenly become clearer. Thus it now appears, de Man says, that the older methods depended upon two models currently in jeopardy: namely, the "intentional" model, founded upon an "identifiable" subject or "self," and the "hermeneutic" model of a "single originary pre-figural and absolute" object or "text." In the face of the uncertainties or indeterminacies presented by literature, these older, Kantian aesthetic and cognitive models predictably avoided "the threat of rhetorical analysis" by mistranslating "rhetorical obstacles to understanding" into "thematic and phenomenal commonplaces."

Along comes this new critical method, built from the semiological concerns that have concretized in France in "structural linguistics" around the work of Saussure, Jakobson, Benveniste, and others, emphasizing the priority of language to both subject and object (and, as a result, thematizing textualization and cognizing reading), and it begins to look—especially to its newest enthusiasts—as if the former "obstacles" are about to be overcome.

"Not quite," de Man observes. Privileging one or another aspect of the classical *trivium*—grammar at the expense of rhetoric or logic, rhetoric at the expense of grammar or logic—literary theory that derives from these French models repeats the same procedures of formalization and interpretation that obstructed the older views. Theorizing literature, which is to say, rendering it "teachable," systematizable, "generalizable," they displace the radical resistance to systematicity constituting literature itself. Far from addressing the "complexities of reading" that older critics avoided, these newer approaches resist them no less thoroughly, if somewhat less obviously, by virtue, moreover, of the very theoretical posture by which they would attempt to overcome such obstacles. "Rhetorical readings," de Man concludes, "like the other kinds, still avoid and resist the reading they advocate. Nothing can overcome the resistance to theory since theory *is* itself this resistance. The loftier the aims and the better the methods of literary theory, the less possible it becomes."[11] Resistance to theory is also the resistance of theory, the resistance or avoidance of literature that theory both practices and constitutes.

Far from shunning, in other words, the "complexities of reading" in primary literary texts for one or another analysis of secondary critical vocabularies, de Man's later essay would appear—in these descriptions of internecine critical battles—to have embraced the question of literary dynamics even more fully than before, although in a manner somewhat unexpected perhaps by his earlier readers. The textual reading advocated in the earlier essay and dismissed implicitly by its new critical practitioners is perceived by de Man as being dismissed no less thoroughly in the later essay, although the expression of this dismissal has now assumed two new and alternative forms: a resistance to theory on the one hand, and a theoretization of literature on the other. And in this current double avoidance of literature (and/or critical reading)—explicit in the first case, implicit in the second—the internal dynamics of literary reading *as* such avoidance or resistance are suddenly highlighted. "Nothing can overcome the resistance to theory," de Man writes, "since theory *is* itself this resistance." Neither therefore can any critical analysis effectively theorize literary language since literature is already also that theorization, the same resistance, in other words, to conceptual and analytic thinking that humanist criticism has been practicing all along and that literary theory has now begun to practice—although undertaken within literature at a greater order of complexity, and somewhat more "deeply embedded" within an avowedly fictional economy. The greater our degree of theoretical sophistication about literary matters, the less our understanding of the literary language from which we have borrowed (without acknowledgment) such sophistication, a literary language that is itself nothing other than an examination of the limitations of such interpretation and formalization, and that thus continues to mirror both our pro-theoretical and anti-theoretical stances all the more clearly as our failures—both to succeed in theorizing it and to perceive these identities—become increasingly evident and costly.

De Man's increased attention to reading complexities in these "secondary," extra-literary contexts, in other words, leads to an enhanced conception of "literature in general" precisely in so far as literature is revealed to be the staging already of the modalities of its own avoidance or resistance, the original literary theory, so to speak, which formal critical response in one manner or another unceasingly and unwittingly rejects and enacts. "The resistance to theory is a resistance to the rhetorical or tropological dimension of language, a dimension which is perhaps more explicitly in the foreground *in literature* (broadly conceived) than in other verbal manifestations . . ." (emphasis added). Literature, for de Man (perhaps to his readers's surprise), needs no supplementary "deconstructive" analysis—as de Man came eventually to call his analytic method, borrowing the word from Jacques Derrida (who borrowed it from Heidegger).[12] Rather, what is required is the recognition and pursuit of the deconstructive analysis in which literature is always already engaging and its application to the multifarious critical contexts—theoretical, humanistic, or other—into which such resistance or theory is repeatedly "mistranslated." "The reading is not *our* reading," de Man insists, in the opening essay to *Allegories of Reading*. "The deconstruction is not something we have added to the text but it constituted the text in the first place. . . . Poetic [or literary] writing is the most advanced and refined mode of deconstruction; it may differ from critical or discursive writing in the economy of its articulation, but not in kind."[13]

One way, then, to describe the volume that follows would be to say that it attempts the "second step" of the project de Man announces in these two passages, to move from the "preliminary" concern with critical texts to the more difficult exegesis of the "complexities of reading" somewhat closer to home—within the domain of "literature in general."

And indeed, at least six of the essays that follow may be said to attempt such a study within some of our most powerful cultural exemplars: in plays by Sophocles and Shakespeare, and in passages from the Hebrew Bible. In each case, these essays are concerned with the way in which the literary or scriptural texts examined constitute a reading, which is to say, a powerful and comprehensive critical examination or staging of the differential structures, the myths or stories, out of which this literature has come and which we in turn bring to its study: an examination, that is to say, less of the stories themselves than of the appropriative gestures in which they function, whether such gestures occur "within" the text, in the figure of its characters—or without, in the figure of critical movements that come along and duplicate or act out the same misunderstandings.

The chapter on Sophocles, for example, stages the way in which certain ideas concerning fate or destiny developed by the first generations of German Romantics for reading the play Aristotle so prized (and for which ideas Hegel may serve as a convenient spokesman) are already at stake within it, within Oedipus's own appropriative mythogenetic response to the enigmatic circumstances surrounding him (by which he determines he is guilty of parricide and incest), and within the Chorus's surprising sacrificial endorsement of that oracular appropriation as evidence of the power of the gods (and especially of destiny, or *moira*) in human affairs.

The chapter on *Richard II* suggests some of the ways in which certain aesthetic and historical critical interpretations developed by humanist Shakespeareans in the nineteenth and early twentieth centuries to account for this dramatization of the medieval English king's deposition are already at work in the play itself, forming in fact the very substance in the early scenes of Richard's damaging conception of his own monarchical authority, then of his struggle with Henry Bolingbroke to retain that authority, and finally of his prisonhouse prophetic speech on the interchangeability of his own (and Henry's) histories, a conception and struggle which in turn Henry systematically repeats.

In the next four chapters, I turn to religious scripture—the Hebrew Bible—to ask whether the same dynamics of inner commentary and outer transfiguration and reenactment are operative in texts where the stake is less fiction or story than revelation. I look at passages on Joseph, Jonah, Job, and the Ten Commandments and at some of the ways in which interpretative readings of these biblical writings—both within and without the major Judaic exegetical traditions (talmudic, midrashic, esoteric, and later rabbinic)—duplicate dilemmas already at stake within Torah. The mimetic and sacrificial dynamics operative initially between Joseph and his brothers echo the opposition of traditional historical and prophetic accounts by which the story has customarily been read. The ongoing and infinite narration by which the revelation of the law of anti-idolatry to Moses at Sinai may be codified into a discrete list of divine commandments or instructions turns out to entail the same issues of distinguishability and hermeneutic principle already at stake within this brief scriptural text. The idolatrous premise by which Jonah would reserve the law of anti-idolatry for the Israelites alone before he is offered God's "object lesson" reflects the traditional interpretative conflict between older rabbinic readings which endorse Jonah's reluctance to prophesy to the Ninevites on historical grounds and more modern readings which take this Yom Kippur liturgical reading as a parable of universal compassion. The successive mythic, institutional, and humanistic contexts by which the Book of Job would appear to question the existence of evil and suffering—before the order of creation and the law of anti-idolatry are revealed—duplicates the mythic, formalistic, humanistic, creational, and even anti-religious terms in which this most familiar of "Old Testament" texts (and by extension Judaism and the Jewish God) is commonly read.

In the remaining chapter, as a kind of test case to a theory of reading pursued thus far within strictly canonic literature and scripture, I wonder whether the same kind of domesticating representational critical readings reproduce themselves in circumstances where the traumatic nature of the founding violence is more intensely historical and "real," moreover, within the community the most categorically affected by such violence. I observe some of the ways in which Yiddish poet and playwright Halpern Leivick "acts out" in his autobiographical writing the same critical dynamics that other Jewish writers at roughly the same moment (for example, Lithuanian French teacher and philosopher Emmanuel Levinas) would prophetically identify as internal to the historical, biblical, and literary contexts about which he is speaking.

There are thus at least three distinct and yet continuous levels on which the studies in this book will be conducted and which the first part of the title reflects. In the first instance, this will be a book about *criticism*, the institutional literary activity we engender around the writing we have constructed as "literature" and that expels or "sacrifices" what it reads, transforming the presumed object of its reading in the specifically differential or mythic manner in which it sees fit to do so. In the second, it will be a book about the inner literary criticism or *commentary* such criticism gives up or expels when it reads in such a displacing and sacralizing fashion. Finally, it will be a commentary about the topic of *sacrificing* itself to the extent that such sacrificial dynamics turn out to make up the very subject matter of such inner commentary, a "sacrificing" thus that literature reveals and that criticism, in reading literary writing sacrificially, enacts.

In this way, the book is offered as a first step toward a comprehensive theory of literary reading. As we have understood literary reading—at least within the Anglo-American community—in primarily Arnoldian terms, such a theory may be seen as an attempt to spell an end to such a sacrificial understanding of terms like "literature" or "criticism," an end pursued by revealing these sacrificial mechanisms as their secret goal or aim. In place of that sacralizing and expulsive understanding I propose reading, which is to say, the consideration of such literary critical dynamics from an anti-sacrificial perspective, one which is in fact already (ironically), I suggest, literature's own. In the conclusion or "afterward,"

I offer, in some seven or so propositions, a rudimentary sketch of such a theory and take up some of the more tricky and weighty questions of method and moment it poses.

But the volume that follows is admittedly not written in a style that either Paul de Man or his followers would readily recognize as familiar. The anthropological language of "sacrificial crisis" and "ritual violence," the psychoanalytic language of "Oedipal conflict" and generational or sibling rivalry, the philosophico-religious language of "prophecy," the "law of anti-idolatry," and the "radical alterity of divinity"—all these ways of talking are much closer to the vocabularies of René Girard, Freud, Martin Buber, and Emmanuel Levinas than to the Heideggerian (and specifically "rhetorical" or "tropological") concerns of the late Belgian deconstructor.

Moreover, to invoke Paul de Man as an authority or predecessor in one's enterprise these days is considerably more risky and complicated a gesture than it was just a short while ago. More than one surprise awaits the sympathetic reader of his work. The revelations at the end of the 1980s by a zealous graduate student of the young writer's wartime journalism lend an unexpected poignancy to this theorist of avoidance, resistance, and duplicity (and to his silence concerning this earlier period), one that intensifies in difficult ways in light of a growing interest today in the effect of the Holocaust upon humanistic study. The "reading lesson" of Paul de Man, or perhaps more succinctly, of the "de Man affair," would seem to constitute something like the limit case for any theory of literary reading that, like the present one, is also concerned with ethics.[14]

Nor is Paul de Man the only theorist of reading on the contemporary theoretical scene. Geoffrey Hartman, Harold Bloom, Jacques Derrida, J. Hillis Miller—to name only the most well known of the so-called "Yale critics" (and to leave unmentioned many other perspectives)—could all legitimately lay claim to this distinction, to a concern with a certain interchangeability of literature with commentary.[15] We need to ask more precisely how de Man's theory of reading differs from theirs or, perhaps more appropriately, how ours differs from either. Such an inquiry will inevitably turn upon the status we attribute to the representational foundation upon which such "tropological" conceptions of language are based, a foundation that may well prove more problematic than we have allowed, and may in fact index a diachronic prophetic logic larger than the synchronic ontologizing logic which, within the Platonic Aristotelian matrix, would transfigure and displace it.

Finally, there remains one further hesitation that must be voiced before too quickly acceding to a characterization of this volume as "de Manian" or, more generally, "deconstructive." It is one that admittedly arises out of my own concern with the ancient Greek and Judaic world and the modality of the prophetic. But it is also one that derives in part from my concern with the profound historical and cultural upheavals to which we have been witness since the beginning of the century in Europe, upheavals which may index larger cultural shifts.

Whatever else it teaches us, the "naturalization" of French critical thinking, as Jeffrey Mehlman once characterized it, that has taken place over the past thirty-five years or so in this country dictates that we need to concern ourselves anew with fundamental questions: about the nature of language, writing, and culture; but also (and perhaps even more pressingly) about the constitution of these systems of distinction locally as power and globally as the sacred and religious transcendence. If structuralist and poststructuralist thought moves us (and I suggest it does so profoundly), if we find in the work of these writers a new access to older European thinking, to Saussure, Durkheim, Freud, Marx, Kant, Hegel, Kierkegaard, Nietzsche, Husserl, Heidegger, and others, I would suggest it is because for some time now we have been slowly awakening from the twenty-year slumber we permitted ourselves following the traumatic appearance in Germany and elsewhere from 1933 to 1945 of the price of Romanticism.

Suddenly, in other words, I would suggest, we are beginning to feel the first stirrings of our implication in and responsibility for the thought that, from Goethe to Hitler, has been in Europe irremediably *our* thought. We are beginning to ask once again the kinds of questions to which two hundred years ago Kant's critical formalism and Hegel's humanistic and apocalyptic theology—to take only the most influential examples—were themselves already a response, questions about the origin of the human community and in particular about the relationship it sustains between survival and violence. It occurs to me that it is at this level that the architects of the religico-philosophical readings of the opening decades of our century need to be examined, that the question of the ontological and the holy on one hand, and of the dialogistic and the ethical on the other, must be posed, and that the most compelling justification and most accurate description for a book in America in the 1990s on the dynamics of critical reading and the end or ends of literature and literary study must be sought.

I
Literary Reading

1

Lēstas Ephaske
Oedipus and Laius's Many Murderers

> The problem of the value of truth came before us—or was it we who came before the problem? Who of us is Oedipus here? Who the Sphinx? It is a rendezvous, it seems, of questions and question marks.
>
> Friedrich Nietzsche, *Beyond Good and Evil*

> Numberless are the pains I bear; and the whole of my people is sick, and they have no weapon devised by thought, with which a man can defend himself . . . one person after another you may see, like a swift-winged bird, speeding faster than irresistible fire towards the shore of the western god. Numberless in these, our city is being destroyed.
>
> Sophocles, *Oedipus Tyrannus*

We are accustomed to believing that we understand Sophocles' treatment of the Oedipus myth.[1] The priest of Zeus appeals to Oedipus for help against the deadly pestilence which is emptying the Theban polis. Learning from the Delphic oracle that the pollution will end when the murderer of the former Theban monarch is found and banished, Oedipus champions Laius "as if he had been my father" (263) and undertakes an investigation on his behalf. He consults the prophet Teiresias, his kinsman Creon, and his wife Jocasta. He summons the lone surviving witness of the Phocial massacre, a man who turns out to be a servant of the house of Laius. And when he discovers at last not only that he is "the killer of the man whose killer [he is] seeking" (362) but that the slain man was his father and the woman with whom he is living (and with whom he has borne children) his mother—that he is, in short, guilty of parricide and incest as the Delphic oracle predicted long ago he would be—he acts swiftly and decisively. He gouges out his eyes. He prophesies disaster for his children. And he demands to be exiled in accordance with his own decree to a beggarly existence on the slopes of Mount Cithaeron.

We feel, that is, that Sophocles' presentation is purely expository, simply an elaboration of the mythic material of which it is composed, material that is in outline at least as old as Homer.[2] Moreover, we seem to agree in general on how the story is to be understood. Elaborating upon Aristotle's notion of *hamartia* in the *Poetics,* we take Sophocles' play as the classic example of the tragedy of destiny.[3] Emphasizing the wonderful divergence between intention and consequence—the fact, for example, that it is ironically Oedipus's efforts to avoid fulfillment of the myth that bring it about—we see in the drama the powers of the gods in human affairs. If we point out, on one hand, its awe-inspiring instruction and, on the other, the terrible price in human suffering that such instruction occasions, we recognize commonly in the play the relentless force of "Greek necessity."[4]

But the situation may be more complicated than it appears. After Teiresias has accused Oedipus of the most baleful crimes and after Oedipus, in response to Jocasta's tale of Laius's death, has confessed his adventures on the Phocial highway and begun to fear "the prophet can see" (747), a curious series of events occurs. Oedipus suggests there is a technical disparity between the account Jocasta has related and his own recollection, and that in view of this disparity he might yet be innocent. His one slight hope (*elpidos,* 836), he asserts, is that the man who alone escaped from the Phocial massacre (and whom he has summoned to testify on the matter) will confirm the circulating account in all of its particulars—that the murderers of Laius were many and not one. If the Herdsman indicates a single murderer, then culpability for the crime would seem to incline uniquely towards Oedipus. But if the Herdsman speaks of many murderers, then it would seem just as clear—since Oedipus acted alone—that Oedipus is innocent of the Phocial guilt. The one and the many cannot be the same (*ou gar genoit' an heis ge tois pollois isos,* 845).

Jocasta assures Oedipus that if in fact the Herdsman does now alter his previous story, he will face the censure of everyone since all the city heard him and not just she alone. Moreover, the Chorus of Theban Elders, who are as eager as anyone to find a solution to the Phocial enigma—and thereby to end the Theban plague—caution as well that whatever hope there is (*ech' elipida,* 835) should be maintained until the full truth of the matter is revealed.

If we were in the genre of detective story, we might expect at this point that the witness would be brought on, questioned on the matter for which he was summoned, and the full truth made plain.[5] But when the Herdsman in Sophocles' play arrives, rather than confirm either the circumstantial version that Oedipus fears or the empirical version on which his salvation hinges, he is completely silent on the matter of the Phocial slaughter. In the interim between his summoning and his arrival, the Corinthian messenger has appeared and shifted the action to the question of Oedipus's origin, to the linking of the history of Oedipus with the house of Laius. And it is to this issue exclusively that the Herdsman's remarks are addressed. It is not that the Herdsman skirts the issue of the Phocial murder but that it never comes up. On the issue for which he was summoned, the issue on which the solution of the play's mystery depends, he is simply never questioned. We know no more after he appears than we knew before. Oedipus may have been right all along. His hope has gone unchallenged. Oedipus may not have killed Laius.[6]

If we find such a possibility rather curious, it may be less that the textual evidence is equivocal than that we have taken our cue from the best of sources—from the one figure in the play who has the most to gain, it would appear, from registering clearly any equivocation the Herdsman has to offer. For Oedipus himself makes no less of a gesture of mythic appropriation than we do. When the Herdsman dissolves the last bit of doubt on the origin of Oedipus in the house of Laius, Oedipus declares the truth he has learned:

> Alas, alas! All fulfilled, all true! O light, let me now look on you for the last time, I who have been revealed as born from whom I ought not [to have been born], associating with whom I ought not, and having killed whom I should not / . . . (1182–85)

Oedipus responds, that is, as if the Herdsman *had* implicated him in the Phocial murder. He declares himself guilty of parricide and incest and anticipates his removal from the Theban populace even according to his own decrees. What is more, the Chorus of Theban Elders who have maintained throughout the play their independence from both the accusations of Teiresias and the portents of Oedipus's confession now join Oedipus in denouncing his catastrophic fortune, and proclaim in a pious Herodotean morality the exemplary pattern, the *paradeigma,* that his life, henceforth, will constitute (1193–94).

What could be Sophocles' interest in constructing his play in such a fashion? What could be his purpose in undermining the mythic pattern to such an extent that if we follow the play closely, it is Oedipus's gesture of appropriation of the myth that comes into focus rather than the myth itself, that it is only if we proceed like Oedipus to read the myth *a priori*, to substitute what we do not see for what we do, that the mythic pattern is revealed?

Sophocles could have resolved the matter simply. Oedipus could have questioned the Herdsman on the Phocial murder, and the old servant, under threat of reprisal for his continued silence, could have uttered the truth: "You yourself would best know the course of these events, sire, for you yourself are the unique murderer." Countless dramatic representations of the Oedipus myth have of course done as much.[7]

Shall we allow ourselves the luxury of believing that the Herdsman's testimony has been lost and that we might reasonably supply it ourselves? It suffices, of course, to consult the edition of Richard Jebb to recognize the remoteness of the Byzantine manuscripts which found most texts from anything like an original Sophoclean copy.[8]

Or, is there another way of viewing what appears to be an antimythic gesture on Sophocles' part, a positive reading of the play on the basis of such a gesture that brings to light aspects of the drama we have simply never read before, that raises serious questions concerning the means by which we have read the play, means that may have inhibited us from reading such a gesture all along?

※　　※　　※

The response of critics to this scene is instructive. Gilbert Norwood, in *Greek Tragedy*, finds the part played by "the aged Theban" in Sophocles' drama "especially pointed."

> The *Oedipus Tyrannus* has been universally admired as a masterpiece, ever since the time of Aristotle, who in his *Poetic* [sic] takes this play as a model of tragedy. The lyrics are simple, beautiful, and even passionately vigorous; the dialogue in language and rhythm is beyond praise; and the tragic irony, for which this poet is famous, is here at its height. But the chief splendour of the work is its construction, its strictly dramatic strength and sincerity. The events grow out of one another with the ease of actual life yet with the accuracy and the power of art. We should note the two great stages: first, the king fears that he has slain Laius; second, that he has slain *his father Laius*. This distinction, so vital to the growing horror, is kept admirably clear and is especially pointed by the part of the aged Theban. When he is summoned, it is to settle whether Laius was slain by one man or by a company; by the time he arrives, this is forgotten, and all wait to know from whom he received the outcast infant.[9]

Certainly, if with Norwood we assume the myth, then Sophocles' constructive skill is masterful. The issue of regicide for which the Herdsman was summoned becomes significantly less interesting once the Corinthian appears, the concern of the inquiry is shifted to the birth and history of Oedipus in the house of Laius, and the singular gravity of the Herdsman's truth becomes evident.

But what if we do not presume the myth? What if we allow the story to unfold as Sophocles has presented it to us? Then Norwood's argument may beg the question it raises, and what Norwood assures us is "forgotten" may become, in fact, curiously conspicuous. In the Sophoclean context in which the Herdsman appears—precisely as the means by which the issue of the many or the one is to be resolved, as the only independent means available for determining whether Oedipus killed Laius at all—what may remain "admirably clear" is the distinction between the mythic pattern we expect and the muddled and equivocal sequence that occurs, between the absolute judgment that Oedipus, with Norwood's approval, makes of his situation, and the empirical obscurities to which we ourselves, through Oedipus, have been made witness.

Is the absence of the Herdsman's reference to Phocis an isolated issue in the play? Are there other means for determining Oedipus's Phocial guilt? Or is the issue of Phocis, perhaps, less important than it would first appear?

Far from isolated, the Herdsman's silence on Phocis is part of a critical pattern. The oracle in Creon's report, upon which so much depends, speaks distinctly of a multiplicity of murderers. "Apollo now clearly commands us to punish with [heavy] hand his murderers, whoever they may be" (*tous autoentas cheiri timōrein tinas,* 107).

Oedipus questions Creon immediately about the death of Laius at Phocis and his kinsman relates that the lone surviving witness of the Phocial massacre said with certainty one thing alone, that the murderers of Laius were many and not one. "He said that bandits fell in with them and killed them, not with a single strength, but with a large number of hands" (*lēstas ephaske syntychontas ou mia / rhōmē ktanein nin, alla syn plēthei cherōn,* 122–23).

Oedipus presses the Chorus for further information on the ancient crime and the Theban Elders confirm an "obscure" story (290) that Laius was said to have met his death at the hands of "certain travelers" (*pros tinōn hodoiporōn,* 292), a report that, Oedipus confirms straightaway, he too has heard. When Teiresias arrives, Oedipus questions the aged seer on the matter and, in the course of elaborating the details of the crisis, repeats the report that the oracle commanded that we punish Laius's murderers. "Phoebus . . . in answer to our question sent a message that deliverance from this plague could come only if we discovered those who killed Laius (*tous ktanontas Laion*) and either killed them or sent them out of the land to exile" (305–9).

Diverted for a time by the curious accusations of the blind prophet and by his own concern that Teiresias and Creon did the deed and have now conspired against him, Oedipus learns, when he turns to question Jocasta on the death of her late husband, the same information he has heard at least three times before. Using the same word that Creon used in reporting the account of the witness (*lēstas*), Jocasta relates that Laius was said to have been killed by "foreign bandits" (*xenoi . . . lēstai*, 715–16).

The point is critical at this moment in the play. For although Oedipus fears from the circumstances surrounding Laius's death as Jocasta has explained them that Teiresias may have been right, it is upon this issue of the number of murderers that he will base his one "hope" (836), that the witness he has summoned will confirm Jocasta's report in all of its particulars (indeed, the report of the oracle itself), that the murderers of Laius were many and not one. "You were saying that he told you that bandits (*lēstas ephaskes*) killed Laius. So, if he still says the same number, I was not the killer; for one cannot be equal to many" (842–45). Jocasta confirms again that this account precisely is the accepted one and that the whole city heard it, not just she alone. The Chorus joins Jocasta to counsel that however "full of fear" (834) these things now seem, hope should be maintained until Oedipus learns fully from the witness what happened.

And when "the man who was present" (835) appears, of course, the full story remains hidden. It is never even requested. If Oedipus assumes he has killed Laius (and if we assume so with him), he makes that assumption, it would seem, not on the basis of what he has learned from the Herdsman or what he has heard previously from Jocasta, from the Chorus, or from Creon, but in spite of these accounts.

Moreover, far from secondary, the ambiguity surrounding Oedipus's role in the Phocial massacre would seem critical. The pattern in which the Herdsman's silence is caught is the dramatic center of the play. Whatever Oedipus's fascination with the accusations of Teiresias or with the confirmation of Teiresias's charges by Creon, whatever inadvertent support Jocasta lends to the prophet's words, whatever gravity the Corinthian's information adds to the testimony that the Herdsman will offer, it is in positive terms around the resolution to the Phocial enigma—whatever the mythic discoveries we expect—that the play is demonstrably built. It is from these moments that its very detective story quality springs.

In the overall dramatic context, then, what is striking is not only that Oedipus may not be the murderer of Laius, but that there is a curious insistence in the play that the murderers of Laius may be many. The oracle, the witness as related by Creon and Jocasta, the Chorus (if we are to believe its information originates elsewhere), all the sources, that is, which are independent of Oedipus's own account, agree on at least one crucial detail. The multiplicity of murderers was the "one thing" (*hen*) about which the witness in Creon's report was "certain" (119) and the witness's testimony is corroborated independently, if we are to believe Creon, by the words of Apollo himself.

※ ※ ※

Are we being a bit hasty in our judgments of the situation? Perhaps we are forgetting the traditional indications in the play on which the myth is founded. What, for example, of Oedipus's repeated references in the singular to the monarch's "murderer" in his speech to the Chorus championing Laius (216–75)? What of the riddling language of Teiresias in his antagonistic exchange with Oedipus which we have always taken as a veiled reference to parricide and incest? Finally, what are we to make of Oedipus's own account? Does not Oedipus's confession of his murderous adventure on the Phocial highway constitute—even by our very demonstration—the only first-hand testimony that we have on the matter?

These matters may not be as unproblematic as they appear. Far from constituting a challenge to the circulating account, Oedipus's speech to the Chorus, in the first place, may lend that account additional support. If Oedipus reduces Creon's account from a plurality to a singularity, it may be less the case that Oedipus implicates himself unconsciously in the guilt (or that Sophocles has ironically foreshadowed that guilt) than that much more consciously he implicates Creon. If Oedipus wonders how the bandit (*ho lēstēs*, 124) could have succeeded without help from the city or why an inquiry was never held (although the oracle in Creon's own words said not to neglect mysteries), or if he pledges to expose the culprit and bring "these things to light" (132) even if the culprit lodges in his own household, it may be that Oedipus already imagines the conspiratorial design with which he will momentarily charge his kinsman, a design which it appears now threatens him (being possessed as he is of Laius's throne and his bed) as much as it once did Laius. The scholiast suggests as much, Bernard Knox points out.[10] Whatever the number in Oedipus's reference here, it is to the plurality of murderers that he refers later in his discussion with the Chorus, and in his address to Teiresias, and of course, the same plurality that he will depend upon with Jocasta.

Moreover, we note that a reference to a multiplicity is already present in this very speech, a reference which would, indeed, be odd if his singular references were to be taken as an unconscious support of the myth. He condemns the culprit whether he be one alone or with others (246–47) and in his rhetorical enthusiasm includes within his condemnation even those who would shield the murderer from prosecution, a shrewd inclusion indeed if the specific terms of his proclamation were designed to catch those who planned the deed in his view (e.g. Teiresias and Creon) as well as those who would execute it (e.g. the Herdsman). If we have been accustomed to regarding Oedipus's conspiratorial accusations as an illusion, it may be that we delude ourselves with regard to their real plausibility and that we dissolve the complicity of Teiresias and Creon only by reading ourselves through the very myth their conspiracy would establish. Even if the mythic account remains convincing, Oedipus's suspicions of capital tyranny, when viewed against the background of fifth-century Athens, Bernard Knox assures us, are fully understandable.[11]

Nor may Teiresias's authority in the play be necessarily disinterested or guaranteed. Unless we privilege Teiresias *a priori* as spokesman for the mythic pattern, we may have no confidence that the knowledge of the practicing mantic is other than professional. What Teiresias knows can be deduced from what is public knowledge if we assume with him *a priori* and apodictically the empirical truth of Apollo's words. If we assume instead Oedipus's conspiratorial design, then we might expect the prophet to respond dramatically to Oedipus's taunts exactly as he does. The forensic tone of an outraged seer, Knox points out, is entirely appropriate.[12] Antagonistically he returns Oedipus's charges verbal blow for verbal blow. It may be such generic and political considerations, for example, that the Chorus has in mind when they initially hail Teiresias as the one man "in whom alone of men truth is innate" (298–99) only to dismiss his charges against Oedipus, after he appears, as unproven and his capacities as a seer no greater than their own prophetic skill (499–512). It is, of course, the Elders who intervene in the agonistic battle between Oedipus and Teiresias to declare that both men have spoken in anger (404–5). And when Creon and Oedipus have fought their battle, Creon has departed, and Jocasta has appeared to question Oedipus on this family conflict, it is the Chorus once again who will simply affirm the purely suppositive character of their mutual accusations, the origin of both positions in the "stings" of injustice (681).

Finally, Oedipus's confession may be less condemning than we have traditionally suspected. The details of Jocasta's account and his own account are strangely incongruent. She identifies the place specifically, he returns only a general affirmation of her words. She lists five members in Laius's entourage, he agrees with her account and then lists only three. She speaks of one who escaped, he says he killed "every man of them" (813). The accounts are so noticeably distinct, in fact, that Richard Jebb sees need to clarify what he calls Sophocles' "neglected clearness" on this point and to introduce in his annotation of the speech what "we must understand" by it.[13]

But more importantly, perhaps, whatever the seeming correspondence between Oedipus's Phocial adventure, the old seer's accusations, and Jocasta's tale, Oedipus finds that correspondence no hindrance to believing that the truth depends exclusively upon the testimony of the Herdsman himself. Even if the Herdsman identifies a unique murderer at Phocis, the guilt, in Oedipus's mind only "inclines" (*rhepon,* 847) towards him. But the Herdsman's testimony is the *sine qua non* of further investigative progress. Oedipus may yet be innocent. Oedipus may not have killed Laius.

❦ ❦ ❦

The situation begins to become more complicated than it initially appeared. What began as a lacuna in the pattern of a traditional reading threatens now, it would seem, to tear apart the entire fabric. Not only may Oedipus not have killed Laius, not only does the empirical situation insist that the means by which we have traditionally condemned Oedipus are themselves questionable and that the murderers of Laius may be many, but the political interactions of Oedipus with Teiresias and Creon begin to suggest that others in the play may be no less guilty than we have traditionally assumed Oedipus to be, that the mythic adoption and the guilt that it determines may, in short, be thoroughly arbitrary. We restore the myth, it would seem, only from the outside and only at the expense of the play Sophocles has given us. The best case we can make for the mythic version is circumstantial, and a case that, short of the Herdsman's appearance, no one in the play is willing to make.

And yet we feel that the mythic version must be founded. The alternatives, we tell ourselves, are unthinkable. It is not simply the tradition of Sophoclean or even classical scholarship and criticism that is at stake here. The power of Freud's suggestion that we continue to find ourselves at the level of desire in Oedipus's position resides less in its novelty than in its appeal to a critical predicament that lies somehow at the heart of Western experience.[14] Parricide and incest, in Lévi-Strauss's words, "express an ancient and lasting dream."[15] To suggest that Oedipus may not have killed Laius is to play havoc with a legend that for twenty-eight hundred years has remained curiously intact. It is to raise serious questions about those for whom the myth has remained constant, whether in Sophocles' world or our own.[16]

Is it possible that Norwood's criticism is idiosyncratic? Surely, we feel, if Jebb's interpretive annotations do not equal his philological erudition and the achievement of his textual presentation, neither should Norwood's criticism, which depends so demonstrably upon Jebb's, be regarded as the model.[17] Other critics, no doubt, more sensitive to the literary value of Sophocles' text and to the rigors of a sound literary criticism, must have taken these matters into account.

The conventional view of Greek tragedy and of Sophocles' play in particular is well known. *Oedipus Tyrannus* is a tragedy of destiny. It is an example of the genus that Aristotle identifies as a "reversal of fortune," the passage of a great man from prosperity to atrocious misfortune.[18] It is particularly "beautiful" (*kalos*) because both the commission of the actions that ruin the hero and the development of the discovery or "recognition" (*anagnōrisis*) of those actions are brought about through naturalistic character. And it is particularly "tragic" because the disaster or "reversal" (*peripeteia*) that follows such prosperity, the fate or destiny (*moira*) that is revealed to have been determined for the hero all along, revolves around a fundamental irony. It comes not simply on the heels or as the result of the hero's actions but as the consequence of those very actions he has undertaken to avoid such a fate.[19]

The panorama of critical interpretations that have remained constant to this conceptual framework is vast. Maurice Bowra finds emphatic the play's religious machinery and takes the conclusion to which Oedipus comes as instructional, as indicative of the poet's "theological intention," as a "salutary lesson" in humility before divine omnipotence.[20] William Chase Greene, among many other critics, takes that same omnipotent force as a function of the ironies of the poet's dramatic technique, as constitutive of the "triumph" of his "artistic manipulation."[21]

But the lesson man learns need not be viewed as positive. Against both Bowra's "piety" and Greene's artistic "triumph," Cedric Whitman, for example, argues the "bitterness" of Oedipus's discovery, the pessimism encouraged by the undeserved fall of such a "keenly intelligent moral conscience."[22] Still other critics, like Jan Kott, who have been influenced by post–World War II continental philosophy, remain dissatisfied with even the credit that Whitman reserves for the gods and take the "evil lot of man" that Whitman unearths less as a discovery than as the allegorical staple of an absurd universe. "All that is left of tragedy," Kott writes, "is the concept of unmerited guilt, the inevitable defeat and unavoidable mistake. But the absolute has ceased to exist. It has been replaced by the absurdity of the human situation."[23]

The difficulties of this approach are clear. The price in human suffering endured far exceeds whatever religious or technical wisdom is gained. Philip Vellacott, who is sensitive to these problems, and less committed to the halters of classical criticism, suggests an alternative designed both to dissolve the difficulties of the tragedy of destiny approach and preserve its insights. In the work of Bowra, Whitman, and most of the older critics, Vellacott argues, Oedipus's innocence is presumed. The worst of which he is usually accused is a hasty temper. The crucial events are said to derive from an accident, an instance of *hamartia,* a mistake, a missing of the mark, an error that cannot be discerned as an error except in retrospect.

"But we can find what we are looking for," Vellacott proposes, namely, "some sin, some fault in Oedipus's character which would justify to men the seemingly cruel and immoral ways of Zeus or of Apollo or of Fate" if we imagine Oedipus's "state of mind when he left the Delphic oracle."

> To avoid heinous pollution, he must make for himself two unbreakable rules: never to kill an older man; and never to marry an older woman. The incident at the banquet makes it clear that these two rules, and not the resolve to keep away from Corinth, would be the probable occupation of Oedipus' thoughts as he left Delphi.[24]

Yet as soon as Oedipus meets Laius, Vellacott says, he slays him and all his party and his fate is assured. "Oedipus has, at the first opportunity, ignored a divine warning. That this man could be his father would be a coincidence so incredible as to be impossible but this was the risk he ought not to have taken. He is guilty."[25]

Vellacott's introduction of a wilfulness into Greek tragedy is bold and attractive. He reminds us that to whatever extent we have accepted the classical line that we are finally in ancient drama the playthings of the gods, we experience that relation as volitional.[26] If older critics find instances of such volition only in the manner in which Oedipus discloses his fateful past, Vellacott locates it at the crossroads, so to speak, of that earlier history. If he waxes a bit theatrical in asking us to envision Oedipus's "state of mind when he left the Delphic oracle," he offers a challenge to more traditional approaches that read such assumed narrative developments in blandly mythic terms.

Moreover, his questions allow us to see things we have never seen before. "The incident at the banquet" which, Vellacott suggests, appears to have been a Sophoclean invention, undermines Oedipus's mythic "resolve to keep away from Corinth" in order not to commit parricide and incest since Corinth was the one place where he had reason to believe his parents were not his own. The incident suggests that there may be other gestures operative on Oedipus's part, gestures that shed light on his behavior later in Thebes, even if in recalling those incidents for us Oedipus dismisses their significance as "not worthy of the deep concern that I showed" (777–78).

But if Vellacott's observations are penetrating, the assumptions on which they are based and the conclusions to which they are put are as mythic as those of the most conservative of classical commentators. He gains the ability to ask such questions only by embedding the play in another moral scheme, one that Hegel admittedly would reserve for modern drama rather than ancient tragedy (and one more familiarly associated perhaps with A. C. Bradley's reading of Shakespeare) but a moral scheme nonetheless.[27] Rather than pursue these questions to the brilliantly anti-mythic possibilities they raise, rather than wonder whether indeed "what we are looking for" in Greek tragedy is some Oedipal *hybris*, "some sin, some fault in Oedipus' character which would justify to men the seemingly cruel and immoral ways of Zeus or of Apollo or of Fate" and stage the appropriative limits of all such dramatic and moral convictions and conventions, he closes down the inquiry he opens no less thoroughly than the most stodgy of his counterparts. He concerns himself with the "probable occupation of Oedipus' thoughts as he left Delphi" and the implications to which that preoccupation leads, a novelistic consideration which, however attractive it might be as a motivating subtext for actors performing the play, sustains the mythic detective story framework within which the play has long been viewed, one in which all questions have unequivocal answers and all enigmas are able to be solved.

We may question, in other words, whether indeed "what we are looking for" in Greek tragedy is some Oedipal *hybris,* "some sin, some fault in Oedipus' character which would justify to men the seemingly cruel and immoral ways of Zeus or of Apollo or of Fate" rather than staging of the limits of such dramatic convictions. And we may wonder why the genuinely critical questions that Vellacott's insights raise and that could open the door for us are abandoned. But whether Vellacott prefers a tragedy of destiny approach or a tragedy of character approach, we would be hard put to deny that he endorses the appurtenance of some mythic structure no less than the most traditional of critics, even if that structure has been novelistically enlarged now to include "the probable occupation of Oedipus' thoughts as he left Delphi."

Another critic who is iconoclastic with regard to more traditional approaches to the play is Bernard Knox.[28] For Knox the difficulty may be overcome by reading the play historically. Oedipus, in Knox's view, is a representation of Periclean Athens, a dramatization of the burgeoning self-understanding in the ancient fifth century of this polis as a kind of cultural *tyrannos.*[29] *Tyrannos,* Knox brilliantly points out, as a reference to the archaic political institution of the *tyrant,* "an unconstitutional ruler, who generally abuses the power he has seized," is in Sophocles' time already a joke. By the fifth century the word had come to assume a much broader semantic field, encompassing the illegitimate seizure or appropriation of power in a wide variety of contexts—all that might be construed as part of the "scientific" or Sophistic or Protagorean revolution.

Oidipous Tyrannos is thus less "Oedipus the King" (which translates the Latin title *Oedipus Rex,* as if the second word in Greek were *basileus* rather than *tyrannos*) than Oedipus who has usurped knowledge and suffers the consequences of his action. *Hybris phyteuei tyrannon* ("arrogance begets the tyrant," 873), the Chorus sing, and Knox draws our attention to the centrality of these words and of the Second Stasimon generally. The riddle of the Sphinx in his view is less a puzzle than a prophecy.

Oedipus himself becomes in the course of the play the monstrous example of the riddle he solves.[30] The play for Knox is Sophocles' critique of the impending fall of Athens, its birth from a kind of Athenian *hybris,* a dangerous pan-Hellenic self-reliance, and the consequences of that *hybris* as the cultural plague it has wrought makes its way throughout the Greek-speaking world. "I, know-nothing Oedipus" (*ho mēden eidōs Oidipous,* 397), Oedipus tells the more traditionally inclined mantic prophet, solved the riddle of the Sphinx, not you. In the end, however, Knox points out, Oedipus becomes equal to his name, "swell-foot," monster-foot, "since while *oidi-* means 'swell' . . . it is very close to *oida,* 'I know'" (183) and the two are superimposed upon each other, knowledge upon deformity. No wonder, Knox says, the Chorus "counts" him finally as "equal to nothing" (*isa . . . to mēden,* 1187).

Like Vellacott, Knox greatly expands our sensitivity to the text before us. He reads the play with an attention to verbal nuance rarely before observed in Sophoclean or classical criticism generally. The language of politics, juridical practice, mathematics, archery, the oracular, the divinatory, and the mantic—in short, the vocabulary of all of the city's institutions—find their expression here. Also, like Vellacott, he eschews older readings that would compel Sophocles to be measured against nineteenth-century moral schemas flagrantly inadequate to the text at hand, and identifies an order in the play which is considerably more satisfying for a modern (and ancient) audience.

Moreover, unlike Vellacott, Knox does not simply apply Hegel in reverse. If Vellacott frees us from considering the play as a tragedy of destiny only to reinscribe it as a tragedy of character or consciousness, Knox invites us to examine the play more independently, to follow the action as it unfolds before us. The play for Knox remains fundamentally critical, an examination of its contextual origins that few other approaches allow.

But the genuinely dazzling insights he offers are achieved only at the price of shifting ground beneath the play in an equally unprecedented way, mapping its movements upon a cultural development taken itself to be primary and that will culminate in the rise (and triumph) of Platonic rationalism a century later. Knox enables us to see the play's "critical" qualities only by displacing the study of literature for the study of history. The play for Knox is cultural and political allegory. He escapes the difficulties of the older moral view neither by dismissing those difficulties, nor by reconstruing the standards by which they come to be measured, but by giving up the study of aesthetics for the study of the humanizing tendencies of the Sophistic enlightenment of which that aesthetic phenomenon is taken to be the document and expression.

Small wonder, then, that many years after the publication of *Oedipus at Thebes* Knox writes another essay in which he suggests Oedipus is not the hero of fate or character but of truth, a truth conceived, moreover, in avowedly Socratic terms.[31] Knox's latest view of the play is less a shift away from his earlier skepticism than an elaboration of the larger philosophic context of which that skepticism was always already a part. He has given up Hegel for Plato, not because he finds Hegel too mythic and the play too critical of the myth, as we would argue, but because he finds Hegel not mythic enough and Plato more comprehensive in that regard. If Knox rejects the myth nineteenth-century critics inherited from German idealist philosophy, it is not because he would see the play as anti-mythic, but rather because he has another myth in mind, a larger one which, far from doing away with philosophy, reintroduces it at a more profound and secure level, a level at which it is one and the same with the scientific and political method known in the nineteenth century as historical research, and from which the literary and interpretive method known as philology emerged.[32]

But whether we read literature as philosophic moralism or philosophic history, we read literature through philosophy and not the reverse. We give up the anti-mythic perspective I would suggest literature offers us for one or another myth by which its challenges may be domesticated. To read Sophocles' play in function of an Aeschylean morality said to precede it or a Platonic philosophic humanist morality said to follow it, is equally to derive our perspective from a myth and not from the challenge to such mythic thinking that the play makes available to us.

The erudition of these critics is not for a moment in question. Our debt to them—and to many others whose work we have not mentioned—is not easily discharged. No one who reads Sophocles with any care remains unaided by their patience and research.[33]

But their adherence to the primacy of mythic expectations is another matter entirely. Whether we consider the scene of Sophocles' morality as theological, dramaturgical, novelistic, or historical, its lesson as optimistic, pessimistic, or absurd, Oedipus's participation in the drama as innocent or guilty, the integrity of the moral or cultural standard by which we have measured such results remains fundamentally and consistently intact. In each case, we have premised our consideration of the play on the viability of the mythic pattern and the moral or historical universe it implies and precluded *a priori* the kinds of equivocation suggested in the present essay. To set aside such questions, to found critical discussion of the play upon their displacement, is to lose more than the increased complexity that the play acquires from their consideration. It is to reproduce the response of Oedipus himself and to become, ironically, subject to whatever examination Sophocles undertakes on the basis of such equivocation.

Can we not develop a more independent stance with regard to the play, one that reads with Sophocles rather than one that is read by Sophocles? Can we not fashion an approach that reads neither with Oedipus's conspiratorial suspicions nor with the expulsion of those suspicions from the insight of his mantic blindness, but rather by juxtaposing one perspective with the other, registers the processes by which Oedipus's systematic exclusion from Thebes both personally and socially is accomplished? Accepting Sophocles' equivocation at face value, and considering the very polysemy that we say we prize as the basis for a new positive reading, can we not, finally, examine the presence of such seemingly anti-mythic elements without invoking in order to explain them the very mythic structures they challenge?

※　　※　　※

Voltaire's reading of Sophocles, contained in the famous "Lettres sur Oedipe" which he prefaces to his own dramatic reworking of the Theban legend, would seem to address the problem of the number of the murderers of Laius more directly and more promisingly than any of the critics we have met so far.[34] After enumerating rather disdainfully Sophocles' imperfections in other regards, and after considering the many "contradictions" and breaches of "common sense" in the matter of the number of murderers ("How can it be," Voltaire wonders, "that a witness to the death of Laius can say that his master has been overcome by a large number when it remains true, moreover, that it is one man who has killed Laius and all his following?"), Voltaire relates the Herdsman's appearance.[35]

> Finally, Phorbas arrives in the fourth act. Those who have no familiarity with Sophocles doubtless imagine that Oedipus, impatient to know the murderer of Laius and to give life to the Thebans, is going to question him straightaway on the death of the late king. No,

indeed. Sophocles forgets that vengeance for the death of Laius is the subject of his play. No one speaks a word to Phorbas concerning his adventure and the tragedy finishes without Phorbas having even opened his mouth on the death of the king his master.[36]

Clearly, Voltaire objects to the same forgetfulness that Norwood found so marvelous. But "it remains true" for Voltaire, nonetheless, "that it is one man who has killed Laius and all his following." If Voltaire raises problems that the tradition dismisses, his reading of the play is no less mythic, finally, than any of the others. He recognizes the presence of such elements only to toss them out with the play itself. If we do not "forget" why the Herdsman was summoned, as Norwood suggests, *Sophocles* in Voltaire's view does. No less than the others, Voltaire wants the myth—another myth, to be sure, a rhetorical myth that prizes "common sense" and "verisimilitude" as the proper decorum for tragic discourse—but, nonetheless, a structure of differences that defines its own system of valuation. And when he does not find this structure, his response will be even more radical than that of classical philologists. He will dismiss the play because of it. He will reestablish the myth elsewhere, in his own dramatic reworkings of the Greek legend, or in other critical literature.[37]

All of our forays into Sophocles' text and into the history of response to that text have led us back only to the questions with which we began. Why does Sophocles undermine the clarity of the empirical situation on which the myth is built? Why does Oedipus adopt the myth in the face of evidence that is inconclusive, that is at best circumstantial and at worst arbitrary? Why does the Chorus, while able to recognize throughout the arbitrariness of Teiresias's accusations, straightaway adopt the same myth once Oedipus adopts it and take Oedipus's culpability as necessary and operative all along? Why, finally, have twenty-four hundred years of critical tradition continued that retrospective view, reading the play from the perspective of the Chorus, or of Oedipus, or of Teiresias, less in spite of Sophocles' presentation, it begins to seem, than because of it?

Our registry of Sophocles' mythic equivocation seems to have led us to an interpretive impasse. We cannot do without such questions. Sophocles has thrust them critically upon us. And yet there seems to be little that we can do with them. No sooner do we register their existence than we face the oblivion to which criticism has in one fashion or another consigned them. We seem condemned, if we are to read the play at all, to choose among a series of equally inadequate alternatives: to dismiss the problems with the mainstream, to dissolve them within some larger neo-mythic (Platonic or Hegelian) framework, or to recognize their existence only to dismiss the play on their basis and reconstruct the traditional myths elsewhere.

Nor may our difficulty be a new one. The gesture of critical exclusion that "forgets" the kind of numerical and technical play that, we have suggested, is at stake in Sophocles seems always to have been part of our critical response in the West, whether we have chosen with Plato to repudiate the mimetic plague of tragedy and institute new structures or with Aristotle to transcendentalize the cathartic perfections of tragic art and identify what is disconcerting with the misunderstandings of critics like Voltaire. Is there no way out of this representational crisis in which Sophocles himself, who played all his life with the prophetic language of pity and fears, may have been embroiled?

*   *   *

There may be a way out of our dilemma. A positive reading of Sophocles' equivocation with the myth may be possible—indeed, much closer than we think—and the prolonged consideration we have given thus far to traditional difficulties may itself provide the key. If we follow a bit longer and observe a little more closely the manner in which criticism fails us, in which it ensures that the ambiguities of Sophocles' text be forgotten, in which it reveals at its origins an idolatry of the Oedipal perspective and at its conclusion a certain self-destructive violence, we may begin to understand both the play to which it is response and the particular relation between them. Moreover, it may be that we need only turn to the criticism of Gilbert Norwood—the work that proved initially such a stumbling block to the positive reading that we wanted—to glimpse in the interstices of his reading, in the expulsive gestures by which he founds that reading, the kinds of genealogical movements that will offer a cornerstone to a new view of Sophocles.

We recall, in the first place, that the kinds of critical issues that we have been considering are not at all absent from Norwood's account. It is, indeed, Norwood who suggested that the "part of the aged Theban" is "especially pointed," that the distinction between the mythic account of Phocis and the account circulating in the city is "vital" to the growing horror. It is also Norwood who highlighted the disparity between what is expected of the Herdsman when he is summoned (viz. "to settle whether Laius was slain by one man or by a company") and what is demanded of him when he arrives (viz. "from whom he received the outcast infant"). If Norwood raises these issues only to resituate them retrospectively as functions of Sophocles' ironic style, his fascination with them, particularly in conjunction with what follows, may hint at a concern on his part which significantly exceeds the demands of the myth of Sophocles' constructive splendor.

Just below his consideration of the Herdsman, Norwood stumbles upon a "flaw" in dramatic construction. The arrival of the Corinthian does not appear as "the direct result of something said or done by Oedipus."

> The arrival of the Corinthian messenger at this moment is purely accidental. Without it, the witness of the old retainer would have fastened upon Oedipus the slaying of Laius (not known to be the king's father) and he would have gone forth from the city, but not as a parricide; moreover, the relation between him and the queen would have remained unknown. Judged by the standard of the whole play, this fact constitutes a flaw in construction.[38]

What is curious in this passage is less that Norwood is able to identify a lapse in Sophocles' technique (although such a discovery is remarkable enough given his lavish praise of Sophocles' achievement) than the fact that the particular blemish he identifies threatens to introduce into the play the very mythic confusions we would suggest are built-in already. Without the Corinthian's information, Norwood asserts, Oedipus "would have gone forth from the city but not as a parricide" and the "relation between him and the queen would have remained unknown." What is "accidental" in the drama is less the manner in which the mythic crimes are committed (which is the view he has just so carefully elaborated) than the attribution to Oedipus of the crimes at all.

Such an observation on Norwood's part would seem less remarkable if the logical context in which it were raised prompted its inclusion. But we note that Norwood feels the need to elaborate at length a hypothetical tangent that has very little to do with the "flaw" he would presumably describe. Rather than discuss how the Corinthian's appearance might have been more effectively motivated, or how else the essential information he holds might be introduced, Norwood ponders the consequences of not introducing the information at all: namely, that parricide and incest would have remained undiscovered, that in some uncanny way the discovery of Oedipus's mythic guilt, in the play we have before us, is arbitrary.

Clearly, Norwood does not suggest that the discovery of the contingent qualities of the attribution of parricide and incest is in any way a function of the Herdsman's silence on Phocis. He does not read the "accident" in function of the Herdsman's appearance at all, only as derivative of the appearance of the Corinthian. Moreover, he does not imagine the notion of "accident" as useful for interpreting the play Sophocles has given us, but rather as a problem Sophocles would have to have faced if the Corinthian were not to appear. He never fears for a moment that even under such circumstances Oedipus would not be guilty of parricide and incest, only that the manifestation of this relation would not, perhaps, have taken place.

But the curious incongruence of the suggestion to the immediate context in which it occurs, and its ironic juxtaposition with Norwood's discussion of issues which, if pushed far enough, would yield the kind of questions we have suggested in this essay, is already clear enough. Does this brief moment of crisis in Norwood's text unveil the origin of his own mythopoesis? Does such reflection upon the potential arbitrariness of the charge of parricide and incest, and consequently responsibility for the Theban plague—even circumscribed as it is within Norwood's strictly mythic coordinates—specify for us the dangers that Norwood finds in Sophocles and to which his tally of flaws and perfections is already itself a systematic response?

No sooner does Norwood raise this hypothetical consideration than he dismisses it as if it had not existed. He subsumes it within the representational structure whose breach he introduced it to elaborate. He identifies for it a naturalistic function he found for the Herdsman just a moment before.

> Why did the poet not contrive that the news of Polybus' death should arrive, and arrive now, as the direct result of something said or done by Oedipus, just as the arrival of the old Theban with his crushing testimony, is due to the king's own summons? No doubt this occurrence is meant to mirror the facts of life, which include accidents as well as events plainly traceable to character.[39]

Norwood's erasure of the questions he has raised may prove decisive both to their establishment and to the critical myth whose limits they highlight. The critical oblivion to which the tradition has consigned Sophocles' equivocation now appears by Norwood's example more systematic, and the intertextual relation between Norwood's work and Sophocles' more intimate, than we have suspected. Norwood repeats Oedipus's response not simply in spite of that response—not merely ironically or coincidentally as if criticism just happens to reproduce the figure it examines—but because of it, in response to it, as part of the definitional and organizing structure of the critical undertaking itself. At the heart of Norwood's text is, in the first instance at least, the rejection of Sophocles'. Norwood articulates the myth of Sophocles' constructive splendor in order to displace categorically and generically the possibility that the tragic discovery is "accidental," to undo the damage that Sophocles' mythic equivocation in the tradition's view has done, an antimythic violence that has accidentally surfaced in the very process of being expelled.

There is another consequence of Norwood's reconstructive gesture. His move parallels closely another case of such forgetfulness to which he himself has drawn our attention. If Norwood manages to raise such antimythic possibilities with the myth intact, in a slightly different noncritical context, and with regard to a play Sophocles never wrote, does he not in fact respond to the demonstrably ambiguous situation confronting him as critic precisely as Oedipus responds to the crisis he faces both at Delphi and, finally, at Thebes?

Have we not, that is, in Norwood's hypothetical deconstruction and reconstruction of the Oedipus myth, the Oedipal response in its entirety? If Norwood assumes, in order to read the Herdsman's appearance in the play, the very myth he is brought on to reveal, if in the face of evidence that Norwood himself can uncover—evidence that would, curiously enough, free him (or prohibit him) from articulating the critical myth of Sophocles' constructive splendor—he "forgets" to measure "new things by old" (916), is transfixed by the Sophoclean speaker "when he speaks of fear and terror" (917), and renders the Herdsman's silence ironically as an indication of the foundation of the myth and of that splendor, if, in short, Norwood substitutes what the Herdsman does not say for what he does, is Norwood's critical *hamartia* not like Oedipus's own mythopoetic gesture before the crisis he faces in Thebes and, perhaps, that Sophocles faced himself in Athens?

As the mantic Oedipal position is reproduced definitionally in criticism, that is, as criticism with Oedipus would systematically "forget" the equivocation which has brought it to this moment of critical decision, we may begin to gain some insight on the nature of the literary text to which it is a response.

If Norwood's position is Oedipal, then it is Norwood's position, and the critical tradition that appropriates that position, that is itself already at stake in Sophocles' drama. If we can remember what Oedipus would "forget," and juxtapose that memory with the moment of its amnesia, if we can read Oedipus against himself even as Norwood reads the Herdsman, and we in turn read Norwood, and uncover behind all of these retrospective transfigurations the displacements which have made them possible, then we recognize in the parallel that it has been a Sophoclean reading of Oedipus that has made possible these very disclosures. Rather than a critique of Oedipus via the myth, Sophocles' play is a critique via Oedipus of us. Norwood reenacts the drama to which the play itself is already a response. It is not Sophocles' text that is the origin of Norwood's, but, to the contrary, Norwood's criticism, in the figure of Oedipus, that is already the origin of Sophocles'.

We can begin to read Sophocles' play, in other words, the moment we give up the "Oedipalization" of Sophocles' text (the retrospective reading that Oedipus himself makes from within his mantic blindness and violence) and join Sophocles in his critique via Oedipus of such a position and such a process, the moment we acknowledge the idolatry and, in the extreme, the blindness and self-destructive violence which have made it possible and which Sophocles has exposed. If Sophocles' play is already about criticism, then it has been our critical posture that has created the difficulty, our assumption of independence, our presumed innocence of any Oedipal reading, that has constituted for us (even as it has for Oedipus) the Oedipal position itself.

The play itself, in other words, already raises all the questions we would ask. It has already undertaken the "deconstruction" we would now "innocently" begin.[40] Translating these questions into a context in which answers are defined, we preempt Sophocles' interrogation for our own. We begin to read Sophocles' play the moment we recognize that we have never not been doing that, the moment we give up the distinction between literature and criticism by which we have "decriticalized" Sophocles' play in order to render the poet's critical activity inspired but mute and the critic's literaturizing activity parasitic but alone fully articulate, the moment we recognize, in short, that our critical position has always already been Oedipal.[41]

The way out of the interpretive crisis in which we found ourselves, then, is to recognize such a crisis as the subject matter of the play itself, to give up trying to explain Sophocles' drama, or to answer the questions the play poses for us, and to turn our attention instead to the arbitrary and potentially destructive premises of such an explanatory posture both within the play and without. Rather than participate in the play's crisis—in the crisis imagined by the play and the crisis that is the play—we might follow instead Sophocles' investigation of the enabling conditions of any Oedipal reading: of Oedipus who manifests the idolatrous and self-destructive limits of such critical blindness; of the Chorus who institute that paradigmatic blindness in traditional morality; and of the classical critical tradition that at least since the nineteenth century has perpetuated that critical Oedipal institution and for which even in our day such blindness and violence continue to assume the status of insight itself.

Suddenly, a new reading of Sophocles' play opens up to us. Sophocles has shifted our traditional focus entirely. Rather than an illustration of the myth, the play is a critique of mythogenesis, an examination of the process by which one arbitrary fiction comes to assume the value of truth. Suspending the empirical foundation on which the myth is built, suggesting as arbitrary the political determination that Oedipus alone is responsible for the "numberless" plague that is depopulating the Theban city, Sophocles undertakes an examination of the logic that assumes Oedipus is the unique culprit. Oedipus discovers he is guilty of parricide and incest—he translates what the Herdsman does tell him into the mythic fulfillment—less by uncovering certain hitherto obscure empirical facts than by voluntarily appropriating an oracular logic that assumes he has always already been guilty. At the genesis of his Teiresian wisdom is an oracular idolatry that has guided his progress throughout and which he will now inscribe in his head forever. Oedipus becomes "Oedipus" by assuming the myth *a priori,* by assuming he has been so all along. Unable to measure new things by old, transfixed by the speaker when he speaks of pity and fear (whether at Delphi or at Thebes), Oedipus invests prophetic language with the power of truth. The truth, Teiresias told him, has power. Apollo is sufficient. The seer, Oedipus tells Jocasta as she trembles, had eyes. The son will kill the father. I am the son. *Ergo,* by mythic oracular definition, I have killed the father. It is the terrible price of this critical wisdom that Sophocles' play weighs in the balance.

To take seriously the suggestion that Oedipus may not have killed Laius, then, is, in the last analysis, to give up Oedipus for Sophocles, to recognize the double of the Oedipal position in ourselves and to follow Sophocles in his critique, via Oedipus, of us. Have we registered Sophocles' equivocation only now to suddenly develop a new myth of Oedipus, to suggest, for example, that Oedipus did not kill Laius or, more cleverly, that someone else did?[42] Or should our examination lead us to decide that the empirical situation is hopelessly mired in obscurity and prompt us either to reject Sophocles' play on the basis of its undecidability or to take our pleasure from the text in an act of unbridled critical indulgence?[43]

Or, rather, does Sophocles not compel us to give up such privileging of the empirical question entirely, to view the empirical issue as less important than the universal matrix of scapegoat politics (in which all are identically "murderers of Laius") in terms of which it functions and for which it comes metonymically (and in retrospective relation to the arbitrary determination of a unique culprit for the plague) to substitute? Shall we not begin, Sophocles demands of us, to examine the limits of our myths, the status of our mythic appropriations in context of the real social relations in which they exist, in context, that is, of the blindness and self-destructive violence that plague identically Oedipus's world, Sophocles' world, and our own?

To read Sophocles, or more precisely to read with Sophocles, is to give up at the extreme the Oedipus myth and the structure of morality and cultural values that it implies for an examination of its genealogy. If Plato can denounce the imitative violence of tragedy and Aristotle in turn applaud the cathartic virtues of the same sacrificial ode, this language of pity and fear, this *legein phobous* (917), and if we in turn can alternately model either Plato's rejection or Aristotle's formal approbation (even as Sophocles, we must assume, modeled Oedipus in his own ambivalent fascination with prophetic language), then, by virtue of the same appropriative freedom, can we not, Sophocles asks of us, give up that Oedipal reading? At the moment of Oedipus's blindness, at the moment when Oedipus's mythic self-definition and self-justification become self-destructive, and our critical insight collapses in the face of its truth, we may continue, Sophocles suggests, the Oedipal response that Oedipus himself would forget. We can retrieve the crisis of "emulous desire" or "imitative rivalry" (*polyzēlos*, 381) that Oedipus himself denounces in his encounter with the prophet and join Sophocles in taking his play, finally, as an autocriticism of all of us.[44]

The stakes of such an investigation are high. Oedipus is part of our language in the West. From Homer to Aristotle to Freud, it is the same old story. Oedipus is synonymous with parricidal and incestuous desire. If Oedipus becomes "Man" in the course of the tragedy, if, as Bernard Knox so astutely points out, Oedipus becomes himself the answer to the riddle he solved, *anthrōpos tyrannos,* even as he becomes in the Chorus's view "equal to nothing" (*isa . . . to mēden,* 1187), then what is at stake in Oedipus—as the answer to an oracle that has become a riddle, as the insistent confusion between the many and the one, as the *paradeigma* (1193) or model whose expulsion will end the "numberless" (*anarithmos,* 167, 178) plague which is the source of the city's woes—is Western humanism at large.[45]

We understand, now, the singular silence of the mainstream of critical tradition on the issues we have tried here to suggest. Substituting the myth for such anti-mythic indications, reading in Sophocles' mythic equivocation ironically the myth itself, repeating Oedipus's mythopoetic construction—the very Oedipal *méconnaissance* that Sophocles' play already "deconstructs"—criticism succeeds in subduing the profoundly critical gesture that it found in literature to begin with, a literature whose very monstrosity—its superimposition of its own mythic conventions upon their arbitrariness—was the source of its uncanny attraction in the first place.[46] If we would raise Sophocles' work with Norwood to the status of a "masterpiece," even as the Greeks themselves sought to elevate this semiheroic playwright to the sacred place of "first prize," we do so less as a way of valuing its beauty than as a way of checking its violence, a beauty which is itself already nothing other than this limitlessness or violence read from a transcendental distance.

Perhaps we also understand now the way in which Freud's appropriation of the "Sophoclean legend" as the program for a scientific institution carries this blindness to a dangerous new level. What is critical in Freud's handling of the Oedipus myth is less that he borrows a Greek myth to describe a psychology of human behavior or that he identifies himself with the most conservative of classical views, than that he introduces a dramatic fiction within the set of cultural fictions by which we govern our everyday lives.

In the famous passage of *The Interpretation of Dreams* in which Freud links psychoanalysis with the Oedipus myth, Freud is astonishingly clear about the relation that he finds between the two. "The action of the play consists in nothing other than the process of revealing, with cunning delays and ever-mounting excitement—a process that can be likened to the work of a psychoanalysis—that Oedipus is himself the murderer of Laius, but further that he is the son of the murdered man and of Jocasta."[47] What is startling enough in the present context is the exclusivity with which Freud collates the play with the myth, the fact that Sophocles' play for the founder of psychoanalysis consists in "nothing other than" the traditional material, that the play, like a detective story "with ever mounting delays and ever mounting excitement," leads to one exclusive truth that will in retrospect make everything fit.

But what is even more troublesome is that Freud in turn has appropriated this classical myth as the program for psychoanalytic therapy. It is the work of psychoanalysis which can be "likened" to this detective fiction and whose truths can be read from the end. If Freud admits, on the one hand, that the play reveals an unanticipated identity between the investigator and the investigated, psychoanalysis, in his view, should be modeled not on this identity but on the replaying of the differential illusions of its drama. The outcome of therapy, for Freud, which we might assume to be open-ended, is thoroughly determined in advance. The difference between the patient and the doctor, the denial of any fundamental identity between them, conditions the very possibility of the therapeutic encounter. The patient for Freud must discover himself Oedipus and must confess his crimes at the level of desire to the doctor who knew that truth in advance and who, with his wise silence and prophetic eyes, has assumed throughout the position of Teiresias.

To be sure, the doctor has not always been free of Oedipal sins himself. But the doctor has already confessed his sins in the Freudian schema. The doctor always already is where the patient hopes one day to be. He has gone through psychoanalysis. If Freud can recognize the arbitrariness of this distinction in other arenas, if he can write in "Dostoyevsky and Parricide" concerning Dmitri's trial for the murder of his father in *The Brothers Karamazov* that "it is a matter of indifference who actually committed the crime" and that "all the brothers . . . are equally guilty," it is curiously the temporal mythic distinction between Teiresias and Oedipus or between the doctor and the patient that Freud insists upon when he reads Sophocles or comes to imagine the psychoanalytic encounter.[48] The confession of Oedipus is more than a theme of psychoanalysis for Freud. The production of an "Oedipus complex," the "Oedipalization" of the patient, would appear to be for him, at least in this formulation, an enabling condition for the psychoanalytic cure.[49]

If we could dismiss psychoanalysis as just another traditionalist reading, we might accept Freud's view of the play as idiosyncratic. We might follow with Sophocles the blindness and dangers of Freud's Oedipal investments as the key to the enigma of Freud's own prophetic concerns.[50] But psychoanalysis has emerged within psychiatric medical practice as the program for a scientific institution.[51] The Oedipus myth in Freud's hands has assumed the status of scientific truth. The imperative to confess one's Oedipal guilt, and the consequences of not confessing to a guilt which is given in advance, are now political. A refusal to confess may result in a declaration of madness and a sentence of imprisonment. This is literary criticism with a vengeance.[52]

Fleeing the myth, Oedipus discovers that he has brought it about. Answering the riddle of the Sphinx, he discovers he has committed parricide and incest. Constructing a theory of tragic irony, we discover that we have reproduced the position of Oedipus himself. Confessing our sins, we discover our Oedipal guilt and unconscious desire. The foregoing analysis and the examination to which it is but a prelude may lead us to a new understanding of Sophocles. It will demand of us that we read Sophocles' text more carefully and that we rethink the theoretical considerations on which our analyses of the past have been based: the notion of an "author" or "writer," the concept of a literary "text" (especially one we qualify as a "masterpiece"), and the relation of both to the real and symbolic worlds in which they function.[53]

At the most profound level, perhaps, it will demand that we rethink the relation of "tragic irony" to violence, that we admit the possibility that the assumption of a position outside of the circle of mythic violence (as sons, as critics, or as patients) is already the gesture that ensures that we are within, and that the seemingly "ironic" conclusions to which we come reflect only the non-ironic relation—the identical violence—in which we have always already taken part and which such distancing gesture itself perpetuates.

To pay attention, however, to Oedipus's status as *paradeigma* or sacrificial model and to the logic of number or *arithmos* (itself, we will suggest, a logic of sacrificial genesis) as the vocabulary in which this oracular crisis is presented is already to reflect the research of the critic who, more fully than anyone else in the contemporary context, has thought out relation of violence to human communities.

* * *

In his essays on Sophocles and Euripides (principally "Symétrie et dissymétrie dans le mythe d'Oedipe" and "Dionysus and the Violent Genesis of the Sacred"), and in his study of the role of sacrifice in primitive culture (*Violence and the Sacred*), René Girard argues the ability of certain works in the Western tradition, principally those that we have called "tragic," to uncover behind the mythic structures from which they are born the violence of their own genesis, a reciprocal violence of "enemy twins" which the conventional distinctions of the work once held in check but now can no longer efficaciously dispel, the same sacrificial violence that once gave rise to the myth itself and is, in fact, the foundative mechanism in the primitive universe of all cultural order.[54]

> The genesis of *myth* can be read in the filigree of tragedy. The ritual expulsion demanded by Oedipus at the end of the play echoes the collective violence which constitutes the true mainspring of mythological creation. . . . The instinct which carries the interpreter to the tragic texts is not false. The poet is the only real ally of the truest and most radical reading, a reading which reassembles the scattered fragments of the defunct reciprocity, which restores the falsified symmetries, which brings together all that the myth arbitrarily separates. . . . The tragic interpretation of the myth, like all truly *critical* readings, is the child of a fundamental crisis.[55]

I have tried to suggest that these insights, and the conceptualization on which they are based, allow us to recognize in *Oedipus Tyrannus* the pervasiveness of mythogenetic violence. Sophocles' equivocation with the mythic determinants has introduced a crisis not simply at the level of the reciprocal antagonisms of Oedipus, Teiresias, and Creon, but in the very heart of the mythic fabric, in the very empirical structure of Oedipus's relation to Laius that we have taken for so long as a cultural given and which has begun to assume the status of scientific verity in our time.

These same insights will also allow us—and here is the area in which their value in our view is decisive—to understand not only the problem but the domain of its solution, to recognize the possibilities for survival in a "post-sacrificial" universe, a universe in which the expulsion of scapegoats no longer works and in which sacrifice has become confused irretrievably with violence itself, to imagine, that is, if only hypothetically, the possibilities for an anti-sacrificial position.

They will allow us to understand, perhaps for the first time, a Sophocles who, in a profoundly critical situation that is not unlike our own, is able to ask in the face of its violence what the Chorus asks in the play's dramatic center, the question of the *choros* or of *choreuein* (896), the question of the efficacy of the dance, of the play, of religious worship itself. If the murderers of Laius are many, if an idolatrous dishonor for Apollo is being substituted for honor itself, if "things shall not fit (*harmosei*, 902) so that all men can point at them with the hand (*cheirodeikta,* 901)," if, in short, the numberless (*anarithmos*) plague cannot end because a *paradeigma* (an example, an oracular model, a one who can stand for many) cannot be found and any attempt at sacrifice (at the establishment of a difference between the one and the many—the principle of number itself) leads only to more violence, then *ti dei me choreuein* (896)? "Why should I dance?"[56]

2

"Being Nothing"
Kings, Mirrors, and Subjects in Shakespeare's Richard II

> Queen Elizabeth would not allow *Richard II* to be performed. Kings and emperors were often represented in the theater as perfidious, cruel, violent men and—as tyrants. The rulers accepted this on the understanding that it did not concern *them*. . . . Theater showed kings having heads cut off; but it was a king whose head they had cut off, and the headless trunk was still a royal trunk. That scene, too, was hallowed by tradition. One thing only could not be tolerated: that a king could cease to be a king. To behead a king meant to break physically the principle of obedience, but to depose a king meant to overthrow authority itself, to abolish all theology, to abolish metaphysics. From such a moment heaven was to be forever empty.
>
> Jan Kott, *Shakespeare Our Contemporary*

I. Double Deposition

Interest in Shakespeare's *Richard II* has never been lacking.[1] But readers in Shakespeare's day seem to have understood the play in a manner very different from our own.[2] Taken in function of the kinds of formal Aristotelian categories in which nineteenth-century historiographers tell us imaginative literature in the Renaissance was often understood, the play could well seem little more than the dramatic rendition of a moment in the chronicle of English kingship that was familiar, we have to believe, to a good deal of Shakespeare's audience. Richard engages in a series of strategic errors that sufficiently weaken his monarchical authority so that Henry Bolingbroke can march an army back into England from exile and compel the king to abdicate. The story was commonplace to Elizabethan popular sensibility, as we learn from the work of Tillyard and others in the 1930s and 1940s, and the larger mythic framework in which that story was understood, the so-called "Tudor myth," seems to have been a common feature of Elizabethan historical writing.[3]

Taken, on the other hand, within the climate of political uneasiness in England at the end of the sixteenth century (about which other historiographers have begun to write), the play could appear considerably more radical. In an age when the English monarch was widely compared with (and is said to have compared herself with) Richard II, a story about the former king's deposition could only be viewed as controversial, as Jan Kott notes above.[4] It is hardly surprising that alongside these more placid accounts of political aetiology and imaginative literature, we have preserved anecdotes of a more unsettling quality. We tell stories of command performances of the play before the soldiers of Essex the night before their rebellion against the queen, or of decisions by the royal authorities and censors to cut the central deposition scene from publication of the script until after the death of Elizabeth, stories, that is to say, of deposition, or attempted deposition, that double those undertaken within it.[5]

In our own age, of course, criticism proper of the play begins with Coleridge.[6] For Coleridge, who looked to Shakespeare with the reverence one often reserves for sacred scripture, as Angus Fletcher once noted, *Richard II* combined Shakespeare's customarily acute treatment of character with "his most purely historical representation."[7] And these two themes, the formal and the historical, have dominated Shakespeare criticism since. By the end of the century, Walter Pater shifted interest slightly from character to the poetic sensibility in which character was embedded, a theme hardly very removed from Coleridge's concerns.[8] In our own century, John Dover Wilson, in his famous introduction to the Cambridge edition of the play, extended these considerations to dramatic genre and even religious ritual.[9] And with the publication in 1944 of Tillyard's *Shakespeare's History Plays,* the historical strain of Coleridgean poetics found a powerful expression.[10] Tillyard argued that *Richard II* depicted the passing of a medieval world order in dramatizing the founding events of the "Tudor myth" of English history and it has become impossible in recent years to speak responsibly about the play without referring to these ideas.

What is the "Tudor myth"? It is the aetiology by which the Tudor family established their historical legitimacy in coming to power on the English throne. *Richard II* is said to dramatize the founding events of the wars between the houses of Lancaster and York, conflicts that concluded only with the defeat of Richard III (the "scourge of English history") by Richmond, grandfather to the reigning English monarch. The critical event of this history was a usurpation, a successful rebellion against the throne, an event that Tillyard assures us Elizabethan popular morality could never abide. The "vile opportunist" Henry Bolingbroke usurped the throne from "that sweet lovely rose" King Richard. And the troubles that Henry in turn experienced in his own reign—both domestic and political—were traceable in this account to his primal foul act as the Bishop of Carlisle had explicitly predicted.[11]

I rehearse these two major traditions in Shakespeare criticism of *Richard II* not because I wish to reopen here an old debate, either to defend a formalist account of the play or articulate a new historical account, or even some combination of these two, but rather to draw attention to the limitations of these views in so far as the play itself does. For whether we have concerned ourselves with generic or referential features, with character or historical representation, with poetic sensibility or politics, we have concerned ourselves with differences, differences within the play, but also differences between the play and our own world, whether those differences are conceived aesthetically or historically. What I would suggest, however, is that the split between these two views is already Shakespeare's subject matter, and that we have built our criticism out of the same mythic materials of which the play itself is constructed, and about which, ironically, the play is profoundly critical.

Peter Ure, for example, the editor of the prestigious Arden edition of the play, draws together these two major trends into what must stand as the representative modern reading.[12] Opposing himself at once to poetical and political approaches that he finds equally reductive (and that he associates with Mark Van Doren and Tillyard), Ure sees the play as reflecting, in a phrase he draws, not unpredictably, from Coleridge—a "history of the human mind," the drama of a "man who was also a king."[13] The play, in his view, is a grand expression of Renaissance humanism as this idea has been employed by Shakespeare critics elsewhere and as Shakespeare is central to our conceptualization of this moment in European history.[14]

Ure's view is compelling and powerful, in large part, no doubt, because it draws upon so much of our common understanding of Shakespeare, literary creation, and even our own history. The notion of a "Renaissance" or of a humanistic revival of classical learning, notions attributed to Jacob Burckhardt and others in the nineteenth century, has accustomed us to seeing Shakespeare's play as the product of a burgeoning new rational social order for which the Cartesian seventeenth century was the formal beginning and the Hegelian nineteenth century the natural culmination.[15]

Yet this conceptualization, like all important conceptual paradigms, is mutable and in the past forty years or so a change has been underway.[16] It began among the medievalists who in the early 1950s set out to rescue the Middle Ages from the "darkness" to which such nineteenth-century conceptions had consigned their field of study.[17] The Middle Ages are only "dark" or "medieval," these scholars argued, when measured against an ancient enlightenment deemed to have passed, and a modern rebirth of classical understanding thought not yet to have begun. Scholars of literature, of the fine arts, and of history alike began to speak of the Middle Ages and even the Renaissance less as a new enlightenment than as the "waning" of an older world order that still held sway within these fields, an order for which the coordinates of Augustinian Christianity were considerably more powerful than the postulates of Hegelian dynamism. The names of D. W. Robertson, Erwin Panofsky, Johan Huizinga, and Wallace Ferguson suffice to invoke these new post-war intellectual currents.[18]

In the 1970s, what might be deemed the second stage of this historical revision was begun. In a little read but brilliant volume purportedly written to defend Burckhardt's original thesis, Joseph Mazzeo had argued that Renaissance historiographers were no less interested in constructing an aetiology of their own historical moment than scholars in the nineteenth century were.[19] The recent work of the so-called "Berkeley school" or new historicism acquires unexpected import in this context. Stephen Greenblatt, Jonathan Goldberg, Stephen Orgel, and Joel Fineman have all powerfully contributed in one way or another to a revisioning of the older orientation.[20] Drawing upon the anthropology of Clifford Geertz and Victor Turner, and the later writings of Michel Foucault, these writers have challenged the notion of a "Renaissance" from the opposite direction.[21] If the medievalists argued that modern notions of self applied less than was thought to their domain, these writers argued that in their field in a curious way it applied more.

Greenblatt, for example, showed that the Renaissance was no less concerned with self-construction or self-fashioning, the embedding of individuals within relations of power, than the most dialectical of modern thinkers.[22] Far from regarding the Renaissance as the birth of a Hegelian dynamism that would reach its maturity two centuries later, these scholars, following the lead of Foucault, would seem almost to argue for a reversal of the traditional view, opening the way to understanding the nineteenth century as in fact the humanistic inversion and usurpation of a metaphysical or theological mode still largely in place, a kind of covert or underground theology, as Meyer Abrams once characterized it.[23]

To revise familiar understandings in this fashion is not, of course, to deny the relevance of a conception like "the Renaissance" to a certain moment in our history as much as it is to suggest a more profound applicability and commonality than we have previously allowed, a commonality with regard to both the urge to mythologize our history and the urge to criticize such mythologizing, a commonality that may also explain, in part at least, why we found such conceptions initially so attractive. Far from suggesting that Shakespeare either reflects his time or transcends it to reflect a movement in European critical thinking four hundred years later (which are the two myths by which we customarily approach his work) we need to consider the possibility, these scholars implicitly suggest, that Shakespeare writes in a cultural climate that is in fundamental ways not significantly different from our own, an identity or identicality we have found it necessary to obviate in constructing the aetiology (literary or historical) of our own perspective. Rather than read either the Elizabethan Shakespeare or the Shakespeare of contemporary critical methodology it may be that what we need to read, what we in effect have always been reading without being aware of it, is Shakespeare's us.[24]

Take, for example, *Richard II*. The difference between Richard and Henry is the cornerstone of modern critical approaches to the play. We differentiate Richard's effusive sentimentalism from Henry's cold and calculating opportunism. The opposition is not always of the same polarity. When we wish to value an artistic sensibility we view Richard's expressiveness as poetic and Henry's calculation as Machiavellian and ambitious. When, on the contrary, we wish to value political savvy, we view Richard's effusiveness as weak and self-destructive and Henry's behavior as pragmatic and resourceful. But the opposition itself remains constant.

Moreover, we distribute this opposition over the course of the play. At any given moment, the characters are seen to contrast not only with other characters, but with themselves at other moments. For example, we draw attention to Richard's behavior in the long central sequence— on the Welsh shore, at Flint Castle, or at Westminster—in which, in speech after speech, he laments his situation as it becomes increasingly clear that his forces are failing him and his mortality is near. "[Let] us sit upon the ground / And tell sad stories about the death of kings" (III.ii.155–56), he remarks at one point. We contrast these speeches with the long ceremonious scenes of the beginning—before the challenge of Bolingbroke and Mowbray, before the lists at Coventry, and at the house of John of Gaunt—in which his ineffectuality is clear and in which he commits the political mistakes with which he has historically been charged.

In a similar if less obvious way we contrast Henry's rigid and politic manner in the central abdication scenes with his anxious, sentimental, almost comic behavior later, freeing his would-be assassin amid a farcical contest between his adviser Old York and the pleas of Aumerle's mother, recoiling before the coffin containing the body of the dead Richard, and finally leaving England to wash from his hands the sins of his accession. We have always treated this behavior lightly—as Shakespearean chronicle, as dramatic parody, or as an anticipation of Shakespeare's plays to come. The stark contrast between Henry and Richard would seem well summarized by their brief direct exchange in the abdication scene:

> *Bolingbroke.* Are you contented to resign the crown?
> *Richard.* Ay, no; no, ay: for I must nothing be.
> (IV.i.199–200)

Yet I think it is possible to show that Richard's behavior in these scenes, when viewed from a certain psychological economy, is indistinguishable from his behavior earlier, and that this current behavior, which culminates in his abdication and deposition from the throne, is but the final step in the progressive substitution of a private, imaginary conception of human relations for a more public, symbolic conception, a substitution that has been going on since the first moments of the play. In the same way, I think it is possible to show that Henry's seeming distance in these central scenes is indistinguishable from his curious vulnerability later.

Moreover, and most important, that the behavior of both Richard and Henry in the play is the *same* behavior. Overtaking Richard, Henry becomes Richard. It is not simply that their actions parallel each other. That much we have always recognized. Their "doubleness," their ability to appear as "foils" for each other at every point, has even been the very foundation of differential readings of the play.[25] But Shakespeare's view of them, I would suggest, is more radical. They double each other not just synchronically or relationally but diachronically or sequentially. They are differentiated or opposed as the two apparent "sides" of a Möbius strip, surfaces that is to say that are genuinely distinguishable at every given point when viewed, so to speak, "side by side," but that turn out, within a larger twisting logic or economy, to be extensions of the same "side." They are for each other the future or the past of the same consistent dramatic figure.

These ideas are, of course, not unfamiliar to students of recent philosophy or contemporary critical theory.[26] The analysis that Shakespeare makes of Richard and Henry would not seem on the surface dissimilar to the reading that Michel Foucault and others have made of a notion that has virtually dominated philosophy in recent years: Nietzsche's notion of the "death of God." Nietzsche's famous aphorism occurs, of course, in the *Gay Science*.[27] "Wither is God?" cries Nietzsche's madman who jumps into the midst of a crowd of nonbelievers, "I will tell you."

> *We have killed him*—you and I. All of us are his murderers.... Do we hear nothing as yet of the noise of the grave-diggers who are burying God? Do we smell nothing as yet of the divine decomposition? Gods, too, decompose. God is dead. God remains dead. And we have killed him.

Foucault's commentary on this passage occurs at the conclusion of *The Order of Things*, in a remark on the relevance of Nietzsche's pronouncement for European humanism, a humanism that since Hegel would heroically take up its place in a universe God has abandoned.[28]

> In our day, and once again Nietzsche indicated the turning-point from a long way off, it is not so much the absence or the death of God that is affirmed as the end of man (that narrow, imperceptible displacement, that recession in the form of identity, which are the reason why man's finitude has become his end); it becomes apparent, then, that the death of God and the last man are engaged in a contest with more than one round: is it not the last man who announces that he has killed God, thus situating his language, his thought, his laughter in the space of that already dead God, yet positing himself also as he who has killed God and whose existence includes the freedom and the decision of that murder? Thus, the last man is at the same time older and yet younger than the death of God; since he has killed God, it is he himself who must answer for his own finitude; but since it is in the death of God that he speaks, thinks, and exists, his murder itself is doomed to die; new gods, the same gods, are already swelling

the future Ocean; man will disappear. Rather than the death of God—or, rather, in the wake of that death and in a profound correlation with it—what Nietzsche's thought heralds is the end of his murderer.[29]

For Foucault this "murderer" is man, and the project of humanism that notion subtends, and he understands "the end" (*la fin*) in two distinct ways: Nietzsche's thought heralds for us at once the secret goal of humanism (to displace God); and at the same time (and by virtue of the success of this displacement) the destruction of humanism.

Foucault argues that Nietzsche's reading is prophetic. Nietzsche recognizes the drama in which the project of humanism is engaged and names in advance the end of it. The "death of God" is less a commentary about the present state of the divine than about humanism and its dangers. Rather than succeed God, rather than heroically show up there where there appears a kind of cosmic vacancy, man has genuinely usurped God's place. The desire to be man is the desire to displace God. You have finally succeeded, Nietzsche's pronouncement tells us (in Foucault's reading), in accomplishing the project in which you have always already been engaged. It is Nietzsche's answer, if you like, to Descartes.

But in the second place, this usurpation is as unstable as it is successful. In the very manner by which man has gained his position he has destroyed forever the possibility of enjoying it. Displacing God, he has displaced necessarily the opposition of man to God, the founding opposition, that is, of metaphysical thinking itself ("the gods are deathless," goes the ancient Greek adage).[30] Thus the condition of his possibility is at the same time the condition of his impossibility. He has only become God insofar as he has destroyed the possibility of being God, in so far, that is, as he has established a fatally fractured position. In an attempt to radically differentiate himself from his other, he has ironically established himself only as a double of that other, and thereby opened the floodgates for others like himself to do the same to him in dutiful emulation of his own divine and rebellious behavior.

If we substitute the figure of the king—God's anointed—for God, then Shakespeare's analysis of the relation between Henry and Richard is nothing else. Bolingbroke's contest with Mowbray within the monarchical framework turns out, when heightened by a series of strategic misjudgments on Richard's part, to be a contest with the monarch himself. And the consequence likewise is the same. Far from establishing a difference between the old and the new, between himself and his predecessor, the deposition succeeds in establishing only the impossibility of such a differentiation. Henry quickly becomes the very model for such impossible differentiation. Before the play is out, he will have had to thwart at least one attempt on his position and Aumerle's will be but the first of many.

Even in this regard, however, Shakespeare has complicated matters for us since Bolingbroke's takeover is already itself only a repetition. He has taken over what is genuinely an empty crown since he is in fact not the first to usurp the throne: Richard has in fact already deposed himself, and Henry is but the first in a long line of imitators of his action. Richard becomes "landlord of England," as John of Gaunt calls him, and leaves a "vacancy" or nothing in the place of the king, long before Bolingbroke makes any move against him. And when Bolingbroke does come along, returning to England on the excuse that he would exercise his rights of inheritance, his "royalty," as York calls it, he does neither more nor less than Richard himself has done in appealing to the power of a kingship that he himself has critically weakened. To some extent Bolingbroke merely emulates Richard's own behavior. He does to Richard what Richard has already done to himself.

But the real structure of Richard's relation to his own kingship appears most clearly only when Henry effectively displaces him. For in overtaking Richard, Henry becomes Richard. More than simply occupying Richard's place, he systematically repeats Richard's every gesture, psychologically as well as politically. Having imitated Richard's behavior to gain the throne—radically displacing Richard as Richard has displaced himself—he now begins to imitate Richard's own internal deposition in his attempts to maintain it, a double deposition that reaches its culmination in the play when Exton appears before Henry with a coffin containing the dead Richard. In what is no doubt Shakespeare's gravest irony, the situation now reenacts the murder of Thomas of Woodstock, duke of Gloucester, the murder scene that set into motion the whole infernal process to begin with:

> *Exton.* Great King, within this coffin I present
>   Thy buried fear . . .
> *Bolingbroke.* Exton, I thank thee not, for thou has wrought
>   A deed of slander with thy fatal hand
>   Upon my head and all this famous land.
> *Exton.* From your own mouth, my lord, did I this deed.

> *Bolingbroke.* They love not poison that do poison need, ...
> The guilt of conscience take thou for thy labor.
> (V.vi.30–41)

To say as much is not, of course, to whitewash Bolingbroke. It is not to reverse the traditional polarities and make Richard a villain and Bolingbroke a creature of circumstance. For such dutiful emulation of the sovereign, such monarchical subjectivity before the actions of the king, is precisely the nature of the problem the play poses for us. Bolingbroke acts like a dutiful subject in a situation in which such action destroys the possibility of being a dutiful subject. His action is therefore no less self-destructive than that of his predecessor, with regard to either Richard's kingship or his own. In fact, the problem the play succeeds effectively in posing for us, though by no means solves, is how to be a dutiful subject in a situation in which there is nothing in the place of the king. Shakespeare articulates this problem for us most intensely in the person of Richard, who, alone in prison in Pomfret Castle, meditates upon kings, subjects, and nothing and the consolation that philosophy may afford.

And in view of these more profound diachronic identities of critical subjectivity, traditional criticism of the play, which insists upon affirming synchronic differences, must be seen at once as mythic and ironic: mythic in so far as it distorts the presentation Shakespeare makes of his characters by resurrecting the kinds of mythic distinctions that inform his sources; but ironic at the same time since it is such distortions or mythic representations that are already Shakespeare's subject matter. The differential reading that criticism affirms, from Coleridge to Ure, is the same reading that the characters themselves affirm with regard to each other. The Tudor myth of differences is less an enveloping structure than the very myth whose limitations the play exists to stage. In the present play the notion that Bolingbroke is a usurper is, of course, the view of Richard and his allies. But before the second tetralogy is out, it will become the view of Henry as well, at a moment when the "boisterous" "snatching" of the crown will appear to him as the central "argument" of all his reign, a moment when his own son Prince Hal, in dutiful imitation of his father's behavior, would take the crown from off the head of the living king (cf. 1 Hen. IV, IV.v.191–98).

Let me be especially clear about this point.[31] It is not that traditional criticism is wrong to recognize the myth in Shakespeare's play, but rather (and perhaps more precisely) that it is not wrong enough: it is insufficient to stop with the recognition. Shakespeare's age and Shakespeare's literature are no less critical than we pride our own as being, whether we take our critical cue from Hegel, Kant, or some other Platonic philosophic framework. To read Shakespeare's plays critically is to read from within Shakespeare's plays, to read his interrogation of the very critical structures by which we would try to encompass those plays.

Which is not to say, therefore, that my own reading thereby escapes being mythic. There are no positions that are not mythic—neither Shakespeare's, nor that of his sources, nor that of traditional criticism, nor mine in this essay. But differing positions may be more or less aware that they are mythic, more or less aware of the limitations of mythic positions, of their origins, their strategies, and their consequences.

In this regard, the relationship of criticism to the play may not be dissimilar to the relation of Henry to Richard. Attempting to differentiate himself from his predecessor, he may succeed only in reproducing him. Reading the play for difference, attempting to master it, to construct ourselves as different from it, we reenact it. We read with the play only in so far as we acknowledge our failures to read it, in so far as we work through the consequences of acting it out, and recognize that Shakespeare is dramatizing the future or past of the critical path upon which we have embarked. It may be less that Shakespeare parallels in his play our positions in criticism (which would be another way of misunderstanding what he has written) than that he traces, prophetically, the conditions that by extension are their origins or ends.

Nor may this be the only time in Shakespeare's career that he takes up such diachronic repetitions. To a certain extent we may say that *Julius Caesar* reflects the same dilemma. Killing Caesar in that play one becomes Caesar. Pompei, Caesar, Brutus, Antony, even Octavius, all find themselves successively occupying the same position and implicated in the same violence. Likewise, Macbeth kills the thane of Cawdor only to find he has become the thane of Cawdor. Like the former "rebel" against the king (whose head he spies, in the Roman Polanski production, impaled upon the stake of his adversaries), so Macbeth will find himself successively rebelling against the king, rebelled against in turn, and finally impaled upon the stake of his own dreaded enemies, enemies who are fated in turn to relinquish the throne to the son of still one more contemporary (Banquo).[32]

In fact, in this regard at least, the liberties taken by Roman Polanski in filming the play would seem entirely "Shakespearean." Polanski creates out of the character of Ross and certain curious textual lapses an entirely new figure: a man who successively elevates Macbeth at his coronation to the throne, a man who is the famed "third murderer" in the scene in which Banquo is killed, a man who "dispatches" the other two murderers in turn once they have outlived their usefulness, a man who leads the attack against the wife and children of Macduff (in a scene conceived as a grisly reenactment of the Sharon Tate murders), a man who is passed over (as Macbeth was initially) when Macbeth rewards his troops, and who makes his way to the enemy camps of Malcolm and Macduff only to help them in turn defeat the rebel and elevate the "rightful" king (Malcolm) to the throne, a man who is, in short, Macbeth's double. In staging the play in this fashion, I would suggest, Polanski has built upon a structure of doubling and violence already fully in place. The film's final shot in which the other son of Duncan—Donalbain—is seen sauntering up to the witches' cave only to begin the whole murderous process again, is only fitting ironic testimony to the endlessness of this structure of deposition and usurpation that Shakespeare set in motion in *Richard II*.[33]

And in our perception of a burgeoning humanism in which we conceive Shakespeare to be writing and that endlessness to be contained, we may similarly give testimony or deposition less to the presence of such an organizational structure than its lack, to the blindness by which in the "Tudor myth" we would seek beyond our own age to construct the conditions of ourselves, both within the Shakespearean context and without. It may be that Shakespeare for his own part has undertaken to stage the limits of such a humanistic usurpation of medieval hierarchies of being and transcendence, one that leaves nothing in the place of the king, and that we for our part have been attracted to such a criticism because we find within it an uncanny resemblance to our own humanistic and nihilistic projects, although we choose to hint at these profounder identities between Shakespeare's world and our own only within the secondary contexts of anecdotes about the play's relation to real rebellions and to the history of real scriptural or textual excisions.

To speak more concretely about such critical subjectivity as Shakespeare's characters share (and we share with them), let us turn to follow more closely the movements of the play itself.

II. Soiled with That Dear Blood

The play opens with a contrast of rhetorical styles that echoes what is to follow.

> *Richard.* Old John of Gaunt, time-honored Lancaster,
> Hast thou according to thy oath and band
> Brought hither Henry Hereford, thy bold son,
> Here to make good the boist'rous late appeal,
> Which then our leisure would not let us hear,
> Against the Duke of Norfolk, Thomas Mowbray?
> (I.i.1–6)

The repetitive alliteration of aspirants ("hither Henry Hereford"), the long-winded ceremonious diction, elicit from John of Gaunt a lean "I have, my liege." In retrospect, Gaunt's response draws our attention to the emptiness of such pageantry both stylistically and dramatically—since Henry is already present—and directs us to Richard's verbal strategies. Richard's language functions less to facilitate exchange than defer it, a deferral, moreover, that seems to repeat an earlier one.

In the sequence that follows, this two-part structure, this coming to nothing of the king's "sound and fury," will in turn be repeated. The appeal of Bolingbroke concerns primarily the murder at Calais of Thomas of Woodstock, duke of Gloucester, one of Edward's sons, and therefore Richard's kin. The charge is overtly directed at Sir Thomas Mowbray. But as Gaunt subtly suggests in his reply to Richard's question, it is covertly directed against Richard. Richard asks for the grounds of Bolingbroke's complaint. Gaunt replies, "some apparent danger seen in him / Aimed at you Highness" (13–14), the ambiguity of "seen in him" suggesting either "that he sees" (that is, in Mowbray) or "that will be seen in him by others as directed against you."

Historians are somewhat undecided about the precise details of Gloucester's death though few exculpate Richard entirely. Let us put aside for the moment the details of the murder. They will come up again in the scene at Pomfret Castle. Whatever Richard's part in it, Bolingbroke's attack against Mowbray is an attack against the throne since Mowbray could not have proceeded in such a gesture without the knowledge and consent of the king. It behooves Richard as monarch, therefore, to act swiftly and strategically.

Denouncing each other as "traitors," the contestants now reflect this application and urgency. After charging Mowbray with the misuse of the king's funds, Bolingbroke remarks, "That all the treasons for these eighteen years / Complotted and contrived in this land / Fetch from false Mowbray, their first head and spring" (95–97).

The charge is, of course, an outlandish one, perhaps purposely so, given that the "first head and spring" of the land is necessarily Richard. Then Bolingbroke adds: "That he did plot the Duke of Gloucester's death" (100). Mowbray answers him, denying any wrongdoing with regard to the king's funds, and disclaiming any responsibility in Gloucester's death. "For Gloucester's death / I slew him not; but, to my own disgrace, / Neglected my sworn duty in that case" (132–34).

What was his "sworn duty in that case"? To pursue the murderer or to execute an action Richard had ordered but that he had not undertaken? He then adds: "as for the rest appealed, / It issues from the rancor of a villain, / A recreant and most degenerate traitor; / Which in myself I boldly will defend" (142–45). "Issues from" could, of course, mean "spoken by," which would implicate Bolingbroke, against whom he will fight ("defend"). Or it could mean "originates with," in which case it suggests Richard, whose "defender" Mowbray, of course, remains.

The situation before Richard, then, is clear and would seem to offer him two courses of action, each of which would serve to improve his situation and consolidate his power. Assuming he allows the fight to proceed, there can be only two possible outcomes: either Bolingbroke is killed or Mowbray is killed. If Bolingbroke is killed, then Richard's problem at least for the moment would appear to be contained. The attack against his throne would seem frontally repudiated. On the other hand, if Mowbray is killed, then Richard would seem in no less of a propitious situation. For Bolingbroke would now be no longer in a position to come before Richard with a claim regarding the death of Gloucester since justice will have been served in that regard. In either case, that is, allowing the fight to proceed would seem strategically the most judicious course to follow.

Which renders what happens that much more strange. Mowbray utters his reply to Bolingbroke (cited above) and now Richard, who earlier seemed to encourage their encounter, suddenly backs off.

> Wrath-kindled gentlemen, be ruled by me.
> Let's purge this choler without letting blood:
> This we prescribe, though no physician;
> Deep malice makes too deep incision;
> Forget, forgive, conclude, and be agreed;
> (152–56)

But this is a conclusion neither likely to be acceptable to them nor is it strategically desirable. Why does he propose it? His proposal, of course, pleases neither of the contestants in whom it provokes a kind of mini-revolution so that Richard ends up proclaiming, "We were not born to sue, but to command" (196). For the moment at least he relents and allows the fight to proceed.

His brief gesture, however, only foreshadows what is to come. The day of the lists at Coventry arrives. The trumpets sound. The ceremonies proceed. And at the last moment, as in the first scene, the proceedings are interrupted. "The King hath thrown his warder down" (I.iii.118).

Why? Why does Richard stop the fight? No reason is offered in the present scene; when the contestants arrive he simply announces their fate. The only clue seems to be Richard's loss of heart earlier. But why should he lose heart initially?

That is not all. Once Richard has stopped the lists at Coventry he treats the potential combatants with a curious inequality, curious to the extent that it is counterproductive to the preservation of his own position, which is presumably the justification for allowing the fight to proceed to begin with.

He turns first to Mowbray.

> . . . our kingdom's earth should not be soiled
> with that dear blood which it hath fosterèd;
> And for our eyes do hate the dire aspect
> Of civil wounds ploughed up with neighbor's sword,
> And for we think the eagle-wingèd pride
> Of sky-aspiring and ambitious thoughts
> With rival-hating envy set on you
> To wake our peace . . .
> And make us wade even in our kindred's blood;
> Therefore we banish you our territories.
> (125–39)

Thomas Mowbray, his defender, he banishes for life, a sentence that leaves his subject in astonishment. "A heavy sentence, my most sovereign liege, / And all unlooked for from your Highness' mouth" (154–55). Then he turns to Henry Bolingbroke. Bolingbroke, his challenger, a man who now is more of a threat than ever, he banishes initially for a limited duration of ten years, and shortly afterwards—upon a certain "look" from John of Gaunt—he reduces that sentence to six years. Even Bolingbroke is amazed at the outcome. "How long a time lies in one little word," he remarks. "[Such] is the breath of kings" (212–14).

What's more, Richard compels both former combatants to swear an oath that they will in exile never plot against him, an oath that both puts into language the natural course of the events he has set into motion, and one that in banishing them he has effectively destroyed the power to enforce.

> Lay on our royal sword your banished hands;
> Swear by the duty that you owe to God— . . .
> To keep the oath that we administer:
> You never shall—so help you truth and God!—
> Embrace each other's love in banishment, . . .
> Nor never by advisèd purpose meet
> To plot, contrive, or complot any ill
> 'Gainst us, our state, our subjects, or our land.
> (179–90)

Why has Richard undertaken such a seemingly foolish course, one that seems to suggest rebellion to his subjects even if such an idea were not in their thoughts already? Shakespeare gives us the answers—as, I suggest, he usually does to the questions he raises—but they are not the ones we expect and not located where we expect to find them. To understand Shakespeare's response, we need to follow more fully his posing of the problem.

Richard's actions at the end of act 1 and the first scene of act 2 are no less bizarre. The environment is now one that is hardly conducive to further abuses. Henry, Richard himself notes, has made himself a popular favorite for his "courtship of the common people." And yet, after curiously concerning himself with Henry's "parting tears" (so that even his aide Green is moved to redirect him to the matters at hand), Richard continues the practices for which he has become notorious in the history books—"[farming] the royal realm" to feed his coffers, and issuing blank charters to supply his needs in fighting the controversial Irish wars (I.iv.45–52).

Then he is summoned to the house of the ailing John of Gaunt. While awaiting Richard's arrival, Gaunt utters his famous death-bed prophecy.

> Methinks I am a prophet new inspired,
> And thus expiring do foretell of him: . . .
> This royal throne of kings, this scept'red isle,
> This earth of majesty, this seat of Mars,
> This other Eden, demi-paradise,
> This fortress built by Nature for herself
> Against infection and the hand of war,
> This happy breed of men, this little world, . . .
> This blessed plot, this earth, this realm, this England, . . .

> Is now leased out—I die pronouncing it—
> Like to a tenement or pelting farm.
> (II.i.31–60)

All the commonplace epithets of English nationalism are there. And when Richard arrives, Gaunt will repeat the conclusion to which they lead him, a conclusion that will turn out to have prophetic power over the play we are to witness at large and over Richard in particular.

> A thousand flatterers sit within thy crown,
> Whose compass is no bigger than thy head,
> And yet incagèd in so small a verge
> The waste is no whit lesser than thy land.
> O, had thy grandsire with a prophet's eye
> Seen how his son's son should destroy his sons,
> From forth thy reach he would have laid thy shame,
> Deposing thee before thou wert possessed,
> Which art possessed now to depose thyself . . .
> Landlord of England art thou now, not king;
> (II.i.100–112)

Gaunt is carried off. His death is announced. What does Richard do? He seizes Gaunt's goods in the name of fighting his Irish wars—precisely, that is, what Gaunt has accused him of doing. "How long shall I be patient?" Gaunt's brother, the duke of York charges. "Seek you to seize and gripe into your hands / The royalties and rights of banished Hereford?" York chides, as if the deposition had already taken place, and it were Richard who were usurping the royalty of Henry.

> Is not Gaunt dead? And doth not Hereford live? . . .
> Take Hereford's rights away, and . . .
> Be not thyself. For how art thou a king
> But by fair sequence and succession? . . .
> You pluck a thousand dangers on your head.
> (II.i.189–205)

What is Richard's response to York? He goes off to fight his wars and leaves York of all people in charge of the kingdom. Having provided the excuse for Bolingbroke to return from exile to claim his rightful inheritance, Richard now offers him, so it seems, the key: the weak, aging, last surviving son of King Edward, who has just charged Richard with the blood of his kin.

Why does Richard do all this? Why does he undertake such egregiously mistaken and self-destructive actions? The situation is not unlike that in *King Lear* where the "mistakes" the king makes in dividing up the kingdom so inequitably and so precariously are of such an outstanding and egregiously evident nature (even to those within the drama) that they begin to argue some "darker purpose."[34]

Shakespeare offers us some clues, some tantalizing hints, in the present scenes that will become fully readable only later. An example is the language with which Richard perpetually greets Bolingbroke, language that is curiously out of place for the context in which they meet and that we have always read as an instance of "dramatic irony." "What doth our cousin lay to Mowbray's charge?" Richard asks, when the contestants appear before him. "It must be great that can inherit us" (I.i.84–85). Or later in the same scene, once the two have spoken, he remarks:

> Mowbray, impartial are our eyes and ears.
> Were he my brother, nay, my kingdom's heir,
> As he is but my father's brother's son,
> Now by my scepter's awe I make a vow,
> Such neighbor nearness to our sacred blood
> Should nothing privilege.
> (I.i.115–20)

That Bolingbroke is, of course, his "kingdom's heir" would hardly escape an Elizabethan audience. And in the present debate, it would be difficult not to see in "my father's brother's son" a reference to an avenging son of Gloucester, with whose murder Mowbray (and covertly Richard) has just been charged.

Or, again, in the fight scene, once the commencement pageantries have begun, Richard "descends" to embrace Bolingbroke. It is a somewhat obsequious gesture that is not afforded his defender, Thomas Mowbray, and performed in language that seems to refer as well to his own "blood" and his own demise.

> We will descend and fold him in our arms.
> Cousin of Hereford, as thy cause is right,
> So be thy fortune in this royal fight:
> Farewell, my blood, which if today thou shed,
> Lament we may, but not revenge thee dead.
> (I.iii.54–58)

Or, on the other side, it is in context of Mowbray's denial of participation in Gloucester's death and his attack against Bolingbroke for making such a charge that Richard would seem moved to stop the fight, as if he heard in Mowbray's attack muted references to himself. "As for the rest appealed," Mowbray charges, "it issues from the rancor of a villain, / A recreant and most degenerate traitor; / which in myself I boldly will defend" (I.i.142–45). And Richard suddenly intercedes: "Wrath kindled gentlemen, be ruled by me. / Let's purge this choler without letting blood: . . . / Forget, forgive, conclude, and be agreed" (I.i.152–56).

Or, finally, in the scene that Shakespeare has interspersed between these scenes, the brief exchange between John of Gaunt and the widow of Thomas of Woodstock in which the duchess asks that Gaunt take action against Richard for the murder of her husband, Gaunt utters some remarks that seem designed to heighten or bring into high relief aspects of the scenes we have just witnessed. "Alas," Gaunt notes, "the part I had in Woodstock's blood / Doth more solicit me than your exclaims / To stir against the butchers of his life" (I.ii.1–3).

These references, in which formalist critics have always found plentiful examples of Shakespeare's "dramatic ironies," and in which psychoanalytic critics have little difficulty discerning the effects of unconscious desire, are troublesome precisely because they seem at once calculated on Shakespeare's part and yet recalcitrant, for the moment at least, to the suggestions they invite us to consider.

Rather than jump the gun, as it were, seeking solutions outside the play or within its formal parameters, let us follow Shakespeare's unfolding of his own analysis. Let us turn to the long middle sequence of the play in which I suggest these earlier passages in retrospect become readable.

III. The King's Two Bodies

Richard feels fairly confident when he lands on the Welsh shore. We will watch him change in this scene from a position of relative security to one of despair as the news of his failing forces reaches him. He opens the scene in language that seems reminiscent of the final words of John of Gaunt. Yet if we look with some care at his language, even in the opening speech, the outcome may seem less than strange.

> I weep for joy
> To stand upon my kingdom once again.
> Dear earth, I do salute thee with my hand,
> Though rebels wound thee with their horses' hoofs . . .
> So weeping, smiling, greet I thee, my earth, . . .
> And do thee favors with my royal hands.
> Feed not thy sovereign's foe, my gentle earth . . .

> Mock not my senseless conjuration, lords:
> This earth shall have a feeling, and these stones
> Prove armèd soldiers, ere her native king
> Shall falter under foul rebellion's arm.
> (III.ii.4–26)

If this passage is placed alongside Richard's language earlier in the play, his style seems to have changed completely. It has become effusive, sentimental, and excessively invested in naturalistic phenomena. It is not unlike, to continue the parallel we noted earlier, the language of *King Lear*, once Lear has been divested of his few remaining soldiers and his shelter. It is so strikingly different, in these respects, in fact, that most critics have sought to divorce it from the earlier behavior we have seen and find in it the emergence of a new poetic or artistic sensibility in Richard, one that these critics find lacking, for example, in his exchange with John of Gaunt. Peter Ure, as we have suggested above, and perhaps with an eye to similar strains within the great tragedies of Shakespeare, sees in this scene the beginning of a Coleridgean "history of the human mind."[35]

> This design must control our understanding of how Shakespeare wished us to read Richard's character. The second scene of the third Act is crucial in any interpretation of this.... The situation in which Richard now finds himself is that of a king, deprived of physical power, who retains a circumscribed personal liberty and the sacred name and attributes pertaining to his kingship.... The rest of this phase of the play is to be concerned with how he gives even these things one by one into the hands of the usurper.... That part of his fall which was political and entailed the loss of power has been accomplished; there remains the aspect of it which trenches upon a sacred tragedy, the divesting of royalty of its mysterious panoply. It is the wish to set this last in a clear and free light, as a thing that happened to a man who was also a king, which we may conjecture, shaped the design of the play as a whole. Shakespeare bundled the narrative of causes away into the first two and a half acts so that he might more fully set forth the drama of the sufferer constrained to reduce himself from king to man by shedding the "great glory" of the Name.... Hence it is that we meet for the first time in this scene the new, expressive Richard.[36]

Ure's reading of this scene, and of the whole middle sequence of the play, in fact, as something of a sacred divestiture seems to draw upon Walter Pater who saw in these scenes what he called an "inverted rite," and perhaps also upon John Dover Wilson who in his own introduction to the Cambridge edition of the play noted above saw in it a parallel to the Christian Passion. In recent years, scholars have pursued this strain.[37] Ernest Kantorowicz, for example, in *The King's Two Bodies: A Study in Medieval Political Theology,* undertakes to study the language of "twin-born majesty" as a curious fiction of English juridical practice in the latter half of the sixteenth century.[38] If we are to situate Richard's behavior in these scenes within the context of the play as a whole, and in particular within those scenes we have dismissed as political, perhaps at this point we should begin to inquire about Elizabethan notions of "subjectivity" for this "man who was also a king." Kantorowicz, who began his own study largely out of his interest in Shakespeare's *Richard II,* seems a propitious place to start.

Kantorowicz cites, as the first example of this curious notion of the "king's two bodies," Edmund Plowden's *Reports*. King Edward VI, while not yet of age, had leased a certain tract of land from the duchy of Lancaster, whereupon the following agreement was made by the crown's lawyers:

> that by the Common Law no Act which the King does as King, shall be defeated by his Nonage. For the King has in him two Bodies, *viz.,* a Body natural, and a Body politic. His Body natural (if it be considered in itself) is a Body mortal, subject to all Infirmities that come by Nature or Accident, to the Imbecility of Infancy or old Age, and to the like Defects that happen to the natural Bodies of other People. But his Body politic is a Body that cannot be seen or handled, consisting of Policy and Government, and constituted for the Direction of the People, and the Management of the public weal, and this Body is utterly void of Infancy, and old Age, and other natural Defects and Imbecilities, which the Body natural is subject to, and for this Cause, what the King does in his Body politic, cannot be invalidated or frustrated by any Disability in his natural Body.[39]

The king, in short, is two distinct bodies with distinct capacities in one person. The distinguishing feature of this conjunction, and what for Kantorowicz makes it sound vaguely mystical, is its double nature. In the first place, this unity, within the confines of this world, was considered indivisible: each of the two bodies was considered contained or "consolidated" within the other. In the second place, the body politic was considered "more large, more ample" than the body natural.

> although [the King] has, or takes, the land in his natural Body, yet to this natural Body is cojoined his Body politic, which contains his

royal Estate and Dignity; and the Body politic includes the Body natural, but the Body natural is the lesser.[40]

Moreover, by virtue of this superiority of the body politic, certain forces are said to act upon the body natural.

> [The King's] Body politic, which is annexed to his Body natural, takes away the Imbecility of his Body natural, and draws the Body natural, which is the lesser, and all the effects thereof to itself, which is the greater.[41]

Kantorowicz notes that the indivisibility of the king's two bodies was no barrier to one being separate from the other at some point in time. The two bodies, for example, can be separated in death. Or, to put it the other way around, death can be thought of precisely as the separation of these two. In this event it was said, not that the body politic dies (for the body politic by definition can never die), but rather that it undergoes a "demise"; it passes from one bodily incarnation to another. The body natural alone dies. The "soul" of the King, as it were, the immortal part of Kingship, migrates from one worldly form to another.[42]

It might be objected, Kantorowicz notes, and on just this kind of argument, that such political language of the sixteenth century jurists was little more than a borrowing from the theological-ecclesiastical realm, and in particular from the doctrine of the two Natures. Kantorowicz acknowledges that a great deal of exchange took place between the two. In the early Middle Ages, for example, he points out that the Church borrowed heavily from the state. By the late Middle Ages, on the other hand, the pendulum had swung the other way and the state borrowed freely from the Church. In the sixteenth century, for example, Christological definitions were being employed with regard to kingship, the king being considered the "head" of state just as Christ was thought to be "head" of Christian society.[43] In explaining the seemingly mystical cojoining of two bodies in one person, Kantorowicz adduces another parallel, the Athanasian Creed, which finally became incorporated into the Book of Common Prayer.[44]

> non duo tamen, sed unus.... Unus autem non conversione divinitatis in carnem, sed assumptione humanitatis in Deum.... Unus omnino, non confusione substantiae, sed unitate personae.
>
> (not two, then, but one.... One however, not by the conversion [or transformation] of divinity into flesh, but by the assumption [or adoption] of mankind into God.... One altogether, not by the con-

fusion [or mixing together] of substance but rather by the unity of person [or agency].)⁴⁵

Such parallels and borrowings exist, Kantorowicz affirms. But we should not be too hasty to see one as the mere extension of the other. Although he never says so directly, Kantorowicz seems to imply that the theological and the political have a relation similar to that of the king's two bodies within the body of the state at large: one not by the confusion or mixing together of the two (or the transformation of one into the other) but by the unity of agency, the political realm being drawn up into the theological.

The distinctiveness of the political and the theological, in any case, helps to explain, in Kantorowicz's view, the difference between English and continental legal practice where a "theology of kingship" was much more customarily maintained. The famous, if apocryphal, "l'état c'est moi" of Louis XIV reflects as much in his view, while in England, by contrast, the king rules only in his capacity as king in Parliament. Thus in England, in extreme situations, it becomes possible to summon the armies of the king (body politic) to fight against King Charles I (body natural), or for Charles Stuart to be executed in the name of the king, and the Puritan cry of "fighting the king to defend the king" becomes reflective of the same distinction.⁴⁶

How does this distinction of the king's two bodies help us to explain the present scene in *Richard II*? Having outlined the above ideas, Kantorowicz devotes an entire chapter to Shakespeare's play, which was his inspiration for the book to begin with.⁴⁷ Richard calls upon the forces of the body politic to defend the body natural. "Feed not thy sovereign's foe," he asks of his kingdom. His gesture is part of Shakespeare's larger strategy, Kantorowicz suggests, which is to depict Richard's progress ultimately from King to Fool to God. And in reading the play in this manner, Kantorowicz attests, he returns to the readings of Pater and Dover Wilson.⁴⁸

But if we read the sequence in light of the distinctions of the first chapter of Kantorowicz's book, a very different understanding emerges. What it reveals, ironically, is the way in which Richard has in fact already deposed himself. In his effusion of feeling, Richard calls upon the forces of the body politic to defend the body natural. But what Kantorowicz has made clear to us is that there is no such obligation within the doctrine of the King's two bodies for the body politic to so act. In fact, to the contrary, the body natural is drawn up into the body politic and it is entirely possible for the body natural to be discarded—even executed—by the forces of the body politic, which is to say, by the king in Parliament, as Charles was.

Richard's appeal, in other words, makes sense only if he has substituted the body politic for the body natural, if he has confused or mixed together the two, in order to make his appeal in the first place. It makes sense only if he has confused his private human body with his public monarchical body, which is to say, only if he has violated the very distinction between the king's two bodies upon which his appeal is founded. The fact that earthly men cannot depose the body of an anointed king does not guarantee that the body natural cannot die. It is only by substituting one for the other, the body natural for the body politic, a substitution that undoes the very condition of the distinction and thus Richard's appeal to the doctrine, that any such appeal can be made.

In the scene that follows, I would suggest, it is this fatal substitution, and its self-destructive and self-usurping consequences, that is made increasingly explicit. Richard's initial appeal to kingship (quoted above) is followed by Carlisle's advice that "that power that made you king / Hath power to keep you king in spite of all" (III.ii.27–28), and his own reiteration of the appeal in starker terms.

> Not all the water in the rough rude sea
> Can wash the balm off from an anointed king;
> The breath of worldly men cannot depose
> The deputy elected by the Lord.
> (54–57)

But Richard's remarks are followed immediately by the news from Salisbury that the Welsh forces have been dispersed. "Time hath set a blot upon my pride" (81), Richard despairs. Aumerle counsels him, "Remember who you are" (82), and the cycle begins again. But this time it proceeds more in questions than affirmations.

> I had forgot myself: am I not King?
> Awake, thou coward majesty! Thou sleepest.
> Is not the King's name twenty thousand names?
> Arm, arm, my name! a puny subject strikes
> At thy great glory.
> (83–87)

Then straightaway Scroop appears. And now, even before he speaks, Richard jumps in. "Say, is my kingdom lost? Why, 'twas my care, /And what loss is it to be rid of care?" (95–96). Scroop delivers his news. Richard's "very beadsmen learn to bend their bows / Of double-fatal yew against thy state" (116–17). Bushy, Bagot, and Green are dead. Richard retorts, "of comfort no man speak" (144).

> Let's talk of graves, of worms, and epitaphs . . .
> For God's sake let us sit upon the ground
> And tell sad stories of the death of kings:
> How some have been deposed, some slain in war,
> Some haunted by the ghost they have deposed,
> Some poisoned by their wives, some sleeping killed,
> All murdered.
>
> (145–60)

After this catalogue, which sounds like a checklist of themes of Shakespeare's coming plays, Richard returns to the theme with which he began the scene. "For you have mistook me all this while: / I live with bread like you, feel want, / Taste grief, need friends—subjected thus, / How can you say to me, I am a king?" (174–75).

But Richard's humanity has never been in doubt. In assuming it was, Richard makes explicit the "double-fatal" substitution that founds it. It is in substituting the body natural for the body politic that such a doubt becomes possible in the first place. Carlisle again counsels that "wise men ne'er sit and wail their woes / But presently prevent the ways to wail" (178–79). Richard cheers up. "This ague fit of fear is overblown; / An easy task it is to win our own" (190–91). Scroop delivers his news. "York is joined with Bolingbroke" (200). And for a third time Richard is undone. "What say you now?" he proclaims. "A king, woe's slave, shall kingly woe obey" (206–10), and he prepares to leave for Flint Castle.

What occurs in the scene, in short, is literally the winding down of Richard's kingship. And what remains when all is done is the oscillation itself from one position to the other: from the doctrinal position concerning the king's two bodies, to one that views kingship from a distance, from the position of king to that of subject. The result of this oscillation is twofold. First, both positions have become rhetorical or theatrical positions with little relation to the power that sustains them. And second, as a result of this emptying out of these positions, they have become interchangeable. Richard's appeal to kingship, founded as it is upon the substitution of the body natural for the body politic, and thus upon the violation of the distinction that enables that appeal, succeeds only in destroying the difference between kingship and subjectivity. They have become in fact one and the same. One is henceforth monarch exclusively of oneself. The monarchy has become another form of theater. Richard has deposed himself.

Understood in this light, Ure's criticism must reveal itself as ironically inadequate. It is inadequate in so far as it takes Richard's "difference" in this scene to be rooted in the "drama of the sufferer constrained to reduce himself from king to man," rooted, that is to say, in Richard's victimage in a scene where we have witnessed the king at least concomitantly depose *himself*. But it is ironically so in that such a partial view—that Richard is victimized—is also Richard's view, and thus the one—the "sad stories of the death of kings"—that the play fundamentally and critically examines.

In the scenes that follow, this theatricalization of monarchy, this interiorization of royal subjectivity, will become increasingly explicit. Richard moves to Flint Castle and initially rebukes Northumberland when he enters with a message from Henry. "We are amazed, and thus long we have stood / To watch the fearful bending of thy knee, / Because we thought ourself thy lawful king" (III.iii.71–73).

But once Northumberland announces the excuse that Richard has earlier offered Henry (by seizing his goods)—namely that "[Henry's] coming hither hath no further scope / Than for his lineal royalties" (111–12)—Richard replies in a tone that seems almost too eager. "Northumberland, say . . . / His noble cousin is right welcome hither, / And all the number of his fair demands / Shall be accomplished without contradiction" (120–23). Even Richard himself is a little embarrassed by these words. "We do debase ourselves, cousin, do we not," he remarks to Aumerle, ". . . to speak so fair?" (126–27). He theatricalizes the situation as he did before. "What must the King do now? Must he submit? / The King shall do it. Must he be deposed? / The King shall be contented. Must he lose / The name of King? a God's name, let it go" (142). For a moment he verges on his former histrionics.

> I'll give . . . my large kingdom for a little grave,
> A little, little grave, an obscure grave;
> Or I'll be buried in the King's highway,
> Some way of common trade, where subjects' feet
> May hourly trample on their sovereign's head.
>
> (146–53)

And once he descends to "the base court" like "glist'ring Phaethon," the transfer seems complete and recapitulated in the brief direct exchange between Richard and Henry.

> *Bolingbroke.* My gracious lord, I come but for mine own.
> *Richard.* Your own is yours, and I am yours, and all.
> (194–95)

Richard has granted him everything and off they go to London. Why? Why does Richard do this? Why, for example, does Richard not choose to remain within the Castle and force Bolingbroke to take him prisoner? The situation seems not unlike that in *Romeo and Juliet*. After Romeo has killed Tybalt, the two lovers conceive of flying to Mantua, not when their plan might have succeeded, but only when it is just about too late and its chances of success are significantly diminished.[49] It would seem that Richard is almost more interested in dramatizing himself than in retaining the kingship.

All of which would seem to spell for Richard the end of his reign, and to leave the actual transfer of the crown somewhat superfluous. It may be just such an expectation, however, that things have been "all wrapped up," that makes what occurs in the central deposition scene that much more disconcerting. Richard's self-dramatizing will continue. But it is as if, now that he is out of power, he can begin to include in that histrionic language both the others who surround him and the conditions of his own theatricalizing. His language will suddenly become intensely critical and incisive. He will seem in the deposition scene to have passed from monarch to something of the prophetic figure that John of Gaunt played for him initially and that the bishop of Carlisle has played for all of them just a few moments ago, a choral role that is as removed from the monarchical position as the ambitious stance that Henry Bolingbroke has until this point adopted.

And by means of that subtle but decisive shift, we may be able to read in a new light all that has gone before. Perhaps, then, those Elizabethan censors who found the central scene particularly objectionable and saw fit to cut it were in a peculiar way more sensitive to its workings than our modern critics who would preserve the text in its integrity for its thoroughly mythic chronicling of English history or the shifts of Richard's "expressive" sensibility. Let us turn, then, to this scene at the center of Shakespeare's play, as the climax to all we have so far witnessed.

IV. Double-Fatal Yew

York enters to announce "plume plucked Richard's" agreement to descend the throne and name Bolingbroke heir. Bolingbroke announces his agreement to ascend the throne Richard has abdicated. And Carlisle denounces the actions of both of them in language that reflects the problem—the inability to separate a subject who speaks from one who speaks to subjects. "What subject can give sentence on his king? / And who sits here that is not Richard's subject? / . . . / I speak to subjects and a subject speaks" (121–33).

Carlisle then delivers, as John of Gaunt did with Richard, his famous attack upon the action they contemplate.

> My Lord of Hereford here, whom you call king,
> Is a foul traitor to proud Hereford's king;
> And if you crown him, let me prophesy
> The blood of English shall manure the ground,
> And future ages groan for this foul act.
> (134–38)

For his efforts, Northumberland promptly arrests him. Then Richard enters. York asks that he resign. "Give me the crown," Richard says.

> Here, cousin, seize the crown. Here, cousin,
> On this side my hand, and on that side yours.
> Now is this golden crown like a deep well
> That owes two buckets, filling one another.
> (180–84)

In the seesawing gesture by which Richard compels Henry to make explicit his appropriation of the crown, Richard's action doubles his talk. His words begin now to play a profoundly critical function. The histrionics remain. But divorced now from royal power, his words begin to explain how they came to be that way, how they came to be emptied, and thereby gain anew a social force.

And the story they tell? That the king, as someone says in *Hamlet*, is a "thing of nothing." Deposing himself before he was deposed, interiorizing his kingship, he drained the external attributes of royalty. Richard has become the absentee "landlord of England" John of Gaunt prophesied he would be. And this crown, with its hole in the center of a circle of gold—a kind of ghost of kingship in itself—makes visible that nothing.

Bolingbroke, of course, misses this point and reads Richard's remarks literally. "I thought you had been willing to resign" (189). "My crown I am," Richard says, with perhaps unintended ironic force, "but still my griefs are mine: / You may my glories and my state depose, / But not my griefs; still am I King of those" (190–92).

Richard's language has become like that of Hamlet or even the Fool in *Lear*. It can be taken in at least two fundamentally different ways: as simple word play, which diverts attention from the issue at hand, or as ironic commentary that enacts its difficulties. Bolingbroke will, of course, adopt the first interpretive approach, and so Richard will explain further. My concern is the lack or "loss" of my kingship. But the kingship itself is only now an empty crown and emptied by my having given it away. Therefore, the more I give it away, the emptier it becomes and the more I lack it, whether I retain it or not. And since you now hold the crown, my thoughts, as they attend the crown, which is empty, are short-circuited. I therefore attend myself. I am "King" of "griefs."

Bolingbroke is frustrated by what he takes to be Richard's inappropriate playfulness, and hopes that by changing terms he can restore Richard's speech to plenitude. He thereby only falls more thoroughly into the trap.

> *Bolingbroke.* Are you contented to resign the crown?
> *Richard.* Ay, no; no, ay: for I must nothing be.
> (199–200)

The word *contented,* which is intended to give plenitude to grief and a care that is loss of care, ends up only representing all three in the notion of nothing, which it comes to designate by representing the others. Yes, says Richard, I am in agreement to give up the crown to you. But in doing so, in contenting or pleasing myself, I empty myself of content (since I was the king) and therefore am "not contented." And without content I must "nothing be." Therefore I must not be content to give up the crown in order to be contented. Moreover, in saying yes or ay, that I am contented to give up the crown, I affirm my discontent, and thus say no. But at the same time in so stating, the I who speaks and says ay has become that no or no-thing or nothing. Therefore "I must nothing be." And if we now include the fact that *ay* can be heard as a pun on *I* and as well on *eye,* the possibilities are suddenly dizzying.[50]

In summarizing these arguments in the following speech, a speech that parallels in words the emptying or nihilating process they describe

("Mark me how I will undo myself," Richard says [202]), Richard is led to a startling conclusion: Henry will become Richard.

> Long may'st thou live in Richard's seat to sit,
> And soon lie Richard in an earthy pit.
> (217–18)

Long may you be king, and I expect (or even hope) soon to die. But also, long may you sit in a usurped seat, and sitting in a seat that is not your own (and therefore an empty seat, and therefore, like Richard, being nothing), soon may you, like Richard, lie in an earthy (or earthly) pit *as* Richard. Like an actor on a stage, soon may you play or "lie" Richard.

The argument is registered by Bolingbroke and Northumberland no more than it is by our modern critical Bolingbrokes who would "snatch" the crown for the fullness they feel it embodies. Northumberland hands him a list of abuses to read and Richard remarks.

> Mine eyes are full of tears, I cannot see:
> And yet salt water blinds them not so much,
> But they can see a sort of traitors here.
> Nay, if I turn mine eyes upon myself,
> I find myself a traitor with the rest;
> For I have given here my soul's consent
> T'undeck the pompous body of a king;
> Made glory base, and sovereignty a slave,
> Proud majesty a subject, state a peasant.
> (243–51)

Suddenly, that is, everything we have said to this point converges. Richard has been handed a piece of paper, a piece of writing, a little plot (a grave plot indeed, Mercutio might say), and in that plot, that drama, he recognizes the perpetrators, those who have arranged things so that this piece of paper gets brought before him. Like Oedipus who recognizes in Creon's report about the Delphic oracle the traces of a plot that once may have taken the life of his forbearer, and may now threaten him, Richard discerns treachery. But unlike Bolingbroke and Northumberland (or Oedipus), who in the plots and props before them recognize nothing personal, Richard also recognizes here himself.

The paper, in other words, functions in two ways at once: as a disturbing mirror of those around him who gave him this document to read; and as a mirror of himself who made such a reading possible, and who, therefore, in a sense they are imitating or mirroring—Bolingbroke having usurped Richard's royalty no more than Richard did his own—in undertaking this action. In a gesture that repeats the situation in front of him, that similarly externalizes the relations in which they are caught, Richard calls for a mirror, a reflecting glass. "I'll read enough, / When I do see the very book indeed, / Where all my sins are writ, and that's myself" (272–74).

I'll read the list of abuses when I get a better look at my face, which is the image of the one who has brought this situation about. Or, I'll read all I care to read when I see the true book of abuses—the image of my face, an image, therefore that doubles the "book" before me even as it will be itself a reflector, a mirror.

And once the mirror that will make reading possible for Richard is brought on, what does he do? He smashes it. He shatters the image before him of his own guilt—"where all [his] sins are writ." He sees in the glass, the reflector, the object before him, an image of himself. And not liking what he sees, he destroys it. He banishes it from his sight. As Lear does Cordelia and then Kent.

And in that gesture of annihilation, the whole of the play may be seen to be reflected. Though it was better strategically that the fight between Mowbray and Bolingbroke proceed, it was preferable from a certain mimetic economy that it be aborted. Within a private economy, Mowbray, Richard's defender, and Bolingbroke, his challenger, functioned less as two independent beings with a certain relationship to political power than as the externalizations of an internal debate within Richard himself. Mowbray may have acted in Richard's defense from within a certain network of social or symbolic relations. But at a more lurid and poignant level for Richard he reflects only his own guilt in the murder of Gloucester. He literally figures for Richard Gloucester's "blood." Similarly, Bolingbroke may represent a severe political challenge to Richard's royalty. But at a more imaginary level he mirrors for Richard an agency ready to do him service, to punish for him what he identifies as the very image of his own guilt.

Therefore Richard stops the fight between them at this level, not because Mowbray may not win, but rather because Bolingbroke may lose. At whatever cost, Richard would rather opt for this dramatization and avoid such a conclusion, even when his very royalty, his ability to continue as king, and therefore to continue distinguishing between these economies, is itself the stake in the battle. He would rather substitute imaginary demands for symbolic demands, even at the price of being able to make such distinctions in the future. In this respect he is a little like King Lear, who would substitute private fantasies of rescue by a fairy-tale daughter for the more public and more enabling dramas of political power, even at the expense of his own future ability—internally or externally—to govern. "No rescue?" Lear exclaims, when he wakes after the storm, and shortly before he is taken captive and his daughter Cordelia is defeated and killed.

Therefore Richard recoils initially from the contest when Mowbray goes on about the murder of Gloucester as having issued "from the rancor of a villain, / A recreant and most degenerate traitor; / which in myself I boldly will defend" (I.i.143–45), before he recovers his strategic senses. Therefore he stops the fight—watching it, as he has been, as a woeful pageant from his royal seat—when it seems as if the contestants are determined to go through with it and he issues the strange decree that he does, proclaiming that "our kingdom's earth should not be soiled / with that dear blood which it hath fosterèd," that "ambitious thoughts" and "rival-hating envy" have "set [the fighters] on" to "make us wade even in our kindred's blood." Therefore, as well, he banishes his "cousin Hereford" from his "territories" for ten years and pronounces upon the duke of Norfolk the "hopeless word of 'Never to return,'" a word that recalls the condition of Gloucester himself. Therefore, looking in "the glasses of [Gaunt's] eyes," he reprieves Bolingbroke from ten years' banishment to six, as if in bringing Henry back he brings back Gloucester, who is no doubt also the object of Gaunt's "grievèd heart" and "sad aspect"—as we have just learned immediately prior to this scene in the conversation between Gaunt and Gloucester's widow.

Therefore, as well, we understand why when Gaunt denounces him as "landlord of England" and charges him with surrounding himself with self-flattering subjects and objects and the vacancy of power he has created, Richard seizes his goods at whatever the cost to him in political stability. He shatters this mirroring discourse, appropriates his place and the wealth that supports it, in the name of fighting his controversial "Irish wars." John of Gaunt, even as he is Richard's father's brother and another son of Edward, has become one more image of those wars, just another disturbance of Richard's "fair Peace," that causes him to "wade even in our kindred's blood." His internal "Irish wars" are of much greater importance to him finally than even the external kingship that enables him to fight them.

And therefore, finally, he leaves York, who has similarly denounced him, in charge of the kingdom. The hostility of York and his weakness in defending the kingdom against attack are not obstacles to Richard's promotion of him but its very point. York has become, in the very moral and chastising theme of his attack, the perfect representative of all of them and therefore of the problem itself. If he cannot silence York (without repeating the murder of Gloucester), he can identify him at once with Mowbray his defender, with Henry (whom he will be too weak to stop), and with the dead Gaunt whose side the duke has just taken—the three representatives, in short, into whom the dead Gloucester has been split. And leave the whole lot of them. As John of Gaunt's prophetic words have equated England itself (this "blessed plot, this earth") with vacancy, he can identify York with his very kingdom (his guilty "blood") and abandon the whole bloody plot.

If we have viewed these actions in criticism exclusively as "political mistakes," as a chronicle of the social conditions under which Richard's deposition occurred, and have seen little or no connection between these scenes and the central sequence in which we feel the "expressive" Richard newly emerges, it may be that we have divided up the monstrous image before us much as Richard himself does (or as Lear does before the nihilating words of Cordelia), a division, that, if we are to take Shakespeare's play seriously, may prove for us no less disastrous.

At the center of the play, in other words, is a mirror, a mirror in which all our sins are writ, so to speak, and that we would critically shatter by substituting formalism or historicism for the "blood" before us, for the nothing in the center of the play or object which implicates us in murder of our own. Richard's shattering of the mirror, even as it duplicates the shattering piece of writing before him, and thereby enables us to read the play to that point, also shatters the illusions by which we have traditionally read that scene. Richard's behavior initially is already the product of the same "double-fatal" substitution that characterizes his actions at the beginning of act 3, a behavior in which the social body politic and the more private body natural, the realm that defines him as a king and the realm that defines him as a man, are already at odds. In the well-ordered state, Kantorowicz reminds us, the two are perfectly consolidated within each other although the second remains subordinate to the first. Richard's behavior on the Welsh shore is but the intensification of a process already "in place," the "expressive Richard" but a manifestation of a drama already fully operational. Critics such as Peter Ure have not simply missed the play's point; they have reproduced it.

Thus Richard's gesture of shattering the reflecting glass enables us to read the play first by identifying a mirror at the center of the object. A piece of paper, a piece of writing, becomes a drama, a traitorous plot, which in turn becomes a book wherein the gazer's own sins are "writ," a transformation made explicit by the substitution for that writing of a mirror, a reflecting glass. It enables us to read second by heightening or bringing into relief as a result the relations Richard has had to people, things, and words around him throughout, all of them props that have similarly mirrored for him his own face, and that he has split into fragments no less divisively (if somewhat less violently) than he has the mirror. Our own division of the play in modern criticism into "expressive" and "historical" components would seem no less delusive in this regard than older approaches that excised the mirror scene entirely. In our modern approaches we are simply somewhat less explicit in its rejection. Like Richard we continue to shatter and fragment that which enables us to read.

But to say as much is to tell only half the story. There is another question we need to ask with regard to the shattering of the mirror. If the mirror functions by revealing itself at the center of an object, what is its relation to subjects? If the mirror for Richard functions within a narcissistic and projective economy that subordinates and thereby empties a monarchical economy it should serve, what is the consequence for others around him of its shattering? From the personal or psychological features of Richard's relations, we must turn now to the larger social or political dimensions and their implications.

V. Mirrors and Models

What in the first place is a mirror? For us a mirror is a reflecting glass, a surface that when illuminated gives us back, as it were, a "reversed" or mirror image of the object being reflected. This explanation, of course, is our modern way of talking about these matters and that way is at least as old as Plato. It is in this sense that aesthetics, for example, has traditionally found in the mirror an analogue for the work of art and of literary production.[51] It is similarly in this sense that Hamlet remarks to the players that art holds "the mirror up to nature."[52]

But there is another notion of mirror or mirroring that was considerably more popular in the Renaissance than it is today and that is reflected in such phrases as "a mirror for magistrates" or "the mirror of all

Christian kings." Quite apart from mirroring or reflecting the objects around it, the mirror was sometimes considered as an object of imitation in itself, as a model or paradigm, and as such, as an independent source of light or radiation or emanation.

What is a model? A model is a pattern through which, literally, things may be seen, a structure that illuminates things other than itself for perceiving agencies other than itself. This sense of a mirror is tricky because it involves to some extent a metaphorical usage of the earlier sense. A mirror is a model to the extent that it can act like an independent light source, which is to say, to the extent that it "mirrors" or emulates a light source by shedding illumination on other objects. Since the ancient world, and in particular since the optical theories of Euclid and Ptolemy, the notion was widespread that light could either enter the eye from the outside or be projected out of the eye from within, and that in such a manner human beings could be the source of such effluences or "extramissions" of "visual rays." "The most popular Renaissance theory of vision," Stephen Booth writes, "held that the eye, like the sun, is a source of light, which it emits in beams."[53] Light in this theory was conceived as a set of beams or rays emitted in the way that we would speak today of "radar," a ray that is to say that is emitted from a source that enlightens by striking and bouncing off (or being absorbed by) an object to be observed.[54]

Thus, for example, kingship may be defined as a modeling relationship. A subject of or to the king can be defined as one who sees through the eyes of the king, one for whom the king provides a radiating or emanating source of light, the king in turn also gilded by and reflecting the illumination of the sun or of divinity, one for whom, in short, the king is a model or "mirror." Thus the sun can become the perfect double for a king in the natural realm, shedding light as if it were an independent light source, and yet at the same time the enlightened reflector of illumination cast by divinity, the commonplace reference to the sun as the "eye of heaven" appearing to capture both senses. In the human realm, the monarch would seem to reflect the same combination of senses, at once the earthly authority who sheds light on others and all things for his subjects, for all those within his kingdom, and yet at the same time, God's anointed, the deputy or place-holder or "lieutenant" of transcendence. As God's anointed, the king is a kind of sun, or mirror, and in this context we understand the reference to the king as "the sun God." Moreover, we understand that the relationship between subject, sovereign, and object is therefore necessarily a triangular one. The beams of light that appear to emanate from a subject to gild or illuminate an object are in fact always necessarily mediated by the king who in his capacity as a stand-in for divinity is the true source of that illumination.[55]

In the context of this larger relation of subjects, kings, and objects we may understand Richard's shattering of the mirror in a new way. It is a shattering not only of his personal kingship but of kingship itself.

Richard as king is model for his subjects. Then Richard deposes himself. "Are you contented to resign the crown?" he is asked and responds, "Ay, no, no, ay: for I must nothing be." The king becomes, as the saying goes in *Hamlet,* a "thing," a "thing of nothing," a veritable ghost (a figure, a shape, an apparition) of a former presence; the presence, in short, of an absence. The ay which agrees to resign the crown, and which yields no I as we saw before, also yields no eye, no radiating beams. I "know not now what name to call myself," he says to Bolingbroke (IV.i.258). Or, to put it another way, he has become indistinguishable from the crown itself. He has become, in the words of his queen, a mere "model." "Thou map of honor, thou King Richard's tomb, / And not King Richard," she says of him (V.i.12–13).

This situation, in which monarchical subjectivity, subjectivity to the sovereign, has given way to another arrangement in which nothing now stands in the place of the mediator of vision, the place of the king, should give us pause. For it would seem that modern subjectivity, at least as we have conceived of it since Kant and Hegel, and in particular since the phenomenologies of being developed by Heidegger and to some extent by Sartre, is nothing else.

Modern subjectivity, in fact, conceived within the terms we have been discussing, would seem to have split off the two possibilities afforded by the collapse of the kind of subjectivity proper to kingship, and to offer us at least two alternatives. In face of the collapse of the model, the displacement of the mediator of vision by nothing, there would seem at least two strategies one could employ. On the one hand, one could entirely exclude the nothing through which we now see and notice only subjects and objects. Such an arrangement, of course, is that of positivism and serves as the basis for all modern science. On the other hand, one could perceive the object via the nothing offered to us as mediator, in which case, optically as it were, such nothing appears either to envelop or to inhabit the object, an object that has become now clearly the presence of an absence, an apparition, a ghost.[56]

Modern subjectivity, in either case, then, would become the product of failed or collapsed mediation, the subjectivity to nothing in the place of the king, a nothing that becomes interchangeable now, literally, with anything. And Shakespeare would seem to have prophetically envisioned, in terms of the collapse of Richard's relations with others, the terms of our own.

Failed mediation, and Bolingbroke's blindness to it, comes in any case to explain both the remainder of Richard's interaction with his captors and the course of Bolingbroke's kingship. For example, in the present scene, having shattered the mirror, Richard remarks: "Mark, silent king, the moral of this sport: / How soon my sorrow hath destroyed my face" (289–90).

How quickly my substitution of personal demands for monarchical demands has destroyed the entire arrangement. Mark, you readers of my progress, who are as well the product of this transformation; those who, like the spectators in Velázquez's *Las Meninas,* have put yourselves in the place of the king; who have internalized royal subjectivity and would pass that narcissism off now as monarchical; mark how soon my concern with personal discontent has left me devoid of content entirely, without the ability to define boundaries or content for myself or others.[57]

> *Bolingbroke.* The shadow of your sorrow hath destroyed
> The shadow of your face.
> (291–92)

Bolingbroke reads literally, representationally. The mirror image is only a shadow, an apparition that your sorrow or discontent at losing the kingship has forced you to destroy. You have destroyed the mirror image because you could not hold onto your kingship. It is a form of weakness, however sentimental or expressive it may be of your delicate sensibilities. You are fighting fantasies, not realities. In doing so you destroy nothing but yourself.

> *Richard.*   Say that again.
> "The shadow of my sorrow?" Ha, let's see.
> 'Tis very true, my grief lies all within,
> And these external manners of laments
> Are merely shadows to the unseen grief
> That swells with silence in the tortured soul.
> There lies the substance: and I thank thee, King,
> For thy great bounty, that not only giv'st

> Me cause to wail, but teachest me the way
> How to lament the cause.
>
> (293–301)

Richard will turn Bolingbroke's criticism of him—in his view, a misunderstanding—into a more profound understanding by loading it metaphorically, and then in turn converting that new understanding into a prophetic account of his own demise. You are right. I was loading my words metaphorically and engaging in histrionics. Destroying the mirror was not getting at the real grief they reflect. What was at stake was not real power but fantasy. And I thank you for teaching me the difference, king, between substance and shadow.

But insofar as you do teach me, and insofar as you do so as a king should, your teaching is at the same time self-defeating. For you have become king only insofar as you have created that grief in me (by displacing the former king). And you teach me the way to answer that grief by your example, which is to say, by displacing you, in turn, as my very words do yours now.

Therefore, your setting of yourself up as model to me as your subject, as one to be emulated, will be your undoing. Your very belief that it is only fantasy and not real power that expresses itself in me, your blindness to the emptiness of what you take to be real power (namely, your own position, which is but another version of the same position I occupy right now, and which is by your very logic, only fantasy) will compel you to repeat my mistakes. Soon will you lie Richard.

In response to which, as Northumberland did to the Bishop of Carlisle before, Henry replies to Richard's prophetic words with an order to convey him to the Tower. He banishes him, shatters him, in other words, as Richard did first Mowbray, then Bolingbroke, then Gaunt, then himself. Refusing to hear Richard's account, as Richard refused to hear Gaunt's account when the deathbed prophet denounced the king's abuses and the vacancy they created, Henry bears out that account straightaway. And the remainder of the play will do little more than complete that duplication and repetition. Mark, silent king, Richard has said, words that Richard has learned to hear at great cost. But Henry hears their special appeal no more than we do in criticism. Shakespeare's "moral" would seem to go unheeded all the more vehemently as his plays insist upon it.

Henry's "fair peace" will be even shorter than Richard's. In order to follow Shakespeare's treatment to its conclusion, let us turn, then, to the completion of Henry's transformation into the king he desires to be, and to the completion of Richard's transformation into the prophetic figure he earlier denounced, and that he himself would excise in prison at Pomfret Castle.

VI. Sacrificing Abel

After Richard abdicates, interest in him flags. We hear that dust has been thrown upon him in the streets and that he has become the object of public derision that he imagined he would be on the coast of Wales, although York finds the procession of both Richard and Henry somewhat theatrical. What takes center stage now is the reign of Henry: his coronation, his thwarting of a plot against him by Aumerle, his domestic troubles, the execution of Richard, and his planned trip to Jerusalem.

We have always read these final scenes as chronicle, as much chronicle in fact as the earlier scenes. My own view, of course, is that our confidence in the existence of a certain symmetry between the beginning and the end of the play has not been misplaced. What I would show is that Henry's actions now reproduce Richard's point by point. Overthrowing Richard, Henry now becomes Richard.

Why would Shakespeare double Richard in this fashion? What is the dramatic function of Henry's duplication? In the first place, it succeeds in making Richard's actions visible to us. It highlights or brings into relief his behavior so that it becomes readable. In the second place, repeating Richard's actions, Henry's behavior enables us to see the consequence of the usurpation—namely, the repetition itself. Overthrowing Richard, Henry becomes subject to the same self-destructiveness and attempts at usurpation.

The doubling starts even before the middle sequence is completed. As Richard stood before Bolingbroke and Mowbray initially in judgment upon their quarrel, so this scene will be repeated three times before the play is out, each time reproducing more of the initial scene it models. At the beginning of act 3, even before Richard has returned, Bolingbroke appears at Bristol, brings forth Richard's favorites Bushy and Green, and "dispatches" judgment upon them forthwith. The scene is brief, almost indiscernible in the wake of the scene on the Welsh shore that we are about to witness. To the extent that we can compare it to the earlier scene, it seems to represent everything Richard should have done but did not. In that respect, it parallels, in fact, the scene with the gardener whose "sea-wallèd garden" is "full of weeds," "swarming with caterpillars," and who advocated "like an executioner" cutting "off the heads of too fast growing sprays" (III.iv).

But the scene will be repeated at the beginning of act 4 once Richard has left Flint Castle for London and just before his abdication and here it is just as likely to be missed. This time Bolingbroke stands before the dispute between Aumerle (who, of course, is Richard's ally) and Bolingbroke's nobles—Fitzwater, Percy (Northumberland's son), and others. And this time the course of events will be more familiar. The issue is explicitly "noble Gloucester's death," and the attack against Aumerle is initiated by Bagot, the only favorite of Richard's curiously excluded from Bolingbroke's previous "dispatch"—as if Bolingbroke may not be above the very favoritism and nepotism that plagued his predecessor. As before with Richard, the lords initially break out in a fight as Surrey, who is Bolingbroke's lord, suddenly turns against Fitzwater. And the outcome is the same as the initial scene. As Richard deferred the feud from coming to trial, so Bolingbroke would have these "differences" "rest under gage" until Mowbray, who is presumably his own sworn enemy, returns from exile with a reprieve, a postponement that is, like the one Richard issued, in effect infinite since Mowbray has died in Italy.

The most striking duplication, however, occurs once Bolingbroke has been coronated as Henry IV. As Richard faced a "traitorous" attack against him and refused to effectively counterattack, so Bolingbroke now learns of an assassination plot against his life and pardons the attacker. As Gaunt initially brought Bolingbroke forth with "some apparent danger . . . aimed at you Highness," so York now argues against his son. "Thou hast a traitor in thy presence" (V.iii.39), he says to Bolingbroke. "O loyal father of a treacherous son!" (59), Henry responds, perhaps thinking of his own "unthrifty son" (1) who "[scrapes] his father's gold" (68). He seems about to "cut off" the "fest'red joint" (84)—in echo of the gardener—when the duchess of York enters and kneels before him to plea for her son's life.

"Our scene is alt'red from a serious thing, . . . to 'The Beggar and the King'" (79), Henry says. Pardoning Aumerle after listening to the pleas of the duchess his mother (that recall, of course, the pleas of Gloucester's duchess to Gaunt to stir against Richard), Henry reveals the same kind of vulnerability to sentimentalism that proved so fatal to his predecessor. We recall that Richard mitigated the sentence against Bolingbroke from ten years to six after what he took to be a "look" from his father, a reduction that failed to please the parent anyway. Freeing his would-be assassin (who now prostrates himself before the king), it would seem he has learned nothing from Richard's mistakes. Aumerle is his Bolingbroke and he will be but the first of many.

But comparisons with the initial aborted contest are not the only suggestions raised by Henry's behavior. As Richard seized John of Gaunt's goods (and therefore Bolingbroke's "royalty," as York notes), so Bolingbroke steals Richard's. And as Richard leaves York in charge of the kingdom (even though York has just finished denouncing him and has reason to feel threatened by him), so Henry restores to "life" the one man who would not fear to oppose him, who has vigorously attacked his actions in taking over the throne, and who he has similarly maligned—the crusty Bishop of Carlisle. "For though mine enemy thou hast ever been, / High sparks of honor in thee have I seen" (V.vi.28–29), Henry says. And once all is said and done, as Richard left to fight his "Irish wars," so Bolingbroke is seen leaving for "the Holy Land, / To wash this blood off from my guilty hand" (49–50).

It is not that these actions are necessarily wrong or strategically unwise, although the pardoning of Aumerle may be imprudent. It is rather that they inescapably recall the actions of Richard, and suggest that the result of the usurpation is a more profound diachronic identity than we have ever imagined, an identity that we blur by dismissing these events as the chronicle of a history book or a play Shakespeare has not yet written.

Lest we think that these comparisons so far are superficial, Shakespeare offers us others. Just as Richard's "conscience" would seem to have overwhelmed his sense of political expediency, and he banished Mowbray, his defender, for life in face of the guilt or "blood" he presents to him, so Henry finally banishes Exton once Henry's knight has completed the task that Exton at least feels has been Henry's bidding. "Great king," Exton says to him, "within this coffin I present / thy buried fear" (V.vi.30–31). And Henry replies, "Exton, I thank thee not, for thou hast wrought / A deed of slander with thy fatal hand / Upon my head and all this famous land" (34–36). The projective economy in which Richard fatally doubled or substituted the body natural for the body politic would seem to have returned.

But Exton will not be so easily put by. For in his view, he did this deed as Henry desired, as Henry's dutiful subject.

> *Exton.* From your own mouth, my lord, did I this deed.
> *Bolingbroke.* They love not poison that do poison need,
>   Nor do I thee; though I did wish him dead,
>   I hate the murderer, love him murderèd.
>   The guilt of conscience take thou for thy labor,
>   But neither my good word, nor princely favor.
>   With Cain go wander through shades of night,
>   (37–43)

Henry does to Exton, in short, what Richard did to Mowbray. And if we assume the "murderer" and the "murderèd" to be internal as well as external references, then he has made explicit the economy by which Richard has been operating throughout, an economy in which he suddenly and perhaps surprisingly finds himself imprisoned and perhaps to which he has just condemned Exton. The primal guilt of "a brother's murder" with which he here describes Exton's actions recalls the terms at the play's outset in which he condemned the actions of Mowbray, terms that, of course, also recall for the reader Claudius's confessional prayer in the middle of *Hamlet*.

> Further, I say . . .
> That he did plot the Duke of Gloucester's death, . . .
> And, consequently, like a traitor coward,
> Sluiced out his innocent soul through streams of blood;
> Which blood, like sacrificing Abel's, cries
> Even from the tongueless caverns of the earth
> To me for justice and rough chastisement.
>   (I.i.98–106)

The same "blood" that plagued Richard returns to plague Henry. And as Richard could tell him (and Macbeth later in Shakespeare's career), no pilgrimage to Jerusalem will effectively "wash this blood off."

If we had only the scene with Exton, we might want to argue that Henry is here being supremely politic, that revolutionaries always destroy first and foremost other revolutionaries. But taken in context of the systematic nature of Shakespeare's duplication, an identification is inescapable. The presence of the box containing his dead kinsman is no less his "buried fear" than either the "blood" or the mirror was for Richard.

And the mimetic quality of Exton's behavior in particular is given great emphasis. Just before Exton does the deed, there is a brief scene in which the imitative nature of Exton's action, the surprisingly appropriative source for the gesture, is made explicit.

> *Exton.* Didst thou not mark the King, what words he spake?
> "Have I no friend will rid me of this living fear?"
> Was it not so?
> *Man.* These were his very words.
> *Exton.* "Have I no friend?" quoth he: he spake it twice,
> And urged it twice together, did he not?
> *Man.* He did.
> *Exton.* And speaking it, he wishtly looked on me,
> As who should say, "I would thou wert the man
> That would divorce this terror from my heart"—
> Meaning the King at Pomfret. Come, let's go:
> I am the King's friend, and will rid his foe.
>
> (V.iv.1–11)

The implications of this brief scene are far-reaching. In the act of doing a deed within the province of the dutiful, as a mimetic appropriation of Henry's desires, Exton turns out to have done a deed of violence against the king, a violence that is in fact faithfully mimetic since it is also the king's own. No less has Henry undertaken such an action against Richard, modeling similarly Richard's own rebellious behavior against himself (as well as others), and finding himself for his labors similarly with the "guilt of conscience," that he now passes on (almost infectiously) to Exton. Both the murder of Gloucester initially and the banishing of the trace of that murder—its ghosts as it were—turn up again, that is, in the present exchange.

And perhaps, finally, that is Shakespeare's point. In what is no doubt one of the greatest of the play's ironies, it would seem that we have now effectively returned to the play's origin: in killing Richard, either by direct order or the mimetic relation proper to a king, Bolingbroke (or Exton) reproduces before us the murder of Gloucester, of Thomas of Woodstock, upon which the entire cycle of mimesis and violence has been founded. If we have never recognized the significance of this identity, it is because we have viewed the play from within a series of critical perspectives that founded themselves upon the very differences this parallel questions, differences between Henry and Richard, or between psychological or political aspects of the play, that are no less the differences conceived by the characters themselves; because, in short, we have modeled or mirrored the characters in a play in which such mirroring behavior has become indistinguishable from violence and it is such violence and modeling relations that the play exists to expose.[58]

It is a profound identity between mimesis, violence, and nothing that Henry learns, if not in the present play, then in *Henry Fourth Part Two*.[59] Near the end of the latter play, Henry gains a rare insight into the prophetic course of his own actions. He is asleep on the throne, and in a gesture that recalls the story of Saul and David in the Bible, his own son Prince Hal, suspecting him to be dead, has taken the crown from off the head of the living king. Henry suddenly wakes up to a scene that has for him an uncanny familiarity.

> *Prince*. I never thought to hear you speak again.
> *King*. Thy wish was father, Harry, to that thought: . . .
>   Dost thou so hunger for mine empty chair
>   that thou wilt needs invest thee with my honors
>   Before thy hour be ripe? O foolish youth,
>   Thou seek'st the greatness that will overwhelm thee . . .
>   God knows, my son,
>   By what bypaths and indirect crook'd ways
>   I met this crown, and I myself know well
>   How troublesome it sate upon my head . . .
>   It seem'd in me
>   But as an honor snatch'd with boisterous hand . . .
>   For all my reign hath been but as a scene
>   Acting that argument.
>   (IV.v.91–198)

There seems, in short, nothing that Henry does that is not systematically a duplication of something that has occurred earlier in the play, nothing, by the same token, that we have traditionally identified as a mistake on Richard's part that is not systematically, if unwittingly, repeated by Henry. What Henry has appropriated is less the stewardship of the kingdom than an empty crown, less the monarchy than an interiorized royal subjectivity that would set itself up as king (and irradiate objects around it with its glitter) but that keeps shortcircuiting—within the narcissistic logic of its economy—back upon itself, less the kingship than nothing. What he inherits, in sum, is less the king's two bodies than a split subjectivity in which one person is called upon to play many people and cannot stop switching from one perspective to another.

But the articulation of this new, monstrous, and reigning subjectivity—this "being nothing" that now defines the relation between subject and monarch—is given by Shakespeare in this play not to Henry but to Richard. Alone in his cell at Pomfret Castle, Richard undertakes a meditation upon kings, subjects, and nothing, a meditation that is often glossed over in the criticism of the play, and yet that may be among the most profound insights Shakespeare offers us (in this play or any other) on the onto-theological conditions of our relationship to authority—insights in whose shadow, as our modern criticism tirelessly demonstrates, we may continue to live.

VII. The Beggar and the King

> *Richard.* I have been studying how I may compare
> This prison where I live unto the world:
> And for because the world is populous,
> And here is not a creature but myself,
> I cannot do it.
>
> (V.v.1–5)

There is no real source for Richard's prison speech in the traditional materials from which Shakespeare has clearly drawn so much else in the play. Ure points out that although Daniel (from whom in Ure's view Shakespeare draws more than from Holinshed or Hall), "like Shakespeare, opens his description of Richard's death with a soliloquy . . . the substance of the two soliloquies does not at all correspond."

Yet to any serious reader of medieval documents, the themes of the speech are inescapably familiar. Alone, in prison, reflecting upon the fortune that has led him to this situation and what philosophy might do to ease him, Richard draws upon the long tradition of medieval humanism represented perhaps most popularly by Boethius's *Consolation of Philosophy*.[60] The speech is Shakespeare's response, in a certain way, to Boethius.

But the speech is far from "Boethian." For if, in Boethius, the conclusion reached is that happiness is a function of directing one's energies towards the supreme being, Shakespeare's theme is the insufficiency of this argument. Richard has been considering how he may find a parity or likeness between his situation in prison and the world, a comparison readily available in medieval theologizing in which our life in this world is but a prison from which we are freed upon death, an idea he would find even within the *Consolation*. But it is impossible, he concludes, not because the comparison is false but because the possibility of such an investigation is foreclosed from the outset: "because the world is populous" and in prison "is not a creature but myself." Imagining the world from within prison one has no guarantee that the world has not been "populated" by one's own thoughts, and that it is not one's fantasies that have been substituted for real social relations.

Why, then, does Shakespeare draw upon Boethius, other than as an available popular vocabulary for describing Richard's dilemma? Because—and here we have what is really the most radical aspect of Richard's remarks—what Boethius sees as "evil" from a traditional Western Christianized Platonized perspective is here seen as the fundamental quality of being itself.

> Nor I, nor any man that but man is,
> With nothing shall be pleased, till he be eased
> With being nothing.
> (39–41)

"Evil is nothing," Boethius writes. "For just as you may call a cadaver a dead man, but cannot call it simply a man, so I would concede that vicious men are evil, but I cannot say, in an absolute sense, that they exist."

> For if our earlier conclusion that evil is nothing still stands, it is clear that the wicked can do nothing since they can do only evil.[61]

But in Shakespeare that "nothing" has become the onto-theological staple of existence itself. The ramifications of such an identity are vast. There where Christian culture would define love—God's relation to the world, the motor force of the great chain of being—Richard locates nothing, which is traditionally associated with evil. The two have become equated in a monstrous identification that occurs again in Shakespeare's work. It will reach its culminating moment in *King Lear*, and in particular when Lear enters with the dead Cordelia in his arms, and is compelled to repeat the word "never" which was so troubling for Richard earlier in this play. The first words out of Cordelia's mouth when Lear demanded a confession of love from her initially were "nothing." And the "nothing" Lear gave her in return issued (in a turn of events unlike the fairy-tale plot on which Lear grounded his "darker purpose") in a new "nothing" from which she will not recover, the "being nothing" of death. The "Gloucester sub-plot" that in *Richard II* remains hidden and to be unearthed, in *King Lear* has become overt. The blindness by which individuals sacrifice real other individuals (their children, their trusty servants) for their own fantasies, and the violence that shrouds that substitution is in the later play pervasive. "Is this the promised end?" Kent asks, a question that may well constitute *King Lear* at large and perhaps as well the Shakespearean canon.

But in a gesture even more immediately relevant for us in our own century, Shakespeare defines such a nihilating nothing there where we would locate the critical center of our own being. From Hegel to Heidegger to Sartre, we have taken as the nature of being a nothing that we identify as desire or death on the one hand, and as appearance or opening on the other. Moreover, we take this recognition to be the hallmark of a tough realistic sophisticated view of things, even though an older European culture would identify it as evil. If we begin to reflect upon that same nothing as failed mediation, as the secret heart of interiorized royal subjectivity, then Shakespeare's world would seem to be fully our own, that part of our world that we have identified as peculiar to our modernity. And it would seem we have not yet begun to plumb the depths, the mimetic foundations, either of our own existential conceptualizations, or of the assistance that Shakespeare (and, no doubt, other "great" writers) may offer us in that inquiry, an inquiry that may constitute the very nature of "great literature," and that we may have displaced or shattered, less in spite of than because of its power to enlighten us.

Let us read Richard's speech, then, with some care, his "philosophizing with a hammer," so to speak, a speech whose appeal may still hold us in its sway.

Having stumbled upon the impossibility of separating the imaginary universe from the symbolic universe, the psychological from the monarchical, the king's body natural from his body politic, Richard remarks, "Yet I'll hammer it out."

> My brain I'll prove the female to my soul,
> My soul the father, and these two beget
> A generation of still-breeding thoughts;
> And these same thoughts people this little world,
> In humours like the people of this world,
> For no thought is contented.
>
> (6–11)

Having decided it is impossible to make the comparison, yet I'll walk through the argument. I'll forge the chain. I'll chisel it out. It will not free me from the prison, either the prison of my body or Pomfret Castle, and in fact it may even create a third prison. It may forge the links whereby I trap myself within my own mind, the globe that is the theater of my head. But I will do it anyway. Mark, silent king, how I will undo myself.

There are, that is, to begin with, two "others." There is the world of real social relations in which people, like Richard, imagine themselves imprisoned within their bodies until they are freed by death. And there is the world of Pomfret Castle in which others are imagined outside the walls only from within. There is no guarantee that Richard's conclusions about the "outside world" will not be self-serving. Which is to say, of course, that there is in fact a third prison, more important than the other two since it predetermines their very possibility for him: the prison of his own mind. "Here is not a creature but myself," he says. The task cannot be undertaken because the other may turn out to be a function neither of social community nor of isolation but of ourselves.

In walking through the argument, therefore, I may not only not hammer myself out of prison or succeed only in walking through an empty argument but I may in fact hammer myself in. My soul I shall spill into my brain and in this act of engendering give birth only to "still-breeding thoughts": thoughts that are stillborn and dead; thoughts that in their very deadly quality give birth to other such thoughts (which is to say, to a form of death or stillness); and thoughts that continue to do so even as I speak. And these monstrous or aborted forms of life shall "populate" this "little world" of my head, this "hamlet," becoming like humors or temperaments indistinguishable from the people of this world.

For no thought is "contented." All thoughts are temperamental. No thought is satisfied. But also, no thought is with content; all thoughts are empty. Again, no thought is clearly demarcated from other thoughts; every thought can only be thought in context of other thoughts. And what in fact constitutes the substance of content is the absence of thought—precisely, no thought. Trapped within Pomfret Castle, Richard will substitute his imaginary economy for an external social or symbolic economy, a substitution that leads to discontent, emptiness, a confusion of boundaries, that explains why the bridge to the outside cannot be made—in answer to Boethius—but that also reflects Richard's history in the play we have just witnessed.

In the next twenty lines, in extending this argument about the impossibility of escaping prison, Richard will exemplify both that argument, and the history of the play to this point. Anatomizing the "discontent" of thoughts, Richard will give substance to his discontent and thereby trap himself within the very myths of content he is exposing. But in the particular anatomy he chooses to discuss—divine thoughts, ambitious thoughts, and flattering thoughts—he will "people" the world he has lived in.

Divine thoughts fail to get us out of prison because they do no more than set the word itself against the word. For every argument that can be summoned to sustain a given point, another can be summoned to rebut it. "Thoughts tending to ambition," thoughts of high design, plot "unlikely wonders" and collapse in their own arrogance and pride. And thoughts designed to create content and contentment beg the end to which they are put. They achieve at best an imaginary victory. Divine thoughts fail to get us out of the prison of the world. Ambitious thoughts fail to get us out of the prisons of social relations. And flattering thoughts fail to get us out of the prison or globe of the individual mind.

But these three strategies for escape are also "people" in Richard's terms and so perhaps we should understand these failures in terms of Richard's real social history. The thoughts of things divine that occur to Gaunt on his deathbed, or to the Bishop of Carlisle at the moment of Henry's ascension, or to Richard at the moment of his abdication and even presently fail to free us because not one of their positions is comprehensive. Each speaks a prophetic voice; but Gaunt speaks for kinship, Carlisle for the Church, and Richard for the monarchy. The heroic discourse spoken by Henry Bolingbroke will end only in Henry's own demise, which has already shown signs of beginning, as will the plots of Aumerle, and as has whatever ambitious thoughts Richard may have had about Gloucester initially. And the self-flattering thoughts whereby Richard would isolate himself within his kingship have only led him to the predicament in which he now finds himself. None of the three modes of practicing power by which the play is permeated—as prince, monarch, or prophet—seem any longer any guarantee for undoing the confusions in which Richard began, the "fatal" confusion that has brought him to this point.

And in the final eleven lines before the music sounds for him, Richard will summarize at once the thoughts upon which he has just reflected and the private history that has begotten that situation in which those thoughts (and failures) take place, a summary with which we may conclude our discussion of the play, and that may stand as the most lucid Shakespeare has written on the themes we are considering.

> Thus play I in one person many people,
> And none contented.
>
> (31–32)

Thus (as I have shown in the above lines, and in the history to which the above lines refer and of which they are a product) play I (enact, but also play at being as one would in a theater) many people (prophetic people, ambitious people, self-flattering people, but also Gaunt, Carlisle, Bolingbroke, Aumerle, and so forth, all of whom in playing various roles I play at being), and none contented (none to any satisfaction, therefore none with any content, and therefore none clearly demarcated from any of the others).

> . . . sometimes am I king,
> Then treasons make me wish myself a beggar,
> And so I am. Then crushing penury
> Persuades me I was better when a king.
> Then am I kinged again and, by and by,
> Think that I am unkinged by Bolingbroke,
> And straight am nothing.
> (32–38)

With startling clarity, Richard recounts the play we have witnessed. Initially he was king before the quarrel of Mowbray and Bolingbroke. Then his treasons with regard to Gloucester make him wish himself a beggar, a mere subject to the king. And so, he stops the trial, banishes Mowbray for life, steals Gaunt's goods, leaves York in charge of the kingdom, and goes off to fight his private wars. Then the poverty of the situation brings him back from the wars to England to make a stand against the invader. Then Bolingbroke appears with his forces at Flint Castle and Richard, thinking himself unkinged by Bolingbroke, steps down and straightaway abdicates the throne. Thinking he is nothing, he quickly makes himself nothing. "Are you contented to resign the crown?" "Ay, no; no, ay; for I must nothing be." Unkinged by himself and by Bolingbroke, he is neither king nor subject. He has literally no place to be. He is nothing, content itself.

But Richard has conceived the above history in the present tense, as if it describes less a history of social relations than the relation between social and imaginary conceptions. And so perhaps we should reread the passage as such. Sometimes I am king. But aware of the emptiness of my position—its purely imaginary status, its status, if you like, as the imaginary that wins, that gets to call itself social and everything else imaginary—I wish myself one of those others, one of my subjects, and so I reconceive of my status accordingly. Now I am a beggar, a subject to the king, but aware of the emptiness of my position, its attractiveness, if you like, only from a position sufficiently removed from its impoverished realities, I recover my former status. But now, aware once again of the emptiness of being king, and yet aware that the position of my others, my subjects, is no better, I imagine that someone else must be responsible for my discontent and that I have been "unking'd" by some "Bolingbroke." And investing him with the power to unking me (for who can wash off the balm of an anointed king?), I stand before him as nothing before God, and as soon as that happens, of course, I am nothing: I lose whatever kingship I still have and very soon afterwards, no doubt, my life.

The heroes of the great European novels of the nineteenth century in their metaphysical anguish have nothing on Richard. And in the final lines of this speech, he carries this thinking to its ineluctable conclusion.

> . . . But whate're I be,
> Nor I, nor any man that but man is,
> With nothing shall be pleased, till he be eased
> With being nothing.
>
> (39–41)

But whatever I be (whether king, subject, or nothing), neither I nor any man who is only a man (as opposed, for example, to divinity, which therefore includes everyone in this play), with nothing shall be pleased (that is to say, shall ever be pleased, contented, satisfied; or taken positively, must learn to be pleased with nothing, which is, in fact, all there is), until he be eased with (reconciled with, until he comes to terms with) being nothing (the being nothing at the end of life, death, but also with the being nothing in the middle of life and that passes as something, as life itself). No man that is only a man shall ever be pleased or find satisfaction, contentment, substance, until he comes to terms with the fact of his own death, a death or nihilation at the end of life but also in the middle of life and that passes as being itself.

Which is to say, in fact, no one will ever be pleased—since the only ease available comes from being nothing or death. Or, there is in fact a way to be pleased, namely, by coming to terms with your own death. Or, there is a way to be pleased, but it necessitates coming to terms with the death or being nothing that passes as content, contentment, and continence in this world.

All of which, in a final ironic twist, succeeds in negatively substantiating the argument of Boethius, since Richard has in fact now found a way to bridge the prison with the world, to recognize the profound identity common to the world, social relations, and his own imaginings (the three prisons in which he lives), an identity, moreover, that concerns a supreme being, a form of transcendent mediation that takes the form for him, if not of God, then of death.

VIII. Issue and Oblivion

In the place of the king, Richard (and Shakespeare behind him) finds a mirror, a model, and in that mirror or model, nothing, nihilation, death. And subjectivity to this new model (or anti-model), to this shattered mirror, this failed mediation, this fragmented image of oneself (of one's being and one's destiny), will henceforth constitute for Shakespeare, and perhaps also for us as well, the problem of subjectivity itself.[62] It is a problem because Shakespeare has identified nothing in the same place where an older cultural formulation would identify love, a nothing that in itself is identifiable in the same cultural terms more customarily with evil. Ontology, therefore, in Shakespeare's rendering, is something like the site of their confusion, a confusion that from Hegel to Derrida, we recognize as the problem of desire and the problem of presence.

Thus we come to understand, by the same token, both the "literature" that would reveal this monstrous identity to us and the humanistic criticism that would displace it. Looming before us, like the Sphinx before Oedipus in Borges's poem, this "monstrous other presence in the mirror" becomes a prophetic account of our own past and our own future.[63]

> At dawn four-footed, at midday erect,
> And wandering on three legs in the deserted
> Spaces of afternoon, thus the eternal
> Sphinx had envisioned her changing brother
> Man, and with afternoon there came a person
> Deciphering, appalled at the monstrous other
> Presence in the mirror, the reflection
> Of his decay and his destiny,
> We are Oedipus; in some eternal way
> We are the long and threefold beast as well—
> All that we will be, all that we have been.
> It would annihilate us all to see
> The huge shape of our being; mercifully
> God offers us issue and oblivion.

Richard II is hardly the last time Shakespeare will explore either this issue or this oblivion. In fact, it could be argued that Shakespeare here opens an investigation that will occupy him the remainder of his literary life. *Hamlet,* for example, may be seen as picking up where *Richard II* leaves off, as an extended meditation on "being nothing." If Richard articulates the nature of the difficulty, Hamlet plays out its implications. Hamlet, we may say, can never come to terms (or "be eased") with "being nothing," with an empty theatricality that he feels scandalously belies "that which passes show." "All the world's a stage" is not for Hamlet a humanistic truism but the statement of a crisis. All the world *should not* be a stage. One should be able to tell the difference between the two. Hamlet's difficulty is not that he cannot act but that he cannot but act, that he cannot give up finding the world at once and indistinguishably real and theatrical.

And when the presence of the ghost, the presence, that is to say, of the absence of his father, upsets his incestuous plotting with its demand to "remember me," he does everything he can to displace that demand. He will studiously "remember" the ghost within a series of fictions—in his writing on the wall, in his antic disposition, in the play within the play (which he says is "something like the murder of my father"), and so forth—remembrances in which at the same time he systematically displaces or "forgets" the violence to which it appeals. And even when he identifies for himself the "supreme fiction" so to speak—to become the very ghost his father was ("Oh I could tell you," he pronounces to Horatio as he dies, echoing his father's opening words to him—"O list, list"), he has no more resolved that dilemma than the play *Hamlet* has for us, a play that, like the tale told by Horatio a moment after Hamlet's demise, continues to haunt us anew in criticism after every attempt to resolve its enigmas. Not unlike Hamlet's own story, Shakespeare's play must remain for us—whatever else it is—his own response, his own way of writing, "So, there you are, uncle!"

The "dullness" of Hamlet's revenge, as he calls it, its "almost blunted purpose," is, then, by this analysis less a criticism of his behavior in Shakespeare's view, than its very point. Hamlet's difficulty is less with trying to trigger one of the many plots in which he finds himself (or in which the critics find him)—revenge plots, oedipal plots, or plots of other kinds—than it is to identify a pattern in which to live at all, a plot so to speak that is at the same time not a plot at all, a piece of theater, but a life. And those legions of critics, therefore, from Goethe and Coleridge onward, who have sought endlessly in the play to explain his famed delay, his alleged failure to act, would seem only to repeat (and thereby compound) this difficulty. Eschewing Hamlet's stated "fight for a plot" (whether that plot be conceived in aesthetic, conspiratorial, strategic, earthly, or mortal terms), they would, like Hamlet himself when he spies his reputed competitor, jump into the newly dug hole in the ground, stage there a fight with their competitor, and cry all the while, "I am Hamlet, the Dane."

If we remain troubled today by a certain monstrous writing that we identify on the one hand as "literary" and on the other as "philosophical"—"Shakespearean" and "Nietzschean"—perhaps it is because the nihilating movement of the criticism that constitutes that writing in either case mirrors us, says to us "remember me," by which it means "recognize yourself in the other"—a demand we are all too eager to translate into a demand either for "revenge" or for art, or ideally for both.

Between the two alternatives Shakespeare's play poses for us, between being and nothing, between "issue" and "oblivion" in Borges's words, between remembering and forgetting, between recognizing ourselves in the other, the monstrous "shape of our being," and displacing that "annihilating" other before a more flattering image we would prefer, it would seem we continue to play out, like Richard before the "blood" of Gloucester, Hamlet before the ghosts of his father, or Lear before Cordelia and his own Gloucester subplots, our literature, our criticism, and our lives.

II
Biblical Reading

3

"I Am Joseph"

Judaism, Anti-idolatry, and the Prophetic Law

> Il est juif et donc, dans son milieu et sa culture, il entend ce qu'il doit entendre, qu'il faut arrêter le sacrifice, qu'il faut un substitut. (He is Jewish and therefore understands what he must understand by his milieu and his culture, that sacrifice must be stopped, that there must be a substitute.)
>
> Michel Serres, *Le parasite*

In 1973 Eric Gans wrote that René Girard's research in anthropology seemed to offer an "Archimedean point" from which the human sciences could one day be rethought.[1] Gans may have underestimated the case. For what has occurred since Girard began writing in the early 1960s is a veritable explosion of interest in his work in all major fields of Western inquiry. By the end of the 1970s, Girardian thinking had gained a foothold in literary studies, classical studies, anthropology, psychoanalysis, and religious studies.[2] More recently, the "mimetic hypothesis" has begun to be extended to fields less commonly associated with the human sciences, fields such as economics and political science, and most recently the hard sciences of physics and biology.[3] If the number and kind of conferences held recently in this country and abroad around Girard's work can be taken as an index to this growing interest, it may not be much longer before we discover in this thought a model for talking responsibly about the conditions for both the humanities and the sciences, a basis for understanding in the most fundamental way the order of behavior and of knowledge in human communities.[4]

My own contribution to this burgeoning Girardian project—both here and elsewhere—will assume the following form. Rather than summarize Girard's ideas (there are already excellent accounts of his work) or "apply" them within my own fields, I would like in the first place to highlight certain aspects of his thinking that I think have been insufficiently emphasized, aspects that I call the "prophetic." And in the second I would like to undertake what I deem to be the next step of this research: to begin to uncover the roots of the Christian revelation which is of such importance for Girard in the source of all prophetic thinking in our culture which is the Hebrew Bible. For that part of my presentation in the present context I will turn to certain texts at the conclusion of Genesis, texts concerning the story of Joseph and his brothers.

I

René Girard's work offers us neither more nor less than a theory of order and disorder in human communities. Emerging as it did from the intellectual climate of structuralism and poststructuralism in the late 1960s and early 1970s in this country, Girard's thinking undertook to deal with the one problem evaded by the proponents both of textuality and of power—the problem of the sacred, a problem, I suggest, that comprehends each of these other two discussions and goes beyond them.

In *Mensonge romantique et vérité romanesque* (1961), Girard proposed that desire is rooted neither in objects nor in subjects but in the deliberate appropriation by subjects of the objects of others.[5] The simplicity and elegance of this theory should not blind us to the enormity of its explanatory power. In a series of readings of five major European novelists (Cervantes, Stendhal, Flaubert, Dostoevsky, and Proust), Girard was able to show that the discovery of the imitative or mimetic nature of desire (in contrast to the romantic belief that desire is original or originary) structures the major fiction of these writers and makes available to us, if we would but read that fiction in context of their total output, an autocriticism of the writer's own emergence from the underground prison of romantic belief.

In *La Violence et le sacré* (1972), Girard generalized his theory of mediated desire to the level of cultural order at large.[6] What is the function of religion at the level of real human relations? he asked. We have long had available to us imaginary theories of sacrifice—such as the kind Frazer and others in the nineteenth century proposed. More recently, with the advent of structural linguistics and structural anthropology, we have tried to explain religion from within a network of social differences or symbolic exchanges—à la Marcel Mauss and Claude Lévi-Strauss. What Girard suggests in their place is a theory of human community that would account for behavior at the level of the real. Religion, Girard suggests, has the function of keeping violence out, of transcendentalizing it, of making it sacred. Thus, the first equation he offers toward this end of understanding the foundations of human community is the identity between violence and the sacred. The sacred he says is violence efficaciously removed from human communities, and violence is the sacred deviated from its divine position and creating havoc in the city.

But what is violence from a human perspective? Human beings argue, Girard asserts, not because they are different but because they are the same, because in their mutual differential accusations they have become enemy twins, human doubles, mirror images of each other in their reciprocal enmity and violence. Thus, violence is none other than difference itself, asserted in the extreme, no longer efficaciously guaranteeing its own propagation. It is difference gone wrong, as it were, the poison for which difference is the medicine. Such is the nature of the sacrificial crisis.

How do these identities offer us a theory of the origin of culture? In the midst of a sacrificial crisis that verges upon a war of all against all, an extraordinary thing can occur: the war of all against all can suddenly turn into the war of all against one. Since within the sacrificial crisis all approach a state of being identical to all, anyone approaches being identical to everyone and can, therefore, substitute for all those that each dreams of sacrificing. Thus, the most arbitrary differences—hair color, skin color—can come to count absolutely. In the wake of the successful expulsion of an enemy twin or double, peace is restored. Since the trouble was never any other than human violence to begin with, the successful completion of the sacrificial project of each in the collective expulsion of an arbitrary scapegoat can restore difference to the human community. A complex network of ritual interactions can now be elaborated to prevent the reoccurrence of such a crisis, a prevention that can paradoxically take the form of its encouragement (in mock or commemorative form—and only up to a point) in order to reacquire its beneficial effects.

In *Des Choses cachées depuis la fondation du monde* (1977) and *Le Bouc émissaire* (1979), Girard carried this development to its natural conclusion.[7] How has our knowledge of these sacrificial dynamics been made possible? Why is this very theory not just another sacrificial theory, protective of our own cultural ethnocentrism? The demystification of the sacrificial genesis of cultural order first makes its appearance in the Hebrew Bible and reaches its zenith, Girard argues, in the texts of the Christian Gospel, in particular the texts of the Passion. Stories such as those of Cain and Abel or Jacob and Esau begin already to make available to us within the text this identity of the sacred with human violence. But the full revelation for Girard comes only in the victimage of Jesus. Jesus, Girard argues, is the first innocent victim, one whose innocence renders visible for the first time the arbitrariness of the victims of primitive sacrificial behavior and shows us where our violence is going.

For example, in the curses against the Pharisees, Jesus says to the Pharisees, in effect, "You say that, had you been there, you would not have stoned the prophets. Don't you see that in distinguishing yourself from 'those who stoned the prophets,' you do the same thing? You put yourself at a sacred remove from them which is neither more nor less than what they already were doing in 'stoning' their adversaries. Moreover, for telling you this truth of your own violence, you will differentiate yourself from or 'stone' me. What's more, those who come after you, will repeat your very gestures. Believing they are different from you, they will stone you in my name, calling you 'Jews' and themselves 'Christians.'" The history of Christianity for Girard is permeated with such sacrificial misunderstandings, misunderstandings ironically of the demystification of sacrificial understanding itself.[8]

What does it mean, then, for me to identify Girard's thinking as "prophetic?" If we understand the notion of the prophetic as the recognition of the dramas in which human beings are engaged and the naming in advance of the end of those dramas, then Girard's thought, which identifies itself with the Gospel reading, is prophetic in the same fashion. Both elaborate for us the total picture of our implication in human violence, showing us where it has come from and where it is leading us, in order that we may give it up.

But where does such a notion of the prophetic itself come from? To ask this question is to open an inquiry of a different sort.

The notion of the prophetic has particular meaning for us in the modern world, one that is associated for us with religiosity or a kind of false theologism, as in the phrase "nouveau prophétisme."[9] I would argue that if we have rarely recognized the true explanatory power of the prophetic, it is because we have lived within the confines of a Platonic essentialism that has barred that knowledge from us.[10] What I want to argue is that the prophetic is more comprehensive than Platonism, that it is, if we understand the notion in its largest sense, the logic of ritual organization itself, a logic, moreover, that we share with every other culture on the planet and yet to which we remain indefatigably blind by virtue of our idolatry of Platonic reason. Therefore, it is a logic that raises as a stake our very ethnocentrism.

In what way? We live in a culture dominated by the thought of the Platonic logos, by discourse, by reason, by difference or decision-making. Within Platonic thinking there have been only two ways that we have been able to conceive of the possibility of knowledge outside of reason. On the one hand, we have imagined it coming to us as the result of divine or providential intercession. Thus, for example, we have imagined poetic inspiration among the Greeks or the language of the Judaic prophets. On the other hand, we have imagined knowledge as possible for us through fantasies, illusion, dreams, in short, all those experiences that we feel to be the product of fiction or of desire. Thus Freud's discoveries, for example, far from unveiling for us a realm which is genuinely new, a knowledge that is other than conscious knowledge, only display for us a region which, from within Platonism was, as it were, mapped out in advance. It is not coincidental that the two theories of dreams with which we are left after Freud hold that they are either prophetic in the strictly literal sense of fortune-telling or the remnants of unconscious desire.

We have, in short, never been able to imagine the prophetic as a reading of the course of the dramas of human relations in front of us, a reading of what Michel Serres might call "the excluded middle."[11] What I want to suggest is that there is such a conceptualization within our culture, one, moreover, that has been misunderstood precisely to the extent that we have felt it to be accessible to us within Platonism. I am thinking, of course, of Greek tragedy and the Jewish and Christian Bibles.

There is no place here to specify how the prophetic makes its appearance within these two domains. Suffice it to say that I do not want to suggest that the Judaic prophetic in the ancient sixth century or Greek tragedy in the ancient fifth century are simply extensions of Assyrio-Babylonian or other Mesopotamian rituals (for example, the mantic enthusiasm of the pre-Socratic philosophers), or even a more profound version of those ritual traditions.[12] Rather I propose that Greek tragedy and the prophetic tradition in Judaism appeared at a moment that Girard would identify as a sacrificial crisis of the possibility of religion itself, a moment when no sacrificial system seems to work, when all sacrifices lead only to more violence and all victimage leads only to more victimage and therefore to the need for more sacrifice. Without trying to pinpoint such a moment historically or culturally, I would suggest that Judaism and to a lesser extent Greek tragedy formulate a response to the following question: how can I live in a world in which there are no longer any gods of the sacrificial kind? How is it possible to be prophetic in the face of the collapse of the prophetic?

Apart from the answer that Greek tragedy would offer, Judaism's response is one that has always been understood from within the Jewish community as an orthodox reading, although the path by which I will arrive at this reading may seem somewhat unorthodox: the law of anti-idolatry.[13] At the heart of Judaism is Torah, the Pentateuch, the five books of Moses, the Law. And all remaining books of Biblical Scripture, the compilations of midrashic, talmudic, and later rabbinic commentaries, as well as the more mystical and esoteric traditions of Kabbala and later Hasidic texts, are centered upon Torah and extend its reach.[14] At the heart of the Law is the Decalogue, the *aseret hadibrot,* the Ten Commandments or ten words. And at the heart of the Decalogue, the Law of the Law, as it were, is the first commandment, the commandment for which all other commandments are themselves extensions, the law against substituting any other God for God, for the prophetic God, for the God of anti-idolatry: *anochiy YHVH eloheycha asher hotzeitiycha meieretz mitzrayim mibeiyt avadiym* ("I am the LORD thy God, who brought thee out of the land of Egypt, out of the house of bondage" [Ex. 20:2]).[15]

The Judaic genius, as readers of Maurice Blanchot and Emmanuel Levinas will immediately recognize, is to have imagined a God completely external to the world, a God for whom nothing within the world is finally sacred.[16] Judaism is "la pensée du dehors," a thought of (or from) the outside or the desert, a thought of exile and of exodus.[17] It is a thought of not confusing anything that is in the world for God, of seeing to the end of the dramas in which human beings are engaged and learning when to stop, a thought therefore of learning to recognize oneself in the other.

Take, for example, the story that Exodus 3 tells of the name of God.[18] Moses is a shrewd and uncanny dealer. He is willing to be a little cagey— even with God. God says to him, "Go back to Egypt and take the Hebrews out of slavery."[19] And Moses responds, "Okay, no problem. Only, who shall I say sent me?"[20] He tries, in other words, to trap God into revealing himself. But God is as cagey as Moses, even cagier. God says, "When they ask you that, here's what you tell them. Tell them *ehyeh asher ehyeh* (or *ehyey* or *YHVH*) sent you."[21] That is, God does not necessarily reveal His name. He simply says, "Here is what you say when they ask you that." The Hasidic tradition which substitutes the word *hashem* ("the name") for *YHVH* is, in this regard at least, as traditional as the mainstream since it presumes as well that God's name has been revealed in this passage (among others)—which is their reason for not pronouncing it (in accordance with the third commandment).

What does *ehyeh asher ehyeh,* or *ehyeh,* or *YHVH* (the third person form of the same word) mean? Here I turn to an insight offered to me by Jonathan Bishop of Cornell University. *Ehyeh* is, of course, an imperfect form of the verb "to be," functioning as a future, and it first occurs in this passage in the first person in the form: *ehyeh asher ehyeh* (3:14–15).[22] Volumes have been written on this sentence. In fact, the kabbalistic tradition takes it as a matter of principle that the unraveling of the name of God is the only important task in Judaism, the one that achieves for us what the Kabbalists take as the primary aim of exegesis, relating the heavens to the earth.[23]

The task may not yet be completed. Here again it may turn out that God is being a little bit cagey with us. Just a moment before Moses asks God His name, God remarks to him, "Go down to Egypt and bring the Israelites out of bondage. And when you do, I will be with you" (3:12).[24] The words employed by Torah for "I will be with you" (*ehyeh 'imach*) contain the same word employed by God a moment later in place of the name: *ehyeh*. The word slips by Moses, of course, who has no reason to fix upon it. But after God's next declaration, we can return to it with renewed interest.[25]

The phrase *ehyeh asher ehyeh* may in context, then, come to mean: "I will be with you in order that I will be with you." Or, inserting the name itself within the name: "I-will-be-with-you will be with you in order that I-will-be-with-you will be with you." And one could continue in this fashion indefinitely. In other words, in the place of the name of God is a promise, the promise of a promise, so to speak, a promise in the first place of future being or accompaniment.[26] To be intimate with God, to know God's name as it were, is simply to follow the Law in order that God will be there with you so that you can announce that name, that promise. The Law of Torah, the Law that is Torah, the Law of God, is thus, the law of survival.

And that is precisely the meaning of the Covenant. The Covenant is the deal, the bargain, that God makes with the human community. You do this and I will do this. You follow My Law—which is the law of anti-idolatry—and you will survive, you will be there to testify to the power of this arrangement. Neither more nor less. Man's part is the law of anti-idolatry, learning when to stop, learning to recognize yourself in the other. God's part is a guarantee of survival—if there is any survival to be had, which is not itself guaranteed.[27]

The Judaic God who promises a future by virtue of this Law, who reveals the way to go on in a world in which there are no gods, who reveals a way to go on in a world defined by the collapse of all possibilities of going on, is, therefore, by definition, as it were, the prophetic God, in fact, the prophetic itself. The notion of the Judaic God and the notion of the prophetic are, in this connection at least, one and the same.

To say, then, that Girard's thought is prophetic is to say that it is a reading from within the Judaic or Hebrew Torah, which is the source of all prophetic thinking in our culture and the source in particular of the evangelical revelation. The Hebrew Bible, the Jewish Law, the Torah, is the first veritable text of demystification in our culture. It is to the project of understanding this text as fully anti-sacrificial (in all the implications of that notion that Girard has made clear to us) that I see the future of Girardian research as necessarily devoted.

But what, more precisely, is the Hebraic prophetic? What is the principle of anti-idolatry, of learning when to stop or of recognizing yourself in the other in its Jewish setting? And to what extent is Girard's anti-sacrificial reading of the Gospels a Jewish reading? It is in the name of answering these questions—answers that will constitute the next step of Girardian research—that I turn now to the texts of Joseph and his brothers.

II

The Joseph story is something of an odd tale for Genesis to end with. It seems curiously misplaced in a book which describes the Creation, the expulsion of man from the garden of Eden, the generations from Adam to Noah to Abraham, and the history of patriarchs. It lacks the monumentalism of the *akeidah,* the story of the binding of Isaac, the tenth trial of Abraham after which God will grant His Covenant with Abraham, or of Jacob's wrestling with an angel, out of which Jacob's name will be changed to Israel. It comes, so far as we are able to tell, from the wisdom literature of the Solomonic courts and seems distinctly prosaic both in subject matter and in style. It seems, in short, little more than a domestic tale of the dotage of old age and of the jealousy and naïveté of youth, on the whole, a story hardly capable of sustaining the weight that its pivotal position within the biblical canon would confer upon it.

The rabbinical commentary would seem to bear out this assessment. The rabbis speak of the story as recounting how Israel came to sojourn in Egypt. They point out that Joseph's dream at the center of the first part of the tale, when he imagines that his sheaves of grain stood up and those of the brothers bowed down to his, is literally prophetic of the end of the story when Joseph will dispense grain as viceroy in Egypt.

What I want to argue is that within the confines of this marginal transitional piece is a veritable deconstruction of sacrificial thinking, one which is all the more powerful for the quotidian and transitory context in which it is offered to us. If we have traditionally read this story in function of the first part—where Joseph is expelled by his brothers, sold to the passing bands of Ishmaelite or Midianite traders—the most important part, I would like to suggest, is really the second part where Joseph has become the right hand man of Pharaoh in Egypt, and in which the sacrificial actions of part 1 are restaged (in the figures of Simeon and Benjamin) and the victim and his executioners are revealed as doubles. "This is because of what we did to our brother Joseph," Judah remarks when things begin to go badly for them (42:21). And at the key moment when Joseph would take Benjamin from them, Judah steps forward and says, "Take me for him" (44:33), an offer that prompts Joseph, of course, to disclose himself with the words, "I am Joseph" (*aniy yoseif* [45:4]).

Joseph's disclosure of himself as their brother, the identification, that is, of the Egyptian viceroy (who is currently their potential victimizer) and their sacrificial victim as one and the same, is indeed the fulfillment, then, of the prophecies of part 1 as the rabbis suggested. But it is so precisely as the complete demystification of sacrificial thinking itself, a demystification that has now become available to us within the very text we are reading. Thus part 2 comes to serve as something of a model for an anti-sacrificial position for its readers, a model that highlights for us the sacrificial actions of part 1 in order precisely that they may be rejected. And the Joseph story, coming as it does at the conclusion of Genesis, can serve as something of a "part 2" to Genesis at large, a "part 2," thus, whose very transitory quality has been no less apparent than that of the part 2 within the tale, and which occurs within a book for which sacrifice or expulsion describe its major themes. Even Torah itself in this regard may be taken as a part 2 to the sacrificial cultures of Canaan and Mesopotamia from which it has come and from which it has taken its own exilic distance.

There is a story, a midrash, told by the Hasidic rabbis (and told to me by Rabbi Aharon Goldstein of Ann Arbor, Michigan) that captures this idea. A woman is sitting upstairs in an orthodox synagogue while the story of Joseph is being recited.[28] When they come to the section in part 1 where Jacob sends Joseph to Shechem to find his brothers and Joseph ends up "wandering in the field" (37:15) as Torah tells us, before someone directs him to Dothan, the woman cries out, "Don't go down there! Don't you remember what they did to you last year there! They are going to sell you!" The joke, the misunderstanding of the story, presumably revolves around what the woman has failed to recognize, which is, in the first place, that it is only a story (so that Joseph could not "hear" her); and second, that for Joseph this has not happened before. For him this is a first time and he lacks the hindsight that by virtue of Torah the woman has acquired.

It may turn out that in laughing at her we unwittingly include ourselves in the same misunderstanding. What if we consider the story of Joseph itself already in some fundamental way a "part 2" to both Genesis and to the sacrificial practices of the culture from which it has emerged? Then, is it not this story, the Book of Genesis as a whole, Torah itself, that says to us finally, "Don't go down there! Didn't you learn from last year? They are going to sell you!" And in laughing at the woman, in asserting that it is only a fiction, and only after all a first time, do we not belie our own implication in the ignorance of such wisdom, a wisdom all the more powerful for its being presented to us within the context of a joke, concerning someone who has been compelled to sit "upstairs" and who has "misunderstood" its teachings?

Nor has the power of this "part 2" been lost on the many generations of Christian exegetes on the Old Testament who have found in it, from within the context of medieval typology, the prefiguration of the Passion. The betrayal of Joseph, his sale for twenty pieces of silver, the twelve brothers (the most pivotal of whom is named Judah)—have all drawn the attention of the Church Fathers. Even the death and resurrection of Jesus finds its earlier counterpart in the ascension of Joseph from the pit and his rise in Egypt to become the right hand man of Pharaoh, the dispenser of Israel's daily grain.

But in thus opposing the Old Testament to the New, in reading the old god as the sacrificial god of vengeance or anger and the new as the anti-sacrificial god of love—a reading that, of course, is central to a certain Christian understanding of the two books—have we not unwittingly already slipped into the very structure we have wished to displace, believing in a new Law or "part 2" which it has already been, by definition, as it were, the goal of the Old Testament itself to reveal to us, an Old Testament that has now proven that much richer by virtue of its having foreseen our sacrificial misunderstanding of it?

To understand the power of part 2 of Joseph's story, and in particular of Joseph's demystificatory disclosure, let us place the sequence in the context in which it occurs.

III

Jacob settles where his father sojourned, Torah tells us, a distinction that leads a number of rabbinical commentators to wonder whether here is not the source of his later misfortunes. Then it tells us that what follows are the chronicles of Jacob. The fact that Torah then proceeds to elaborate only the story of Joseph leads the rabbis to suggest that this story is the most important of the chronicles of Jacob from this point on.

At seventeen Joseph was a shepherd with his brothers, the sons of Leah, but a youth with the sons of Bilhah and Zilpah, the slaves of Jacob. Again the rabbis wonder whether some distinction is to be drawn in this regard, keeping in mind that Joseph is the only son of Rachel, Jacob's favored wife, and whose only other son will later be Benjamin. The distinction between the sons of Rachel and the sons of Leah will recur later in Egypt when Judah proposes exchanging himself for his half-brother Benjamin.

Torah tells us that Joseph "brought evil report" of his brothers. Rashi, the foremost medieval Jewish French exegete, undertakes to tell us what these reports were: eating meat torn from living animals, treating maid servants as slaves, engaging in immoral behavior, etc., all the charges, in short, that will later be brought against Joseph in the house of Potiphar. Ramban, who represents another great exegetical tradition, suggests that we cannot even be sure it is the sons of Leah Torah is talking about at this point; it may be the sons of Bilhah and Zilpah.[29]

Torah then notes that Jacob loved Joseph more than any of the other children because Joseph was a "son of his old age," and that he made for him an aristocratic tunic. What is the meaning of the phrase "son of his old age" (*ven-z'kuniym*)? The rabbis are undecided. Is it the child of Rachel, Benjamin being too young to attend Jacob? Or simply one who attends Jacob in his old age, as opposed to the others? Or some special distinction that we are to confer upon Joseph from this privilege? Moreover, the words for "coat of many colors" (*k'tonet pasiym*) mean a tunic suitable for royalty rather than the "coat of many colors" of folktale fame. The brothers saw the tunic, Torah tells us, recognized that it was Joseph whom their father loved most, and they hated Joseph all the more for it.

All of these details of the first few sentences of part 1 are about to become important in the second part of this sequence. Joseph dreams a dream and says to his brothers: "Behold, we were binding sheaves in the field, and lo, my sheaf arose, and also stood upright; and, behold, your sheaves came round about, and bowed down to my sheaf" (37:7). The brothers answer, "Shalt thou indeed reign over us? or shalt thou indeed have dominion over us?" (8) and they hated him, Torah tells us, all the more.

There are two traditional interpretations of this sequence, although I would like to argue that they are in fact two versions of the same interpretation, one, moreover, that is decidedly partial. The brothers say to him: "So you would reign over us!" They see his dream as a sign of arrogance, that he would feel himself superior to them. What do the rabbis say? Rashi, among others, says in effect, "Look, this dream is prophetic of the future—all dreams in the Jewish exegetical tradition have something prophetic about them—since Joseph's history will involve grain when he is viceroy in Egypt. Moreover, they will bow down to him since he will be the right-hand man of Pharaoh and dispenser of that grain and so in the long run they will have Joseph to thank for saving them."[30]

In other words, both interpretations identically regard the dream as Joseph's assertion of his own superiority, the brothers simply translating that assertion into concealed arrogance or desire on Joseph's part while the rabbis find in it a sign of providential intercession and read the anger of the brothers toward Joseph as reflective of their own jealousy of that status. Neither reading, however, relates the dream to the real dramatic or social context in which it appears.

There may, however, be another way to read this sequence, one that places it clearly within the ongoing contextual dynamics and therefore encompasses both of these views. Here I avail myself of an insight offered to me by Walter Gern of New York City. The dream is prophetic, Gern suggests, but it has less to do with the end of the history (although it may prophesy that as well) than with the more immediate situation to follow: in particular, Joseph's expulsion by the brothers in the very next scene. The key, Gern suggests, is the reference in the dream to the sheaves rising up. The action of making something into an uplifted thing, of course, is not foreign to students of Torah since it is the action that defines the very word used in the sacred context for sacrifice itself, for the burnt offering: the word *alah,* to cause to ascend, to rise up. This is the word used commonly in the Abraham and Isaac story, for example, when God asks Abraham to prepare Isaac as a "burnt offering," an *olah.*

What is the significance of this connection? The word *alah* (or *olah,* in the noun form) is not actually used in the language of Joseph's dream. Rather Torah offers us the much more prosaic and everyday words *kamah* ("arose") and *nitsavah* ("stood upright"). In fact, for a story as clearly about an expulsion as the Joseph story is, the absence of the word *alah* would seem somewhat surprising. It is used only once in the story and then in an anti-sacrificial sense, at the moment when the sacrifice is to be aborted and the sale substituted, when the brothers are lifting Joseph out of the pit, drawn up to be given to the passing bands of traders.

How, then, is this reference within Joseph's dream to an uplifted thing the key? If we had only the two final sequences of part 1—the dream and the expulsion—I would have to argue that it was not, that Gern's suggestion was only another reading of the traditional prophetic kind, finding a literalizing linkage not only to Egypt but to the action at Dothan as well, and not a very strong linkage at that. Yet I am going to argue that it is the very weakness of the linkage, the very dearth of references to sacrificial language, the very anti-sacrificial and quotidian quality of the story that confers upon it its greatest power. But to make that argument I have to introduce another aspect of the dream, the context of Jacob's favoritism.

We recognize, of course, that Jacob's view of the situation is important. Torah tells us that when Joseph repeats essentially the same dream, this time with the sun, the moon, and the eleven stars bowing down to him, Jacob at first joins in the chorus of the brothers. "Shall I and thy mother and thy brethren indeed come to bow down to thee to the earth?" he asks (10). But when the brothers "hated Joseph yet the more for his dreams," Torah tells us, Jacob "kept the saying in mind." Moreover, we know that Joseph made clear his dream to both his brothers and to Jacob for in both tellings he repeats emphatically words meaning "listen to what I say," "behold" (*v'hineih,* for example).

Why does Joseph do this? Joseph has seen that he is the apple of his father's eye, the object of his father's desire. How do we know that? Torah tells us specifically that Jacob loved Joseph more than all the other brothers, that he was the child of his old age. But we also know it because he was the recipient of the special coat that his father had given him. Joseph recognizes, in short, that his father sees him as aristocratic, as special. Wanting to please his father (he is, we recall, seventeen years old), he begins acting the way his father thinks of him. He puts on his father's "coat of many colors" as it were, he thinks of himself as special just as his father thinks of him, he mimes or imitates his father's view of him.

Thus we come to understand his giving "evil report" to Jacob about his brothers. It is less important that we determine precisely what the brothers may or may not have done to deserve such report than that we recognize that the action of giving it is a mimetic appropriation on Joseph's part of his father's view of the situation. For his father indirectly has already given evil report of the brothers by favoring Joseph to begin with, and Joseph is simply enacting Jacob's desire in return.

In the same way we come to understand Joseph's dream as a similar dramatic representation of what Jacob's desire has been all along: to have the brothers bow down to him as one would before royalty. Joseph's dream is a prophetic representation, a going to the end of the road, of Jacob's desire. It is what Freud might call a rebus, a figuration of the total dramatic context in which Joseph, Jacob, and the brothers all identically find themselves.

We also understand Jacob's hesitation when Joseph tells his second dream, his sense that there is something uncannily familiar about Joseph's narrative. Jacob is moved to "keep it in mind." And we understand the limitations of both the view of the rabbis who see only the literal representation of the dream, ignoring the social situation in which it was produced and that it figures. And as well we understand the limitations of the view of the brothers who recognize accurately that desire is behind the dream but see it uniquely as Joseph's desire rather than Jacob's and equally ignore the implication of their own actions in the situation— that it is their very jealousy that will render that "end of the road" possible. Neither group, that is, has taken into account the "excluded middle" sequence that is the mimetic appropriation of Jacob's desire by

Joseph and the substitution—by Joseph first and later by the brothers—of Jacob's desire for their own.

This excluded middle, these dynamics of mimetic appropriation and substitution, may now explain for us how the final sequence of part 1 is linked to Joseph's dream and why Joseph's reference to an "uplifted thing" is so powerful. In formulating his insights in the form of a dream, Joseph has substituted for Jacob's favoring of his son over the brothers his own desires. Rather than saying Jacob is the author of this desire, he says that I, Joseph, am its author. Similarly, rather than blame Jacob for what Joseph has said, the brothers blame Joseph. Their condemnation of Joseph for what they perceive to be his arrogance is, moreover, but another substitution of the same kind as Joseph's.

The dream sequence, in other words, enables us to read the first sequence by highlighting its structure through a controlled repetition of it. If there were no dream sequence, and we proceeded directly to the expulsion—Jacob singles out Joseph for favoritism; the brothers become jealous and take action against him—the tale would be little more than the story of jealousy and dotage we have popularly taken it to be.

By the same kind of displacement we can now understand the relation of the dream to what follows. In the face of Joseph's sheaves, that "rise up and also stand upright," those of the brothers now "come round and bow down." What is the act of "bowing down"? It is, of course, sacralization—differentiation and exaltation. But in this context it is a repetition of the action of the sheaves of Joseph. It is, that is to say, by an inverse action, a gesture that makes Joseph's sheaves into an uplifted thing. In his dream, that is, Joseph imagines not only Jacob's desire but his brothers' response. In good rabbinical fashion he imagines the end of the drama—that the brothers will sacralize him. But he does so in the specific way in which Torah has imagined for us making something into an uplifted thing. In what is perhaps another example of the Hebraic demystificatory genius, we come to understand that action as an act of radical separation, of destruction, of violence, of sacrifice: a burnt offering.

And in the connection that Torah has offered us between the action of the sheaves within the dream and the action at Dothan that immediately follows we can now perceive how the final sequence links up with the first. The two actions are linked in the text for us directly. The brothers see Joseph approaching and say, "Behold, this dreamer cometh. Come now therefore, and let us slay him . . . and we shall see what will become of his dreams" (19–20). The action of expelling Joseph is but a duplication of the same kind already imagined within the dream. Substituting Joseph's dream for his sheaves and Joseph himself for his dreams, they will simply intensify the same kinds of displacements to which we have already been witness. Joseph will himself be made into an uplifted thing—literally drawn out of the well—as a mimetic imitation or acting out of the dream language itself. Far from opposing Joseph's dreams, that are, after all, only the acting out of Jacob's dreams, the brothers in expelling Joseph violently enact them.

The notion of "uplifting" within the dream, then, draws our attention less to the dispensing of grain at the end of the tale—as we have traditionally read it—than to the sacrificial victimage immediately to follow. Or rather, it draws our attention to the dispensing of grain but only as the result of that victimage. And the dream sequence as a whole links for us the beginning and the end, mimetic appropriation with sacrificial victimage. It deconstructs for us the sacrificial thinking that constitutes part 1 in its entirety. The final sacrificial substitution is but the violent culminating intensification of the mimetic displacements that have taken place throughout and of which the dream sequence itself is already a primary example. What the dream has revealed to us above all is that mimesis, sacrifice, and substitution are continuous with each other. The dream is prophetic, which is to say that it offers us an account of the total dramatic context in which all are implicated. Just as the Joseph story does of the Book of Genesis that precedes it and the Book of Exodus that follows. Just as the Hebrew Torah does of the sacrificial cultures from which it has come and the Platonic culture to follow.

To answer the questions with which we began, let us turn quickly to the end of part 1—to the sale of Joseph—and then briefly to part 2 of the story, in which part 1 gains its greatest power.

IV

Joseph is sent by his father Jacob to Shechem to check on the welfare of his brothers. Does Jacob already perceive their intentions, and is he sending Joseph as a lamb to the slaughter? Joseph, of course, does not find them at Shechem. He is spotted by another man, Torah tells us, "wandering in the field," and sent instead to Dothan. Why has Torah substituted Dothan for Shechem? Is there a textual corruption here, as even the greatest of traditional biblical scholars have imagined? Or is there a principle of textual coherence, an editorial perspective, that sees fit to include these sequences within the "story of Joseph," a perspective whose criteria of selectivity we can unravel?[31] In what follows we may begin to discern the answers to these and other such questions.

For what follows is a series of extraordinary substitutions that constitute the entire fabric of the end of part 1. The sequence in which Joseph is sold may veritably be described as substitution gone wild. The brothers see him and conspire to kill him. "Behold, this dreamer cometh," they say. "Come now therefore, and let us slay him, and cast him into one of the pits, and we will say: An evil beast hath devoured him; and we shall see what will become of his dreams" (19–20). They would substitute Joseph for his dreams, and murder for his language. Moreover, they would then substitute another story—that he was killed by a wild animal—for what they contemplate. Keep in mind that later, when they bring the bloodied tunic to Jacob, he will imagine that Joseph has been devoured by a wild animal. It is as if the brothers already know what would count as a plausible explanation for Jacob of the fate of Joseph. Jacob and the brothers are in harmony, it would appear, on the topic of Joseph's death.

Reuben objects and tells them to "shed no blood." Let us "cast him into this pit that is in the wilderness but lay no hand upon him." Reuben had the intention, Torah tells us, to save Joseph and return him to his father. How are we to understand this remark? Is Reuben suggesting that they not kill him or only that they not shed any blood in killing him? Later, when they cast him into the pit and sit down to eat, Judah will say, "Let us not kill him," as if their intention were still to do so. In any case, we recognize that Reuben would substitute another solution for the one proposed. To suggest that Torah may already begin to dissociate Reuben—or Judah—from the sacrificial behavior of the others in part 1, a dissociation that will reach its culmination in part 2 when an anti-sacrificial position (the substitution to end all substitutions) comes to be substituted for the earlier one, is not to weaken our thesis, I would suggest, but to strengthen it. It is as if the kind of rabbinical commentary that looks forward prophetically to the end of the story and reads from that perspective has come to be inserted in advance and in a fragmentary form within the text itself.

Joseph arrives, and the brothers take his tunic and cast him into the pit. Then they sit down for a meal. That is, having substituted the suggestion of Reuben for their own, they make another. They substitute eating for dismemberment. What, after all, is eating but the substitution of food for the victim (sometimes they are one and the same) and ingestion for expulsion?

Then the Ishmaelites arrive, and Judah suggests that they "shed no blood" (has Torah substituted Judah for Reuben?), but instead sell Joseph to the Ishmaelite traders. Such a sale would thus substitute commercial transaction for murder, commercial transaction itself being already founded upon the possibility of equivalency or substitution. The brothers agree, and suddenly there are Midianite traders rather than Ishmaelites, Torah having substituted the former for the latter. Then, Torah tells us, "they" drew Joseph out of the well and sold him to the Ishmaelites for twenty pieces of silver. Who drew him out of the well? The brothers? The Midianites? The Ishmaelites? And who sold him to the Ishmaelites? The Ishmaelites, it seems, have been substituted for the Midianites, who were substituted for the Ishmaelites to begin with. The text leaves the matter undecided, as if the important thing were less to determine who was substituted for whom, who the specific agencies of action were, than to put substitution itself on display. The long traditions of biblical scholarship that have read in this passage an example of textual corruption may reflect this situation more than resolve it for us, substituting in turn their notion of textual "corruption" for the sacrificial substitutions the text may already be revealing to us.

In any case, Joseph is handed over in exchange for twenty pieces of silver and comes to be brought to Egypt. But the sequence does not end there. The chain of substitutions will return unto Jacob, where it all began. Reuben returns to the pit, and notices that Joseph is not there (a moment that echoes Joseph's earlier trip to Shechem), and tears his garments. He substitutes self-mutilation for mutilation of the other and garments for himself. He says, "The child is not; and as for me, whither shall I go?" as if in some fundamental way the fate of Joseph were a stand-in or substitute for his own.

The brothers then proceed to kill a goat in place of killing Joseph. They smear the blood of the goat, which substitutes for the goat itself, upon Joseph's tunic, as a substitute for smearing it upon Joseph. Then they return this same tunic to Jacob in place of returning Joseph. They ask him, "Do you recognize this tunic? Is it Joseph's?" ("This have we found. Know now whether it is thy son's coat or not" [32]). Just as Judah will be asked later by Tamar with whom he consorted, "Do you recognize whose pledge this is?" ("Discern, I pray thee, whose are these, the signet, and the cords, and the staff" [38:25]). And just as Joseph will recognize the brothers later in Egypt but they will not recognize him, and similarly disclose himself to them: "Do you recognize me? I am Joseph." Do you recognize, in other words, the brothers say to Jacob, Joseph through this series of substitutions? Do you recognize your coat, your aristocratic tunic, the object of your desires, as the origin of this substitutive violence?

The bloodied tunic, in other words, is the return unto Jacob of his own violence, of their violence against Joseph, of their violence against Jacob. Do you recognize your own violence? Here it is. This is the end of the road of sacrificial violence on which you are traveling, the death of your favored son. The Joseph story is a counterpart in Genesis to the story of Abraham and Isaac.

What is Jacob's response to this prophetic presentation? "An evil beast hath devoured him; Joseph is without doubt torn in pieces" (33). Far from recognizing himself in the other, his own violence in the violence of the other, he externalizes it, he dehumanizes it. A savage beast did it. He repeats the explanation the brothers imagined originally. Like father, like son. And then he tears his clothes, as Judah did, as if he would rather go on with the traditional substitutions than demystify them, even at the cost of his own son.

The conclusion of part 1 of the Joseph story, in short, brings us back to the beginning. It demystifies sacrifice for us. It reveals the substitutive nature of the mimetic displacements with which the story began and the sacrificial violence in which it concludes. It shows us the end of the road we are traveling in order that we may give it up. It says to us, "Do you recognize yourself, your own violence, in this tale?" in order that we may put an end to sacrificial substitution, that we may give up idolizing sacrifice.

Why, then, is part 1 insufficient? Why does there need to be a part 2? Is part 2 just a repetition of what is already available to us in part 1?

In a sense, yes. In the sense that all of the Hebraic biblical narrative is structured as a replaying of the same drama. The whole was already contained in the first sequence of part 1 when Jacob favored Joseph, Joseph gave evil report of his brothers, and they acted against him, hating him all the more. All traditional Jewish writing, I would suggest, is so structured, which is why, in a sense, we can begin anywhere.

At the same time, part 2 is necessary. To this point in the story, the anti-sacrificial position that the text presents for us, the demystification of sacrificial thinking, has occurred to virtually no one within the text. There are hints of it in the words of Reuben and Judah, but no more than that.

Yet the Hebrew biblical text exists—and here is perhaps my main point—to make it available to the characters themselves within the text, which is what makes it what I have called a text of demystification. It has to do this necessarily since what it asks of us primarily is whether or not we recognize ourselves in the text, whether we recognize that the text is already the world in which we live. We have never been outside of the text. Rather than a parallel to our lives (which is analogous, perhaps, but never contiguous with it), the text is a veritable extension of our experience. The inside of the text is to the outside as the two apparent "sides" of a Möbius strip that are really extensions of the same side. The text is the prophetic future of the dramas in which we ourselves are already engaged. In watching characters come to find themselves implicated in their own sacrificial gestures, their own texts, so the text is demystified for us. It is this gesture of demystification that offers us a way out of a crisis. Part 1 deconstructs sacrificial violence for us. It enables us to recognize ourselves in the other, to recognize that the other is only the future or the past of the same, of where we are. Part 2 will offer us a model for what to do about it, namely, to fictionalize it, to regard our sacrificial violence from a distance in order that we might abandon it.

There is no place here to pursue the intricacies of part 2 by which the knowledge of the identification of sacrifice with violence becomes available to each of the major characters. Judah learns it when he consorts with Tamar, after denying her his third son by the rites of Levirate marriage, and she identifies the man with whom she has played the harlot as Judah himself. He says, "She is more righteous than I; forasmuch as I gave her not to Shelah my son" (38:26). Joseph learns it in the house of Potiphar, where he is subjected to the same kinds of unjust accusations concerning morality to which he presumably subjected the brothers initially (he is treated "measure for measure," the rabbis note). The brothers as a group learn it in the sequence in Egypt when they come to ask for grain.

In the final scene of part 2 there is a famine in Israel. Jacob sends the brothers to find grain in Egypt, where Joseph has become the chief dispenser of that grain and the right hand man of Pharaoh. Joseph recognizes them, but they do not recognize him. It is as if Joseph has become himself the text in which they must learn to recognize themselves, their own brother. He takes Simeon as hostage and demands Benjamin—Jacob's youngest son and the only other remaining son of Rachel—before he will give them grain. On their way home they discover that the money they paid Joseph has been returned to them, that they too now are potential victims of unjust accusations.

They tell Jacob what has happened, and he says, "First I lost Joseph; then I lose Simeon; and now you tell me you want me to send with you Benjamin!" But first Reuben intercedes: "Thou shalt slay my two sons if I bring him not to thee" (42:37). And then Judah: "I will be surety for him; of my hand shalt thou require him; if I bring him not unto thee and set him before thee, then let me bear the blame for ever" (43:9). Finally, Jacob agrees, and they return to Egypt.

Joseph now prepares a huge meal for them with Benjamin getting the largest portions. He sends them away for a second time. Now he has guards intercept the brothers and accuse them of theft. When they look in their sacks the money is back and this time so is the cup Joseph gave Benjamin. The brothers return, and Joseph asks them for Benjamin. At this point, Judah steps up and says: "If we return to Israel without Benjamin, it will kill my father. Take me for the boy." At which point, of course, Joseph discloses his own identity to them, all rejoice in the discovery, and Jacob comes to Egypt with the remainder of his family and blesses the two sons of Joseph.[32]

From his position as Egyptian viceroy, Joseph has in effect restaged the sacrificial activity of the earlier sequence in its entirety. The unjust accusation, the money in the sack, recall the silver for which he himself was sold. The taking of Simeon and the threatened appropriation of Benjamin recall the sale of Joseph. This time, however, the demonstration is not lost on the brothers. For when things begin to go badly, they say, "This is because we sacrificed our brother Joseph" (42:21). They link the troubles into which they have fallen to human behavior, to their own violence.

At the key moment everything converges upon Joseph's disclosure: "I am Joseph" (*aniy yoseif* [45:3]). The Egyptian viceroy who is their lord, who controls the stage as it were, turns out to be the same as their victim. "I am Joseph," he says to them, "whom you would sacrifice." Moreover, their victim, who is also their lord, is also their brother, identical to them by family origins and identical to Benjamin, the other son of Rachel, for whom Judah would now exchange himself. The disclosure of Joseph's identity is a demystification of sacrifice itself, revealing the identity of victim, master, and sacrificers, all as doubles, all as brothers. And in the context of Judah's offer, it shows us the way out: to acknowledge our identity, which is to say, our identicality with the other, to recognize that the other is the same, that the other is us.

Does Joseph recognize this dynamic? Has he staged this earlier sacrificial activity deliberately? Not necessarily. I would even suggest that there must not be total recognition if Joseph is to be fully like us. Joseph's disclosure is still to some extent an echo of his new masters. We recall that Pharaoh said earlier, in calling Joseph from the prison, "I am Pharaoh" (41:44). Even in the act of disclosing himself, he takes away their responsibility for the sacrificial gesture. "I am Joseph your brother, whom ye sold into Egypt. / And now, be not grieved . . . for God did send me before you to preserve life / . . . God sent me before you to give you a remnant on the earth, and to save you alive for a great deliverance. So now it was not you who sent me hither, but God" (45:4–8). Demystifying the text for us, and perhaps for Judah, Joseph remains to some extent still within it, as he must. What is important is that the possibility of a demystification of sacrifice has become available within the text, which is, thus, a perfect mirror of our own world in which the possibility of a demystification of sacrifice has become available to us by the same process in the form of the Hebrew Bible.

Joseph, in the last account, is not dissimilar to Torah itself, to the Hebrew Law in which the story has been told, to the very biblical text. And in that Law we must come to recognize ourselves. The text says to us: here is the bloodied tunic which is the end of the road you are on. Do you recognize yourself in it? Do you recognize this as your own violence so that you may give it up? Joseph, Torah, Jewish culture itself, asks no less of us.

I conclude as I began, with a midrash. There is a story, told by Gershom Scholem, of the medieval Jewish mystic Abulafia who describes the culminating moment of the prophetic ecstasy in the following way.[33] He says that the talmudic scholar is sitting in his study reading Talmud and he suddenly sees himself sitting in his study reading Talmud. He comes, in other words, to see his own double, to recognize himself in the other, to recognize the other as himself. Moreover, he understands that other as his own past or his own future, the road he is already traveling. And having had this vision, he comes finally, at the critical moment, to distance himself from it. He fictionalizes it. He tells a story about it, a midrash. The substitution to end all substitutions, as Michel Serres has said.³⁴

The Judaic Law, the law of anti-idolatry, the prophetic law, is nothing else. And if today the thought of René Girard strikes us as trenchant, perhaps it is because it functions in the same way as the Joseph story does, as a part 2 to the sacrificial qualities of our own critical thinking, as the text that says to us, "I am Joseph."

4

Reading the Ten Commandments
Torah, Interpretation, and the Name of God

> Hear, O Israel: the LORD our God, the LORD is one.
>
> Deuteronomy 6:4
>
> Blessed be the name of His glorious majesty forever and ever.
>
> Liturgy

Biblical studies would seem to have fallen upon hard times these days.[1] To take the Bible seriously outside the university has come to be regarded—even among the otherwise most liberal of counselors—as at best a cause for suspicion and at worst a cause for outright alarm. And within the university, in fields like sociology, anthropology, psychology, philosophy, and even departments of literature and religious studies, to read the Bible seriously has come to be regarded as little short of scandalous. We may look to Biblical Scripture for documentation on the social organization, the cultural history, the psychology, the belief system, or the aesthetics of cultures other than our own—or even of our own culture at some remote point within its own history. But we are never to regard it as a living, breathing presence among us, never as a source of wisdom or critical intelligence equal to (let alone greater than) our own.[2]

Things, of course, have not always been this way. For more than fifteen hundred years in Western Europe it would have been as scandalous not to speak seriously of the Bible as it is today to speak of it. Even as recently as two hundred years ago, when the discipline we now recognize as literary criticism was born, it was from the methods and procedures appropriated from biblical commentary and exegesis that this new field took its guidance, a guidance that, if we are to believe some of the cultural historians currently writing about it, has never entirely been suppressed.[3] If we find ourselves embroiled today in controversies concerning authorial intention, the role of the reader in the literary process, or the special nature of literary language, it may be instructive to recall the biblical contexts in which these discussions take their origin and perhaps in which they assume their greatest force.[4]

Moreover, the sands may once again be shifting. If the spate of books published recently in this country alone on biblical matters can be taken as any indication (books by Michael Fishbane, Robert Alter, Geoffrey Hartman, Susan Handelman, Gerald Bruns, James Kugel, David Stern, and Phyllis Trible, to mention only a very few), it would seem this religious silence is at least beginning to be broken.[5] When a leading American exponent of the critical avant-garde can discover in the planning of a session on Torah at a recent meeting of the English Institute a cause for alarm, it would seem a new seriousness of biblical reading is imminent.[6] And it may not be very much longer before the last two hundred years or so in European history will appear to us in retrospect as a developmental phase in our ongoing cultural life, a moment of temporary religious amnesia that will have passed away from us (to borrow Foucault's phrase for the demise of humanism, a phenomenon to which this amnesia may not be unrelated) like a figure drawn in the sand at the edge of the sea.[7]

While we still remain, however, within the throes of that amnesia—even if within its death throes—we might find it useful to try and cull from our recent experience some lessons. The lessons I have in mind, however, concern less our silences on biblical matters per se than the silences behind our silences, so to speak, the kinds of omissions we have constructed within our practice of biblical reading, perhaps even as the condition of that practice, at least within the university. René Girard has remarked on numerous occasions that the absence of serious discussion of biblical texts, far from certifying the final triumph of secularism and scientism over mythology and religious faith, may reflect the intensity of the latter's hold upon us, a "sacrificial" hold that differs in form alone from the sacrificial misunderstandings that in Girard's view have marked the history of Christianity in the West.[8] One of the most elusive and yet decisive examples of such a hold, I would suggest, is the way in which Christians and Jews have traditionally perceived the texts they study.

Take, for instance, the notion of the "bible." The English word comes from the Greek word (*ta*) *biblia,* meaning "books" or "the books," a word that, scholars tell us, was the diminutive form of *biblos* (or *bublos*).[9] It seems to have referred to the papyrus or scrolls on which the sacred scriptures were written in the ancient Near East, and was taken from the name of the Phoenician port, Bublos, from which Egyptian papyrus was exported to Greece.

In Hebrew, the word *tanakh* (which refers more or less to the same body of texts identified in the Christian tradition as the "Old Testament") has no such derivation. The word *tanakh* is an anagram of three Hebrew words designating the three major collections constituting this body of texts: the Torah (*torah*), the books of the prophets (*n'viyiym*), and the collections of the holy writings (*k'tuviym*).[10] But even here the analogy breaks down. For these texts are not, taken together, equivalent, say, to the Christian Gospel. Within the Jewish tradition it is unquestionably one text alone—Torah, the five books of Moses, the books of the Law—that constitutes the key text, the one for which all the others are, in one fashion or another, merely extensions.[11]

This distinction is more than semantic. Behind the difference between these two words are concealed two vastly different conceptual schemas. The common notion that the Bible is really a library or a plurality of "books" is decisive for a Christian understanding that believes there are in fact two books—an Old Testament and a New Testament—with a highly ordered, strictly hierarchical relationship between them.[12] The "Old Testament," in this view, although capable of being considered an advance over social organizations anthropologists commonly call "primitive" or "closed," is regarded as fundamentally deficient and in need of completion.[13] And the "New Testament" is (not surprisingly) precisely that completion, that fulfillment, that bringing to fruition of everything the Old Testament has undertaken without full success.[14] In place of an Old Law demanding blind obedience to a God of wrath and vengeance (so a common doxa goes), the New Testament substitutes a "New Law" of faith, hope, and charity—in short, of love.[15] Consequently, any correspondence we are able to demonstrate between the Old and the New Testaments can be understood within a Christian framework as temporal anticipation, as a prefiguration or foreshadowing, of a more complete revelation yet to come.[16]

The Hebrew perspective is entirely different. Within the Hebraic tradition there is, in the first place, only one text of preeminent importance—the Torah. That text is full and complete in itself, and if it requires endless interpretation, it does so not because it lacks anything or is deficient in any way but in order to extend the wisdom of the Torah into the nooks and crannies of everyday life, to make the text accessible to the ever-changing conditions of the world in which we live.[17]

In the second place—and this point is part and parcel of the first—from a Jewish point of view, these two perspectives are not independent notions but in fact the second is already an interpretation of the first. The Christian is already itself a reading of the Judaic, an episode within the history of the Judaic. The notion that there is an old and a new Law is already itself a displacement of the idea that there is only one Law, that the Torah is the unique Word of God.[18]

Let me be especially clear about this point. The Jewish reading is not that the Old Testament has been inadequately or incompletely represented within the literature of Christianity. It is rather and more precisely that there is no "Old Law" to speak of, unless we mean the sacrificial laws of Canaanite and Mesopotamian cultures from which Judaism progressively differentiated itself. The very conception that there are old Laws and new Laws has supplanted the idea that the Torah is sufficient.

This point is particularly sensitive for defining the contours of any discussion between Christianity and Judaism. For if there is one stumbling block to such a discussion, it is not, I would suggest—as Jewish and Christian thinkers alike have often maintained—the issue of the coming of the Messiah. Gershom Scholem, for instance, one of the most eminent and revered historiographers of Jewish mystical and messianic traditions, has argued that the one issue par excellence dividing Christians and Jews is the issue of the coming of the Messiah.[19] I would argue to the contrary that there is a more fundamental issue, one from which in fact the coming of the Messiah derives. Here I align myself with thinkers like Martin Buber and Emmanuel Levinas.[20] If the issue were only the claim among Christians that Jesus of Nazareth was the Messiah, Judaism would have much less difficulty. Moses Maimonides, for example, the great medieval philosopher and religious thinker, relates that the talmudic sage Rabbi Akiba regarded Bar Kochba as the Messiah.[21] The doctrine on the coming of the Messiah is not the issue dividing Christianity and Judaism.

Rather, the problem lies in the definition of a Messiah who, rather than returning us to Torah study (as Maimonides, for example, says he will), is presented as the Word of God himself, a new Word of God, that is to say, one that displaces what now must be interpreted as an "old" testament. For Judaism, Torah alone is the Word of God, and only on the basis of that assumption could Judaism ever relate itself to a belief community other than its own.[22]

The new biblical hermeneutics that I envision, therefore, would concern itself less with either Old or New Testament studies than with the silent assumptions on which those studies were founded, the notion, on the one hand, that there *are* old and new testaments, and, on the other, that there is only one unique and privileged Word of God. To offer an example of how such a new hermeneutics or new critical reading of the Bible might look, and perhaps to shed some light as well on how in particular we might speak of Jewish-Christian relations in this context, let me turn to one text that has been read in both traditions fairly regularly and consistently—the Ten Commandments. And let me adopt a notion that I have begun to develop elsewhere and that I would offer as a useful tool for looking at a good deal (if not all) of scriptural writing, what I have called "the two part structure."[23]

※ ※ ※

The text of the Ten Commandments, the *'aseret hadibrot*, the "ten words" or "ten utterances," would seem an especially propitious place to start if we wish to sharpen our perception of the principles necessary to a critical reading of the Bible since there seems to be so much common ground between Christian and Jewish understandings of this text.[24] We may differ on how to count the Ten Commandments—the main problem being that the sentence "You shall have no other gods before me" in Exodus 20:3 seems to slip from one commandment to another. But most readers of the text would agree that there are three primary groupings: those concerning one's relationship to God (one through three in the Jewish rendering), those concerning one's relationship to family via God (four and five), and those concerning one's relationship to the surrounding social community (six through ten).[25]

Moreover, although debates raged throughout the nineteenth century over which version of the two texts we have for the commandments was more authoritative (that of Exodus 20 or that of Deuteronomy 5), over whether these precepts should be taken as elements of an ethical or a legal system, and over whether these ten seemingly succinct formulations were to be regarded as the entirety of a system of beliefs or only the tip of an ethical or legal iceberg (Buber's famous essay on the Ten Commandments summarizes these debates), most readers today would agree that what we have is a list of precepts that form, in part or in full, the building blocks of a value system that we recognize within broad outlines as our own.²⁶

Nor do I in any way wish to challenge that characterization. Rather I would like to raise a different question: namely, what does it mean to read a list as a text? What does it mean to come across this list of moral, legal, or ethical precepts, in Exodus or Deuteronomy, and read it in context of an ongoing narrative structure? The question clearly turns upon the nature of textuality itself and we shall return to this problem later. The answer, I suggest, is that, in this connection at least, context and sequence are everything and that given a discrete textual unit, we are compelled to read it in terms of what precedes and what follows, and to reevaluate all that has occurred in its light.

Take, for example, the first commandment: *anochiy YHVH eloheycha asher hotzeitiycha meieretz mitzrayim mibeiyt 'avadiym* ("I am the LORD thy God, who brought thee out of the land of Egypt, out of the house of bondage" [Ex. 20:2]). Taken in itself this commandment has been read from within both traditions as the major statement of Hebraic monotheism, although with slightly differing emphases.²⁷

Within the Christian tradition (and particularly that aspect of the Christian tradition under the influence of Greek thinking and the notion of *arithmos*), the commandment has been read as the opposition of the one to the many: "I alone am the Lord, not those many gods who have been proposed in my place." Whatever the advantages or disadvantages of setting up a system of divinity that does away with the polytheistic pantheon of the Greeks and other cultures in the area, the ancient Israelites, we are invited to believe, set up such a system of belief in one unique God and here is its great statement.

Within the Jewish tradition, the interpretation of these words is not significantly different. For here the sentence is read as the unity of manifold manifestation. The Lord appears to us in many ways and under many names, we are told. Sometimes He comes as *YHVH* (which we read as *adonay,* "lord"), sometimes as *elohiym,* sometimes as *el shaddaiy,* and so forth. These names reflect the various aspects of God—His capacity as a God of mercy, as a God of justice, as God the almighty, and so forth. What the commandment affirms is the unity of all these manifestations: in all these cases, the same God speaks to us, the God of our fathers, God of Abraham, of Isaac, and of Jacob.

So far, so good. If we had only this much of the text, there might be little to quarrel with. But we are now confronted with a second commandment, and with its introduction the problem of interpretation becomes somewhat more complicated. The second commandment begins with these words: *lo-yihyeh l'cha elohiym acheiriym 'al-panaiy* (Ex. 20:3). They translate: "Thou shalt have no other gods before Me." The commandment continues as follows:

> Thou shalt not make unto thee a graven image, nor any manner of likeness, of any thing that is in heaven above, or that is in the earth beneath, or that is in the water under the earth; thou shalt not bow down unto them, nor serve them; for I the LORD thy God am a jealous God, visiting the iniquity of the fathers upon the children unto the third and fourth generation of them that hate Me; and showing mercy unto the thousandth generation of them that love Me and keep My commandments. (Ex. 20:4–6)[28]

Once again, this commandment seems fairly straightforward and transparent in its meaning. Is this not the famous commandment against the making of graven images, the commandment against idolatry? Taken together with the first, does it not constitute the do's and the don't's so to speak—monotheism and anti-paganism—of ancient Israelite religion?[29] If we are puzzled as to why such a taboo against sensorial representation was so important to Hebrew culture (and explain it to ourselves as reflecting the historical circumstances out of which Judaism emerged—for example, the Canaanite ritual practice of idol worship), we accept it nonetheless fairly uncritically as the statement of the law of anti-idolatry.

A midrash, taken from the collection *Midrash Rabbah*, may help both to explain the importance of this commandment and situate it as a text within the narrative context in which it occurs.[30] Terah, we may recall, was Abraham's father, and he owned an idol shop in which his son Abraham worked. One day when Terah was out for the afternoon, Abraham got an idea. He took a hammer and smashed all the idols in his father's shop with the exception of the largest one. When the destruction was completed, he placed the hammer in the lap of the largest idol, which was seated in the center of the room. His father returned home and when he inquired about what had happened to cause such terrible havoc, Abraham told him a story, a kind of midrash within the midrash. "My father," he said, "while you were out, the most incredible thing occurred. The large idol sitting in the middle of the room over there suddenly took a hammer and smashed every one of the smaller idols to bits, so jealous was he of their competition with him." Abraham's father, you can imagine, was not very amused by his son's account, and he replied: "But how could that idol do such a thing? You and I both know that it's made of stone. It hasn't the power to do what you say it did." "Ah," Abraham replied to his father, triumphantly, "then why do you serve it!"

The story draws our attention, in the first place, to the centrality of the law of anti-idolatry in Hebraic religion.[31] Abraham is destined to become the father of Judaism. He will be granted the covenant by God that his descendants shall fill the earth, and that by them the entire earth shall be blessed. The dominant themes of the stories surrounding Abraham concern his exodus from Mesopotamian lands and his giving up of the idolatrous ways of his forebears. And this story in particular highlights dramatically that iconoclastic reputation.

But in the second place, the anecdote suggests something about the function of storytelling itself that may be useful to us in the present context. Abraham stages his father's beliefs, we may say, in order that his father may see them and give them up. The story Abraham tells his father, the "white lie" he employs, functions as a kind of "part 2" to the idolatrous beliefs of his father, which now function as a kind of "part 1," although there is some indication that his father Terah was already predisposed to be receptive to such an idea. Terah, we recall, is represented as a dealer in the idols of others rather than as a believer himself; moreover, he will later accompany his son on his migrations from their native regions. Given that Abraham's internal midrash functions in this fashion, the entire story now—both the iconoclastic sequence and the earlier suggestion of Terah's activities as the keeper of an idol shop—comes in a concatenated fashion to function itself as a "part 2" to the biblical passage in Genesis by which its implications may be staged.

In this way can we not now understand the function of the second commandment in relation to the first? Understood in sequence with the first commandment, the second commandment stages the first; it creates the context in which the statement of monotheism (or unity of manifold manifestation) can in retrospect be understood. "*I* am the LORD thy God, who brought thee out of the land of Egypt, out of the house of bondage," rather than those other gods—rather, in particular, than those gods of idolatry whom you worship. The issue now, in other words, in the first commandment (read from the point of view of the second) was never the one versus the many, or unity versus diversity, but an internal god versus an external god. Rather than simply either monotheism or the unity of manifold manifestation, what the first commandment *now* asserts to us is the radical externality of divinity, the radical alterity or otherness of God before these internal forms of transcendence we have been worshiping.[32] The first commandment is monotheistic if and only if we already understand that monotheism as anti-paganism, which is to say, as the law of anti-idolatry.

Do we understand, then, why scholars have had so much trouble counting the commandments, and in particular so much difficulty confining the sentence "You shall have no other gods before me" to one commandment or another? The sentence seems to want to slip between them, to migrate from one to the other, as if in some way it is genuinely a part of both. First it is a part of the second. But then, understood retrospectively as qualifying the context of the first, it is taken to have already been a part of the first all along. Our difficulty at the scholarly level reflects perhaps a more esoteric movement that is fundamental to the constitution of the text itself. It is a part of the second commandment, we understand now (from our reading of the second commandment), only in so far as it is at the same time (and more fundamentally) already a part of the first.

Perhaps we also understand now in a new way a potential danger in what we were doing all along when we read the first two commandments as independent of each other. To read them discretely, to read them as if they are complete and sufficient in and of themselves, without the addition of further interpretation, is to read them as if they are idols—in short, to violate the very law of anti-idolatry about which they are talking in the process of talking about it.

The implications of this process of rereading, or perhaps simply of reading, are far-reaching. It enables us to understand, in the first place, the relationship between text and interpretation in the Jewish biblical context. Interpretation of Torah in this view is neither more nor less than the practice of anti-idolatry itself. Interpretation must exist in order that the text not be regarded as an idol. At the same time, what interpretation makes available to us is what has always already been contained within Torah to begin with.[33] We have only made a little more evident what was always already there.

Can interpretation end? Is it possible that we shall one day be able to say that we have made manifest all that Torah—or even a single part of it—has to offer us? To say as much would be to claim that we were able to determine the limits of a text, to examine it as if it were both thoroughly independent of us and yet within our world at the same time—as if, in short, it were an idol. To say, as is often said within Judaism, that interpretation is endless because the function of interpretation is to make Torah available to the present hour and the present hour is always changing, is but the flip side of saying that interpretation is the practice of anti-idolatry.

On the other hand, and by virtue of what we have shown, we also begin to understand what it would mean to read anti-idolatrously, what a critical reading of the Bible in the spirit of the Bible itself would look like. To read anti-idolatrously would be to read any text as if it were always already a "part 1" of a "part 2" yet to be disclosed. To say—as is often said—that Torah is the "blueprint" of the world, is to say that we read any text as if there were always something more to learn, as if Torah will be fulfilled and complete, requiring no further interpretation, only when the world and Torah are one and the same.[34]

In the remainder of my essay, I will develop some of the implications of these ideas for reading more of the Ten Commandments and for beginning to trace the contours of the relationship between Judaism and Christianity at large.

※ ※ ※

From the first two commandments we have now suddenly been able to generate three: a commandment exhorting monotheism, a commandment condemning idolatry, and a commandment in which monotheism is understood already to be a version of anti-idolatry and to contain the latter sense within it. We understand, moreover, from what we have just said, that this collection of commandments is at once an accurate representation of the text we have before us, and at the same time incomplete. The fact that there is always more to be said, that another reading will necessarily develop new possibilities within the text we are already reading, does not prevent any given reading from being accurate and complete in the context under consideration.

How far can we go in this direction? What, for example, about the third commandment against taking the name of the Lord in vain? *lo tisa et-sheim-YHVH eloheycha lashav kiy lo y'nakeh YHVH eit asher-yisa et-sh'mo lashav.* "Thou shalt not take the name of the LORD thy God in vain; for the LORD will not hold him guiltless that taketh His name in vain" (Ex. 20:7). Taken in itself as before, this commandment sounds appropriate enough. Do not misuse the name of divinity in your speech.

We recognize immediately the appeal of the idea even if we are not sure how this dictum has made it into the three major commandments concerning one's relationship to transcendence.

But once again, as soon as we place the commandment in relationship to what has occurred, a new explanatory power becomes evident. For now the commandment against idolatry in the second verse can be understood less as a commandment against the worshipping of stone idols than as a condemnation of the idolatrous appropriation of language in general. For Judaism, it is above all within language, in our conceptualizations and our discourse, that we create idols, that we place others before God, before YHVH. For example, in the very idea that we have gained access to God's name.

Concomitantly, within the context of this new and "enriched" reading of the second commandment (to borrow a modern metaphor), we now have a doubly enriched reading of the first—enriched initially by the second, and now again by a second that has itself been enriched by a third. "I am the LORD, thy God," the first commandment *now* tells us, not that God you thought you recognized from the various names attributed to Me, from the way language thinks that it has hold of Me or designates Me, that it knows My name. The law of monotheism that is also the law of anti-idolatry is as well the law prohibiting the representation in language of the name of God. The Hasidic tradition that derives its prohibition against pronouncing the Tetragrammaton even as *adonai* (and further substitutes the word *hashem,* meaning "the name") from the third commandment does so, we now understand, by way of the first.[35]

There is more in the first two commandments already suggesting the prohibition of idolatrous designation, references that only in retrospect are we able to read. An echo hidden within the very words of the first two commandments reveals such a prohibition to us, and here again I turn to an insight offered to me in conversation by Jonathan Bishop. In the passage earlier in Exodus 3 on the name of God, God says to Moses, in effect: "When they ask you what My name is, here is what you say." And what follows is the famous formula *ehyeh asher ehyeh* (Ex. 3:14). The moment in Exodus is an extraordinarily important one, and we saw in the last chapter the way in which that formula may be understood in the context of what God had said earlier concerning Moses's return to Egypt to bring the Israelites out of bondage. "Go down to Egypt," God says in effect to Moses, "and when you do" (*kiy-ehyeh 'imach*), "Certainly I will be with thee" (Ex. 3:12).[36] This earlier context in which we understand the word *ehyeh* (in context with *'imach*) as "I will be with thee," allows us to introduce the word *'imach* for "with thee" two lines later (in Ex. 3:14), when *ehyeh* occurs without it. Thus we understand the *drash,* the interpretative rendering, that Rashi (the foremost medieval commentator on Torah) makes upon the divine name, translating *ehyeh* when it occurs later as "I will be with thee."[37]

What is important for the present context is that the word *ehyeh,* an imperfect form of the verb "to be" given in the first person, and in the future (not the present tense as it is often rendered), is straightaway abandoned by God when He first substitutes for the formula *ehyeh asher ehyeh* the word *ehyeh* alone, and then in turn the word *YHVH* (from which in the Christian tradition we get *Jehovah*), the third person form of the same word. In other words, for "I will be with thee in order that I will be with thee" (or alternatively "I will be with thee what I will be with thee"), God substitutes simply "I will be with thee," and then simply "He will be" (the "with thee" to be added if we read the tetragrammaton in context as a substitute for the former name of God).[38]

What is the relevance of this passage on the name of God to the Ten Commandments? In the first two commandments, the same substitution seems to occur. *anochiy YHVH eloheycha,* the first commandment begins: "I am *YHVH eloheycha,* the LORD thy God," which is to say, *YHVH.* The second commandment begins *lo-yihyeh l'cha elohiym acheiriym 'al-panaiy*: "Thou shalt have no other gods before Me." Hidden within the wording of the first two commandments (taken together and considering the possibility of verbal echo) is the dictum *anochi YHVH eloheycha . . . lo-yihyeh*: "I am *YHVH,* your God . . . not *ehyeh,"* the *same dictum,* in other words, that God offered to Moses initially. Exodus 20 in other words bears out literally what Exodus 3 promised. "I will be with thee in order that I will be with thee." Where? In language. In the Law. In the Ten Commandments itself. In the language designed to ensure survival—if there is any survival to be had (which is not itself guaranteed). When the Law is given, "I will be with thee" (*ehyeh asher ehyeh* become *ehyeh* become *YHVH*) will be with thee (in the Ten Commandments, in language) in order that "I will be with thee" (God) will be with thee (You will survive). To follow the Ten Commandments is to be with God, which is also to say, to say God's name.

That's not all. We have long understood the unutterability of the name of God since the collapse of the Second Temple to be a staple of Jewish liturgical practice (in the Temple service, the ineffable name *was* pronounced every year ten times by the High Priest on the occasion of Yom Kippur).[39] We commonly explain that taboo with the suggestion that the correct pronunciation has been lost.

The above insight offers us a new way of understanding that taboo. What is unpronounceable with regard to the "name" is less the third person form, *YHVH,* than the first person form, *ehyeh,* and here again I cite the insight of my colleague, Jonathan Bishop. Who among us can pronounce the name of God as an auto-reference? If the name is unpronounceable, is it not because no one can pronounce the divine self-reference as a legitimate claim about the world? The tradition that refuses to pronounce the *third* person form—which is already a substitute for the first person form (itself in turn a substitute for the longer form)—simply acts out in the world the same Toradic distinction. Not pronouncing the third person form of the name, substituting another word for that name (whether *adonai, hashem,* or some other), enacts the textual substitution of one word for the other, the third person form for the first. It thus confirms their interchangeability. It affirms that "He will be with you" is the same as "I will be with you," which in both cases is "God will be with you," an identification offered in an exchange between God and Moses, between I and you. It affirms, in short, that in the case of God, third person relation, like second person relation, is the same as first person relation.

The "unpronounceability" of the name of God, in other words, is less a reflection of the name, the words used to reflect the name, God, or some deficit in our modern understanding of any of these than of the relation of God to the world. It expresses the alterity, the radical otherness or externality, of God to the world, which is to say, the status of God as otherwise than being. The unpronounceability of the name of God and the law of anti-idolatry are, in this respect at least, one and the same. Levinas's famous remark that politics and justice are always a matter of the three (the neighbor of my neighbor), and that ethics is always a matter of the two (the other individual before me whose face I encounter), yields in this context a new understanding: revelation is a matter of the one. It is the encounter in which each of these relations and their identicality to each other is disclosed. The first three commandments, which are given in Exodus 20, and which correspond to God in third, second, and first person contexts (in language or politics, in face to face social relations, and in revelation), offer a commentary on Exodus 3. They exhibit this trifold aspect of the holy name—"I am the LORD thy

God . . . ," "You are not to worship idols . . . ," and "Do not use the LORD's (His) name in vain . . ."—as part of the same God, the same name, and the same relation. He is a God who is as good as His name, for whom relations with others are the same as our relations with Him, and whose name may be given as "I will be with you."

The commandments have begun to add up. What began as two has suddenly become three. And what were three commandments have now become six: the three commandments we previously enumerated, the first commandment enriched by a second which is enriched by a third, the second enriched by the third, and the first enriched by the second. The total number of commandments has begun to multiply geometrically. By the time we get to ten, we can already easily see we will have enumerated many more than ten. If each in turn simply rereads all those that have preceded it, we will have generated more than fifty.

Why stop there? What if we were to read each of these "fifty" commandments in light of what has preceded the giving of the Law—the "ten words" or "ten utterances"—on Sinai? After all, the Law has been given, not in Genesis where we might have expected it, but in Exodus, in book 2 of Torah. Or, alternatively, what if, having read each of the commandments in light of all preceding commandments, we then reversed the procedure and derived each of the commandments from all that preceded it, each concretizing and manifesting those others? The second commandment, for example, would now derive its power from the general law of anti-idolatry, which the first spells out, and rather than two commandments initially, we would have at least four.

Do we begin, in short, to understand the logic of the tradition that tells us that there are six hundred and thirteen commandments, or *mitzvot*, in Torah? The number six hundred and thirteen, of course, is cited throughout the rabbinic literature and linked with a number of mnemonic devices: the numerical value of the Hebrew word *torah* plus two, the number of bones in the human body added to the number of days in the year (a mnemonic device that spells out in particular the positive and negative commandments), and so forth.[40] If we have been puzzled, for example, by the precision of the number—that Moses Maimonides writes a book in which he lists and explains each of the six hundred and thirteen commandments (neither more nor less than six hundred and thirteen)—do we not begin to see at least the thinking (if not as yet the precise calculation) behind such a claim?[41]

Moreover, we can no doubt readily see as well where the idea that all the Ten Commandments are contained in the first one originates. If we were to continue our analysis the way we have proceeded so far and expand it to include each of the Ten Commandments, we would arrive at the idea that all that we have been able to derive was already available to us in the first commandment, in the identification of God as *our* God who brought us out of the land of Egypt, out of the house of bondage.

And finally, and here is perhaps the most important point, in view of what we have said, in so far as Torah as a whole can be said to be contained within the Ten Commandments, can we not say that Torah as a whole is already contained within the first commandment?[42] We recall the Judaic commonplace that the Law was said to have been given to Moses in *one* utterance, and that the Law within the Law—the ten utterances or ten words—were equally said to have been given in one utterance.[43] If the commentators are fond of saying that the entire Torah is but an extension of the Ten Commandments, that the Ten Commandments are something like the Torah of Torah, and that the larger Torah is something like an interpretation of that smaller internal Law (in the same way that the Talmud, the Midrash, and the later tradition of rabbinic commentators are said to interpret Torah), then have we not begun to uncover the logic of the preceding ideas?[44]

If we were to stop at this point, we might be tempted to say that we had described the overall structure of Torah, one that paralleled, moreover, the overall structure we might attribute to interpretation itself, an ordering, that is to say, of its revealed content. Numbering, interpretation, and the name of God would all seem to entail in this respect the same logic. But precisely at these points, the esoteric tradition—which brings out what was hidden in Torah, as opposed to the more exoteric traditions of talmudic and rabbinic commentary, which develop what is given on its surface—cautions us: why stop here?[45] Could not the entire history of interpretation—talmudic, midrashic, esoteric, and so forth—be seen to do to Torah what Torah does to the Ten Commandments? As a result could not the entire history of interpretation, a history thought to be the accumulation of gestures by which Torah is made accessible to an ever-changing present hour, be seen already to be contained within the Ten Commandments, indeed within the first commandment?

And if we keep in mind that the first commandment taken as a whole—"I am the LORD, thy God, who brought thee out of the land of Egypt, out of the house of bondage"—is itself but an extension or interpretation of the first two words of that commandment—*anochi*

YHVH, "I am the LORD, I am YHVH"—then cannot the entire history of interpretation be said already to be contained within these first two words? And do we not now have a way of understanding in a profound way the kabbalistic principle that there is only one task to be accomplished in the study of Torah—namely, the spelling out of the name of God? Torah in its entirety, the Kabbalists are fond of saying, is nothing other than the name of God.[46] All of Torah, all of biblical interpretation, all of the world (which by fits and starts finds itself—through interpretation—contained within Torah which is its "blueprint") may thus be said to be nothing but that divine name, a name which in the above manner may be said to be contained already within the first word (since *YHVH* is itself already only an extension of *anochi* which is the divine self-identification), indeed, within the first letter of that first word, which is, appropriately enough, an *aleph*.[47]

❦ ❦ ❦

To read the Bible critically, to read the Bible in the spirit of the Bible's own inner reading or commentary, is thus to read neither esoterically nor exoterically but rather anti-idolatrously, prophetically, to read in advance what will turn out to have been contained within all along.

With this observation we may return to the considerations from which we began. To what extent do our remarks about the Ten Commandments (and in particular about the "two part structure") apply to the relationship between Judaism and Christianity? It will not be possible, of course, to give more than the sketch of an answer here. To put the matter more specifically, just as we have claimed that Torah requires interpretation, that Torah (though complete and sufficient in itself) can never completely disclose its meanings without interpretation, can we not say that Christianity undertakes—in its own particular way and for its own particular community—that monumental Toradic task? Is not, in short, the text of the Christian Gospel, a "part 2" to Torah's "part 1"?[48]

The answer, I suggest (and this may come as a surprise), is affirmative, provided that we include one qualification, and upon that qualification everything hinges: namely, that the interpretation Christianity offers be understood as making manifest what was fully contained within Judaism all along.[49] Judaism is capable, I suggest, of accepting Christianity as continuous with it so long as that continuity—even one that is outside the domain of traditional Judaism—is understood, in the manner of all good interpretations, as making Torah accessible to a particular time and place.

What is problematic for Judaism in Christianity, in other words, is not the ethical system it proposes. The commandment of Jesus of Nazareth to his disciples to "love the LORD your God with all your heart and all your soul" is a quote from Deuteronomy. Nor, from a Jewish perspective, is the identification of Jesus of Nazareth as the Messiah. Bar Kochba, Sabbatai Sevi, and many others have made similar claims.[50] But the displacement of the Word of God that is Torah with another *is* a stumbling block. For Judaism there is only one Word of God, one revelation—that given to Moses at Sinai. Any and all others are, in one fashion or another, at their best, interpretations.

In this spirit, moreover, I would like to suggest that René Girard's reading of the Gospel is primarily a Jewish reading, and that the role of Jesus of Nazareth in his perspective is accordingly a prophetic one. Jesus in Girard's understanding shows us where our violence is going in order that we may give it up, speaking first to a Hellenized Jewry that is felt to have become alienated from its origins, and later (and perhaps most significantly) to a larger non-Jewish community.[51]

Whatever the differences, however, between Christianity and Judaism, they need not stop us, in principle at least, from working together toward the world to come, toward a moment—one that may last a thousand years and may not differ except politically (if we adopt Maimonides' view of the matter) from our own—when we will all return to Torah study, when the way of anti-idolatry will seem the only way and the "light of nations," the only way to stave off the sacrificial violence and mimetic rivalries (to use Girard's terms) in which we will all no doubt continue to participate, a moment, that is to say, when we shall all feel identically the inner necessity, the unimpeachable logic, of the words of Deuteronomy (6:4) and of a prayer attributed to Jacob (Israel) on his deathbed and recited by observant Jews twice daily, in which number, interpretive commentary, and the name of God are inextricably linked:

sh'ma° yisraeil YHVH eloheiynu YHVH echad
baruch sheim k'vod malchuto l^xolam va°ed

HEAR, O ISRAEL: THE LORD OUR GOD, THE LORD IS ONE.
Blessed be the name of His glorious majesty forever and ever.[52]

5

"Out of the Fish's Belly"

Prophecy, Sacrifice, and Repentance in the Book of Jonah

> "The Torah warns us," a disciple of the Holy Jehuda and Rabbi Bunam, namely, Rabbi Mendel of Kotsk, said, "not to make an idol even of the command of God."
>
> *Martin Buber*

The Book of Jonah is something of a misfit in the scriptural context in which we encounter it.[1] It is, of course, post-Toradic, one of the Books of the Twelve Israelite Prophets. But it clearly lacks the monumentalism—the historical and cultural urgency—common to so many of the other prophetic texts—the Book of Isaiah or of Jeremiah, for example.[2] Although commentators continue to debate the accuracy of the historical details of the story (noting that a "Jonah the son of Amittai" is mentioned in 2 Kings [14:25] as having prophesied during the reign of Jeraboam II), the story seems less concerned either with denouncing Israel for its persistent refusal to give up idolatry or with establishing the historical circumstances of the life of this particular prophet (as those other books are) than with getting Jonah to prophesy at all.[3]

In fact, the folksy almost anecdotal tone of the story would appear to render it somewhat anti-prophetic, more like the wisdom literature of the Solomonic court (cf., for example, the Book of Job) than the accounts of the pre- or post-exilic prophets. Perhaps it is this unsettledness of Jonah within the prophetic canon, a certain uneasiness about the scriptural locus of this parabolic fable, that we reflect when we memorialize it in the popular imagination (and to the scorn of most commentators) as a kind of biblical Pinocchio, the story of a man who was eaten by a whale.

Even if we accept the narrative in its own terms, however, its make-up is somewhat odd. God calls upon Jonah to prophesy to the Ninevites and straightaway he flees to Tarshish, to what appears to count in the ancient world as the other end of the earth. Although as a narrative entity the book is already among the shortest in scripture, the whole first part is spent just in getting Jonah back to the point from which the story can begin again.

And when it does, and Jonah proceeds at God's instruction to Nineveh to prophesy destruction ("Yet forty days, and Nineveh shall be overthrown" [3:4]), and is, moreover, successful beyond his wildest expectations, occasioning a mass repentance of unprecedented proportions, he is strangely angered by his success and he retreats to a hillside to brood about it. Then there occurs a lengthy exchange (one-fourth of the entire book) between God and Jonah concerning a gourd (or "kikayon" plant) that has arisen to shield the prophet from the heat of the sun, an episode undoubtedly interesting as a generalized moral commentary (even interesting perhaps as a glimpse into Jonah's personal psychology), but fairly remote from anything occurring around it, a kind of "Jonah story" within the Jonah story, so to speak.

What kind of prophetic instruction are we to gain from such a tale? What is the relevance of the long opening sequence in which everything this reluctant prophet does seems only to further isolate him from the task at hand? What is the relevance of the second half of the book in which, having uttered barely a sentence of prophetic instruction to a non-Israelite audience, he broods for the remainder of the story, first about his success and then about his loss of personal comfort?

The story has, of course, long been submitted to interpretation. But neither of the two major exegetical traditions in which it has been read appears to engage these questions without begging them, without neglecting some part of the story for another in a way that calls attention to the limitations of the approach itself, a preparatory and supplementary interpretive process that, thus, turns out not unlike the partial and self-limiting perspectives observable within the story.[4]

Take, for example, the question of narrative structure. Any understanding of the story requires that we grapple with Jonah's initial flight from the site of the divine command—from the *shechinah,* the divine presence in *eretz yisrael.* This flight clearly dominates the first part of the story and eventually comes to dominate the second. When Jonah retreats to the hillside and is angry about what has occurred, he says to God, "Was not this my saying, when I was yet in mine own country? Therefore I fled beforehand unto Tarshish. . . . Therefore now, O LORD, take, I beseech Thee, my life from me" (4:2–3). It would appear that Jonah's behavior after the prophecy is not unrelated to his behavior before.

Yet, neither of the two major traditions of interpretive response seems to have given this coherence much attention. Rather they seem to have divided the sequence between them and thereby, implicitly at least, discouraged consideration of its integrity. One tradition would emphasize the final episode and read the whole as a parable of the "mystery of compassion," largely to the exclusion of the narrative to that point (in which the primary "prophetic" action occurs). "God's answer to Jonah," writes Rabbi Abraham Heschel in a famous account, "stressing the supremacy of compassion, upsets the possibility of looking for a rational coherence of God's way with the world. . . . [B]eyond justice and anger lies the mystery of compassion."[5]

The other tradition which is equally venerable would concern itself with almost equal exclusivity with Jonah's refusal to prophesy to the Ninevites initially, a reluctance it deems, if not precisely positive, then certainly redemptive.[6] Like all of the great figures of the Jewish tradition to whom he is compared (Abraham, Moses, David, Elijah, and others), this reading would argue, Jonah has sacrificed his personal needs for the greater needs of the community at large.

Jonah knows, this argument goes, that if Nineveh repents (which undoubtedly it will), things will look bad for Israel who in other of the Prophetic Books has stubbornly refused to repent. Scoffers will then surely denounce Jonah as a false prophet (since the destruction he prophesied will not have come to pass), and cast aspersions upon the institution of prophecy itself. Finally, since in the distant future, Nineveh is destined to become the "rod of God's wrath" against Israel (as part of the Assyrian Empire), Jonah knows that undertaking such an action will aid and abet that future event and therefore refuses to offer that assistance.

We can appreciate the difficulties to which each of these readings responds. The older approach (which is probably the less familiar one to modern readers although it has informed talmudic, midrashic, and later rabbinic readings) responds to the curious lack of historical detail in this tale—the kind that we find elsewhere in the Prophetic Books—by attempting to fill in the blanks. The tale *is* historical it seems to say. It is like other prophetic texts in offering us both Jonah's message and an intimate biographical account of his relation to his task, although that account needs to be teased out of it.

Similarly, the modern approach appears to answer for the curiously skimpy and conventional nature of the instruction (in comparison, say, to the message of a Jeremiah or an Isaiah), and to the curiously supplemental and psychological orientation of the narrative in which it is presented by elucidating the message and revealing the relevance of what appears secondary. The addendum *is* relevant, it tells us. It discloses the need for compassion for all God's creatures in the same way that God's message to Nineveh (through Jonah) did, thus developing further both that message and Jonah's relation to it.

But it may be argued against the modern view that Jonah never doubted God's compassion, that it was because he knew that God was compassionate—as he himself tells us—that he was angry in the first place. And it may be argued against the older view that Jonah's concern with Israel and Nineveh may not be entirely separable from his personal investments (he employs, for example, the same words, to describe his reaction to both) and that if his identification with Israel were the book's center of gravity, it might have concluded with Jonah's repentance and successful prophecy. Such "midrashic" attempts to defend scripture by supplying what is missing also succeed necessarily in calling attention to the necessity of their own construction and thus to the textual lapses that inspired their addition.

Moreover, whatever the power of these "historical" and "parabolic" readings (and their influence has been considerable), neither attaches any special importance to the continuous narrative sequence we are offered—the fact that the two parts of the story are presented as connected. The modern reading treats the final episode as if it constituted the entire story and as if the "object lesson" conducted by God were able to engulf the entirety of Jonah's history. And the older approach treats the historical identification of Jonah with Israel (and with Israel's history) as if *it* constituted the story as a whole and as if Jonah's experience on the hillside were ornamental or extraneous and able to be excluded from consideration.

Is there no way to read this tale in a manner that is sensitive to the terms in which it is offered, a comprehensive reading that can recognize the machinery of such sacrificial engorging and expulsion as already its subject matter?[7] Traditions are not "wrong" in their readings, even if they necessarily distort what they read for their own purposes. Undoubtedly there *is* something "parabolic" about the story of Jonah we have to believe, and somehow compassion is at the heart of it. Undoubtedly the historical relation between Nineveh and Israel—both currently and within the imagined future of their relations—*is* critical to the story's understanding, and Jonah is right to "think ahead."

Are we sure that the terms "parabolic" and "historical" need be understood as restrictively as we have traditionally conceived them? The historicism and literalism of the older reading and the abstraction and formalism of the modern reading are equally unsatisfactory. Perhaps we can benefit from these approaches if we allow the synchronic and representational logics they reflect more fluidity, if we allow history and parable to mingle, perhaps as the Bible itself does.

What if "historical" were to describe not simply the external synchronic empirical circumstances enveloping the tale but a diachronic continuity within it, a diachrony, that is to say, between "Ninevitian" and "Hebraic" conditions or moments within an ongoing spiritual development? Likewise what if "parabolic" were to describe not simply the supplementary anecdotal and personal psychology of Jonah (or its translation by analogy into the story's generalized prophetic content), but the same internal spiritual continuity between Nineveh and Israel, to which the various concrete histories within the story—that of the Ninevites, that of the sailors, even that of Jonah himself to a certain extent—bear paradigmatic witness?

Such considerations would necessarily enlarge our perspective on the Jonah story, prompting us to inquire about the status of the interpretive strategies within which we customarily read it (whether in formal exegesis or more subtly in the gestures of biblical canonizers), strategies, paradoxically, that may not be quite as remote from the scriptural story as they initially appear.

But such interpretive difficulties are hardly the only ones with which a serious reader of the Book of Jonah must grapple. For the liturgical context in which this little tale has customarily been appropriated settles the matters we have been raising no more satisfactorily. As if the place of this story in Scripture and in exegesis were not already confusing enough, the entire congregation of Judaism turns annually to recite the book on the holiest day of the Jewish calendar, the day of Yom Kippur, the day of atonement or repentance.

What has the story of Jonah to do with repentance? The notion of repentance or *teshuvah* in Judaism (as understood, for example, by Maimonides) is the notion of return and of the abandonment of sin, the giving up of one's evil ways and the return to the ways of God. The only enduringly repentant figures within the story of Jonah, however, are non-Jews and God Himself. The sailors on the ship bound for Tarshish repent after Jonah requests to be tossed overboard and the sea is suddenly and strangely calmed. They give up their pagan ways, the commentators point out, and turn to the religion of the Hebrew God. And no sooner does Jonah enter the city of Nineveh and get a word out of his mouth than the entire city puts on sackcloth and sits on ashes and the king decrees that even the beasts of burden should be compelled to fast. So extraordinary, in fact, is this turn of events that some commentators have wondered whether some of the sailors who threw Jonah overboard have somehow slipped into the city in advance of his arrival. And, of course, God Himself, upon seeing the true repentance of the Ninevites, relents of His planned destruction of them.

Jonah, on the other hand, seems constitutionally bent upon pursuing his own path from beginning to end. Fleeing the divine command initially (suppressing a prophecy, the Talmud tells us, is an offense punishable by death), Jonah advises his own expulsion from the ship less as a return to God than as a benefit to the sailors, as a measure he undertakes in order that the sea might be calmed for them again and thereby that they might be saved.

If, in fact, he does repent after three days within the belly of the great fish (and the psalm-like language of his prayer is treated by the mainstream of Jewish tradition in such a fashion), then the value of that repentance seems curiously in jeopardy later when, upon observing the salvation of the Ninevites (a goal for which presumably he has worked in good faith), he declares to God: "I pray Thee, O LORD, was not this my saying, when I was yet in mine own country? Therefore I fled beforehand . . . it is better [now] for me to die than to live" (4:2–3). His repentance, in other words, within the belly of the great fish seems to have changed nothing of his initial feelings of discomfort and the whole issue must now be taken up again in the final exchange. His position seems to have come full circle and returned to the point from which he began.

Nor does the traditional halachic or legal context for the day of Yom Kippur clarify these interpretive difficulties for us. For Yom Kippur is traditionally regarded by the rabbis, through a pun on the word *purim* (lots), to be the day of the lots, or *kippurim*. It recalls the days of the Temple when the High Priest of Israel would choose by lots between two identical goats, one of which was to be sacrificed in a procedure of ritual slaughter, and the other of which was to be expelled from the community, led off to Azazel into the wilderness.

The notion of lots, of course, appears throughout Scripture (one thinks of the story of Joshua and the theft of cattle, or the story of Esther told on the festival of Purim, a name derived from the same word), and the theme of lots turns up within the Jonah story as well. The sailors draw lots to see who is the cause of the trouble the ship is having.

But nothing of the arbitrariness that accompanies its appearance elsewhere is found here. The arbitrariness of the casting of lots in Scripture is often understood to assure that the result is a message from God and not the function of human intervention. And yet, although the lots (here *goral* not *purim*) are cast three times on the ship, and the result is always the same (Jonah is indicted), the sailors refuse to act upon that determination until the last moment and until Jonah himself requests them to do so.

What has the story of Jonah to do with sacrifice anyway? Sacrifice is clearly a dominant theme in Scripture, and certainly on the day of Yom Kippur, but what does it have to do with the story of Jonah? The only sacrifices in the story are those that the sailors offer after Jonah is expelled from the ship and those pagan sacrifices offered before Jonah arrives in Nineveh. The story would seem almost anti-sacrificial in this regard, more a history of expulsions than of sacrifices, more properly akin either to the Book of Job or the Books of the Prophets (where sacrifices fail) than to the Book of Leviticus. Why have the liturgists seen fit to link this story, we must wonder, with the most austere of Hebraic ritual procedures?

Is the Jonah story an anomaly within these traditional contexts, a kind of freak of scriptural, exegetical, and liturgical history? Or are these frameworks critical to its truths in ways that we have yet to perceive? In answering this question we may be in a better position to consider others that are often raised in these discussions, larger questions concerning Jewish and non-Jewish relations, and (perhaps somewhat unexpectedly), questions concerning the one biblical theme in which each of the above contextual frameworks—prophecy, interpretation, sacrifice, and repentance—converges: the coming of the Messiah.

There is no place here to follow the text in its entirety. We will content ourselves, therefore, with summarizing the narrative structure of the story as a whole and focus upon the final exchange.

I

That the story of Jonah is dominated by Jonah's reluctance to prophesy to the Ninevites is acknowledged by even the most casual of readers. That this reluctance structures the story systematically—setting up an intricate pattern of repetitions and transformations—is less commonly acknowledged.

The story is divided into two major narrative segments, the second of which is a repetition and development of the first. The first segment may be described as a negative version of the Oedipus story. As in the case of Oedipus (at least as we have the myth from Sophocles' play in the classical reading of it), the very efforts Jonah makes to avoid enacting the behavior God has decreed for him are the very efforts that bring it about, although in the Hebrew context—in contradistinction to the Greek—that fulfillment is regarded as positive rather than negative.

The prophetic call comes and Jonah flees to Tarshish. But his presence on the ship only intensifies his difficulties and he arranges to be removed from the scene once again, thrown into the sea, the sailors on the ship, as a kind of narrative aside, converting to the religion of the Hebrews upon his departure. No sooner, however, is he tossed free of the ship (in the middle of a tempest) than he is engulfed by a large fish. Miraculously preserved after three days within the belly of the fish, he thanks God for all He has done for him and he is suddenly expelled from the fish onto dry land, the same land, in fact, from which his odyssey began, only to face the prospect of the same divine command. As if in echo of the sailors, it is the rabbinical commentators themselves, this time, who convert Jonah's prayer of thanksgiving into a prayer of repentance, citing his words as an instance of the "prophetic past."[8]

The second part of the narrative continues the same ironic conjunction of cause and effect. But now it is his fulfillment of the divine mission that renders him increasingly unhappy. The call comes to Jonah a second time and this time—as if in negative imitation of his initial flight—he goes. He preaches to the Ninevites and is successful beyond all measure. But that success is repellent to him and he retires to a hill to await the outcome. A gourd grows to shelter him from the heat and he rejoices over it, and when, on the next day, it withers he is even more upset than before. Finally, God speaks to him about his experiences and, once he has expressed his anger at the salvation of the Ninevites and the loss of the gourd, God delivers His final speech in which He puts into perspective all that has occurred.

At the same time, and independent of this forward diachronic movement, there is a clear pattern of repetition and intensification that we have already in part suggested. Each scene reflects in some fashion all that has preceded it. Jonah flees God's prophetic call and the elements of that initial scene—the issuance of the word of God, the tempestuous conditions of Nineveh with its fruitless religious appeals, the implementation of an institutional or ritual practice, the removal of Jonah from the scene—are repeated in scene 2 two times in paganized form: once before he arrives, and then once again during his presence on the ship.

The breath of God is issued. A storm is raised in which the sailors fruitlessly call upon their gods, offer sacrifices, and expel cargo. The word of the commander to "arise" comes to Jonah (who has fallen asleep in the innermost hold of the ship). A process of ritual selection takes place (the questions and the casting of lots) in which a certain arbitrariness of the circumstances is displayed, and the sailors are unsure who is to blame. And finally Jonah is thrown overboard.

Similarly, the scene within the water reproduces in significant measure the same four elements. God designates a sacrificial monster from the tempestuous depths to engulf Jonah who offers a religious prayer of thanksgiving for past salvation that results in his expulsion from those depths. From religious and pagan encounters we have moved to environmental encounters of the most intense kind.

Part 2 plays off of this pattern to opposite narrative effect. The opening scene echoes the opening of the story. The word of God comes regarding the stormy conditions in Nineveh. The call appeals to Jonah's sense of religious duty, and this time he removes himself from the premises to fulfill his mission. The second scene of part 2 similarly echoes its counterpart in part 1. The word of God arrives through Jonah to a tempestuous city. The city is responsive to his words, and engages in the appropriate religious behavior. And Jonah leaves—although, as before, the religious response and his departure are in appropriate measure to the situation at hand.

The third scene on the hill similarly recalls the conclusion of part 1 within the depths. God exchanges words with Jonah. The heat of the day oppresses him. Jonah builds a booth (is the booth the gourd, and has the narrative doubled itself? or, in contradistinction to the gourd, is it the product of his labor?). The gourd arises to protect him and quickly withers, an event that induces Jonah's anger once again. God delivers a final speech that recapitulates all that has occurred, closes off the narrative, and becomes the touchstone for rabbinical commentary upon the tale.

What is the function of this curious narrative structure in which an unmistakable and continuous forward movement results in diametrically opposed encounters? Or, to put the question the other way around, how are we to understand two decisively contrasted sequences that turn out to be continuous with each other? Moreover, what is the function of the final exchange between God and Jonah upon the hill that at once continues this narrative development and yet seems at the same time to include within it all that has occurred.

To set the stage for an examination of this final exchange, let us turn to the sequence leading up to it.

II

> And the word of the LORD came unto Jonah the second time, saying:
> "Arise, go unto Nineveh, that great city, and make unto it
> the proclamation that I bid thee."
> (3:1–2)

The opening words of part 2 echo unmistakably the opening words of part 1 (1:1–2). The word of the LORD came to Jonah and this time he goes. Why? Jonah had achieved repentance in the belly of the fish, the sages tell us, and in order for repentance to be complete, the penitent must be tried in circumstances similar to those in which he previously failed.[9] His faith alone is insufficient. He must be tried in the fires of experience. The word of the LORD comes and this time he goes without a moment's hesitation—like Abraham to the sacrifice of Isaac. His repentance would seem just about complete.

As if for a kind of bonus, his efforts are successful beyond his wildest expectations. Barely has he stepped foot in Nineveh—which was "exceeding great" (3:3) and "of three days' journey" across (3:3)—and barely has he offered his proclamation—"'Yet forty days, and Nineveh shall be overthrown'"—than his appearance occasions a repentance of unprecedented proportions. "The people of Nineveh believed God; and they proclaimed a fast, and put on sackcloth, from the greatest of them even to the least of them" (3:5).

No sooner does the word of Jonah's appearance in the city reach the king than he decrees repentance into state law. "He arose from his throne, and laid his robe from him, and covered him with sackcloth, and sat in ashes" and issued a city-wide proclamation: no one—neither men nor cattle—shall eat or drink, but rather they shall "be covered with sackcloth" and pray to God (3:6–8).

> Let them turn every one from his evil way, and from the violence that is in their hands. Who knoweth whether God will not turn and repent, and turn away from His fierce anger, that we perish not? (3:8–9)

So intense and deeply felt are these penitential gestures that even the cattle are kept in a fast. If ever Jonah contemplated the fears to which the commentators allude, his experience in Nineveh should have dispelled them completely. Their repentance is massive and genuine. Moreover, they repent without in any way challenging either Jonah in particular or the institutions of prophecy of which he is representative. They are fully aware, it seems (as the sailors were before them), that God sometimes turns from the destruction He plans when He sees that the human community turns from its evil ways.[10] It is a gesture more expected of Israel (in Jonah's view) than Nineveh—which has been compared in the commentaries to the cities of Sodom and Gomorrah—and bound therefore to astonish him.[11] Jonah seems, in fact, to have very little to do with what occurs. It is as if all that was needed was the prophet's appearance in the city for a movement of staggering proportions to begin—which may be in part why commentators sometimes suggest that sailors from the ship from which Jonah was expelled had made their way to Nineveh before him and got things started, so to speak.[12]

What is the response of God? The LORD sees the depth and breadth of their repentance and calls off the disaster He had in store for them. He relents from destroying them. Jonah's success, in short, would seem the completion and reversal of all that has occurred in part 1. All that would be left to include—as a kind of parallel to the end of part 1—would be some kind of prayer on Jonah's part to God, thanking Him for all He has done for the human community, declaring His greatness—His universal glory, mercy, and justice—the kind of prayer, in fact, which the liturgists saw fit to tack on to the reading of the Book of Jonah on the afternoon of Yom Kippur from the end of the Book of Micah.

> Who is a God like unto Thee, that pardoneth the iniquity,
> And passeth by the transgression of the remnant of His heritage?

> He retaineth not His anger for ever,
> Because He delighteth in mercy.
> He will again have compassion upon us;
> He will subdue our iniquities;
> And Thou wilt cast all their sins into the depths of the sea.
> Thou wilt show faithfulness to Jacob, mercy to Abraham,
> As Thou hast sworn unto our fathers from the days of old.
>
> (7:18–20)

It is as if the liturgists of Yom Kippur are mindful of the developments we have been suggesting and draw them to their natural conclusion.

All of which makes what in fact follows the repentance of the Ninevites and God's relenting of His planned destruction so strange.

> But it displeased Jonah exceedingly, and he was angry. And he prayed unto the LORD, and said: "I pray Thee, O LORD, was not this my saying, when I was yet in mine own country? Therefore I fled beforehand unto Tarshish; for I knew that Thou art a gracious God, and compassionate, long suffering, and abundant in mercy, and repentest Thee of the evil. Therefore now, O LORD, take, I beseech Thee, my life from me; for it is better for me to die than to live." (4:1–3)

The very qualities for which the prayer from Micah praises God—compassion, slowness to anger, kindness, mercy, etc.—which are, moreover, the very qualities Jonah anticipated that God would display, are the very reasons Jonah cites for his anger against what has occurred and, moreover, for his flight initially from *eretz yisrael* to Tarshish.

Why is Jonah angry at his success? Moreover, why is he so intensely angry that he asks God to take his life, that he asserts "it is better for me to die than to live?"

What is strange about Jonah's anger in the first place is that it seems to cast doubts upon his entire history up to this point. Jonah fled from the *shechinah* initially. But presumably he began to realize that he was doing something worthy of criticism when in the tempest-tossed vessel he asked to be thrown overboard and finally, within the belly of the great fish, he offered a prayer of repentant thanksgiving. That he reveals now that his response to the salvation of Nineveh has been the same that he had initially ("was not this my saying, when I was yet in mine own country? Therefore I fled beforehand unto Tarshish") suggests either: (1) that he was never fully repentant (or repentant in bad faith); or (2) that his true repentance has suddenly and curiously lapsed and he is in need of it again. In either case, that is, the question that was posed initially, the question of his flight from his native land and the prophetic call, seems from the current vantage point not in fact ever to have been answered and to be fully open once again.

But in the second place, if the question is raised this time, it seems to be raised once and for all. If everything in the narrative to this point seems to converge upon the final scene of part 2, the exchange that now takes place between God and Jonah seems to resolve those issues in some way that remains to be elucidated. The final scene takes up Jonah's flight—his reluctance to prophesy to the Ninevites—as its central concern. Jonah is angry with God. God responds. Jonah retires to a hill to watch what is to happen to Nineveh. And God undertakes an action that is designed to explain His own behavior (and perhaps Jonah's as well) with regard to Nineveh and so in looking at the last scene we are finally in a position to read the story in its entirety.

There is something else. Jonah withdraws to the booth he has constructed to watch what will happen and God now gives him an "object lesson" with the gourd (or castor oil plant). The final scene, that is, reproduces to some extent, in miniature as it were, the whole of the Jonah story thus far. It restages the Jonah story from a certain distance so that its contours become clearer. It is thus a kind of "Jonah story" within the Jonah story and, as such, parallels the end of the first part. It operates much the same way, for example, as the episode in the belly of the great fish (with its series of thoughts and cries and remembered prayers)—which is to say, a reflection of both the narrative to that point and the narrative to come, and a staging of the relations between the "insides" of the story and the multiplicity of concatenated or engulfing frameworks within which those "insides" or entrails reside (the fish, the tempest-tossed sea, the Jonah story, the Books of the Prophets, Hebrew Scripture, Judaic culture, the world, etc.). It stages those relations from without as the former does from the depths. It provides a "part 2" to the Jonah story that is not dissimilar to the "part 2" in which it is contained. Thus as we saw in chapter 3 it parallels certain other scriptural texts in which a "part 2" is followed by a "part 2" that restages the earlier sequence in such a way that its salient features become apparent—both to readers of the story and to the characters within it (who are thus rendered like those readers).[13]

Let us turn, then, to this Jonah story within the Jonah story upon which everything seems to converge.

III

The Ninevites repent. God relents from the disaster He has planned. And Jonah is greatly displeased and retires to the hill to watch what will become of the city. ". . . was not this my saying, when I was yet in mine own country? . . . Therefore now, O LORD, take, I beseech Thee, my life from me; for it is better for me to die than to live."

The first part of the exchange draws into the fore the central movement of the narrative so far. The envisioning of just this conclusion was what led him to flee God's request initially, Jonah relates. And his offering of the ultimate sacrifice ("It is better for me to die than to live") reflects presumably what was already present to his thoughts when he was aboard the tempest-tossed vessel and asked that he be thrown overboard. It is in fact this offer that redeems him in the eyes of most traditional commentators since in the face of a perceived embarrassment to Israel (the suppression of a prophecy, the Talmud tells us—citing Jonah as an example—was a crime punishable by death) he does what all major leaders of Israel—Abraham, Moses, David—have done.[14]

Moreover, the offer puts to rest any speculation that Jonah fled because he feared God would not be compassionate or that the Ninevites would not repent of their ways. In function of a logic that remains to be elucidated, he flees precisely *because* of God's compassion and *because* he knows that the Ninevites will repent.

The second part of the narrative stages in turn the first part. God draws Jonah's attention to what he has said, to his own words, registering Jonah's response. "And the LORD said: 'Art thou greatly angry'?" There may even be something slightly ironic about God's response, perhaps even sardonic, given the fact that Jonah is angry that He has just saved a city full of people from disaster. "Does that, indeed, bother you?" God seems to be saying. "Let Me get clear on exactly what it is you are telling Me," as if God is a kind of prosecuting attorney and there is more to follow.

Which, of course, there is. The first exchange having set the stage for what is to come, God will now make His own move: he will deconstruct Jonah's anger and reluctance to prophesy in a gesture calculated to inspire in Jonah (and perhaps in us) a profound repentance.

> Then Jonah went out of the city, and sat on the east side of the city, and there made him a booth, and sat under it in the shadow, till he might see what would become of the city. And the LORD God pre-

pared a gourd, and made it to come up over Jonah, that it might be a shadow over his head, to deliver him from his evil. So Jonah was exceeding glad because of the gourd. But God prepared a worm when the morning rose the next day, and it smote the gourd, that it withered. And it came to pass, when the sun arose, that God prepared a vehement east wind; and the sun beat upon the head of Jonah, that he fainted, and requested for himself that he might die, and said: "It is better for me to die than to live." And God said to Jonah: "Art thou greatly angry for the gourd?" And he said: "I am greatly angry, even unto death." And the LORD said: "Thou hast had pity on the gourd, for which thou hast not laboured, neither madest it grow, which came up in a night, and perished in a night; and should not I have pity on Nineveh, that great city, wherein are more than sixscore thousand persons that cannot discern between their right hand and their left hand, and also much cattle?" (4:5–11)

These final verses of the Jonah story have puzzled readers for as long as they have been read. The scene seems clearly to be of climactic importance in the narrative to this point. Yet it is so parabolic and oblique in its reference to the details of the story we have witnessed that it has given rise to a variety of partial and (for that reason) insufficient readings.

The most common reading (cited earlier) is that God teaches Jonah an "object lesson" in compassion. God sets the scene by generating in Jonah the same response that he felt for the impending salvation of the Ninevites and then pointing out, "You felt compassion for a gourd (or castor oil plant, a "kikayon") for which you did not work, that is not your handiwork, and that is as transitory as the wind. How much more compassion should I feel for the people of the great city of Nineveh— who *are* My handiwork, for whom I *have* worked, and whose repentance may sow seeds for the repentance of others in the future?" The rhetorical form, of course, is that of the *kal vachomer*, or *a fortiori* argument, that is used commonly in Scripture and so lends an added familiarity and strength to the words.

There may, however, be another reading, one that suggests a more subtle and complex strategy on God's part, in function of which, in fact, the more common reading is itself implicated.

What is striking above all in the context in which the verses appear is the repetition of Jonah's response, a repetition that draws our attention to what has changed. "Are you so deeply grieved over the *kikayon*?" God asks, at once in repetition of the sentiment on Jonah's part that God registered earlier and in a kind of amazement, offering Jonah as it were a way out of the corner in which he has lodged himself. But Jonah will not take that exit and repeats himself with an emphasis that can leave no doubt about his intentions. "I am greatly angry, even unto death."

What God is showing Jonah, in other words, in the first instance is that what has troubled him—"even unto death" as he says—is nothing more terrible than a matter of personal discomfort. What "angers" him, in one case as in the other, is the loss of his own personal protection from the heat of the sun, the fear of his own exposure in the light of day. What has angered him in the salvation of the Ninevites is the loss in some way of his own security, the threatened exposure of his own weaknesses and failings, the loss of his shielding "kikayon." The traditional reading of Jonah's reluctance to prophesy—for fear of exposing Israel who will not repent in the other Books of the Prophets—gains validity in this light if we substitute for the threat to Israel at large the more immediate danger to Jonah in particular.

But why has God chosen to reveal the real object of Jonah's concern in this particular way? Why a "kikayon" plant? What in the first place is a "kikayon?"

There are many conjectures among the commentators as to the particular plant to which the text refers. Some identify it as a kind of gourd, others as a castor oil plant. Rashi, the foremost medieval commentator within the rabbinic tradition, identifies it only as a "plant containing many leaves, that provides shade," presumably in concert with those who feel it unnecessary to identify it more specifically, since such "speculation diverts from the lesson of the narrative."[15] It is, in that connection, the commentators assert, not unlike the great fish who swallowed Jonah. It is not the salvation of Nineveh at all that draws Jonah's attention, God seems to be saying, but something else: let us call it a "kikayon." Perhaps our difficulty in knowing how to translate this word reflects the more profound difficulty of identifying the nature of this substitute (and of the substitutive logic in general).

The function of the "kikayon," that is, may be in part at least, to signify that Jonah has invested his energies precisely in an object, a thing of this world, an idol. As God elicits from Jonah the intensity of his investment ("It is better for me to die than to live," Jonah says; "I am greatly angry, even unto death"), the status of that object becomes clear for us: it has become for Jonah a kind of divinity. Quite apart from a perceived threat to his own exposure, what describes Jonah's relationship to Nineveh is a form of idolatry.

In what way? The late Rabbi J. H. Hertz, in the excellent commentary to this story that he includes in a widely used liturgical text, draws our attention to this aspect of Jonah's relation to Nineveh. His suggestions are shrewdly insightful and worth following at some length. "The Book of Jonah is the most ill-used and least understood of all the Books of the Bible," the commentator writes.

> The purpose of Jonah's adventures is to teach him by experience, and through him Israel and mankind, a lesson which had to be learned. The lesson cannot be only, as some have maintained, that God accepts repentance; if that were all, chapter four would be irrelevant and unnecessary. Nor can it be only the lesson that the Gentiles too are God's creatures, and worthy of pardon if sincerely repentant. Jonah knew and understood that lesson; his very reluctance to deliver his message was based on the fear that the Ninevites might repent, if warned, and be forgiven, and that he would therefore be the agent of their salvation.[16]

Dismissing the traditional accounts, the commentator subtly draws our attention to the absolute difference upon which Jonah's view is founded.

> The essential teaching is that the Gentiles *should not be grudged* God's love, care, and forgiveness. It is this grudging which is so superbly rebuked throughout the Book, and most of all in the final chapter, which must rightly be considered the climax of the story.[17]

Jonah has refused to prophesy to the Ninevites, in other words, because he would reserve salvation to the Israelites alone. He would make an idol, ironically, of the law of anti-idolatry itself. But what God would teach him, what the Book of Jonah would teach us, is that to begrudge salvation to the Ninevites is not simply snobbish: it is anti-Jewish.

For who are the Jews? They are not some people who are indigenous to the region in which they live and who happen to have been given some kind of special handling by God (and the Nazi appropriation of this idea within a monstrous context reflects just such a misunderstanding). They are, precisely, those who have left, those who have given up the sacrificial ways of the lands from which they came in order to be Jews in the first place.

The Jews, in other words, are ex-Ninevites and by this same understanding, as those who have given up their sacrificial and idolatrous ways and turned in repentance to the religion of the LORD, the Ninevites are the new Jews. To turn against the Ninevites, therefore, is to turn against the Jews. Likewise either to justify Jonah's flight (on the basis that it saves Israel) or to criticize it (on the basis that he must have compassion for the non-Jews)—both of which positions we adopt in criticism—is equally to participate in Jonah's own misunderstanding. It is to preserve in either case the difference between the two, between the Israelites and the Ninevites, the very difference that the story is working prophetically to undo. It is to make an idol of the law of anti-idolatry once again—just as Jonah himself did.

And if we can identify this new idolatry—which is given in the face of the revelation of the law of anti-idolatry—as itself "Ninevitian," a new form of sacrificial thinking that founds itself once more on the very distinctions Judaism founded itself upon rejecting, then we may say that Israel and Nineveh (or Judaism and sacrificial modes of thinking) are distributed along an axis that is neither historical nor parabolic, neither diachronic nor synchronic, but rather that occupies the two apparent "sides" of a Möbius strip in which there is really only one side, one continuous and twisting path between them. The Ninevites are the "other" of the Jews at every point if and only if they are at the same time the future or the past of the Jews, the future or the past of where the Jews already are.

There is a third understanding of the final scene that needs to be made explicit, one that in fact combines each of the first two. This understanding derives from God's final words to Jonah. The scene with the gourd reveals to Jonah in the dreamlike language of parable the source of his anger at the salvation of the Ninevites—the fear of his own exposure. And the particularity of that language helps us to specify the nature of that relationship from a biblical perspective: Jonah is reenacting the very idolatry whose rejection enabled the Jews to give up their sacrificial origins and become Jews in the first place. To turn against the Ninevites is to turn against the Jews. It is to fall into a Ninevitian sacrificial mode of a new and more dangerous order since it is to do so in the wake of the revelation of anti-idolatry. It is to make an idol of the law of anti-idolatry itself.

But why the particularity of the *kikayon* with regard to Jonah individually? God's final words give us the clue: "Thou hast had pity on the gourd (or *kikayon*), . . . and should not I have pity on Nineveh?" (*chas'ta 'al-hakiykayon . . . va'aniy lo achus al-niyn'veih*, 4:10–11). But Jonah never "had pity" on the *kikayon* in the narrative we have. He was "exceeding glad" because of it when it offered him shade, and was "greatly angry" over it—even to the point of wishing for his own death—when it was lost, but never "pitied" it (the Hebrew word is *chus*) in the narrative we have. Why has God seemingly altered this description?

In a sense, in substituting the *kikayon* for Nineveh as the object of Jonah's concern God has acted somewhat in the manner of a primitive shaman with him. The object has functioned both to clarify and delineate Jonah's relation to Nineveh prior to this scene. But lest this object in itself gain undue attention in Jonah's eyes, God is about to snatch that away as well. Having shown him what his anger is (viz. a "kikayon," an excuse, a defense, an idolatrous substitute for his own fears of exposure), He will now show him what this *kikayon* is: namely, a substitute, in turn, for his own self-condemnation and self-judgment.

"It is better for me to die than to live" is the clue. The intensity with which Jonah greeted the loss of the gourd reflects a depth of personal involvement that far exceeds either an onerous prophetic task he perceives God to be giving him or an idolatrous perspective with regard to non-Jews. And it is that depth of internal involvement that God reflects when He characterizes Jonah's relationship to the *kikayon* retrospectively as one of "pity." You have seen yourself in the *kikayon,* God tells him implicitly, your own transitory nature, and your own impending demise, and it is that that you have pitied—the *kikayon* within the *kikayon,* so to speak.

Behind Nineveh, in other words, behind the *kikayon,* is the real object of Jonah's fascination, which is himself—a self he has not created, for which he has not labored, and that will perish overnight. "It is better for me to die than to live" is a resonant judgment not only of Nineveh but also and above all of himself. And it is in these terms that Jonah's response to Nineveh finds its greatest source of power. At root, Jonah has made an idol not only of Nineveh, that great city, but of the language by which he describes his own capabilities.

Why is taking himself, or more precisely the language of his own capabilities, as an idol, bad? Because it is that, above all, that is "Ninevitian." It is that that Jews left in order to be Jews. You are angry at saving the Ninevites, God tells Jonah implicitly, because you are in danger of being embarrassed, in danger of being exposed as a Ninevitian yourself, a new Ninevite no doubt, one who has made an idol of the law of anti-idolatry (rather than one who has not yet discovered that law), but a Ninevite nonetheless. And in fleeing My prophetic task, you do that once again.

Yet, having characterized Jonah's relation to the *kikayon* as one of pity (and thereby a revelation of Jonah's self-indictment and its consequences), God will now make the boldest stroke of all: He will offer Jonah (and those for whom the story of Jonah is their "kikayon") the way out of that dilemma. "Leave the pitying to Me," He tells this reluctant prophet. "Don't take over My position. Did you create the universe? Let Me decide who is worthy of pity and who is not. Let Me alone make human beings in My image. The excessive gladness over *kikayons* and the anger over their loss is My job, not yours. You do yourself and Me a disservice by usurping My role in these matters, in creating idols of earthly concerns, in fashioning *kikayons* after your own image."

"And should not I have pity on Nineveh, that great city?" To give up "pity on" the Ninevites is to give up "pity on" the Jews who are the new Ninevites. God's final pronouncement, in other words, completes the deconstruction begun at the outset of this final scene. By your own argument, God in essence is telling Jonah, should I not do what you would rather I refrain from doing, namely, save the city of Nineveh? Should I not save them precisely by imitation of your example, by thinking of them as *My* "kikayons," pitiable in the same way in which you would take yourself as an object of "pity?" And is it not better, after all, that *I* should make "kikayons" rather than you? And that you render back unto Me what was Mine to begin with, what you appropriated idolatrously from Me—ironically, in your manner of defining yourself as anti-idolatrous? In appropriating My role from Me, it is you who now reside in Nineveh, in "that great city, wherein are more than sixscore thousand persons that cannot discern between their right hand and their left hand, and also much cattle." In cutting Me off from Nineveh, you are cutting Me off, in the same gesture, from yourself, from the hidden Ninevites, that is to say, as well as the exposed Ninevites. *Va'aniy lo achus al-niyn'veih?* ("And should not I have pity on Nineveh?")

IV

The profound diachronic continuity between Israel and Nineveh, and the radical difference between idolatry and divinity that at every point sustains that continuity, will answer for us all of the questions we have raised. The story of Jonah is among the Prophetic Books not because it relates (or fails to relate) the historical or cultural circumstances of Israel's relation to its prophets but because it demystifies for us the prophetic spirit itself, the spirit that in the sixth century before our era canonized the biblical texts and thus in some very real sense "wrote" the Bible.

What is prophetic thinking? We have always had difficulty from within a Platonic perspective imagining as genuine any knowledge issuing from sources other than reason or decision making. And we have accepted this alternative claim only in those realms where it can be declared to have come from beyond conscious human relations—from the intervention of some outside agency (for example, divine providence) or from the interruption of our everyday lives by some inside unconscious agency that we can attribute to our own desires.

What the prophetic calls upon us to imagine on the other hand—within both the pre-Socratic Greek context and within Israel in the centuries during which the biblical texts were canonized—is the "middle" that has been excluded from these considerations, the matrix of human relations in which we were immersed before invoking this ratio separating the differentiable from the undifferentiable.[18] In particular, it calls upon us to recognize the dramas, the ritualized patterns of behavior, in which human beings are always already engaged and to name in advance the end of those dramas.

To think the relation of Nineveh to Israel prophetically, therefore, is to think in transformational and sequential terms that do not derive from some external synchronic grid against which such developmental changes can be measured. Israel is what Nineveh is becoming as it turns away from the idolatrous sacrificial ways of its past and, moreover, what it is in danger of becoming again should it make an idol of that transformation itself. To insist upon the difference between the two—even in the wake of the revelation of the law of anti-idolatry—is to make an "object lesson" or *kikayon* of that very revelation, to participate in a new idolatry, one that is, in a sense, even more dangerous than the first, since there is no longer any revelation of which it is not already cognizant. It is to fall into a new sacrificial mode that is identical in kind (if not in detail) with the old sacrificial mode, the one rejected in order to formulate that revelatory difference in the first place.

And it is preeminently this danger, the danger of making a *kikayon* of the law of anti-*kikayons,* that the story of Jonah is about. Coming in Scripture after the giving of the Law, it concerns less the nature of anti-idolatry per se (as do the books of the Torah proper) than the kinds of idolatrous traps into which we can fall even after we are in possession of that Law. Jonah is the Israelite who would reserve the revelation of the law of anti-idolatry for himself, and God's interaction with him serves to deconstruct that position—to stage its limits—in two distinct ways: in such a way that Jonah can understand it (with the *kikayon*), and in such a way that through Jonah's recognition we can see it as well, we who have made a *kikayon* or object lesson of the story of Jonah within the Books of the Prophets no less than he has. The story of Jonah is to the Books of the Prophets what the scene of the *kikayon* is to the story of Jonah, each in fact functioning the same way that the Biblical Scripture does for us.

Moreover, perhaps we now also understand why the story of Jonah "feels like" wisdom literature—for example, like the Book of Job. It may be that the story of Jonah locates itself at the same place in the history of sacrificial thinking as the wisdom texts, at those moments when the wisdom of the Hebraic God and the Law He reveals, comes itself under fire. To make an idol of the law of anti-idolatry is to feel oneself to be in possession of a truth denied to others, denied in particular to non-Jews, and therefore to have subsumed in some fashion divine revelation under the aegis of human history. It is to make a *kikayon* of ourselves before God, to do, that is, precisely what God chastises Jonah for doing in "pitying" the gourd. If we have traditionally erected two explanations of Jonah's behavior—that he is acting on behalf of Israel when he rejects his mission to prophesy to non-Jews and that he needs to learn the mystery of God's compassion for all creatures—have we not constructed our readings upon the same premises, turning either to the historical situation or the parabolic context of human values in order to found our case, the two grounds, that is to say, whose appropriation the story is primarily challenging?

Perhaps in recognizing the ways in which, within the history of interpretation, we have reproduced the humanistic usurpation already at stake within the narrative, we come to understand as well something of the dynamics of interpretation itself in the Jewish context. In some fundamental way, the traditional exoteric readings of the text serve to actualize potentials that are already preserved within the narrative (and therefore they remain true to the text, so to speak), but potentials in particular that the narrative has raised in order to challenge. To view Jonah's behavior as redemptive or lacking in compassion is to construct a view not incompatible finally with Jonah's own, although it is the

"Ninevitian" or sacrificial qualities of such a view that God and the narrative have displayed for us (and for Jonah).

At the same time, the construction of such interpretation is as well a break with the text, a refusal to take seriously the radical otherness that the text as text would demand of us, a making accessible of its intricacies (and thereby an extension of it) to the present hour and to everyday life.[19] To read the text from within is to perform the text. When Rashi tells us that the *kikayon* must be understood as a "plant containing many leaves, which provides shade," he is not throwing up his hands before an empirical reality too obscure to be discerned. He is telling us something about our construction of and reliance upon such a notion. He is performing the fact that the *kikayon* for Jonah has become an idol, pure language, independent of any narrative universe of which the text would convince us. In tracing the diachronic conditions of that performance—both within the text and within the world in which the interpreter himself functions—we learn something about that interpretive process.

It is in this way preeminently that the Jewish conception of interpretation differs from the Platonic conception—for which there are always true and false readings (those that have being and those that do not), and the contractual preservation of a difference between the inside and outside of the text. For Judaism there are no true or false readings (in the sense of transcontextual truths), not because all readings are partial and the puzzle remains to be solved, but rather because there are always new puzzles, because the function of interpretation is to make the text accessible to the present hour and the present hour is always changing. In this way, therefore, many interpretations (which are mutually exclusive) may come to be regarded as equally "true" readings (those of Rashi, Maimonides, and so forth) and interpretation may be construed necessarily as endless. Interpretation, in this regard, has become a version of the practice of anti-idolatry itself.

Idolatrous, therefore, and anti-idolatrous, sacrificial and anti-sacrificial interpretation within Judaism is a kind of coded communication, a communication that at once offers us the domain in which an anti-idolatrous reading is to be found and yet necessarily "gets it wrong" so to speak. Breaking with the text, performing it, it recreates the text in interpretation. The strength of the traditional reading that takes Jonah's reluctance as redemptive, for example, is that it recognizes that it is Israel that is really at stake in "Nineveh," although it reads this identity as historical rather than developmental, and social rather than individual. In the same way, the real strength of the more modern view that reads Jonah's anger as lacking in compassion is to have recognized in Nineveh a certain profound identity with Israel although it postulates that identity within the very humanistic framework the story is challenging, in terms of the very "pity" or "kikayonic" activity that the final speech of God reveals as so dangerous.

Perhaps within this understanding of the doubleness of interpretation, we also understand the wisdom of the liturgists who saw in the story of Jonah a text appropriate to both the traditional legal practices of the day of Yom Kippur and the notion of repentance or *teshuvah* that is taken as the central theme of that day. Like the ancient halachic Temple practices of the day of Yom Kippur itself (the practices of ritual scapegoating, for example), the story must be understood as profoundly antisacrificial.

Theories of sacrifice and sacrificial structuration depend upon a distinction between violence, expulsion, and crisis on the one hand, and sacrifice, sacralization, and the difference between the sacred and the profane on the other.[20] Yet the story progressively intermixes the two. God calls upon Jonah to prophesy to the Ninevites (a gesture that must be understood as a summoning of Jonah to his sacred duty) and Jonah responds by expelling himself from the premises. Then, in the second scene, expulsions and sacrifice begin to become confused. There are gestures of expulsion and violence on one side (the tempest, for example, that may be construed as the sea trying to expel the ship, or the tossing of cargo overboard to lighten it) and the gestures of sacrifice on the other (the sacrifices to God that the sailors make, for example, after Jonah is removed). But there is also the confusion between the two when Jonah asks them to expel him in order to save them and they first reject (or expel) the idea and then finally carry it out.

Then in scene 3, the mixture becomes even more apparent. There is the great fish that is undoubtedly an image of sacrificial mechanism on the one hand, and the prayer of Jonah who is caught within that mechanism, a prayer which is equally without doubt a gesture of holiness. And the result is an expulsion (literally, a vomiting up) that is also identically a salvation (or rescuing) that makes possible for Jonah a new beginning.

Then, in part 2, there seems to be both a continuation of this intermixing of sacrificial and expulsive gestures and (by comparison with part 1) a new conceptualization. Jonah in the first scene this time refuses to disobey God's command, in a kind of negative imitation of part 1. The Ninevites likewise immediately turn away from their former behavior and towards the ways of the God of Israel. Even God gets into the act, as it were, and upon seeing the Ninevites give up their sacrificial ways gives up His planned destruction of them. And once this success is achieved, that success is itself rejected. In the third scene, Jonah rejects his success and returns to his old objections: he rejoices in his booth on the hillside, and then laments its loss. Whereupon God turns Jonah's attention first from Nineveh to the *kikayon,* and then from the *kikayon,* to himself, and finally back to divinity.

In short, the story in its entirety seems to reenact the history of Israel itself, from "Nineveh" to "Jerusalem," or from Egypt to the land of Canaan. For it traces the transformation from a sacrificial perspective to an anti-sacrificial one, conceived as a form of turning away from the idolatrous ways of one's past and a turning to the ways of God.

In the same way, in fact, that the day of Yom Kippur itself does. Interspersed with texts that recall the scapegoat rituals of the High Priests in the Temple in Jerusalem, the services of the day turn more and more focally upon the theme of *teshuvah* or repentance. The very name of the day "Yom Kippur" refers doubly to the "day of the lots" (those cast during the scapegoat ritual in order to determine which of two identical goats was to be led off to the wilderness, to "Azazel," and which was to be sacrificed in the ritual slaughter) and the "day of atonement or repentance."[21]

What is *teshuvah*? The notion of *teshuvah* (or repentance) has been traditionally understood (for example, by Maimonides) as an abandonment of sin and a return to the ways of God.[22] But if we conceive of this notion broadly enough, it may be seen to encompass all that we have identified as the conditions of Judaism itself—both its birth from cultures in which sacrifice no longer works, and the ongoing motor force of Judaism at its most individual and personal level. The linkage, therefore, of the story of Jonah with the notion of repentance and the ancient halachic practices of the day of Yom Kippur—the holiest day of the Jewish calendar, the day on which (the Sages say) human beings may purify themselves and become as angels—may reproduce for us, in fact, precisely the circumstances within the story. The story of Jonah becomes then *our* parable of the *kikayon* through which the dangers of our own idolatrous behavior may be narratively staged in order that we may stop and return to the ways of God.

In what way? Repentance is the abandonment of sin and the return to God, the giving up of those energies devoted to paths that take us away from God and the return to God of what properly belongs to Him, that one has inappropriately usurped as one's own. In historical terms, therefore, it is the giving up of the sacrificial ways in which one has lived and the turning back to the ways of the LORD. Perhaps in this connection we understand why the Midrash lists repentance as one of the seven conditions in which the world was created: without repentance, the Sages say, the world would inevitably perish in the face of God's judgment.[23]

But repentance is also the motor force of Judaism. To turn (or more precisely to turn back) is to presuppose that one has stopped, that one has given up—even fleetingly—the path one was following in order to pursue another. The notion of stopping or resting is built into the cycle of Jewish life. It is the foundation for the notion of the Sabbath or day of rest (*yom hashabbat*), a day that reproduces the action of God after the universe was created (or in other renderings after the creation of the universe was begun) on the seventh day. It describes, in a slightly different connection, the period of mourning following a death for a specified period of time, sometimes a period of seven days referred to as "sitting *shiv*ˣ*ah*" or "sitting seven." The day of Yom Kippur itself, of course, is conceived along similar lines as a day of stopping and turning, a day on which one ceases or gives up all of the activity that may take one away from God, and devotes oneself exclusively to rest, prayer, and study of Torah, and a day that the Sages are fond of calling the "sabbath of sabbaths." The very word *teshuvah* (from *shuv*, to turn back, return) and a whole series of other words—*shiv*ˣ*ah*, or *sheva*ʿ (seven), *shava*ʿ (curse, swear, literally, bind oneself by "seven" things), *shavat* (cease, desist, rest), *shabbat* (sabbath, seventh day, a day of rest), and so forth—are often played upon by the rabbis in this connection.[24] Thus, for example, the Sabbath that falls between the High Holidays is called the *shabbat shuvah*.

It is, however, and perhaps more significantly, the condition of Jewish spiritual life as well.

> They asked Wisdom, "What is the sinner's punishment?"
> It told them: "Sinners—let them be pursued by [their] evil"
>   (Proverbs 13:21).
> They asked Prophecy, "What is the sinner's punishment?"
> It told them: "The soul that sins—it shall die!" (Ezekiel 18:20).
> They asked Torah, "What is the sinner's punishment?"

It told them: "Let him bring a guilt-offering and gain atonement!"
They asked the Holy One, Blessed Be He, "What is the sinner's punishment?"
He told them: "Let him repent and gain atonement!"[25]

Do we understand, then, the logic by which the Sages saw fit to link the notion of repentance to the day of Yom Kippur? Repentance is the regenerative force par excellence in Judaism and therefore appropriate to the one day ordained since creation, in the view of the Sages, for purification, for the separation of light from darkness, the sabbath of sabbaths, so to speak.

But why the story of Jonah? The thematic correspondence is manifest. The idolatry and pagan sacrifices of the sailors during the storm, the repentance of the sailors after Jonah is tossed overboard, the repentance of the Ninevites and of Jonah within the belly of the great fish—all these sequences reproduce the themes of the day.

Even more significant, perhaps, is the ritual or "performative" context in which the story is introduced. Listening to the story of Jonah within the synagogue service, watching Jonah have his own history staged before him, first with the parable of the *kikayon,* and then in God's speech to him about the *kikayon* and about Nineveh (a history in which he turns out to be an extension of those he would consider his bitterest enemies), we encounter our own history enacted before us as well. This history—within Judaism at large, within our individual lives, within our very experiences of the day of Yom Kippur—is staged before us in the same manner in which Jonah's is staged before him, a history that turns out similarly to be the record of our diachronic continuity with those elements of that history that we might consider to be radically foreign to our own experience—Biblical Scripture, for example. We find ourselves reenacting, in short, the very patterns with which the narrative is already primarily concerned, in the very act, moreover, of engaging that narrative and that concern. The story of Jonah comes to instruct us in repentance within the congregation in the same intensely personal way in which the words of God instruct Jonah within the story.

There is something else. The hearing of the Jonah story in synagogue at the beginning of *minchah,* or afternoon service (just after the morning Torah reading from Leviticus 18 which is permeated by liturgical texts in which God recalls the emergence of the Hebrews from Egypt and exhorts Israel to give up idolatrous and imitative practices of both the place from which they came and of the place to which they are coming—

the land of Canaan), and in the service shortly after *yizkor* and *musaf* (when the most devotional and confessional portions of the day have just been recited) focuses the individual encounter with God in such a way that the third reading we have suggested of the final scene is enacted as well. In this setting it is not the historical, nor the universalist, nor even the ritualistic character of the story that is foremost, but the deeply personal. Repentance in this reading of the Jonah story comes to mean the giving up of self-condemnation and self-judgment.

And once again the traditional interpretive strategies by which we have engaged the story offer us a coded version of this understanding. "Why did Jonah flee?" begins the commentary of Pirkei d'Rabbi Eliezer. "He passed judgment upon himself."[26] The modern reading observes that judgment is at stake but presupposes the difference between the Ninevites and the Israelites and believes the indictment concerns the non-Jews. In context of the synagogue service we now understand we must have compassion, the story tells us, in the first instance, not upon the others but upon ourselves, or, rather, upon others but precisely in so far as we recognize already ourselves in those others. We must give up the judgment of ourselves, the self-condemnation, upon which the fashioning of *kikayons* is based. We must, in short, engage in self-forgiveness, and it is the lack of self-forgiveness (expressing itself first as anger against the salvation of the Ninevites) that is above all finally reflected in Jonah's resonant words, "It is better for me to die than to live."

In this manner we come to understand how the traditional historical reading instructs us in the potential future of that dangerous self-judgment. The Ninevites will turn to God and we (who maintain the difference between Israel and Nineveh) shall be implicated by their conversion. Moreover, if we continue on this path, we shall soon witness the rise of scoffers who will challenge the very institutions from which we have come. And in the far distant future, the consequences will be even more drastic. Empires shall swallow up Israel and the Temple itself shall be destroyed. The history of Judaism relative to Hellenism, Christianity, and the modern world seems here already to have been imagined.

We have come a long way. And there remains more to be said. But it is already clear that the question on the horizon concerns the relation of Judaism to Christianity. Does not this relation turn, finally, upon the same questions of prophetic understanding, of sacrificial behavior, and of repentance in context of which we have examined the story of Jonah? And does not the familiar phrase "until the conversion of the Jews," a phrase used with haunting resonance throughout the Middle Ages (and well into the seventeenth century, in fact) to refer to "the end of time," bear all the mystery? Turning as it does upon the difference between Latin and Hebrew, between *conversio* and *teshuvah,* does not the phrase designate less a historical moment than a metaphysical one, a moment when those who are Jews (and are denying that Judaism) give up that denial and return to Judaism itself, a moment, that is to say, when Jewish anti-Jewishness (either within or outside of institutional Judaism) begins to take cognizance of itself? Such a moment will no doubt spell the end of historical time as we know it.

Moreover, do not these eschatological considerations lead directly to the door, so to speak, of still another one—namely, the coming of the Messiah? Is not the debate between Jonah and God, between one who would give up his life for Israel and one who would deconstruct the limits—the conditions, the strategies, and the consequences—of that perspective, the same debate?

Perhaps we have always known all of this. Have we not in fact encapsulated just such an understanding within the least likely of places—hidden away within a child's fable about a man who is swallowed by a whale? Is not the very anecdote that we are so fond of telling (and universally repudiating) about the story of Jonah in fact a rebus, moreover, a rebus concerned precisely with prophecy, sacrifice, and repentance? Does not the image of the great fish (or *dag gadol*) that has swallowed Jonah reproduce in pictorial language the very relationship we have discerned between Nineveh (that great city or *ha'ir hagdola*) and Israel, a prophetic relationship, that is to say, in which Israel has been engulfed by the sacrificial mechanisms of its own Ninevitian ways and can emerge from this idolatrous or "kikayonic" condition only by a prayer, a Hebrew prayer uttered in genuine repentance and as thanksgiving for a salvation that has either not yet or already occurred, and within a verbal construction commentators would readily identify as "the prophetic past"?[27]

This misfit, then, within Biblical Scripture and Jewish liturgy, that is the Book of Jonah, would turn out already to have contained that scripture and that liturgy—even the world itself—within its entrails. And the real butt of the joke we tell ourselves may turn out to be less those who take it to be the story of a man swallowed by a whale (or man-eating shark) than those who, from within the sacrificial and idolatrous mechanisms of their own tempestuous interpretive depths, would dismiss such a fiction as the fable of an uncomprehending child.

6

"The End from the Beginning"
Evil and Accusation in the Book of Job

> I am God, and there is none like Me:
> Declaring the end from the beginning.
>
> Isaiah 46:9–10

> The "Where were you when I founded the earth?" of Job 38:4, at the beginning of the discourse attributed to God, reminds Job of his absence at the hour of creation. But does it only upbraid the impudence of a creature who allows himself to judge the Creator? Does it only set forth a theodicy in which the economy of a harmonious and wisely arranged whole harbors evil only for a look limited to a part of this whole? Might one not understand in this "Where were you?" a denunciation of being wanting [*un constat de carence*], which can have meaning only if the humanity of man is fraternally solidary with creation, that is, is responsible for what was neither one's self nor one's work, and if this solidarity and this responsibility for everything and for all, which cannot occur without pain, is the spirit itself?
>
> This uprightness is called *Temimut,* the essence of Jacob. Integrity, taken in its logical meaning and not as a characteristic of a childlike disposition, indicates, if it is thought through to the end, an ethical configuration. . . . *Temimut* consists in substituting oneself for others.
>
> Emmanuel Levinas

> In Thy goodness Thou renewest the work
> of creation everyday, constantly.
>
> *Liturgy*

I. Prologue: Job and the Problem of Evil

The Book of Job, we are told, is the most exquisite example in all of biblical literature, perhaps in all of Western literature, of the "problem of evil."[1] Job is the wealthiest and most upright man in all of the East and one day, for reasons unknown to him, he is the victim of the most terrible calamities. His livestock and servants are stolen or slaughtered by invading tribes. His seven sons and three daughters, all of whom are visiting him at the time, are suddenly killed in a freakish elemental disaster. He himself is suddenly and inexplicably afflicted with the most terrible physical ailments. And yet throughout it all, Job remains upright and without sin. "Dost thou still hold fast thine integrity? Blaspheme God, and die," his wife counsels. And Job retorts, "Thou speakest as one of the impious women speaketh. What? Shall we receive good at the hand of God, and shall we not receive evil?" (2:9–10).

As if to compound his difficulties, his three friends, Eliphaz, Bildah, and Zophar, now appear, and after commiserating with him in silence for the appropriate period of time, engage him in a long series of exchanges or colloquies on this strange turn of events. "Let the day perish wherein I was born," Job tells them initially in his frustration (3:3). But these events are only the product of your own iniquity, they counsel, the product of a retributive justice in which you have sinned. "Who ever perished, being innocent? . . . they that plow iniquity, And sow mischief, reap the same" (4:7–8).

But "I *am* innocent" (9:21), Job protests (italics added). "Cause me to understand wherein I have erred" (6:24). And "if I have sinned . . . why dost [God] not pardon my transgression . . . ?" (7:20–21). Moreover, your taunts only add to my misfortunes. "To him that is ready to faint, kindness is due from his friend." Yet "my brethren have dealt deceitfully" (6:14–15). I will continue to believe in God to my death and I will continue to believe that there is some justice in all of this, but I would like to know exactly what it is. I am prepared if necessary to defend my case as in a court of law and I am confident that I am right. "Though He slay me, yet will I trust in Him; / But I will argue my ways before Him." And "I know that I shall be justified" (13:15).

The action is diverted for a while by the unexpected arrival of a fourth interlocutor, a young man who chides both Job and his elderly companions in terms oddly similar to both what precedes and what follows, so similar in fact that most commentators suspect the speeches of Elihu to be a late interpolation. And then the most extraordinary thing happens. God answers Job. God speaks to him from the whirlwind.

> Then the LORD answered Job out of the whirlwind, and said:
> Who is this that darkeneth counsel by words without knowledge?

> Gird up thy loins like a man;
> For I will demand of thee, and declare thou unto Me.
> Where wast thou when I laid the foundations of the earth?
>
> (38:1–4)

How do you answer a question like that? What do you say? Out? I had other things to do? Call me next time? God's opening question is quickly followed by a long series of questions of similar kind regarding the elemental and natural universe. "[W]ho shut up the sea with doors . . . ?" (38:8). "Hast thou commanded the morning since thy days began . . . ?" (38:12). "Canst thou draw out leviathan with a fish-hook?" or yoke behemoth? (40:25). "Whatsoever is under the whole heaven is Mine" (41:3).

And Job's response to this divine effulgence? "Behold, I am of small account; / what shall I answer Thee? / I lay my hand upon my mouth" (40:4).

> I know that Thou canst do everything,
> And . . .
> Therefore have I uttered that which I understood not, . . .
> I had heard of Thee by the hearing of the ear;
> But now mine eye seeth Thee;
> Wherefore I abhor my words, and repent,
> Seeing I am dust and ashes.
>
> (42:2–6)

That is, he appears to put his tail between his legs and, after bowing several times, scurry out of there.

Nor is that all. God now curiously rewards Job's behavior. He reproves Job's three friends, who "have not spoken of Me the thing that is right as My servant Job hath," and blesses "the latter end of Job more than his beginning" (42:7–12). He puts the final icing on the cake, so to speak, paying Job off in public for what appears to be his servile obedience.

I draw attention to this climactic (or anti-climactic) encounter between Job and God in chapters 38–42 in the facetious manner in which I have—somewhat in the manner of a Woody Allen comedy—because that genre seems to me to convey something of the tone this exchange has often elicited for us in the modern world, a tone which suggests that in some important way God's response to Job is deeply inadequate, that God has simply marched out the celestial armed forces, as it were, and bullied Job into submission. "He destroyeth the innocent and the wicked" indiscriminately, Job observes at one point (9:22). And then later, more poignantly, "the just, the innocent man is a laughing-stock" (12:4), while "The tents of robbers prosper, / And they that provoke God are secure" (12:6). "Wherefore do the wicked live, / Become old, yea, wax mighty in power?" (21:7), Job wonders, while the righteous, on the other hand, have become the outcasts of the outcast, and the brothers of jackals (30:8–10).

And what is God's response to these inquiries? "How dare you presume to question Me! Come back when you can do what I can do and then I shall pray to you." Far from proving to be either the God Job has imagined Him to be (who might at least be able to explain—if not to justify—all these things) or even the God of his three friends (who would affirm a more formalistic religious theology in the face of Job's challenge), the God of these final passages seems to signal a return of the God of the prologue, the divinity who set these strange trials in motion to begin with, a God of primitive savage power who would test the loyalty of the righteous on the strength of a Satanic bet. Scholars are quick to note that the divine name employed in these middle verses is the same as that which is employed in the prologue and epilogue but not in the dialogues or the Elihu speeches.[2]

To claim, in other words, that the Book of Job is about the "problem of evil" or human suffering is to claim that in some fundamental way Job's questions resonate more powerfully for us than God's answers, as powerfully and deeply for us in fact within the last two hundred (and especially the last fifty) years of European history as we have to imagine they once did for the exilic or post-exilic historical community from which these words are presumed to have come. If we are puzzled as to how so forceful and radical a challenge to traditional Judaism made its way into the literature of the "Old Testament," we remain content with the surprising fact that it has and compare its presence to that of other texts (Ecclesiastes comes to mind), texts that seem similarly to have escaped the censorship of more formalistic theologies.

Such a reading has certainly not been the only one we have made of the Book. Biblical scholarship—and especially the long nineteenth-century tradition of the so-called "documentary hypothesis"—has been relatively content to regard it as an old story, probably of folkloric origin, that reflects the simple yearnings shared with so much other literature classified as "wisdom" writings—Proverbs and Lamentations, for example. The long tradition of talmudic, midrashic, and later rabbinic writings within the Judaic tradition has commonly regarded God's reply as a matter of mystical faith—the designation of the arena in which an answer to the problem of human suffering is to be found in anticipation of a more satisfying response at a later date, an implicit admonition, in other words, that we glimpse only a part of the total picture and should be cautious in our criticism of it.

But at least since the beginning of the nineteenth century in Europe, more secularized thinkers of the literary and philosophic tradition have felt a less submissive and more openly critical reading to be unavoidable. Christian theologians of course had long turned their attention to this book, finding in it an expression of the inadequacy of the Old Testament God of the Hebrews and a prefigurative anticipation of a New Testament God of love, mercy, and forgiveness for whom such inquiries regarding human justice would be fully answered. In the wake of European Romanticism, while Protestant and even Jewish scholars constructed the so-called "high biblical criticism," these more secularized investigators proposed more deeply unsettling questions that risked doing away with religious perspectives entirely in favor of more humanistic approaches. It is these more secularized accounts that have formed the basis of our modern approach. Jung's famous *Answer to Job* would be one such account.[3]

My intention in the present essay is not to contest so powerful a modern reading, either to replace it with what I would deem a "better" interpretation, or even finally to affirm one or another older interpretation at a higher level of comprehension. In the first place, because one does not challenge so powerful a reading as much as elaborate or explain it. To challenge the reading of the Book of Job as "the problem of suffering" is a little like disproving Freudian psychoanalysis. It has become a part of our language in the West. It seems more fruitful to take account of that fact and ask about its implications. I would also like to avoid challenging our reading of the Book of Job for another reason. Whatever particular value the modern interpretation has for us, it is also endemic to the biblical text itself. It is powerful as a reading, among other reasons, because it makes audible and articulate an interpretive potential already operative within the text, namely, that of Job himself.

Rather than challenge this modern reading, what I would like to do is situate it, elaborate the conditions of its possibility, both within the biblical text and without, which is to say, within the historical context within which that position is constructed. For once we realize that this modern reading is also Job's, we are led to notice other positions within the book, and in particular one other that is at least as powerful as Job's, but that has been subsumed by the former—namely, the position of God.

The God of chapters 38–42 and of the epilogue, I would argue, is identical in character neither to the God of the prologue nor to the God of the three friends, nor to Job's God, and yet we have never seriously listened to His speeches. The speeches are important, I would suggest, not only because of the dramatic situation to which they respond within the story, but also because of the dramatic situation by which we enact that story. If in our interpretive behavior we reproduce Job's position, and remark, for example, that the story itself fails to respond adequately to the exigencies of the modern world, we put the story in the same position that Job puts God. Dismissing the speeches of God is a little like dismissing the Book of Job.

Both God and the Book of Job, I suggest, may have more to say to their respective interlocutors than we suspect. They may in fact both stage for us the relation between such internal and external interlocution, between the primitive, formalist, humanist, and creationist perspectives from which we—along with the characters within—have for so long read the story, indeed in some ways from which we have read the Bible at large. To examine more carefully the encounter between God and Job in chapters 38–42, I will turn to the reflections of three thinkers who have meditated extensively upon these matters and whose words no doubt are already resonating in much of what I have been saying: Martin Buber, Emmanuel Levinas, and René Girard.

II. Colloquies with Friends

No one who approaches biblical study as I do from the vantage point of literary criticism can fail to be struck by the unparalleled service offered to students of the text by Marvin Pope's magistral edition and commentary in the Anchor Bible series. Pope's erudition is uncannily expansive and his knowledge of Ugaritic materials and concerns especially helpful in the present context.

Moreover, his scholarly writing seems to abound in reasonableness and good sense. The text of Job, in all of the received versions, seems particularly mangled in some spots. The most famous examples are the brevity of the third speech of Bildah, the absence of any explicit reference to a third speech of Zophar, and the inappropriateness of a series of remarks that are given to Job and look as if they should belong elsewhere, perhaps even to Zophar. Pope has undertaken to remedy this situation. He has redistributed lines and speeches in these sections with the aim of producing a coherent and continuous narrative order that is, in his words, "the simplest and most satisfactory."[4]

In fact, were the question before us how best to construe the literary or narrative unity of the Book of Job, Pope's answer would seem a perfectly satisfactory one. But in adopting his strategy, I wonder whether we might not be falling into the very trap of which Job accuses his three friends, namely, that of substituting formalistic criteria for the existential facts before us. I wonder whether, in other words, in altering the text as it is given to us, in rearranging it, in making the conclusion tally nicely and symmetrically with the rest of the narrative, we have not reproduced in our scholarly endeavors—our historical and formal enterprises—something of the same judicious calculation that the text we read is examining, a calculation that Job for one finds particularly insensitive to the experiences he has undergone.

I am not suggesting, of course, that the text as we have traditionally received it is better as a narrative organization than Pope's emendations, but rather that perhaps we should give up worrying about narrative organization in this fashion and ask instead how the text has set us up, so to speak, how it invites us in our scholarly and interpretive enterprises to reenact its contents. What is interesting, it seems to me, is not what the Book of Job originally looked like (I am not even sure that question has much meaning in the present context) any more than what was important before was determining which of the two accounts of God in the dialogues—Job's or that of the three friends—is more accurate, but rather what it means for us to undertake such formalistic or interpretive quests at all, and how that behavior parallels or deviates from the very drama we are watching and whose dangers above all the text is prophetically staging for us. Rather than adopt either Pope's text or the received text, let us examine the enabling conditions—the origins, the strategies, the consequences—of any textual or interpretive appropriation, even as the story itself does.

※   ※   ※

For some time now, Martin Buber has occupied a curiously double status within the field of Jewish studies, a field up until recently more univocally dominated, I would suggest, by the more rational and judicious style of Gershom Scholem.[5] Scholem notes that for a long time Buber had been associated with a movement known as "religious existentialism" (and with the movement associated in Europe with the names of Heidegger and Sartre and the notions of nothingness and responsibility). Buber's work in particular on Hasidism, Scholem notes, that last living vestige of Jewish mystical life, had become for the general audience synonymous with Hasidism itself. It was high time, Scholem felt, for a more historical and more critical stance towards these materials, time to recognize, as he put it, that Buber's understanding of Hasidism was in fact only an interpretation, a gesture that made its own subjective selection of materials, and that other understandings, even understandings that offered a more comprehensive view, were possible.

Scholem's position has for the past twenty-five years or so held the day. If Buber is regarded within the Hasidic community as something of a popularizer, he is regarded, curiously enough, within the mainstream of academic Jewish studies as not secular enough, too committed to his position, a position that, in the extreme, is identified with mysticism and emotionalism.

But Scholem's position, I would like to suggest, may have run its course (at least for the time being), and we may be on the verge of a new reversal of the arrangement.[6] After regarding Buber for so long from within a Scholemic perspective, it may be that we are about to view Scholem, and in general the historical and critical perspective of which he is so eminently the representative, from a more critically Buberian approach. Although there is no place here to elaborate the terms of such a reversal, it is already apparent what form it will (and will not) assume. For it may be that this episode is but the latest round in a continuing saga of the battle between Hebraic and Hellenic forces within Judaism, between prophetic thinking and a Platonic essentialism that has characterized thinkers before in Jewish history.

The new arrangement will clearly not take the form of a retreat to a new mysticism or subjectivism (although its opponents may very well designate it as such) but rather a move away from the rational and dialectical oppositions in which such terms are contained (and in which we have spoken for so long). It will be a view, I suggest, less concerned with the differences between rational and irrational ways of organizing the universe than with the continuities between such ratios and other forms of Jewish spiritual life, and in particular with the more primary integrities from which such differential splits have been carved.

❧ ❧ ❧

Buber's essay on the Book of Job, contained within a longer chapter entitled "The God of the Sufferers" in *The Prophetic Faith,* is a good example of this prophetic criticism to come and will set us on our way toward listening to the speeches of God.[7] The wicked prosper and the innocent are slaughtered. That is the experience, Buber asserts, from which the Book of Job is born. It is a supraindividual experience, probably born of the moment of the exile, when the answers pronounced in Deutero-Isaiah and Psalm 73 were not yet part of the tradition, and it is, Buber suggests, a new question, "the first clothing of human quest in the form of speech."[8]

The poem, Buber says, is really four poems, four independent relationships between God and man, strung together by the poet to form a pathway from the first to the last. The first is largely mythological. The faithful sufferer is engaged by the gratuitous God who would wantonly test man to make manifest what He already knows is true. The second is the relationship to God proposed by the three friends, and Buber calls the God of that relation an ideological idol. Here is a rationalistic and calculating God who distributes responses according to a strict system of cause and effect and who is more appropriate to the dogmatics of Ezekiel. Job suffers; therefore, he has sinned. The tight theological imperatives of this system made universal render it for Buber the ashheap of religion when applied as a universal principle, a purpose, Buber claims, for which it was never intended.

The third relationship we observe is that between God and Job. God is now hidden from man, as He is in both Isaiahs, Buber says, and man experiences at once the formal system of divine justice and the reality of human suffering. He believes both in God and the truth of human wickedness around him but does not see how the two will ever be reconciled. He will believe in God despite the fact of suffering, although the abysmal absence of God's presence leads him at times to the brink of despair.

The fourth relationship between God and man provides, Buber suggests, the bridge over that abyss. God now reveals Himself and Job "sees" God, a vision only granted to non-prophetic individuals before on Mount Sinai. Moreover, there is more to this revelation than the announcement either of the mystery of divine order or of the eternal riddle of creation and the natural universe. It is specifically a matter of justice and creation offered to us as revelation. Everything in the universe is set within its appointed boundaries and the fulfillment of those boundaries constitutes a communication between Creator and Creature. God thus reveals Himself *as* the answer to Job's question. In the final sequence Job becomes a *nabi,* a servant of YHVH, just as Abraham, Moses, and David were. He has become God's witness on the earth as God proves his advocate in heaven, the God of sufferers he has long sought.

Buber's essay is extraordinarily rich and suggestive, though it is not immediately clear how all of the arguments he makes cohere. The identification of four distinct relations constituting the "inner dialectic" of the poem seems decisive, as does his suggestion that in some fashion in reading the book we move from one to another, although again it is not precisely clear how that movement takes place. Moreover, although the relation between God and man in the first three relations seems fairly straightforward and reflective of the text we have, the fourth is less so. How precisely is the final section, for example, a matter of justice? How is God's panoramic presentation of differential relations and of natural and elemental power a response to Job's question about human judgment and wickedness? How is the answer constituted in or more precisely *as* the presentation? Is Buber merely repeating the traditional rabbinical response that there is an order to creation although it is incomprehensible and mysterious to man, that it is effectively "in place" although we cannot make judgments on the matter until all the evidence is in, so to speak? How in this manner does Job become God's "witness" on earth, the suffering servant of YHVH, while God becomes the God of the sufferers? Finally, what does it mean to call the question thus answered by the Book of Job a "new" question? Is that not the modern view to which we referred before, that Job represents something of a challenge to a more traditional orthodox theology, the very position that Buber asserts is transcended in the fourth relation?

These three sets of questions, questions of form, of meaning, and of history, will set the stage for our inquiry. What is the logic that impels us from one part of the narrative to another? How is God's discourse on the order of creation in chapters 38–42 a matter of justice and thus an answer to Job? What is the historical status of such creation as a response to human suffering and is the question it answers really a new question? Reading the discourse of chapters 38–42 in these contexts will enable us to situate more precisely the problem that the Book of Job has always posed for us.

❦   ❦   ❦

The work of Emmanuel Levinas, in particular, may offer the turning point. More, perhaps, than anyone else on the contemporary scene, and to a much greater extent than has been appreciated, Levinas picks up where Buber leaves off.[9] Up until very recently, Levinas was probably best known in this country for his work on philosophy through two rather lengthy essays written about him by Jacques Derrida.[10] And yet for years, prior to his coming to teach philosophy at the Sorbonne, Levinas taught in a series of Jewish normal schools in France, the most notable of which is probably the Ecole Normale Israelite Orientale. His many volumes on Jewish studies and biblical and talmudic exegesis attest to the primacy of these concerns in his thinking alongside his more strictly philosophic writings. It is interesting that although most of his philosophic works were translated some time ago, we have only recently translated *Difficile liberté, Quatre lectures talmudiques, Du sacré au saint, L'au-délà du verset,* and *A l'heure des nations.*[11]

Like Buber, Lacan, Sartre, Merleau-Ponty, and so many others of his generation, Levinas was decisively influenced in his intellectual life by the philosophy of Martin Heidegger and in particular Heidegger's ontological reading of Husserlian phenomenology. More than anyone else, perhaps, Levinas has taken upon himself the project of thinking out philosophically the status of religious transcendence, a project already announced in *Totalité et infini.*[12] Divinity, he argues there, must be thought as radically other, as radical externality or alterity. In *Autrement qu'être, ou au-délà de l'essence* and in numerous other works, he discloses such radical alterity on the human plane as responsibility for the other individual and places this notion at the center of both Judaism and of an ontological critique of Platonic essentialism.[13] If we understand this notion in religious terms as the law of anti-idolatry, it will make readable for us the Book of Job.

The particular text of Levinas to which I am going to refer initially, however, does not concern the Book of Job directly but the Holocaust and thus makes overt a concern that is never far from the subject under discussion in Levinas. Everything in my biography, Levinas tells us, in a section of *Difficile liberté* entitled "Signature," "est dominée par le pressentiment et le souvenir de l'horreur nazie," and by the kinds of questions one may raise concerning Judaism and being "le lendemain des exterminations hitleriennes."[14] As that experience stands, however, for

Levinas (and perhaps for us as well) in the place where Job finds his own encounter with the triumph of the wicked, Levinas's remarks in one case may apply in the other.

The particular passage to which I am going to refer is part of an essay entitled "To Love the Torah More than God" ("Aimer le Thora plus que Dieu") and concerns a text reputedly published (anonymously) in an Israeli newspaper and translated into French (by M. Arnold Mandel and for *La Terre retrouvée*) under the title "Yossel, fils de Yossel de Rackover de Tarnopol, parle à Dieu."[15] "The text presents itself to us," Levinas tells us, "as a document, written during the final hours of the Warsaw Ghetto Resistance. The narrator would have been witness to all the horrors; he would have lost his young children under conditions of atrocity. As the last survivor of his family and with only a few moments left, he bequeaths to us his ultimate thoughts."[16]

> What is the meaning of this suffering of the innocent? Does it not bear witness to a world that is without God, to a land where man alone measures Good and Evil? The simplest and most common response to this question would lead to atheism. This is no doubt also the sanest reaction for all those for whom up until a moment ago a God, conceived a bit primitively, distributed prizes, inflicted sanctions or pardoned faults, and in His kindness treated human beings as eternal children. But with what narrow-minded demon, with what strange magician did you thus populate your sky, you who now declare it to be deserted? And why under such an empty sky do you continue to seek a world that is meaningful and good?
>
> Yossel ben Yossel reveals to us the certitude of God with a new force under an empty sky. For if he exists so alone, it is in order to feel upon his shoulders all the responsibilities of God. On the path that leads to the unique God there is a relay point which is without God. True monotheism must respond to the legitimate exigencies of atheism. A God of adults manifests Himself precisely through (*par*) the emptiness of the sky of a child. This is a moment when God withdraws from the world and conceals His face (according to Yossel ben Yossel).[17]

The Holocaust, in other words, according to Levinas, like the experience of Job, could lead us to conclude in atheism, if we were to imagine a God who distributed awards and punishments, such as the God of Job's three friends. But who said God was like that? It is only by positing such a God to begin with—and thus distorting Judaism—that we can arrive at such a conclusion. The absence of God in the world or in the sky, the concealment of God behind a veil, far from signifying His non-existence, is itself the surest proof, in fact the certitude, *of* that existence. For it is this very absence of God to the world that confers upon man all responsibility for his own existence, his own destiny. It is not that there is no God, but that there is no God to the world. That is the meaning of the law of anti-idolatry, of the externality or radical alterity of transcendence. We must function *as if* there is no God, as if all responsibility for human behavior and human relations falls upon man himself. That is what it means to be an adult as opposed to being a child and to have a religion of adults rather than a religion of eternal childhood. The possibility of atheism is the necessary step in the process of assuming responsibility for one's own behavior. This is the meaning of the hidden God who conceals Himself behind a veil.

Thus Levinas has answered Job's complaint in the very terms that Buber describes it. The hidden God, "le Dieu qui se voile," far from a stumbling block to Job's lament, is in fact its very answer, an answer we may want to argue God explicitly reveals by appearing to offer Job the discourse of His otherness, His exteriority to man.

But Levinas continues. And in a brilliant series of remarks extends this analysis of the hidden God to the precise terms of Job's human experience of justice, an experience of suffering and of victimage.

> A God who conceals His face is not, I think, a theological abstraction or a poetic image. It is a way of talking about the hour when the just individual no longer finds any external recourse, when no institution protects him, when the consolation of divine presence in childish religious sentiment is similarly of no avail, when the individual can no longer triumph except in his own consciousness (*conscience*), which is to say, necessarily in suffering; a specifically Jewish sense of suffering which never at any moment assumes the value of a mystical expiation for the sins of the world. The condition of being a victim (*le position des victimes*) in a world in disorder, which is to say, in a world where the good does not triumph, *is* suffering. It reveals a God who, renouncing all helpful manifestation, appeals to the full maturity of the integrally responsible man.... The suffering of the just for a justice that is without triumph is lived concretely *as* Judaism. Israel—historic and carnal—has become once again a religious category (italics added).

The God of Judaism is neither the simple-minded God of the three friends and their abstract theology, nor the hidden God of Job and his poetic imagery, but a God who confers complete responsibility for our own actions upon the integrally responsible man, the man who gives up the perspective of a child and assumes upon his shoulders the responsibility for full consciousness. And that consciousness precisely is always necessarily one of suffering.

Suffering, in other words, within the Jewish perspective is not a mystical purgation or substitution for the sins of the world, but a reading from the position of the victim, which is to say, from the position of one who is in the midst of struggle, a struggle in which justice does not triumph, in which what triumphs, perhaps, are precisely the childish perspectives of the friends or the atheistic and nihilistic perspectives of the Jobs who carry their own position to an extreme (and who are thus the negatives of the perspective of the friends). Suffering is the consciousness gained from the victim that finds the certitude of God in His seeming absence and thus which enables that responsibility which escapes childishness and atheism to be assumed.

The answer to Job's question, in other words, for Levinas, is Judaism itself. The God of the sufferers (to use Buber's phrase) is the Jewish God, and has in fact never been any other. If we have imagined the Jewish God to be other—and thus able to be scandalized by the existence of evil or of human suffering in the world—it is because it is we who have distorted Him in conceptualizing Him as such to begin with. Far from it being the case that Judaism is scandalized by evil or human suffering, radical evil and human suffering are that to which Judaism and the Jewish God have always already been a response by definition, as it were. The Jewish God is the God of suffering par excellence and only by substituting for that God another candidate have we been able to pose our problem at all, a problem with which we then ironically charge God! "The suffering of the just for a justice that is without triumph," Levinas writes, "is lived concretely *as* Judaism."

In certain ways Levinas has thus constructed an answer to at least one of the questions raised by Buber. The Jewish God is the God of the sufferers, the God of victims par excellence. The "hidden God" leads not to despair and the abyss Job feared but to revelation, to the revelation of the hidden God *as* the answer. The God of chapters 38–42 who shows up and speaks largely of the creative order is the speaking of the hidden God, the showing up, so to speak, of the impossibility of God showing up. But Levinas's reading has also constructed for us an answer—and, moreover, a rather unexpected one—to another of Buber's questions. If the Jewish God, in Levinas's reading, has never not been the God of the victims, Job's question is not "new" at all. Judaism is in fact already a response to precisely such a crisis or world in "disorder." If it appears "new" to Buber it can only be because Buber, like Job, in this capacity at least, has in some way already displaced that primary and fundamental identity.

At the same time, Levinas's analysis raises new questions. How is the God who discourses on nature, the elements, and the creative order of the universe this same God of suffering? Is it simply a matter of discourses on the "otherness" of God from human relations, a kind of negative of man as we hinted earlier might be argued? Otherwise than being in Levinas's terms is not being's other but otherwise than the ontological question itself. Moreover, apart from Job's experience of evil and of suffering, how is it specifically an experience of victimage? We realize that Job may be regarded as the victim of God (or of Satan) and of the argument of his three friends. But how is he the victim on the human level in the fundamental and foundative way in which Levinas speaks? And thirdly, of course, we have not yet answered the questions of literary or narrative form.

❦ ❦ ❦

For the answer to this second question—a startlingly new answer within Jewish studies—we turn to the extraordinary work of René Girard. All his intellectual life, Girard has concerned himself in one context or another, with the problematic effects of desire and human violence. In his earliest book, *Mensonge romantique et vérité romanesque,* he argued that mimetic desire—the imitative appropriation of the desire of another and the violence and conflict into which it issues—proves the motor force of all of the great European novelists (from Cervantes and Stendhal to Flaubert, Proust, and Dostoyevsky) both within their books and within the circumstances that produced those books.[18]

In *La violence et le sacré* Girard extends this analysis to human cultures designated by anthropologists as "primitive."[19] Religion functions in these communities, he suggests, to keep violence out, to transcendentalize it, to make it "sacred." The mechanism for the expulsion of violence specifically is sacrifice, in particular, sacrificial substitution, the collective transfer of a generalized reciprocal violence against a unique member of the community who is perceived in the wake of his removal as different from others but who has been in fact a human double, an enemy twin, a surrogate victim.

In *Des choses cachées depuis la fondation du monde,* and *Le bouc émis-*

saire, Girard carries this analysis to its natural conclusion in our own culture in the modern era.[20] How has it become possible within our own culture to understand such mechanisms of cultural production and structuration? The answer for Girard is the Judeo-Christian tradition that reveals to us the full operation of violence and its generative and degenerative effects. From one end to the other, the Judeo-Christian Bible is a deconstruction of sacrificial victimage, a movement that culminates in the Christian Passion. Jesus offers himself, in Girard's reading, not as a substitute for our sins which purchases salvation on our behalf (which would be but a new way of sacrificially misunderstanding that offer) but as a way of revealing prophetically to us where our violence is going in order that we may give it up.

In *La route antique des hommes pervers* Girard extends this analysis backward to the Book of Job.[21] We have never read seriously the long middle section, the dialogues, of the Book of Job, he tells us. We have never heard the real object of Job's complaints, which is not the ills that come from the outside, the failure of God to account for evil or human suffering (as we have traditionally understood those passages), but the ills arising from purely human origins.

> Unto me men gave ear, and waited,
> And kept silence for my counsel.
> After my words they spoke not again;
> And my speech dropped upon them.
> And they waited for me as for the rain;
> And they opened their mouth wide as for the latter rain.
> If I laughed on them they believed it not;
> And the light of my countenance they cast not down.
> I chose out their way, and sat as their chief,
> And dwelt as a king in the army,
> As one that comforteth the mourners.
> (29:21–25)

Job was the sought-after of the sought-after, the communal mediator or model of desire. He "chose out their way and sat as their chief." But then suddenly God's affliction strikes and all that is changed.

> But now they that are younger than I have me in derision,
> Whose fathers I disdained to set with the dogs of my flock . . .
> They are the children of churls, yea, the children of ignoble men;
> They were scourged out of the land.
> And now I am become their song,
> Yea, I am become a byword unto them.

> They abhor me, they flee far from me,
> And spare not to spit in my face . . .
> I am become a brother to jackals,
> And a companion to ostriches.
>
> (30:1, 8–10, 29)

From the center of the circle Job has been projected to its outermost reaches. He has become, suddenly, the expelled of the expelled, the outcast of outcasts, alien even to the human community itself. These are not idle images, Girard suggests, conventional descriptions that the author of this book has included to give dimension to the suffering Job is experiencing. These are realistic reflections on the course of human relations from someone who has lived thoroughly within them. From the object of communal admiration, Job has become (as a consequence of the arbitrary imposition of disaster upon his life from the outside) the victim of those around him, their scapegoat, the one they blame for the troubles they are currently experiencing.

And yet rather than hear Job's complaint, Girard suggests, we have concerned ourselves with other aspects of his situation, with the actions, for example, of God in setting the conditions in which such behavior occurs. Not unlike Job's friends, in other words, we have substituted something else for the analysis Job is offering us. We have even outdone the friends in this substitution since we discredit what he is saying in the course of pretending to credit it. We conceal the displacement we effect behind a feigned attention to him while the friends at least denounce him openly by attributing the source of his misfortunes—through a chain of cause and effect—to God.

Girard's reading of these passages, I would suggest, is an extraordinarily subtle one, all the more so because a critique of victimage is what by now we have come to expect from his readings. While we might have expected the identification of the processes of sacrificial substitution with which he works so extensively elsewhere, what is surprising is how powerfully his ideas open up for us lines which are entirely familiar. Within the above parameters they offer us a trenchant and decisive analysis of lines we have rarely read before in this fashion.

Moreover, in context of the present discussion, his suggestions make explicit for us the ways in which the long central colloquies bear out (thematically at least) what Buber and Levinas have been saying. The perspective of the victim, the consciousness of a justice which is without triumph and which is the experience of suffering (*la souffrance*), is not the experience of an outside intervention but of a form of sacrificial behavior originating entirely from within human relations. That reading enables us to further refine what it would mean to listen to the God of chapters 38–42. It would be in particular to listen to a God for whom the creative order of the universe is itself the answer to the question of human suffering conceived as a matter of human victimage. It would be, to use Girard's words now, to identify "un Dieu des victimes."

Curiously enough, however, the God of chapters 38–42 for Girard is not such a "Dieu des victimes." After reading the central sections with unmatched brilliance and pursuing a more radical approach to them than anyone, Girard returns in his consideration of chapters 38–42 and the epilogue to the most conservative position of all.[22]

Here is the full passage in Yvonne Freccero's translation:

> The God who finally breaks silence and answers Job "from the heart of the tempest" does not make the slightest allusion to the questions posed in these two passages (16:19–21 and 19:25–27), or to Job's protestations of innocence. He does not seem to understand that Job is the victim of his community; or perhaps he is pretending. Job, for his part, is an individual who is engaged in a metaphysical protest without valid reason. With this speech, he cuts short the whole problematic of the scapegoat. This God poses the problem in the deceptive way that has prevailed ever since: he pushes aside anything that has to do with Job's relations with his community—the best way of neutralizing the subversive force of Job's speech. The words remain, but their meaning becomes almost inaccessible. This is much more effective than reducing Job to silence by a too-obvious physical violence.
>
> To escape the formidable hornet's nest of human relationships, this God takes refuge in nature. . . . A little astronomy, a little meteorology, and a lot of zoology. . . . The poetry of this bestiary should not conceal from us that it constitutes a display of irresistible power. This God demonstrates his strength so as not to have to use it. He is no longer the God of the friends, who openly oppresses against scapegoats. He no longer brandishes the celestial armies against the rebel.
>
> He resorts to cunning and wins his case: Job is finally docile and silent, full of terrified admiration for the ostrich and Leviathan. . . . It is difficult to take this farce seriously.[23]

The God who speaks to Job in Girard's view is little more than the God of the prologue, the God of ruses and of the celestial armed forces, a divine "charlatan" (209) and "hypocrite" (209) who bullies Job—less overtly perhaps than by subterfuge—into submission, in short, the God of our modern reading who fails to understand anything about evil or about human suffering or of its foundation in human violence.

Why should Girard avoid the identification which seems so evident in context of the argument he has been making? The one thinker who has gone further than anyone else to reveal the sacrificial dynamics of cultural life and who identifies in particular the biblical tradition as the repository for that revelation, becomes curiously sacrificial and expulsive at the one moment from which the misunderstanding of Job's humanism—indeed, the humanism from which we must assume the Book itself emerged—might itself be revealed. It would seem too facile to argue that Girard discredits the revelatory power of the God of chapters 38–42 because at this moment in the text another candidate for a "Dieu des victimes" suggests itself to him. But there may be a way in which Girard's abrogation of the analysis he himself has so powerfully inaugurated nonetheless points us to a larger issue concerning the relation of Judaic to Christian thinking about these matters.

For within the Gospel text as Girard reads it, it is precisely from the Judaic that Jesus draws his most profound inspiration. To obscure one of the moments within the Judaic in which the "Dieu des victimes" becomes the most explicit (in Girard's sense) is to obscure in effect the condition from which Girard will later derive the Christian itself, to render the Christian in other words originary in a manner Girard will later explicitly repudiate. If Jesus is particularly powerful for us, Girard tells us in *Des choses cachées,* it is because he is "prophetic" in the Jewish sense, because he shows us where our violence is leading, offering us his own body as a "teaching tool" so to speak, because he announces the end of the sacrificial and violent road upon which we are traveling, a lesson Girard feels that has in fact already begun to be revealed to us within the Hebrew Scriptures but that has never before been announced overtly or carried to its completion. It is not for the sake of the Judaic in other words, I would suggest, that Girard needs to read chapters 38–42 as revelatory but rather for the efficacy of his reading of the Christian Gospels as he himself so powerfully opens them up for us.

What does Jesus have, in Girard's view, as a "Dieu des victimes" that the God of chapters 38–42 does not? Here we touch upon what may in fact be the central concern of this Book for both Jewish and Christian readers alike. In the distinction Girard makes between the two figures we may begin to see in a more focused way the stakes of both. The disqualification in Girard's view of the earlier figure is that he fails to take up the question of the scapegoat mechanism in the manner of the latter. In its place, Girard asserts, the God of chapters 38–42 offers us the panorama of the elemental and natural universe, the panorama of the order of creation. Such a God remains for Job, in the final account in Girard's reading, not the God of victims, but the God of ostriches.

But what if the God of ostriches is the God of victims? "I am become a brother to jackals," Job says, in the passage Girard quotes, "And a companion to ostriches." Job doesn't like ostriches. He feels he shouldn't have to live with them. He wants to remain among the in-crowd, the beautiful people, all of whom once regarded him as their model. "But now they that are younger than I have me in derision," he says, "Whose fathers I disdained to set with the dogs of my flock." What if God's communication to Job couched in terms of the elemental and animal universe (the "dogs of [his] flock") is a deconstructive one, suggesting that in rejecting the ostriches he is in some way rejecting God of victims, identifying himself privately with the very persecutors and predators whose ways he would publicly denounce?

In other words, what if Job's words in 16 and 19 reveal the scapegoat mechanism as Girard so powerfully shows (although Job has no cognizance of that revelation and says what he says simply because he wants back the power and admiration he lacks), and God's presentation of the creational order of chapters 38–42 extends the exposition of that scapegoat mechanism, not by implementing it as Girard suggests, but by revealing it, a revelation that proceeds not through theme certainly but through effect, through a prophetic demonstration of its very expansiveness and power? What if, in short, far from a mythic superimposition upon the revelation of sacrificial substitution in the dialogues, these passages are, via the law of anti-idolatry, an extension of the question of human suffering and justice in *precisely the terms* in which we have now come to understand their sacrificial implication (viz. creation), an extension or extremity we have barred ourselves from observing by the ways in which we have conceived of the difference between creation on the one hand and suffering or victimage on the other.

How so? We are accustomed to localizing creation diachronically as a unique event at the outset of history, an event that took place once and for all, and that remains now a part of the primeval past. By the same token, we are accustomed to isolating suffering or victimage synchronically as an alternative that is distinguishable from among other possibilities (and in particular the possibility of not suffering). In thus separating creation from suffering, have we not constructed a system of differentiation that is already the product of the very history it is being called upon to trace? Have we not, in short, adopted the distinctly Christian postulate that we enter history posthumously in order then to account historically for the passage from the Judaic to the Christian?

Girard's analyses, in other words, even by virtue of the curious turn they take at this point, would seem to lead us to the door of a much more radical reading and identification than we have before been willing to make, one that is fully in keeping with the necessities of his own argument, one which, taken in context of Buber and Levinas, will enable us to answer all the questions we have raised in this essay relative to the Book of Job.

III. Interpolated Prophetic Wisdom

The key to opening that door, I suggest, will be the notion of anti-idolatry and a text that may help to focus that notion for us in the Judaic context is the text of Deutero-Isaiah. The text of Deutero-Isaiah, the Book of the Consolation of Israel, is hardly foreign to the reader of Job. Although Buber suggests that Deutero-Isaiah cannot yet have been part of the traditional response to the problems raised there (any more than Psalm 73 can have been), most scholars would date the text to coincide roughly with the Babylonian exile and nothing we have said so far would reject that suggestion. What is clear is that all three texts have come from the same general crisis, the crisis out of which the Hebrew scriptural canon itself was born.

Moreover, were we to ask more broadly if there were a candidate in Hebrew scripture who would fulfill the exigencies with which we would constrain the God of chapters 38–42, our task would have been much simpler. For we then should simply have turned straightaway to chapters 52–53 of Deutero-Isaiah and the fourth song of the suffering servant of YHVH to find all these elements in evidence.[24]

> He was despised, and forsaken of men,
> A man of pains, and acquainted with disease,
> And as one from whom men hide their face:
> He was despised, and we esteemed him not.
> Surely our diseases he did bear, and our pains he carried;
> Whereas we did esteem him stricken,
> Smitten of God, and afflicted.

> But he was wounded because of our transgressions,
> He was crushed because of our iniquities:
> The chastisement of our welfare was upon him,
> And with his stripes we were healed.
>
> (53:3–5)

All of the elements of Girard's theory of sacrificial structuration and victimage are there. The victim is a marginal member of the community, one "acquainted with disease." The victim is generally rejected and expelled. He was "despised and we esteemed him not." And in the process of his removal from the community we attributed the violence we were inflicting upon him to biological or supernatural origins—to disease or God—but never to ourselves. Thus we "did esteem him stricken, smitten of God, and afflicted." But in fact the violence was our own, human violence. He was "wounded because of our transgressions . . . our iniquities." And in his removal our communal bonds were strengthened. "With his stripes we were healed."

Moreover, the relationship of the suffering servant to God and to creation is also clear. God, Judaism, and suffering are perfectly in harmony in this poem. The relation is primarily eschatological and refers to a moment of a new covenant when Israel shall become a "light of nations" and so the passage describes at once the relation between the faithful and a God of the sufferers and the final redemptive form of a historical order that began with the Creation.

The term in which these two notions—creation and suffering—seems to be commonly grounded is that of the Law itself, the law of anti-idolatry. Throughout the Book of the Consolation of Israel, the creation of the universe, anti-idolatry, and the redemptive power of the Jewish God in the midst of suffering of the exile are profoundly identified:

> Who hath measured the waters in the hollow of his hand,
> And meted out heaven with the span,
> And comprehended the dust of the earth in a measure,
> And weighed the mountains in scales,
> And the hills in a balance? . . .
> To whom then will ye liken God?
> Or what likeness will ye compare unto Him?
> The image perchance, which the craftsman hath melted,
> And the goldsmith spread over with gold,
> The silversmith casting silver chains? . . .
> Know ye not? hear ye not?

> Hath it not been told you from the beginning?
> Have ye not understood the foundations of the earth?
> (Is. 40:12–21)

He "who hath measured the waters in the hollow of his hand" is the same God to which no one or nothing may be "likened." These verses are extremely powerful and they are only a very small portion of a great many. The insistence, the urgency with which they speak of our lack of knowledge, as well as the thematic content that rhetorical urgency envelops, must strike us as familiar. "Hast thou not known? Hast thou not heard? / That the everlasting God, the LORD, / The Creator of the ends of the earth, / Fainteth not, neither is weary?" (Is. 40:28).

> Remember this, and stand fast;
> Bring it to mind, O ye transgressors.
> Remember the former things of old.
> That I am God, and there is none else;
> I am God, and there none like Me;
> Declaring the end from the beginning,
> And from ancient times things that are not yet done.
> (Is. 46:8–10)

But this same God "who laid the foundations of the earth," is included with a "Book of the Consolation of Israel."

> Comfort ye, comfort ye My people,
> Saith your God.
> Bid Jerusalem take heart,
> And proclaim unto her, that her time of service is accomplished,
> That her guilt is paid off;
> That she hath received of the LORD's hand
> Double for all her sins . . .
> Thus saith the LORD, Thy Redeemer,
> The Holy One of Israel;
> I am the LORD thy God,
> Who teacheth thee for thy profit,
> Who leadeth thee by the way that thou shouldest go.
> Oh that thou wouldest hearken to My commandments!
> Then would thy peace be as a river,
> And thy righteousness as the waves of the sea;
> Thy seed also would be as the sand,
> And the offspring of thy body like the grains thereof;
> His name would not be cut off
> Nor destroyed from before Me.
> Go ye forth from Babylon,

> Flee ye from the Chaldeans;
> With a voice of singing
> Declare ye, tell this,
> Utter it even to the end of the earth;
> Say ye: "The LORD hath redeemed
> His servant Jacob." . . .
> There is no peace,
> Saith the LORD concerning the wicked.
> (Is. 40:1–2; 48:17–22)

Like Job, Israel (or Jacob) will receive "double" for her sins if only she will follow the commandments and live a life of Torah, which is to say, a life of anti-idolatry. The Abrahamic promise is available at any and every moment. It is available since we participate with God in creation by living such a life. On the other hand, the end of the wicked is also available. "For lo," says the psalmist, "those who are far from Thee shall perish; Thou dost put an end to those who are false to Thee" (Ps. 27). A life of anti-idolatry is by the same token the way in which Judaism has devised to live in the face of suffering. To question suffering as a problem is to question Judaism, to question the law of anti-idolatry, to question creation itself, which is constituted in Judaism as a response to that problem.

But Isaiah 53 is not Job 38–42 and so while we may turn to Deutero-Isaiah for confidence that Judaism can conceive a compatible relation between creation and suffering via Torah, that confidence does not explain for us specifically the Book of Job and it is to that text that we must now return.

IV. The Meeting

The exchange between God and Job takes the form of two colloquies. God speaks (38:1–40:2) and Job replies (40:3–5). God speaks again (40:6–41:34) and Job answers a second time (42:1–6). Moreover, there is a progressive pattern discernible in both God's speech and Job's reply. God speaks initially of creation (the foundations of the earth, the sea, the morning, death, light, and darkness), of the elemental universe (snow, hail, wind, rain, ice, stars, clouds, lightning), and of the animal universe (the lion, the raven, the goat, the wild ass, the wild ox, the ostrich, the horse, the hawk, and the eagle). And in the second speech, as if continuing this enumeration, he speaks of man (and Job in particular), of land creatures more powerful than Job (behemoth), and of creatures of the sea more powerful than Job (leviathan). Job, in his first reply, says, "I am insignificant, I have no answer, I have spoken before but I will not do so again." And in his second reply, as if in annotation of the first, he asserts "I know You can do these things (and I am insignificant and have no answer for You) and that I spoke in ignorance (when I spoke before) and I will not do so again." And he adds, "Before I spoke about God from hearsay. But now I see you face to face and I despise myself and repent 'in dust and ashes.'"

Beyond the thematic content of these colloquies, however, what is clear is the rhetorical structure in which they are embedded. "Who is this that darkens counsel by words without knowledge?" God says initially. "Gird up your loins like a man, and I will question you and you shall declare to Me." The response that God makes is understood in the first instance, by God at least, as a direct response to what Job has been saying, a response that God feels will correct what He perceives to be an error or misapprehension on Job's part and that will uncover Job's strategies, whether or not Job is aware of them. "Now I will do what you have been doing but I think it will go less well for you than it has for Me." If there is an evasion on God's part (as we have traditionally said), it is not one that God has intentionally undertaken. His intention is to answer Job point for point, moreover, in the very terms in which Job has posed the challenge—whether or not we are finally satisfied with that answer, which is another question.

What is God's answer? In the answer He gives, God appears to lay out a panorama of the created order of the universe as a rhetorical attack upon the illegitimate appropriation of knowledge and power that Job in his view has undertaken. In the first discourse, this attack concerns mainly what Job presumes to know. "Where were you when I laid the foundations of the earth? Tell me if you have understanding (as your position would seem to imply). Who determined its position—surely you know!" Or later, "Have the gates of death been revealed to you, or have you seen the gates of deep darkness (as your words seem to imply)? Have you comprehended the expanse of the earth? Declare if you know all this."

In the second discourse, particularly in His opening address to Job, God attacks more specifically what forces Job presumes to wield.

> Gird up thy loins now like a man;
> I will demand of thee, and declare thou unto Me.
> Wilt thou even make void My judgment?

> Wilt thou condemn Me, that thou mayest be justified?
> Or hast thou an arm like God?
> And canst thou thunder with a voice like Him?
> Deck thyself now with majesty and excellency,
> And array thyself with glory and beauty . . .
> And tread down the wicked in their place . . .
> Then will I also confess unto thee
> That thine own right hand can save thee.
>
> (40:7–14)

This is pretty strong language. In questioning Me, God appears to say, in accusing Me as if we were together in a court of law where you were the plaintiff and I the defendant, you have put yourself in My place. You have usurped My position. Quite apart from the merit of your argument, in the way in which you have responded you have assumed that you know what I know and that you can do what I can do as a condition for mounting your accusations in the first place.

Has Job been doing that? How has Job been claiming omniscience or attempting to wield divine power? In the face of extreme adversity, an adversity that we have seen, moreover, to be of deliberate and unsavory origins (although Job doesn't know those origins), Job has called upon God to defend His own system of justice. He has not challenged the existence of God or even the efficacy of His justice as He might well have done; he has simply suggested that the grand design of such justice remains somewhat obscured. Could you clarify things for me a little? Job asks. Provoking Job in the extreme, and eliciting from him little more than a grumbling about his circumstances—"I call upon God to defend me against God," Job says at one point—God responds, it seems as if Job were about to steal the whole show.

Little wonder then that we have found God's words to be inadequate, as the words of a threatened child or obdurate parent more than those of the ruler and creator of the universe, or that we have felt Job's questions to linger beyond God's reply and felt the need to pose again the questions God seems not to have heard. Far from answering Job's questions about human justice and suffering, God would seem eager to pull rank upon him, to attack his right to ask such a question at all.

But what if God has heard Job? What if God's response is less an attack upon Job's right to speak than an analysis of the interrogation itself? What if, in a way we have not yet perceived, Job *has* in fact displaced God, usurped His position, less by conscious declaration than by the structure of presuppositions upon which his questioning depends?

In proclaiming God's response to be evasive, we have always presumed Job's questioning to be innocent. We have presumed that justice remains to be explained no less than Job has. But what if God is right, and if, in adopting Job's position (inside or outside of the text), we have obscured the presuppositions of our *own* interpretive appropriation, presuppositions in which we have already settled in advance (and adversely to God) the very questions we would then presume to ask?

Moreover, and perhaps most importantly, what if the tone in which we have constructed God's response to Job is skewed, if God is not speaking as Zeus throwing down lightning or even Odysseus closing the gates upon the suitors but in a tone somewhat closer to the "still small voice" of which Buber speaks after the Holocaust? God's response may be less confrontational and Job's behavior more questionable than we have allowed ourselves to perceive.

Suddenly, the whole series of forays we have made into the work of Buber, Levinas, and Girard appears decisive. For what have each of these thinkers been arguing in one fashion or another if not that Judaism has never not been an answer to precisely the questions Job has raised, that Judaism is constituted already, as it were, as a response to human suffering? Has not the Jewish God for Buber been par excellence "the God of the sufferers?" Has not God for Levinas been conceived as radically other than the world—by definition, so to speak—so that the responsibilities of man for his own actions, for his own suffering, and consequently his own salvation, are made available to him? "The suffering of the just for a justice which is without triumph," writes Levinas, "is lived concretely *as* Judaism" (italics added). And is not Judaism for Girard, and in particular the Book of Job (at least if we subtract chapters 38–42), the deconstruction par excellence of sacrificial thinking (even if Job remains unaware of it as such), and of the thinking that for Girard produces suffering in human culture, which is to say, mimetic desire and a crisis of victimage?

In asking the questions he asks, in other words, God would then be suggesting to Job that Job has already displaced the answer he seeks, the answer already fully available to him within Judaism itself, and that in displacing that answer he has displaced Judaism as well. To assume that there is a question to be asked is already to have displaced the answer Judaism would provide, the answer that is constituted as Judaism, which is to say, as the law of anti-idolatry. It is not in questioning human suffering or God's justice that Job's response is problematic but rather in assuming that it has not always already been questioned, in dismissing implicitly the questioning and answers that Judaism has always already offered to those questions, an interrogation and response that are in fact constitutive of Judaism. To the extent that we persist in reading the Book of Job as "the problem of evil" we continue to do the same. Perhaps this is what the rabbis really mean when they say that Job is not Jewish.

There is a second half to God's response. It is not simply in challenging Job's presuppositions that God's words respond to him. In obscuring the primary identification of Judaism with a response to suffering, we obscure what follows from that identification; we assume that since Job's question is genuine, God's response must be disingenuous. God must be pulling rank. God's response continues, and in the second portion of it we come to understand more fully His introduction of the created order. What God has told Job in the first instance is that he has usurped the role of Judaism, substituted another ethical system for the one Judaism provides, a humanistic system founded above all on the primacy of suffering as viewed from within the universe of which it is also a part.

In the second instance what God tells him—and here is our particular contribution to this discussion—is that such a course of action is acceptable, that Job can do that if he wishes to do so (it has certainly been done before), but that he may wish to consider what follows from such a gesture. Namely, he might want to consider that since what is implicated in Judaism is not only human suffering but the entire created order, he had better be ready to replace that created order as well. Is Job fully confident, God wonders, that his new system of justice will effectively take care, for example, of the monsters of the sea and of the land (leviathan and behemoth). If not, then perhaps he had better not go forward with this plan of his or not go forward so quickly. If he does not have a way of dealing with the natural universe, then the world will surely collapse in an instant.

The implications of this identification—between Judaism and a critique of human suffering on the one hand, and between Job's questioning and a suppression of Judaism on the other—are far-reaching and will enable us to answer all of the questions that we have raised. The God of chapters 38–42, I would suggest, stages prophetically the sacrificial implications of Job's position in order that Job might assume responsibility for his words and that position and choose to implement their consequences or not as he wishes. Far from evasive, God's words in this context would seem a direct response to the position Job has articulated.

God has staged diachronically the implications of that position. Here is where you have come from, here is what your strategies are, and here is where you are going. Are sure you want to do that and to go there?

If there is an evasion to be observed in these matters, it would seem to be less that of God in this context than that of Job. God mirrors Job's own questioning process, just as in part God's words echo the speeches of Elihu to Job—although the speeches of Job's younger adversary do not extend these words to their implications for creation. In fact, to the extent that we read God as pulling rank, we read Him as simply a supernatural Elihu, which is another reason the question of the panorama of the created order is so important in this connection. It is the revelation of the creative order that makes explicit the diachronic continuity of a gesture Job would imagine as synchronic—namely, the identification of suffering as a problem. Suffering is a perspective in Levinas's words, one, moreover, that is part and parcel of the creation of the universe, and the creation of the universe is similarly both a discrete historical gesture located in diachronic relation to the present and yet available to us at each and every moment via the law of anti-idolatry, the Law of Torah.[25]

In fact, via the Judaic Law, suffering and the creative order of the universe are two sides of the same Judaic coin, or perhaps more precisely, the same side of a Judaic conceptualization that can only be conceived in the manner of a Möbius strip in which what appears at every point to be another side (and separated from the same side by an "edge" that is not traversable) is in fact—through a twist that is difficult to perceive—the future or the past of where you are. The twist in the case of Judaism is the notion of anti-idolatry and perhaps at this point, in an effort to further clarify what we are suggesting, it would be helpful to consider briefly this enigmatic and foundative notion.

✻ ✻ ✻

The revelation of the creative order of the universe is a revelation of the identity between Judaism and a critique of human suffering only if there is a common ground between them, a missing middle term that we have not previously identified. I would suggest there is and that the common ground is the notion of anti-idolatry.

It is clear immediately, I think, how Judaism as a response to suffering and wickedness is constituted as an extension of the law of anti-idolatry. The law of anti-idolatry, the radical otherness or alterity of divinity to the world and to being in the world, as Levinas explains that idea, is the Jewish Law par excellence. "I am the LORD, thy God," say the *aseret hadibrot,* the Ten Commandments, "Thou shalt have no other Gods before Me." Monotheism and anti-paganism are thoroughly interpenetrated by each other, as we have suggested in an earlier chapter. Judaism is monotheistic if and only if the Jewish God is conceived as other than the stone Gods of pagan worship. The history of God as supreme being or as having any of the attributes medieval scholasticism consigns to this figure is a non-Jewish history.

Moreover, this anti-idolatrous God is everywhere presented as the Redeemer of Israel. The place of the wicked, says the psalmist in Psalm 73, is "slippery."

> ... as for me, my feet were almost gone;
> My steps had well nigh slipped.
> For I was envious at the arrogant,
> When I saw the prosperity of the wicked.
> For there are no pangs at their death,
> And their body is sound.
> In the trouble of man they are not;
> Neither are they plagued like men.
> Therefore pride is as a chain around their neck;
> Violence covereth them as a garment.
> Their eyes stand forth from fatness;
> They are gone beyond the imaginations of their heart.
> They scoff and in wickedness utter oppression;
> They speak as if there were none on high.
> They have set their mouth against the heavens,
> And their tongue walketh through the earth ...
> Surely in vain have I cleansed my heart,
> And washed my hands in innocency;
> For all the day have I been plagued,
> And my chastisement came every morning ...
> And when I pondered how I might know this,
> It was wearisomeness in mine eyes;
> Until I entered into the sanctuary of God,
> And *considered their end.*
> Surely Thou settest them in slippery places;
> And hurlest them down to utter ruin.
> How they are become a desolation in a moment!
> They are wholly consumed by terrors (italics added).
>   (Ps. 73:2–19)

The speaker of the poem could be Job. And it is not hard to see how Buber could have seen in this text and portions of Deutero-Isaiah echoes of Job. Only if you return to the way of the LORD and abandon the way of sin—which means in this case reading from the beginning to the end—will you escape the fate of evil men. And even then there is no guarantee. The anti-idolatrous God is the God of repentance or *teshuvah*, the God of turning back, the God who commands you to recognize the path you have been following in order that you may give it up.

Likewise the creative power of the universe is also a matter of anti-idolatry. Here perhaps is where my view will sound most different from familiar academic accounts. In the midrashic literature, the Torah—the law of anti-idolatry—is one of the seven entities said to be present before the creation of the world. Torah in this literature is considered a kind of guidebook, a "blueprint" or model, a kind of computer manual, in context of which the creation of the world actually takes place. The world, the rabbis are fond of saying, is created in accordance with Torah.

Even in more familiar accounts, the creative act itself is understood as a matter of anti-idolatry, the radical separation of God from the world. The very conception of creation, as it appears, for example, in Genesis—the separation of the heavens from the earth, the waters above from the waters below, the seas from dry land, and so forth—may be construed as the inverse of the separation of God from man. The very first creative act registered for us in Rashi's account—*vayomer elohiym y'hiy-or vay'hiy-or* ("And God said 'Let there be light.' And there was light" [Gen. 1:3])—is an act of separation. God's action regarding the separateness of things and pronouncements concerning the separateness and the fitting or appropriate nature (*tov*, "good") of things continues to characterize the whole first sequence of Genesis.

Thus to live in accord with God's Law in this account, to live according to the law of anti-idolatry, is to participate in God's creative act, to create the world as God did via Torah. To fulfill man's role as man, in other words, to live "in the image of God" is to partake of the same distinctions that made possible the world itself, distinctions that issue specifically from language and in particular the language of Torah. It would be to live in accordance with the Torah, which is to say, to live prophetically and to assume full responsibility (as Levinas says) for the creation of the universe, to assume, that is to say, the responsibilities of God. "And thou shalt love the LORD thy God with all thy heart, and all thy soul, and all thy might," Torah tells us (Deut. 6:5). To live anti-idolatrously is to live from the point of view of God, from the perspective of the Creator, from the creative source of the universe.

These notions, I suggest, comprise the formal (if unfamiliar) identifications Judaism would make. There is no doubt that Judaism is the religion of the sufferers. There is equally no doubt that Judaism's Law is the law of anti-idolatry. And if the third component of these equations seems more uncanny from a traditional perspective—that the law of anti-idolatry as the Law of Torah should also be the creative source of the universe—we may be ready to acknowledge that such is what is said within certain more orthodox religious contexts.

What is the motor force of these equations? Without an explication of the logic of these identifications we are left somewhat unsatisfactorily with a solution to a puzzle that may seem more imposed than derived, not unlike God's own celestial machinery. To answer this final question—upon which all else seems to hinge—will require something of a final brief excursus.

*   *   *

From a perspective within a Girardian account of the sacrificial dynamics of culture and of cultural history, Judaism appears as an answer to the question, "how can I go on in a world in which there are no longer any gods of the sacrificial kind?" The answer that Judaism offers to this question is straightforward: "live anti-idolatrously." What can this mean? It presupposes at once an analysis of a problem and its solution. The problem is idolatry, namely, that sooner or later, all social structures, all sacrificial structures, will become identical with violence. In a universe in which there are no stops, in which all difference and sacrificial behavior become inseparable from violence in its assertion in the extreme (since all the rituals that would inhibit such transformation have collapsed and become themselves new sources of its continuance), in which all sacrifice and violence, that is to say, are finally indistinguishable, idolatry is the identification of a moment. It is the moment at which the transformation occurs, at which what is sacrificial and helpful becomes violent and destructive, at which medicine becomes poison.

In the face of this "sacrificial crisis," in Girard's terms, the law of anti-idolatry proposes an ethical response: learning how to stop, learning how to follow the sacrificial only up to a point (one, moreover, that is never determinable in advance), up to the point precisely that it turns violent and from which one may turn back to another path, a path that is itself admittedly no less violent when asserted in the extreme but that is not equatable with violence at that particular moment. Regarding in advance the path we are on, recognizing the dramas in which human beings are engaged and naming in advance the end of those dramas in order that we might give them up and turn back, reading that is to say, prophetically, the law of anti-idolatry offers itself as a way out of the crisis, a way that carries with it no guarantees but that proposes a way out if one is to be had.

Idolatry, then, in this context must be understood as a reading, a prophetic or diachronic account structured to offer the possibility of stopping or turning away from destruction and back towards the way of God. Where does this Law originate? Since it identifies in all human structure the potential for violence, for difference gone wrong, it must itself of necessity be conceived from a point equidistant from all structure and all being, a point of retreat or withdrawal from the world which is nowhere and nothing in the world. In so far as this retreat or withdrawal creates the possibility of the world, it must be conceived as originating from some "otherwise than being," some radical externality or alterity or Otherness. The law of anti-idolatry, we may say, is thus a learning to read from some otherwise than being in the world, from which perspective all worldly paths in the extreme are identical with violence.

Within such a conception, it is perhaps clearer how this Law is identical at once with the existential experience of human suffering or wickedness and the creative source of the universe. Suffering is a position, a consciousness, a perspective, *the* perspective precisely that says that sooner or later all roads lead to misery if followed long enough and in enough extremity. To say as much is not to offer an identification of any essential truth of the world or of a being in the world beyond appearances. Nor is it to propose as an alternative some non-suffering position, although these alternatives are the two ways suffering is customarily thought. Suffering is not a synchronic phenomenon but a diachronic perspective. Idolatry and suffering in this respect are one and the same. Judaism is nothing if not an identification of the roads by which suffering appears in human relations (down to the nooks and crannies of everyday human experience) in order that we might, if possible, avoid their more destructive outcomes.

On the other hand, creation is not so much a diachronic occurrence as a synchronic gesture. In so far as the law of anti-idolatry enables survival—and that is its final function—it genuinely creates the possibility of the world. And not only in a negative fashion. It is clear enough how such an ethical mechanism serves to ward off the excesses into which we can sometimes fall. But the claim of this Law is considerably more radical. Its claim is that in so far as the "world" of our experience is already only given to us via the registers in which we live—imaginary worlds in which we create an "I," symbolic registers of law, language, and systems of exchange by which we ensure the promotion and production of such "I's," real registers in which death occurs and in relation to which such social and imaginary systems function—it creates or enables that world itself. To partake in the law of anti-idolatry, to live a life of Torah, which is to say, a life of anti-idolatry, of learning when to stop, of learning where suffering is likely to appear and to stop before it does, is to partake of the possibility of human relations within that context. To learn how to stop, to rest, to punctuate the week with the Sabbath, is to partake with God or the radically Other, in the creation of the universe in an ongoing and sustaining fashion. It is in the extreme, Levinas tells us, to assume responsibility not only for the life of the other individual but for his death. In the most extreme circumstances, it is to be ready to substitute one's own life for his.

Will that creative process ever stop? Is there ever a moment at which creation may be regarded as a completed or past event? At precisely the moment when all roads are understood as leading to idolatry, and in which there is no other study but the study of anti-idolatry, at that moment when Torah will be shown to be larger than the world, since it will be shown to have contained the entirety of the world. At such a moment, the Sages say, we will read (in Levinasian translation) via the Otherwise than being on the earth. Revelation will have led us to the moment when Israel—the community of Torah—will be the center of the world and the "light of nations." The route from the world via Torah to a relation with transcendence will have been completed and the Mashiyach, or Messiah, will have arrived. It is the moment that Franz Rosenzweig (from whom Buber and Levinas derive so much of their understanding of these matters) reserves for the completion of the revelation of creation and which he designates redemption.

※ ※ ※

We may return then to the Book of Job. From the above perspective it is clear then why the *only possible* response God can make to Job—who would view suffering as a problem—is the revelation of the creative order of the universe. Creation is larger than justice, God says to him. "You may found the universe upon the perspective of human justice if you like.

In that case, creation will become for you either a metaphor or an event that occurred long ago but is not ongoing. Are you sure you want to do that?" God asks. Job's position in this regard is no different from that of his friends who also found the world upon justice but assume that such justice must operate at a level beyond appearances.

Job's questions, in other words, presuppose that he has transferred suffering from a diachronic perspective to a synchronic mode. "I am innocent" Job protests constantly. To assert as we do that Job is guilty, that he is guilty by virtue of his protestations of innocence alone (if nothing else), is not to claim as the friends do that there is some violation Job must have committed. It is rather to identify the synchronic outlook in which for Job one can be either guilty or innocent of causing suffering. To claim one is innocent of such behavior is to presuppose that there is some position from which, all things being equal, no suffering should arise. The thrust of their questioning of him is to assume that suffering surely issues from some violation, although not from the pursuit of the right way. The thrust of his position is the same. They assume he must have done something. He is sure he has not. But both assume that only in that fashion would suffering occur. Otherwise it need not be explained. If Job were to assume suffering were a perspective or consciousness through which all roads pass (though not necessarily at the same time or in the same way), he need not inquire about its appearance. It would not have the feel to him of a scandal or an outrage. Things happen. This is a lesson that Job learns at great cost.

And in relinquishing that perspective and that Jewish understanding of suffering, he gives up what it does—namely create the possibility of the world: create the natural or elemental universe of animals and sea creatures, and create the universe of man. There is nothing wrong in Job's doing that, and God's response is often misunderstood to be a rebuke. Judaism itself does no less up to a certain point. For Judaism has itself been nothing other than the decision to live otherwise than by the being of the sacrificial structures of the worlds in which it appeared. Job's "creativity" in this regard, his abandoning of a religious route that for him has become sacrificial, in suspending the possibility of the Judaic explanation, is no more than Judaism itself did initially in separating itself from surrounding cultures. Job can certainly do that, God tells him, if he wishes.

But is he sure he really wants to? If you suspend the law of anti-idolatry, if you propose an alternative response to the sacrificial crises of experience, are you really confident your new humanly engendered law will do for you all that the law of anti-idolatry has done? Judaism is far from the only way human cultures have learned to cope with the collapse of sacrificial systems. There is nothing sacrosanct about Judaism's way from a larger perspective. Eastern religions, for example, have done so quite differently. But will a system founded as yours is—simply upon human justice—do the trick? God asks. Are there not enormous difficulties to be encountered, monsters of the sea and of the land to be grappled with, over which one may have less control than one hopes or even suspects?

In the face of this inquiry, the only possible response Job can make is: of course not! He has never imagined that he was displacing the law of anti-idolatry (he may not even have identified Judaism as the law of anti-idolatry), let alone substituting another in its place or evaluating the viability of that substitution vis-à-vis the former system. Now that he has seen what he has been doing, that it has been called to his attention and he has been called to account for his behavior, now that he has been made to own responsibility for what necessarily exceeds choice and been shown the connections between where he is and the future to which it leads (and thus the future he has displaced by substituting that new place), he may choose more effectively.

And as such connections have been made for Job from a response to suffering to the creation of the world, so they have been made for us: from accusation to its renunciation, from mythological interpretation, through institutional reasoning, through humanistic outrage, to readings that link survival to the creation of the world and responsibility for the other individual. From the Satan who embodies accusation to the figure of Job who finally renounces the accusatory structure in which he participates.

V. Epilogue: Evil, Accusation, and Reading

We are in a position to bring our essay to a close and to return to the questions with which we began. The answer to Buber's questions about the relation between human suffering and the creative order of the universe is clear. To pose a question about human suffering is to displace a Judaism that has already posed such a question, and which is already constituted itself as an answer to that question. The Law of Judaism, the law of anti-idolatry, is the same in this context as the creative source of the universe. The only possible serious response of God to Job is to say: look at what you have done. Are you sure that you want to continue doing it? You can form a new religion based entirely on human justice if you wish. But are you sure you can sustain the obligations it will impose upon you? Can you catch leviathan on a fishhook or yoke behemoth? Will your humanism trod down the wicked where they stand? The last two hundred years of European history should convince us—if nothing else does—of both the urgency of this question and the insufficiency of the answers we have chosen to erect in response to it.

The presentation of the creative order of the universe, in short, is a response to human suffering since human suffering and the creative order have never not been part and parcel of the same Judaic Law. God has staged Job's position prophetically—where he has been, the strategies he is employing, where he is going—in order to avail him of the freedom not to do that. But in observing this staging, we have come upon the answer to Buber's second question concerning the novelty of the interrogation posed by the Book of Job. If we identify anti-idolatry as the common ground to the creative and moral orders, we now understand that Job's question is not "new" at all, and that here, perhaps, we glimpse Buber's own romanticism. Judaism has never not been a response to such a question. The migrations of the Abrahamic tribes in the Mesopotamian region in the beginning of the second millennium before the common era already took place, we have to assume, within the same cultural climate, one of profound sacrificial and cultural crisis. These populations were already exiling themselves from the idolatrous ways of their ancestors for a new law, one that offered them respite from the kinds of persecutions and victimage with which we must assume the time was rife. The composition and circulation of the Book of Job in the ancient sixth century must be understood as a reemergence of an old problem, the oldest in the book as it were, the one from which the book was constituted. Perhaps that is what scholars like Martin Noth have in mind when they find traces of Hebraic style in the text that are as old as the beginning of the second millennium.[26]

Far from a successor to Judaism, to a Judaism that has become unresponsive to the miseries of life around it, Job's humanism is the articulation of its very predicate, the condition from which and in response to which Judaism first arose. Do we understand in this connection the process from which the scriptural canon was formed? The canonization of biblical texts in the ancient sixth century, I would argue, must be understood as part and parcel of the same critical spirit. At a moment when the religion of Judaism began to be confused with the humanistic movements taking place everywhere in the ancient Near East (one thinks, for example, of the demythologizing and desacralizing currents in Miletan Greece), and in the midst of a historical crisis that destroyed the Temple and condemned the Jewish population to a Babylonian exile, the Book of Job, Deutero-Isaiah, some of the Psalms, and other texts appear to proclaim that current conditions are the same from which Judaism originated, and commentators suddenly seize the opportunity to "write down" the Toradic Law. The fact that questions concerning the creative order of the universe, the law of anti-idolatry, the response to human suffering, and the question of eschatology all show up within these texts should hardly surprise us. It is a moment in which Judaism is reborn from precisely the dust and ashes that would seek to bury it, a moment that exegetes and philologists alike—and not without good reason—have designated as "prophetic." It is a moment no doubt not unlike the moment six hundred years later when the need would once again be felt to write down the oral Law and from which the talmudic and other exegetical texts have come. Perhaps it remains the same moment in which, in the shadow of Auschwitz, we continue to think, write, and read once again today.

Do we understand, then, Job's brief reply to God's prophetic presentation?

> Then Job answered the LORD and said:
> I know that Thou canst do every thing.
> And that no purpose can be withheld from Thee.
> Who is this that hideth counsel without knowledge?
> Therefore have I uttered that which I understood not,
> Things too wonderful for me, which I knew not.
> Hear, I beseech Thee, and I will speak;
> I will demand of Thee, and declare Thou unto me.
> I had heard of Thee by the hearing of the ear;
> But now mine eye seeth Thee;
> Wherefore I abhor my words, and repent,
> Seeing I am dust and ashes.
> (42:1–6)

You are right, he says. I have spoken in ignorance. I am nothing. I heard of You before from others. But now I see You myself, face to face, and I repent in dust and ashes. What does it mean when Job says he sees God (in Buber's reading) face to face, that "mine eye seeth Thee?" It is among other things, to see God as not even the prophets have seen Him, as in fact only one individual before was said to have seen Him—Moses on Sinai. Having renounced his idolatry and returned to the way of God, having done *teshuvah,* Job's initial good fortunes are now "doubled." He has become, as Buber notes, a *nabi*. This narrative of "wisdom" literature turns out to be another version of the prophetic writings.

Perhaps in noticing Job's repentance we are finally in a position to answer Buber's third question as well concerning the progress of the narrative from one relation between man and God to another. If God has staged Job's position diachronically—prophetically—perhaps the Book of Job at large has staged the progress of the reader in a similar fashion.

How so? Job's response to God's revelation is clear. You are right. Before I heard of You through others. Now I see You face to face and I repent in dust and ashes. Yet there is someone in the Book of Job who does not repent, someone for whom accusation is written into his very name, so to speak. We have always viewed the prologue as something of an addendum, as a "late addition" (or "early addition" depending upon how we read and how we think about what we read), extraneous by virtue largely of its mythological trappings. What if, far from secondary or marginal, the prologue is in fact strategic, the indispensable origin from which all else in the Book proceeds?

What I would suggest is that in fact the Book of Job may be considered a duplicate of the prologue, that the Book at large—the colloquies of Job and his three friends, the speeches of Elihu, the speeches of God, and the epilogue that follows—is a prophetic extension of the interchange between God and the Satan initially, a "part 2" to the prologue's "part 1," a duplication that develops the contours of the earlier sequence so that new possibilities may be seen from that sequence. I have discussed in other chapters the generality and potency of this two-part structure in Hebraic scriptural literature.[27]

The fact that God baits the Satan has long been acknowledged. The Satan even resists this baiting initially perhaps from long experience with divine craftiness. "Where have you been lately?" God asks, and the Satan replies succinctly, "Around." Can God not know where the Satan has been or that the Satan is the Satan, literally, in Hebrew, the accuser? We are not dealing here with Othello and Iago, but with the perennial accuser and the omniscient and omnipotent divinity. Not only must God know it, but we know it as well. It is written into His very name, into who He is at the level of linguistic understanding.

We must assume, therefore, that when God raises the issue of "My servant Job," He does so for strategic reasons, and that far from being surprised by the Satan's response, God depends upon the Satan responding exactly as he does. The Satan's reluctance to answer God's inquiries directly, far from Satanic craftiness, may reflect a kind of exasperation at his dawning perception of the strategic task to which God will now put him. If we have read the scene as the Satan's hoodwinking of God, we have done so only by first reducing God to a candidate for such a deception and as a result it should come as no surprise that the God who appears at the other end of the Book appears similarly impoverished.

Why would God be strategic in this fashion? Precisely, I would suggest, to offer us a choice and teach us a lesson. For in the drama that follows, up to a certain point, the same interaction is reproduced. A seemingly unjust action by a demonic controlling agency is followed by accusation piled upon accusation. The Satan proceeds from the mythological to the institutional to the existentially human before it is finally unmasked in the creational. The fates rain down their miseries upon Job and he accuses God of not making clear the design in all of this. He calls God to account as one would in a court of law. After God speaks and reveals to Job the dimensions of his humanistic appropriations and displacement, Job repents. The Satan on the other hand does not.

Perhaps we feel that this is a cruel lesson for us to learn at Job's expense. But to say as much is to reveal our own vulnerability. We reveal that we too feel that the Judaic Law will not fully win out over the wicked. Perhaps we feel that the Book of Job is a product of wisdom literature, not history. But the law of anti-idolatry, the prophetic law, cannot fail in its terms to achieve its goal, any more, for example, than the angel in the story of the binding of Isaac can fail to arrive in time in the face of Abraham's complete obedience.[28] Job will always be rewarded "doubly" for his efforts. If we have allowed ourselves to be seduced by the familiarity of his situation to our own and to reverse the outcome of his trial, then perhaps it is because, rather than recognize the difference between Job and the Satan, we would collapse their accusatory structures within each other and continue accusation even beyond the point where Job himself has abandoned it. We read from the point of view of a perennial accuser in a situation ironically where it is the very difference between a perennial accuser and one who first accuses and then gives it up, between the Satan and Job, that is being traced for us.

The God of the prologue, therefore, is neither the innocent dupe of

Satan's wiles nor the demonic strategist who would play havoc with man's fate for His personal amusement, but the same God we have seen throughout, one who offers us a choice between the accuser who would feed upon himself interminably, and the accuser who, taking cognizance of his own strategies, gives up the accusation itself. The only available positions in this Book are accusatory ones. The difference between Job and the Satan is not that one is accusatory and the other is not, but that while one is accusatory, the other at some point assumes responsibility for the accusation in which he has all along been engaging.

There are thus in the Book of Job finally two positions: those that are accusatory of God, and those that are aware of their accusatory structure and attempt ownership of that structure and genuine repentance for it. There are no non-accusatory positions to be had. The position of the three friends is no less accusatory of God than any of the others, even if their accusations are presented in inverted form, in the form of institutional approval. Expelling God from real human experience, making experience a matter of nice calculation, the three friends construct a position that in effect does without God entirely except as a kind of ancient memory. The relation between God and man has been abrogated no less here than elsewhere. Job's insistence upon the existential realities of human miseries and the Satan's insistence upon cynicism and accusation are merely explicit externalizations of the accusatory structure upon which the idealized forms of the friends are based.

Perhaps that is why, finally, God credits Job in the last instance and denounces the friends. Only if they obtain Job's blessing can God's anger at them be ameliorated. To say as much of the Satan would be a tautology. But it is important to see the friends on the side of the Satanic—which we have rarely done. "My wrath is kindled against thee [Eliphaz], and against thy two friends; for ye have not spoken of Me the thing that is right, as my servant Job hath" (42:7). The questions Job has raised, the question of human suffering and justice, are the only important questions worth considering, and it is those questions that in the first instance God endorses. The friends would expel those questions as the product of a messy non-institutional imagination.

But in the second instance, even the position that poses these questions must not take itself seriously since it has been from Judaism—from the religion of this God—that the necessity of posing these questions at all has arisen. To stop with the posing of these questions would be like making an idol of the law of anti-idolatry itself; it would be in a sense the most dangerous form of idolatry since to what other agency than itself would it appeal? After posing these questions what is required of Job is that he give up insisting upon the sanctity of his own position, that he humble himself before the condition of his own possibility, indeed the condition of the possibility of the universe itself, and return to the way of God.

The Book of Job, in other words, is also within the Book of God. Within the story, God suddenly breaks this structural boundary and speaks directly to Job. In the same way, we are within the world of God and yet here is the Book of Job that is part of the Word of God to Moses at Sinai that speaks to us directly about Judaism at large. In the final analysis, the choice becomes our own as readers. Reading becomes a form of ethical activity. If it were only a matter of Job's choice, the prologue would be unnecessary. It is in order to teach us a lesson, to reveal to us the difference between the Satanic and the Job-like, that the Book is developed in the fashion that it is. The Book remains for us a "scene of instruction," to use a phrase literary critics have employed in other contexts. We are offered the possibility of tracing a path from mythological thinking, to institutional thinking, to humanistic thinking, to the thinking from which the universe has been created, to follow, in short, the path of accusation from beginning to end.

The Book of Job is the end of the path of accusation and within the Book its history is told from the beginning. Accusation reveals itself to be the truth of the "problem of evil," just as the colloquies between God and the Satan regarding Job turn out to be the truth of the colloquies between Job and his friends. To find suffering to be a problem and a scandal, to displace the creative potential of Judaism as a response already to suffering, is to accuse God, to partake in the modality of the Satanic as the second set of colloquies reveal that mode to us. Evil in this book has been fully exposed for us in four manifestations: (1) as victimage by mythological forces; (2) as the product of sin or error; (3) as the product of injustice and oppression; and (4) as the product of elemental and natural monstrosity. In all cases, it turns out to be the product of inclination, the viewing of the world and of God from the perspective of a deviated transcendence, the idolatrous perspective of the *yetzer hara*.

In all cases, in short, it is the rejection of rectitude, uprightness, proximity to God, which define for us the *yetzer tov*, the inclination which is not an inclination or deviation at all but an approach. Levinas's argument in the epigraph to this chapter makes this point. Occurring in the course of a review of Philippe Nemo's book, *Job et l'excès du mal,* the passage reveals to us less the inadequacy of the two traditional ways of understanding Job's experiences—crediting those experiences before a delegitimized inadequate and impotent divinity, discrediting those experiences before a mystified transcendent perspective—than the necessary giving up of "adequacy" itself as a measure, and the making of *un constat de carence,* a statement or declaration of deficiency or deficit of assets (a "denunciation of being wanting" in Lingis's translation).[29] If in no other instance, the alterity of God, the radical Otherness of God to man, to man's absence, shows up in the moment of creation. And with that alterity comes responsibility. Where were you? God asks Job, in echo of the question He asked Adam. Job can understand suffering and its relation to justice if and only if he understands it in the limit case, at the moment of creation, when he could not possibly be there, and when it was once before a question of accusation. Job is responsible for the other individual, he comes to learn, for everyone and for everything, even for the death of the other individual, for what was not in oneself and not in one's work, even at the moment of its greatest impossibility. He comes to understand his responsibility for the other individual via a creation with which he is "fraternally solidary." Moreover, he comes to understand that this responsibility is inevitably painful, and that this pain and this responsibility are constitutive of the world as Judaism understands it.

In short, he comes to learn that were God to answer Job in the synchronic terms or script in which Job has cast him, he would not be God. God offers Job the only possible response—the impossible voice of the absolutely Other, the only terms in which an answer is possible, the terms that reveal to Job the alterity, responsibility, and consequent pain that his questions would insistently evade. Where were you when I handed out universes? Don't you know that people get sick and die, that natural disasters occur? I could put an end to the wicked in a second. How would that change your situation in the slightest? It would even make it worse. You speak as a child. Your questions to Me about justice and fairness suggest that you don't know that it's really about creation and responsibility.

Could one object that Job never agreed to such a universe, to carry such a burden on his shoulders, that such a "prior alliance" with commandment and responsibility "was not freely chosen?" "But one reasons," Levinas writes, "as though the ego had witnessed the creation of the world and as though the world had emerged out of its free will. This is the presumptuousness of the philosopher. Scripture makes Job a reproach of it."³⁰

God's revelation in other words comes in speaking or saying itself, in the meeting that occurs between God and Job in which a speaking occurs face to face. "To hear a voice speaking is *ipso facto* to accept obligation toward the one speaking," Levinas writes.³¹

> Consciousness is the urgency of a destination leading to the other person and not an eternal return to self. . . . Prior fidelity . . . is an innocence without naivete, an uprightness without stupidity, an absolute uprightness which is also absolute self-criticism, read in the eyes of the one who is the goal of my uprightness and whose look calls me into question. It is a movement toward the other which does not come back to its point of origin the way diversion comes back, incapable as it is of transcendence—a movement beyond anxiety and stronger than death.
>
> This uprightness is called *Temimut*, the essence of Jacob. Integrity, taken in its logical meaning, and not as a characteristic of a childlike disposition, indicates, if it is thought through to the end, an ethical configuration. . . . *Temimut* consists in substituting oneself for others.

The Book of Job is finally to us as God's speeches are to Job. It stages before us our position and our responsibility, not in order to accuse us or to judge us, but to avail us of our options, speaking to us, as it were, face to face. Which is to say, as God did with Job, and with Moses. It summons us to our own responsibility, first as readers, but secondly (and by way of that reading) as ethical individuals, as witnesses. If we have refused to accept this communication and this understanding, this testimonial obligation, if we have persisted in accusing God or the Book of Job with being unfair, implicitly or explicitly, if we have persisted in reading the Book of Job as the "problem of evil," it is to the Satanic or accusatory origins of that position and the fraternal solidarity with others via creation which such a position would reject that this Book would finally direct our attention.

The Book of Job remains for us a scene of instruction if we would but avail ourselves of its opportunity. It stages our idolatry from beginning to end. Rather than offering us one position contrasted with another, Job's with the Satan's or with that of the three friends, or God's with Job's, it offers us the twisting and continuous path between them. That path is multi-dimensional. If we can trace the path from beginning to end and not read simply the end or the beginning independently of each other, we can also follow it as well from inside out: from mythological thinking, to religious and institutional thinking, to humanistic thinking about justice and suffering, to creational or creaturely thinking about fraternity and repentance. If we get stuck along the way, speaking of the Book as a non-Jewish fable, dutifully writing the formal histories of its religious institutions and philology, passionately admiring from a position of moral outrage or primal sympathy Job's humanistic accusations, before accepting it as an opening to creation of the world and responsibility for the other individual, it remains for us, for our instruction, that the Book of Job continues to be available.

Fifty years after "planet Auschwitz," the resources of that creation and that instruction may not yet be fully exhausted.

III
Modern Reading

7

"Writing on Fire"
The Holocaust, Witness, and Responsibility

> "Ye are My witnesses, saith the LORD."
> Isaiah 43:10

In his brief introduction to Ellen Fine's shrewdly insightful book on the work of Elie Wiesel, *Legacy of Night,* Terrence Des Pres offers the following rather extraordinary observations.[1]

> The Holocaust would seem to have no end. The destruction of Europe's Jews stopped in 1945, but the spectacle of the death camps continues to haunt us, and not merely as a fading memory or as a bad dream that lingers. This memory does not fade, this nightmare goes on and on. The Holocaust *happened.* That in itself is the intractable fact we can neither erase nor evade. And the more we think of it, the more it intrudes to occupy our minds, until *l'univers concentrationnaire* becomes a demonic anti-world that undermines our own. After Auschwitz, nothing seems stable or unstained—not the values we live by, not our sense of self-worth, not existence itself. We dwell in aftermath, and I do not think I exaggerate to say that the Holocaust has forced upon us a radical rethinking of everything we are and do.[2]

Des Pres's remarks, of course, largely summarize an argument he articulated some years earlier in an essay entitled "The Dreaming Back" (a title he borrowed from Yeats) and that he wrote for a special Holocaust issue of the journal *Centerpoint.*[3] But their reproduction here—at the head of a book on the work of Elie Wiesel—changes their impact, I think, decisively. For it becomes clear now (although Des Pres never makes the claim explicitly) that it is Wiesel himself who is their primary interlocutor. Who more than Elie Wiesel in the late 1950s and 1960s in this country came increasingly to be identified with the suggestion that we "remember the Holocaust," that, as the rabbis say, "in memory lies redemption," and that the gravest danger we face after an event of such magnitude is that we return to "business as usual"?

What is extraordinary, in other words, in the first instance is that Des Pres's words constitute a fundamental and polemical reply to the position Wiesel had been arguing almost singlehandedly for some twenty years. Contrary to what we have been led to expect, Des Pres suggests, this memory does not fade. If there were ever a time in which we were in danger of forgetting, that danger no longer obtains. This dream lingers. This nightmare goes on and on. Indeed the more distant we get from the event, the less easy it would seem to avoid or evade it. Far from there being a danger that we might forget the event, the danger would seem to arise from the opposite direction—that we cannot let go of it, that the further away we move from it, the more intensive and intrusive it becomes until it begins to assume the status of a "demonic anti-world that undermines our own."

Writing in 1982, Des Pres may have been one of the first to make this particular claim. Increasingly in recent years, however, others have begun to argue similarly. Jürgen Habermas, for example, is reported to have remarked in 1985 that the memory of the Nazi epoch "had somehow remained" for him "untouched by the passage of time." "[Forty] years after the war, this past still appeared as present, whereas [the events of his adolescence] four decades earlier seemed to be distant history."[4] And Saul Friedlander notes, at the outset of a recent essay, that when in the summer of 1986 the *Frankfurter Allgemeine Zeitung* published an essay by historian and Heideggerian Ernst Nolte entitled "A Past That Refuses To Go Away," both Habermas and Nolte, in Friedlander's view, "were pointing to the as yet massive presence of the Nazi epoch in contemporary German memory."[5] In fact, Friedlander remarks, "notwithstanding an explicit yearning for a 'normalization' of the Nazi past, this epoch is more present than ever." With regard to the so-called "historian's controversy," the *Historikerstreit,* Friedlander concludes (with an echo of Des Pres), "those who wanted Auschwitz to fade away, failed."[6]

In context of these new reflections, some new conclusions are beginning to be drawn, many of which Des Pres's essay already anticipates. It is not just that—in the eyes of some recent thinkers—this "unmasterable past" has begun to get a bit out of control and begun to seem somewhat intrusive, as if we need try only a little harder and we may succeed in putting these matters to rest. It is rather that this "endlessness" (to build upon Des Pres's word) has begun to seem curiously endemic to the nature of the devastation, built-in, so to speak, to its very fabric.

In what way? "The Holocaust *happened,*" Des Pres writes. "That in itself is the intractable fact which we can neither erase nor evade." What could not happen, did happen. The Holocaust, the unthinkable, the impossible occurred. And once it occurred, the world within which it occurred was changed decisively. Since it happened once it could happen again. New measurements are necessary. The fact that it occurred constitutes a break with the past, a discontinuity as Foucault used to say, a *nova* as Fackenheim calls it (or *caesura* in Arthur Cohen's vocabulary, which deconstructionist Lacoue-Labarthe echoes).[7] Since we dwell, as Des Pres writes, in its "aftermath," in its shadow, "nothing seems stable or unstained." "It has forced upon us a radical rethinking of everything we are and do."

At the same time, since what we do in this aftermath, this "after"-ward, is live, dwell, reside, a strikingly new realization is suddenly forced upon us—namely, that in fact we are not "after" the Shoah at all, but within it, that the Holocaust is not over but ongoing. Although the overt killing of the Jews stopped in 1945, other forms of annihilation have displaced and replaced that more overt form of devastation, and these other forms continue to interpenetrate with—in fact, to constitute—critical parts of our daily experience.

To take just one example. In a recent essay on the survivor testimonies Lawrence Langer points out that in so far as we refuse to listen to the survivors and substitute instead the heroic conceptions of the world that a writer like Victor Frankl would suggest to us, we continue to impose the silence to which the Nazis themselves would reduce the Jews.[8] The silencing of the survivors after the war, the "double dying" to which we submitted them, was already an observation that Elie Wiesel himself had made in his famous plea for survivors.[9] What Langer adds is that this silencing, this literal termination of the interview, continues even in those contexts in which we avowedly want to listen. And in so far that the Nazi project so to speak was the same silencing, in context of the virile and heroic Greek sense of Western self, we continue that enterprise, more "tastefully" perhaps, but no less decidedly.[10]

Is it possible that in formulating the problem in this fashion we have stumbled upon an answer to at least one of the questions that plague us in these domains? Is it possible, for example, that at least one of the reasons we have had difficulty constructing the Holocaust as a theme of memory or an object of knowledge (even the very idea of "a" Holocaust or "the" Holocaust is suspect here as numerous writers have remarked) is that we are only able to re-member something that was fully "membered" so to speak in the first place (or that we are able to construct as "membered" in order to later construct it as re-memberable). Yet we are, in this particular region, so to speak, not out of the woods. The sentiment often expressed by survivors to describe their current experiences with regard to the Shoah—that words fail them, that words cannot describe their experience and are inadequate to the horror—may tell us less about either the weakness of words to do their job or the intensity of the horror these survivors experienced than about the construction upon which each of these notions depend, and the fundamental incompleteness and incommensurability that survivors who use these words repeatedly encounter.

Let me elaborate. One of the observations researchers have made increasingly about the war years concerns the so-called "progressive revelation" of the final solution, the fact that at every stage *each* solution was thought to be final only to be replaced by another in turn. Raul Hilberg makes this point repeatedly, and his student, Christopher Browning, has begun to make the same point with regard to the very decision to establish deathcamps. It would not seem inappropriate in this context to speak of a collapse of "object-formation," both on the part of the perpetrators and on the part of their victims. Such behavior on the part of survivors today, then, such expression of the incommensurability of the experience, may to some extent simply repeat or continue that collapse, may constitute only one more episode in an ongoing serial drama.[11] Apart from describing the Holocaust, in other words, such language about its unrepresentability also partakes within it, continues it, reproduces it, reflects by extension as it were one of its most troubling aspects. Apart from constituting a memory about it, these words index its wounds.

But the silencing of the survivors (or their silencing of themselves in the above manner) is far from the only way in which the Holocaust continues and in which we are still within it and exemplify it. In the relation between survivors and their children, a no less troublesome silencing may persist. In a brilliant article on post–World War II French Jewish writers, Ellen Fine makes some rather astounding observations about the dilemmas in which "post-genocide children" find themselves.[12]

> Afflicted by the unhealed wounds of memory, those born in the aftermath of genocide continue to bear its burden. They have inherited the anguish, yet at the same time feel excluded from a universe they can never know. This sense of being shut out of a momentous era

compels writers of the second generation to fill the void created by the Holocaust. They are confronted with a difficult task: to imagine an event they have not lived through, and to reconstitute and integrate it into their writing—to create a story out of History. . . . They are haunted by the world that has vanished; a large gap exists in their history, and they desire to bridge this gap, to be informed about what occurred, to know something about members of their family who perished. However they feel frustrated by the impotence of incomprehension; the past eludes and excludes them. Repeatedly met with the silence of their parents and relatives—who transmit the wounds of genocide, and not the memory—they grow up in "the compact void of the unspeakable," as Nadine Fresco affirms in her "Remembering the Unknown," an analysis of how young Jews born after World War II relate to a traumatic event they have not experienced. These Jews, she says, are like "people who have had a hand amputated that they never had": they inherit the pain, but it is "a phantom pain in which amnesia takes the place of memory. . . . One remembers only that one remembers nothing."[13]

And this struggle to remember nothing is then compounded when on occasion the parents of these children sense their dilemma and confront them with it. "This sense of nothingness caused by the deprivation of memory, or by memory that is concealed, refused, or forbidden," Fine writes, "is intensified by the survivors themselves."[14] Elie Wiesel has frequently made the observation, "Who has not lived through the event, will never know it." And Fine adds in a footnote Wiesel's reply to her questions about this dilemma in an interview she conducted with him.[15] "The Holocaust is a sacred realm. One cannot enter this realm without realizing that only those who were there can know. . . . One can never know and yet one must try."[16] "Yet the message is contradictory," Fine notes, "and therein lies the predicament." She quotes Maurice Blanchot's remark in *L'Écriture du désastre*, adding her own emphasis: *"At the same time one can never know, one must know, and one must not forget."*[17]

How far can we go with this thinking? How systematically can we apply this notion of "trauma" that Nadine Fresco introduces or of "contradiction" that Fine introduces?[18] Is it possible that what we have been examining first as a horror that is repressed for some twenty years and then explodes into consciousness not as an object but as the force constituent of consciousness, as condition of the possibility of everything we are and do, follows the pattern at a social level that thinkers like Nadine Fresco would immediately recognize in psychological terms; that we might appropriately speak of the Holocaust in context of the culture from which it comes to count as a "model" (and for which it will probably remain the model for some time to come), as collective trauma?[19] Is not "trauma" the appropriate term to describe the divorce between wound and memory in this context? Is not the very distinction between wound and memory what informs the way in which the Holocaust continues to survive?

Our paradigms for talking about the Holocaust, in short, are changing. It seems to be less remembering that is critical to our discussion of these matters than surviving—living on and living through. Or, rather, only in taking stock of the ways in which we continue to re-member, endlessly, so to speak, do we gain cognizance about such survival. It is less memory per se that concerns us than the wounds it stages—its silences, its absences, its voids.

On the one hand, then, Claude Lanzmann.[20] Rather than package the Holocaust as an aesthetic object—for example in the manner that Renais in *Night and Fog* did for one decade and the TV broadcast of *Holocaust* did for another—Lanzmann chooses to expose the packaging itself, the dreaming back, the "fatal aestheticizing" that Geoffrey Hartman says, after Benjamin, "gave fascism its false brilliance."[21] Rather than clothe his characters in archives, Lanzmann offers us a prolonged view—nine and a half hours worth—of the one archive we have in so dressing them forgotten and at the one moment we have for the most part deigned not to look—the survivors in their present context, those who were there and can still talk about it in their own language. Rather than represent memory for us—as Tony Brinkley and Steven Youra show in their brilliant essay on the movie—he constructs it.[22]

On the other hand, Raul Hilberg. Rather than offer us generalities on the distinctiveness of the Holocaust from other modes surrounding it—on its barbarousness or monstrosity—Hilberg offers us the considerably more ominous studies of the continuities of its machinery with the entire fabric of contemporary bourgeois life.[23] He undoes forever, as commentators have remarked, the possibility of the innocent bystander. He lifts the transparent interpretative veil of the historical statistic to disclose in the non-representational forms of the fragment the presentness of the past—the railway timetable, the survivor's diary.

In both cases, then, in historical studies and in aesthetics, the difficulties of remembering the event, of taking it as even a subject matter for memory—let alone for memorializing it—are evident. The survivors, the "living documents," the writings of the times, so to speak, undo our sense that this event has ended, and draw our attention instead to the ways in which the Holocaust shows up, indexes itself, traces itself in Levinas's terms, in everything we say and do.[24]

To make more concrete some of the ways in which the Holocaust continues to "show up" I would like to examine two texts: one by Yiddish poet and playwright Halpern Leivick and another by philosopher and teacher Emmanuel Levinas. Afterward I will return to some of the themes I have been raising in this introduction.

※　*※*　*※*

The particular text of Leivick to which I want to refer occurs within a series of social contexts that turn out themselves not unrelated to the remarks that he offers. Yiddish literature, of course, has never been a stranger to the question of suffering, and Halpern Leivick in particular may be said to be (in this regard at least) something of a Yiddish poet's Yiddish poet. Throughout his life, in poems, essays, plays, and virtually every literary form in which Yiddish writers of his generation published, Leivick was obsessed with the idea of suffering and the many texts he wrote on the biblical "sacrifice of Isaac" or "the trials of Job" attest to that persistent concern. The passage we are going to look at is no exception.[25]

Moreover, here, in 1957, in one of the last talks that he gave—he fell sick very shortly after the talk and the following year suffered a paralyzing stroke that left him "helpless and speechless" for the remainder of his life—Leivick arrives in Israel to speak at a writers conference that takes place in Jerusalem, at the foot of Mount Moriah, which of course is the site of the biblical *akeidah,* the binding of Isaac, on the occasion of the tenth anniversary of the founding of the State of Israel, a date not unrelated to the Shoah.[26] And within the speech, after recalling the kinds of discussions that accompanied the foundation of the State of Israel—the relation between the Jew of the *galut* (the exile or Diaspora) and the Israeli Jew—he offers what seems to be a truce.

> I have seen—we have all seen—six million Isaacs lying under knives, under axes, in fires, and in gas chambers; and they were slaughtered. The angel of God did come too late. Six million slaughtered Isaacs are beyond my comprehension. But I can comprehend one Isaac waiting to be slaughtered and thereby living through the horrors of six million slaughtered, as though he were himself slaughtered six million times. . . .
> Have we not had enough of sacrificial altars?

Why compound our difficulties? he asks. Have we not all witnessed enough tragedy in the world around us that we should give up squabbling among ourselves? Let us recognize the sanctity of the individual Jew wherever he is and treasure whatever individual experience he brings to his Judaism.[27] The title of the talk, "The Jew—The Individual"("*Der Yid—Der Yichud*"), plays in Yiddish on the word "*Yid*" that is both contained within and frames the word "*Yichud*," a wordplay that thus echoes in good rabbinic fashion the talk's theme. Let me acknowledge the importance of Israel, Leivick seems to be saying, and let the Israeli Jew recognize the importance of the Diasporic Jew. To support this argument he will offer an anecdote from his childhood, an individual experience that "left a permanent imprint upon my entire life and became the undertone of all my later poems and plays."

In the chapter that follows, I will look at some of the ways in which Leivick weaves together these four motifs—the Holocaust, biblical reference, childhood experience, and his career as a writer—in the anecdote that he tells as a way of handling this decisive "event." Then I will compare Leivick's response to alternative approaches to the same themes within other more philosophically or historically grounded writers.

Although the passage is lengthy, I will quote it in its entirety, then offer some comments upon it.

> And now, may I conclude by telling you something about myself as an individual and as a Jew, something that has followed me for a lifetime. It happened when I was no more than seven years old, and now, when I am on the eve of seventy, it stands as fresh before me as if it had occurred today. . . .
>
> Yes, I was about seven. One day I went off to *kheder*. It was a bright, sunny winter day, cold and quiet, as often happens in the towns of White Russia. And I walked, in the early morning, to the *kheder* on the synagogue street. I passed a large market square and turned off into the street on which stood the Polish church. As I passed the church entrance a tall burly Pole bounded over to me, slammed his fist across my head, tore my hat off and threw both it and me to the frosty ground. He beat me, shouting, "Dirty Jew! When you pass our church you have to take your hat off! You dirty Jew!" I got up with difficulty, grabbed my hat from the ground, and ran off to *kheder* in tears. My heart cried out within me: Why did that big Pole beat me, a child of seven years? And why is it that when he, a gentile, passes a synagogue, no one makes him put on a hat?
>
> I walked into the *kheder,* choked back the tears, and sat down to the study of the Pentateuch. The teacher began the lesson for the

day, the verses about the sacrifice of Isaac. Isaac accompanies his father Abraham to mount Moriah, and now Isaac lies bound upon the altar waiting to be slaughtered. Within me my heart weeps even harder. It weeps out of great pity for Isaac. And now Abraham raises the knife. My heart is nearly frozen with fear. Suddenly—the angel's voice: Abraham, do not raise your hand against your son, do not slay him. You have only been tested by God. And now I burst into tears. "Why are you crying now?" the teacher asked. "As you see, Isaac was not slaughtered." In my tears I replied, "But what would have happened had the angel *come one moment too late?*" The teacher tried to console me with the reassurance that an angel cannot be late. But the fear of coming too late stayed with me.

After *kheder* I went home. It was already evening. I walked past the spacious courtyard of Count Yassevitch. I stole inside. I had been told that in one of the rooms of the Count's palace his demented son was kept locked behind bars. I was filled with eagerness and with a strange fascination to see this unfortunate man behind bars. I wanted to see this man of pain and suffering. And then I saw him. I stood before his grated window and looked at him through the bars. He stood inside, near the window, and looked at me. Silent and motionless, he stood looking at me. Great terrifying eyes. The man himself—a giant, the black hair of his head and face dishevelled, wild. I stared at him as if entranced, as if gazing into an abyss that drew me. Our eyes met. My knees began to buckle. To save myself, I thought up a trick. Near the window hung an iron pole with which they closed the shutters at night. The pole was frozen. I wanted to show this terrifying man that I wished to do something to make him joyous, to amuse him; I put my tongue against the frozen iron. The tip of my tongue stuck to the iron, froze to it. I tore my tongue away and it began to bleed. The blood filled my mouth and dripped down onto my clothes. I ran home in terror and came into the houses spattered all over with blood. And soon after, I fell into a great fever.

As you see, four moments, four sharp experiences in one day in the life of a seven-year-old child. They would be too much even for an adult. How much more so for a child. But it seems there is no such thing as "too much" for a Jewish child! These four events of a single day left a permanent imprint upon my entire life and became the undertone of all my later poems and plays, the undertone of my existence as a Jew and of my fate as a Jew. . . .

Yes, I was seven years old at the time and now I am nearly seventy, and these four events are happening to me again today no less fatefully and no less tragically but also with no less decisiveness and no less honor.

I still feel afresh the pain of that Pole's—that gentile's—fist across my face, a blow for no wrong of mine. I still see the terrifying eyes of the man behind bars, bars behind which later on, in Czarist jails, I spent long years. Why? For wanting freedom. For wanting a world without bars. I see that incarcerated man, wildly unkempt, sunk in loneliness, in darkness—forlorn. I still bear within me the desire to test nature, that icy, frozen iron, the desire to place my tongue against nature's essence, to savor its taste, and savoring it, to feel my own warm blood dripping over me. But most of all I am pursued by Isaac's lying bound upon the altar, his looking at the raised knife till the angel of God announced that it was but a trial; and like a decree as well as a refrain my childish question still pursues me: "What would have happened had the angel come one moment too late?"

It pursues me because I have seen—we have all seen—six million Isaacs lying under knives, under axes, in fires, and in gas chambers; and they were slaughtered. The angel of God did come too late. Six million slaughtered Isaacs are beyond my comprehension. But I can comprehend one Isaac waiting to be slaughtered and thereby living through the horrors of six million slaughtered, as though he were himself slaughtered six million times. . . .

Have we not had enough of sacrificial altars? I ask have we not had enough?

On the surface of it, things are reasonably clear. The anecdote is inserted within the speech explicitly to amplify his offer of truce. Have we not had enough tragedy *not* of our doing so that we should not add to our difficulties by fighting we *can* control. Leivick inserts his argument in a biblical vehicle. The Holocaust is like a sacrifice of Isaac gone wrong, a holocaust, that, by mistake, as it were, *did* take place, because the angel of God was tardy. The use of biblical imagery to make a point is of course common in Yiddish literature and contrasting scriptural imagery negatively with the world is a similarly familiar tactic. Although Leivick never explicitly says "God died at Auschwitz," his proclamation that "for us the angel did not arrive in time" is tantamount to the same assertion.

There are, moreover, tonalities to the proclamation he does make that resonate within a larger arena. In contrast to the "world of our fathers" (where all eventualities by a strict talmudic interpretation may be understood as having been contained within Torah), there are some eventualities in *our* world that Torah (and perhaps Jewish Orthodoxy at large) has not foreseen. Leivick's sentiment, of course, shares a much larger, if not strictly anti-Jewish, then certainly anti-Orthodox attitude that pervaded a good deal of Yiddish writing of his generation.[28]

Finally, the foundation of this culminating declaration upon a childhood experience developed as a kind of model is equally familiar. As the boy of seven, so the man of seventy—who is significantly ten times as old. As the boy of seven learns the world through an experience that is blithely dismissed before the rigors of a talmudic education, so the man of seventy has learned his lessons through the more severe constraints first of political oppression, and later of religious oppression. The hero of each narrative is in fact a little like Job arguing his humanism against the formalist theology of his three "teachers." For those of us who have learned our lessons from life, they each seem to say to their well-intentioned rabbis, the angel of God did not arrive in time. The tardiness of God is more resonant for us than His greatness. Theirs is not an atheistic view any more so than Job's challenges are atheistic. But like those challenges, their view chides God for not living up to His name and calls Him to judgment as one would perhaps a divinely recalcitrant father who remains negligent of his earthly charge.[29]

Moreover, when we turn to the anecdote itself, things continue to seem fairly uncomplicated. The three different experiences of the child of seven are strikingly similar. In each there is an adult and a child—the burly Pole and the child of seven on the street, the old Hebrew school teacher and the young Torah student in the classroom (as well as Abraham and Isaac within the story they are reading), and the demented son of the count and the curiously fascinated observer at the gate of the house he visits. In each there is an action of some kind, a form of violence, that leaves the child in tears or bloody. The Pole's fist across the child's face brings him to the ground in tears. The story of Abraham and Isaac reduces the Torah student—who has just been beaten up on the street—to tears. And the incident at the iron gate—where the child applies his tongue and pulls it briskly away only to discover his mouth filled with blood—issues in blood, flight, and fever. In each the central action is accompanied by a series of questions or responsive thoughts—the child's questions about the justice of the gentile's behavior on the street, the exchange of questions between the rabbi and the student about the potential lateness of the angel of God in the biblical story, the child's thoughts about the tricks he might perform to please this man of pain and sorrow at the gate of the count. In addition, each scene occurs, in one way or another, around Hebrew school: on the way to *kheder*, at *kheder*, after *kheder*.

Against the background of these structural similarities, Leivick has set up a number of striking thematic contrasts. The differences in the first encounter are the clearest. The older aggressive gentile confronts a passive Jewish child. Violence is introduced by the older male that causes the child to burst into tears, while the child's relation to that violence is more or less arbitrary. He happens to be walking past. In the wake of the violence, the child poses to himself a series of questions that challenge the motivation of the burly Pole and the justice of his action, questions that contrast sharply with the Pole's relation to him.

In the second, there are also older males and children. But now the first older male is Jewish, he is significantly older (presumably aged), and his "aggressive nature" is manifest in his responsibilities as the child's teacher or rabbi, while the second is a father (in fact the progenitor of the Jewish people) and viewed at one of his most trying moments. The child is again brought to tears but this time not by the adult but by the biblical story both he and the teacher are dutifully reading, and whatever violence is threatened within the story never in fact occurs. Following the reading and the outburst, questions again take place but now it is the rabbi who asks the questions first, and the questioning that ensues is styled as a commentary upon the story.

The contrast between the first two episodes—between the antisemitic attack and the Torah lesson—could hardly be more pronounced. Furthermore, Leivick has heightened the comparison by doubling the external circumstances within the particular story they are reading—the story of Abraham and Issac, a story in which the same violence that the child experienced on the street (between an adult and a child) threatens to erupt. To be sure, the violence within the story does not occur—Isaac is *not* sacrificed—but the differing dimensions of the story are similar enough—at once to the attack the child has just suffered and to the more academic interchange in the Hebrew school classroom—that the story can serve as a reflection of both.

Such doubling or repetition on Leivick's part enables us to see the whole second episode as a kind of transformation of the first: the aggressive threatening features of the older male (and the genuinely threatening situation of the child) are segregated from the more instructive and rational elements that are reserved for the interaction between the rabbi and his pupil. It is a interesting reversal that the classroom interaction should provide the instruction while the biblical reading (Abraham and Isaac) should furnish the naturalistic or humanistic representation of the street experience, but it is one that retains power for Leivick and for other Yiddish writers.

Were these first two anecdotes all that Leivick had offered us, we should have little difficulty, I suspect, in generalizing from them to the final paragraph in which they reappear. The incidents seem entirely sufficient to sustain the analogy from personal experience that Leivick wants to draw. The first offers the content—the antisemitism of the gentile toward the Jew—while the second offers the vehicle—the Judaic (and in this case biblical) image in which he will clothe his ideas. The idea of the Holocaust as a massive example of antisemitism undertaken as a kind of Abraham and Isaac story gone terribly wrong seems readily constructed and it derives a great deal of its energy from collapsing the first anecdote into the second, and enacting the first in the terms of the second.

Moreover, if the boy of seven feels the rabbi is not responsive to the specificity of his experience, how much more so does the man of seventy feel that way who has seen "six million Isaacs"? The scene in the final paragraph, in other words, is not unlike the scene in the Hebrew school. The internal drama that both teacher and student observe is similar (in potential at least) to the antisemitism the writer has experienced throughout his life (and most recently in the Holocaust). Just as the student feels the teacher's assurance misses the point, so the seventy-year-old appeals to fellow Jews to join him in honoring—despite their differences—their common Jewish individuality, whatever the well-intentioned rabbis have to say about it. And what better place to do so than in Jerusalem, at the foot of Mount Moriah, on the anniversary of the foundation of the State of Israel? Leivick's mode of argument even employs the familiar *kal vachomer* structure in ironic imitation of his rabbinic forebears.

Leivick's anecdote, however, does not stop there. The speaker sees fit to relate a third episode that seems to him equally part of the events of that important day and it may be that in observing what appears at a cursory glance a fairly inconsequential and anomalous addition to the child's experience, we may be drawn to reflect upon a set of concerns that cast a decisively new light on all we have seen so far.

To be sure, although we have not spoken a great deal about them, there are already elements of some confusion in the first two episodes. In the first, for example, the questions that the child poses are already slightly out of kilter with our expectations and hardly the first questions we would have imagined the child to pose. After being accosted the way he was, slammed across the face, the utterance "you big brute" or a much more forceful expletive might have been more natural than the child's reasoned reflection on the Pole's motivation or the fairness of the action.

In the second anecdote, the questions articulated seem even more out of place. We must presume the child is visibly upset when he enters because of the encounter just a moment before on the street and understandably moved to fear and anguish by the appearance before him in the biblical story of a situation threatening to reproduce his own. And when he burst into tears and the rabbi—who ascribes his tears to a misreading of the biblical passage—points out that the biblical victim is not hurt and he replies by wondering aloud what would have happened if the angel had come one moment too late, again the child's response is understandable, as is the rabbi's explanation from a strictly talmudic perspective.

But what "stayed with him" was not the fear of violence or destruction attendant upon the angel's belated arrival (as we might have expected) but "the fear of coming too late," as if belatedness itself were somehow the problem and a source of danger. It is this "fear" that Leivick will later reiterate when he speculates on the relation of the day's events to his subsequent life ("what stayed with me throughout my life was the childish question 'what would have happened if the angel had not arrived on time?'"), and when he recapitulates the entire day in relation to the Holocaust ("The angel of God did come too late"). The "fear of coming to late" bears for him a curious resonance that exceeds the parameters of the circumstances in which it is embedded.

In the third episode, the elements that seemed in the earlier anecdotes somewhat puzzling come to predominate. Why is the child strangely fascinated after his experience in the classroom to see this demented son of the local count? Why, once he views this figure face to face, does it engender such a powerful effect upon him that his knees give way and he feels "entranced" and "drawn" to "gaze" into an "abyss"? Why, once he experiences this weakness (and the "abyss" that "draws" him to this figure), does he respond by attempting to perform a "trick" to amuse or please that figure? And why in particular, once he has made this decision to amuse or please the man, does he engage in the particular action of putting his tongue to the frozen iron—once again, hardly the first gesture one would contemplate after witnessing such a figure—and a gesture, moreover, that can only result in the blood, flight, and fever that ensue?

Far from remaining tranquil and predictable, in short, things in the third episode get entirely out of hand, so much so that the transformational and differential structure established by the first two anecdotes begins to come undone. Again, it is a matter of a gentile adult and a Jewish child. But this time it is the child himself who is strangely "fascinated" by the man and it is he who inaugurates the trip to the count's house to view "this man of pain and suffering." Presumably the child sets out to see the son behind bars much as he has just observed the son, Isaac, bound upon the altar and behind the "bars" of the biblical writing. Yet when he arrives and confronts the terrifying eyes in the world, it is clearly more the father ("a giant") that he encounters in this face to face meeting. Again, there is a victim and blood. But this time the violence is inaugurated by the child himself in a response to the abyss he feels drawing him and it is he who finally inflicts it upon himself: he traps himself in his own efforts to please or amuse or placate.

In short, all of the categories with which the child was earlier concerned—gentile/Jewish, adult/child, father/son, persecutor/victim, justice/unfairness—seem curiously vitiated and the third episode begins to assume something of a regressive and hallucinatory quality, as if the second scene were suddenly superimposed upon the first. And this confusion of the earlier categories confuses the valorization that results. It is not clear whether it is the father or the son who is the aggressor (or, to the child, who it is who stands before him). It is not clear to the child whether the victimage originates from the outside or the inside of the bars (or which is which). And it is not clear finally whether the questions the child asks are genuinely independent reflections or defensive attempts to amuse or placate.

The net effect of such devalorization is to render the final rearticulation of Leivick's position profoundly enigmatic. If the final image of the Holocaust as the Abraham and Isaac story gone wrong re-presents all of the elements of the first two anecdotes with exemplary clarity, the third offers the same distinctions within a context that thoroughly confuses them. If in the final paragraph it appears that the shared public history of the Jewish people is of primary importance to the speaker, by the end of the third anecdote it begins to appear that the child's private experience has supplanted the public or domestic dimensions of the earlier encounter.

But what is the nature of that private experience? Why does Leivick introduce the third anecdote at all? How are we to understand this strange turn of events, these anomalous questions that Leivick says "stayed" with the child of seven as he moved from one experience to another, this extremely odd behavior in the third?

> And now, may I conclude by telling you some*thing* about myself as an individual and as a Jew, some*thing* that has followed me for a lifetime. *It* happened when I was no more than seven years old, and now, when I am on the eve of seventy, *it* stands as fresh before me as if *it* had occurred yesterday (italics added).

The "four events" of the day in the eyes of the seventy-year-old are recalled as a single event and I propose that we read that equation literally and register the child's movement from one episode to another, rather than as a movement through a sequence of different experiences, as a movement through the *same* experience, which is to say, one that is progressively transfigured or transformed in some fashion by a logic that remains to be elaborated. The child is beaten up on the street and arrives at Hebrew school visibly shaken by what has just occurred—upset both by the physical attack and the unfairness—and presumably bearing a sense of the injustice of the attack. Then, at Hebrew school he discovers another experience—the story of Abraham and Isaac—in which the same violence threatens to recur. What appeared an attack upon him from the outside now shows up as an attack from within as well—both within the biblical reading and (once the teacher misunderstands him) within the classroom. The anger with which presumably he arrived turns to fear that the salvation that he expected—here in his own community—may not occur. The situation at home—within his own texts and contexts—may be no less problematic than his experience away.

He wanders back into the community to get a closer look at a real-life Isaac who has been imprisoned by his own father, and his discovery there is even more terrifying. For the attack now turns out to originate not even from within the community from which he expected support (i.e. Judaism)—and found only invasion (on the part of the father) and abandonment (on the part of the teacher)—but from within himself. The figure of the son turns out to be the figure of the father. And before this imprisoned father it turns out to be the child who initiates violence—as the result of an attempt to please or amuse that goes wrong. The whole terrifying experience drives him to a fever and collapse.

The recollection of this progressive revelation—as if through a series of four successively descending levels or layers—is recast in the final paragraph as the story of Abraham and Isaac gone wrong that in turn comes to define for him the Holocaust. The story of antisemitism has given way before a deeper battle within Judaism, between father and son and between teacher and student. And that battle in turn has given way before an even more intensely personal encounter in which persecutor and victim, father and son, adult and child, are one and the same and equatable in fact with himself. The anger has turned to fear which has turned to guilt of personal exposure (and the "abyss" it opens) and that guilt returns as the view of a failed God who partakes in an experience that is at once powerfully invasive and powerfully abandoning.

What is it that "pursues" him about this experience, that "haunts" him, that provides the "undertone" of all his life as a writer and for which even the incomprehensible murder of six million Isaacs provides only an extension? What is it about "one Isaac waiting to be slaughtered" that is so powerful for him, that leads him so ineluctably to the question, "what would have happened had the angel come one moment too late?" and in his view remains the motor force of everything he does and is—from his experience at the age of seven to his experience at the age of seventy? What, in other words, provides the vehicle for the collapse of all ego boundaries before an abyss that draws him, frozen, as he gazes terrified onto its figure, beyond the gentile with his fist, beyond Abraham with his raised knife, beyond the silent eyes of the giant, wild, and disheveled son?

The attack by the antisemite against the son is clear. The potential violence of the father against the son is equally clear. But what is the nature of the violence of the son? What has he done that he so fears exposure and that the "fear of coming too late" seems so powerfully to index? It must be great enough in his own mind that he would flee in terror at its appearance and yet commemorate its memory—even through the displacements of this narrative—as the foundation of his career as a writer and of the view of the Holocaust he now articulates for us—which is to say, his very Jewish individuality.

To answer that question, we need to turn briefly to one more text and to introduce a piece of information with which Leivick has not provided us. In his chapter on Halpern Leivick, Charles Madison makes the following remarks concerning Leivick's childhood.

> In his fifth year the boy began going to *kheder*, and made great strides in his studies. Two years later he experienced a series of traumas. One morning he saw his little sister of four accidentally scald herself to death: "a young, live body scorched, twisted, haphazardly,

thoughtlessly." The cruelty of the child's fate long tormented him. That same day in deep winter, he was passing a church on his way to *kheder* when suddenly a tall Pole tore off his cap, knocked him down, and shouted: "*Zhid*, when you pass our church you must doff your hat, *zhid!*" This early taste of antisemitism pervaded his memory. In school that morning, he studied the story of Isaak's sacrifice with deep apprehension and burst into tears at the end. When asked by his rabbi why he was crying, Leivick exclaimed: "But suppose the angel was a minute late!" The assurance that an angel was never late did not satisfy him: in his imagination he saw Isaak slain by his own father! On his way home he passed a Polish palace and was curious to see for himself if the rumor that the noble's demented son was chained in his room was really true. As he approached one of the windows he saw a giant of a man standing disheveled and wild-eyed. Feeling sorry for him and wishing to make him laugh, he stuck his tongue out and pressed it against the iron bar. It became frozen to the metal, and when he finally managed to tear it loose it bled copiously. Years later he wrote: "These four experiences in one day lay a permanent stamp on my entire life and became the susurrus of all my later poems and plays."[30]

It seems hard to doubt that Madison is referring to the same series of events Leivick is describing here in his Jerusalem speech. But if we accept that assumption, then an astounding conclusion follows. In his speech before his Israeli audience in 1957, Leivick excluded what was undoubtedly the most important event of that winter day, one that confers upon everything he has just said an entirely new significance, namely, the death of his four-year-old sister by fire. Whatever else it suggests, the seven-year-old child's concern that "the angel" might have been late is now no longer separable from his own inevitable feelings—founded or unfounded—regarding his own implication in and culpability for that death.

And this unexpected exclusion adds an entirely new dimension to some of the narrative anomalies that we have already noted—as well as others we have not. Does it not offer us a powerful new way for understanding, for example, his refusal to be calmed by the rabbi's assurance that the biblical angel cannot be late? Moreover, does it not account for an otherwise curious numerical confusion to which Leivick seems to return to repeatedly. "As you see," he says, "*four* moments, *four* sharp experiences in one day in the life of a seven-year-old child. . . . These *four* events of a single day left a permanent imprint upon my entire life and became the undertone of all my later poems and plays, the undertone of my existence as a Jew and of my fate as a Jew" (italics added). But there were only three: the incident outside the church, the emotional outburst during the Hebrew lesson, and the incident on the way home from school outside the house of the count. Leivick himself seems to feel the need to reiterate the "four moments."

> Yes, I was seven years old at the time and now I am nearly seventy, and these four events are happening to me again today no less fatefully and no less tragically but also with no less decisiveness and no less honor.
>
> I still feel afresh the pain of that Pole's—that gentile's—fist across my face, a blow for no wrong of mine. I still see the terrifying eyes of the man behind bars, bars behind which later on, in Czarist jails, I spent long years. Why? for wanting freedom. For wanting a world without bars. I see that incarcerated man, wildly unkempt, sunk in loneliness, in darkness—forlorn. I still bear within me the desire to test nature, that icy, frozen iron, the desire to place my tongue against nature's essence, to savor its taste, and savoring it, to feel my own warm blood dripping over me. But most of all I am pursued by Isaac's lying bound upon the altar, his looking at the raised knife till the angel of God announced that it was but a trial; and like a decree as well as a refrain my childish question still pursues me: "what would have happened had the angel come one moment too late?"

"I still feel the pain of that Pole's ... fist"—one. "I still see the terrifying eyes of the man behind bars"—two. "I still bear within me the desire to test nature"—three? But there was no such "desire" in the narrative as he has given it to us. Shall we imagine that the seven-year-old boy felt such a desire or is that the desire of a much older man, perhaps one who is languishing in the Czarist prisons?[31]

And then, having excluded it from the recount (and having substituted a "moment" that did not appear), he can include the scene of biblical reading. "But most of all I am pursued by Isaac's lying bound upon the altar." And it is this image that leads him to find in his personal experience a way of talking about the larger instances of antisemitism they have all experienced.

> [Isaac's lying bound upon the altar] pursues me because I have seen—we have all seen—six million Isaacs lying under knives, under axes, in fires, and in gas chambers; and they were slaughtered. The angel of God did come too late. Six million slaughtered Isaacs are beyond my comprehension. But I can comprehend one Isaac waiting to be slaughtered and thereby living through the horrors of six million

slaughtered, as though he were himself slaughtered six million times....
    Have we not had enough of sacrificial altars? I ask have we not had enough?

In other words, if we supplement the information Leivick has given us with the information Madison supplies, or perhaps more precisely, if we understand the image of Isaac lying bound upon the altar waiting to be slaughtered as an image of his sister "of *four*" burning in the fire on that winter day (or waiting to die over a period of months), a "death by fire" for which the child of seven may feel some very real implication, then the final words—"the angel of God did come too late. . . . I can comprehend one Isaac waiting to be slaughtered and thereby living through the horrors of six million slaughtered"—whatever their relevance to the real events of the historical horror, and whatever their relevance to an ongoing relation to his father, begin to assume a self-dramatizing and intensely personal character that is now itself indissolubly linked to all of the multifarious world historical contexts in 1957 in which those words are explicitly seen to function and that we have thereby identified.

How does this revelation enable us to read the passage as a whole? The Holocaust about which Leivick writes is a powerfully private holocaust in a number of important ways. The public discussion in Jerusalem concerns a generalized humanistic response to the *golus*/Israeli debate and to the Holocaust characteristic of a good many other writers. But what fuels that more public concern with Jewish/gentile, father/son, teacher/student relations concerns the death of his sister (and his personal implication in that death), a death that, if we follow this logical pattern to the end, structures for Leivick everything he does and is.

The external Holocaust, in other words, is subsumed finally within the private battles in which he imagines himself as the belated angel, a battle that aligns itself with the distinctly private transformation the writer relates in the movement from a clear distinction between victim and victimizer to a state of their thorough confusion. The final image of the Holocaust in which the angel did not arrive on time begins to sound in this perspective less like an attack upon a negligent father than an attack upon a monstrous, disheveled, terrified, and wide-eyed son and the conflagration for which he feels in some real way—founded or unfounded—fundamentally responsible.

Nor is that all. The excluded material persists in other ways. Does not the surrealistic scene at the count's gate reenact, to some extent, the conflagration itself? The child approaches the bars out of curiosity and fascination with the imprisoned son. What he sees terrifies him. He is transfixed, as if gazing into an abyss. His knees buckle. And in an attempt to respond positively he traps himself. Moreover, the disfigurement and tearing of flesh that results from his placing of his tongue against the frozen bars is experienced (because of the temperature differential) as burning. Blood flows and the end result of this fascination and good will gone wrong is collapse and fever.

And if permanent disfigurement (and finally death) predominate in the biographical scene, has not that same twisting or scarring or branding, a blurring of boundaries between what is within and what is without, begun to appear to some extent *as* the text, as its frozen bars, so to speak?[32] Is not the mistake Leivick makes in substituting the characterization "four" for the three episodes he has recounted the same "branding" or "blurring"? His insistence that there were "four moments" exceeds our demonstration that there were only three. The fourth event is no doubt the morning's tragedy. But there is an odd urgency or intensity to the word "four" that suggests it functions as much to describe which events as how many, and it is this adjectival or ordinal intensity (in contrast to the cardinal and more broadly numerical intensity we expect) that the sister's age—of "four"—seems most resonantly to explain. "These 'four' events," he repeats, "are happening to me again today no less fatefully and no less tragically. . . ."

Are we over-reading? Are we making too much of this admittedly biographically grounded information? Here is a poem Leivick wrote for a volume published in 1955 (two years before the current Jerusalem speech), a volume also containing a poem on his sister, and one in which fire, fathers, and writing all play a part.

In Fire

The long dark night is fire.
My head on a pillow of flaming fire.
I inhale and exhale fire
Through open doors and windows of fire.
My hand reaches out and makes signs in fire,
Writing in fire with fire on fire.
I ask for mercy, seek defense in fire,
I pray: Oh, save me, save me, fire!
And I hear voices blazing in fire:
    I am your father—your father of fire.
    I am your mother—your mother of fire,
    Your father who made you a Jew in fire,

> Your mother who nursed you, an infant, with fire.
> Remember your cradle—hung on ropes of fire.
> Once, in a hut, at the dawn of fire;
> Remember, how the ropes fluttered in fire,
> The ropes reaching the ceiling of fire,
> Remember how we caught you in fire
> And ran with you between fire and fire,
> Ran from fire, through fire, in fire.
> Now we return to hug you with fire,
> To swaddle you again in diapers of fire.
> To raise you again, to carry you in fire
> From fire, through fire, to fire—
>
> I hear the voices in nightly fire,
> Until the beginning of dawn in fire,
> And what will come—no one knows but the fire
> Drawing with fire in fire on fire.³³

"I inhale and exhale fire / . . . Writing in fire with fire on fire." These words may stand, I suggest, as a title for Leivick's lifelong project. I will return to Leivick and to the complexities of his position. But in order to set the stage for the contrast that I would like to develop—between two very different attitudes toward the Holocaust—I would like to turn momentarily to another text, one that was also first delivered orally (in fact two years earlier than Leivick's) on the French television broadcast *Écoute Israel* that aired on April 29, 1955. At times the words of the second earlier address seem to be forecasting Leivick's with astonishing accuracy.

The second talk, delivered by Lithuanian French Jewish teacher and philosopher Emmanuel Levinas, was entitled "Aimer le Thora plus que Dieu" ("To Love the Torah More than God") and appeared in his collection *Difficile liberté*.³⁴ I have already commented on this text in my discussion of the Book of Job. I recall it in the present context as a way of developing the biblical resource for our own moment.

> I have just read a text that is both beautiful and true, true as only fiction can be. Published in an Israeli journal by an anonymous author, and translated under the title of "Yossel, son of Yossel Rakover of Tarnopol, speaks to God" for *La Terre retrouvée*—a Parisian Zionist periodical—by M. Arnold Mandel, it . . . translates an experience of spiritual life that is at once profound and authentic.
>
> *The text presents itself to us as a document,* written during the final hours of the Resistance of the Warsaw Ghetto. The narrator would have been witness to all the horrors; he would have lost his young children under conditions of atrocity. As the last survivor of his family and with only a few moments left, he bequeaths to us his ultimate

thoughts. This is literary fiction, of course; but fiction in which each one of us who are survivors may dizzily recognize his own life. . . .

What is the meaning of this suffering of the innocent? Does it not bear witness to a world that is without God, to a land where man alone measures Good and Evil? The simplest and most common response to this question would lead to atheism. This is no doubt also the sanest reaction for all those for whom up until a moment ago a God, conceived a bit primitively, distributed prizes, inflicted sanctions, or pardoned faults, and in His kindness treated human beings as eternal children. But with what narrow-minded demon, with what strange magician did you thus populate your sky, you who now declare it to be deserted? And why under such an empty sky do you continue to seek a world that is meaningful and good?

Yossel ben Yossel reveals to us the certitude of God with a new force under an empty sky. For if he exists so alone, it is in order to feel upon his shoulders all the responsibilities of God. On the path that leads to the unique God there is a relay point which is without God. True monotheism must respond to the legitimate exigencies of atheism. A God of adults manifests Himself precisely through (*par*) the emptiness of the sky of a child. This is a moment when God withdraws from the world and conceals His face (according to Yossel ben Yossel). . . .

A God who conceals His face is not, I think, a theological abstraction or a poetic image. It is a way of talking about the hour when the just individual no longer finds any external recourse, when no institution protects him, when the consolation of divine presence in childish religious sentiment is similarly of no avail, when the individual can no longer triumph except in his own consciousness (*conscience*), which is to say, necessarily in suffering; a specifically Jewish sense of suffering which never at any moment assumes the value of a mystical expiation for the sins of the world. The condition of being a victim (*la position des victimes*) in a world in disorder, which is to say, in a world where the good does not triumph, *is* suffering. It reveals a God who, renouncing all helpful manifestation, appeals to the full maturity of the integrally responsible man. . . . The suffering of the just for a justice that is without triumph is lived concretely *as* Judaism. Israel—historic and carnal—has become once again a religious category (italics in the final paragraph added).[35]

In the wake of an experience like that of the Holocaust, atheism or the death of God might seem the most natural (perhaps even the most reasonable) response. But we make that response only if we have held up until this moment a particularly childlike conception of God—of one who inflicts injury and awards prizes, a God, that is to say, of eternal children. On the other hand, if we expand our conception of transcendence, if we allow God at least the same sophistication we grant ourselves, alternative possibilities appear. His very absence, for example, may be taken less as a sign of abandonment than as an index of our own responsibility for (and implication in) human behavior. It may lead to the recognition that suffering is not an interruption of human experience from the outside—as if a condition independent of suffering were achievable under the right circumstances—nor an experience to which may be attached any symbolic value whatsoever—as if, for example, it were redemptive—but an inevitable extension of that experience in a dilapidated world where the good and the just do not triumph. Moreover, that in the face of that ineluctability what we *can* do is respond, trace the path of our own implication in the fortunes of the neighbor, the other individual, whose absolute alterity from us I have attempted to objectify and master. "The suffering of the just for a justice that is without triumph is lived concretely *as* Judaism."

It is hard in the present context not to read these words in connection with the text of Leivick we have just been examining. Does not Leivick's lament that "for us the angel did not arrive in time" invite us to adopt the very childlike humanistic perspective that would subordinate the social Holocaust to the private holocausts of personal guilt? Is it not Leivick who chides God for not doing enough, who would require of God that He be the responsible God of the children (who are His charge) and who takes up the mantle of responsibility only in and by virtue of its perceived abandonment by God?

But if we make that assumption, a rather astounding conclusion follows. Holocaust scholars have begun to speak of the Holocaust less as an event in which a peaceful moral Europe was suddenly invaded by demonic elements from the outside than as the becoming monstrous or going wrong of a certain style of humanistic thinking recognizably European in origin—the equation, for example, of humanism in the extreme with nihilism and with murder, the enactment we may say of romanticism with a vengeance. What Levinas enables us to conclude is that what died at Auschwitz was not God but humanism, the possibility that when all else failed one could rely upon a reservoir of man's common humanity, the very humanism upon which Leivick's remarks depend. "Premodern philosophy was prepared to posit," Fackenheim writes, "a permanent human nature that was unaffected by historical change."

> More deeply immersed in the varieties and vicissitudes of history, modern philosophy generally has perceived, in abstraction from historical change, only a human condition, which was considered per-

manent only in so far as it was beyond the humanly impossible. At Auschwitz, however, "more was real than is possible," and the impossible was done by some and suffered by others.[36]

In the wake of that collapse of the human, Leivick's appropriation of a certain humanistic style of thinking as commentary about the Holocaust is more than "inadequate." Ironically continuing the very position at stake within it, the view of which the Holocaust is itself the explosion, Leivick's position reenacts those internal dynamics. More than a commentary, it becomes itself a symptom, a trace, an index, an evidentiary display of the very event it would describe, a repetition of that event founded this time not upon difference or analogy but on sameness and continuity. Watching Leivick watch those events, we ourselves witness them. Moreover, we do so from the "inside," so to speak, since it was nothing other than the articulation of such a reconstructive view in the face of its own inadequacy that constituted that "inside."

Watching Leivick substitute for the outer historical Holocaust—in which no institution protects the just individual who can no longer triumph except in his own consciousness, which is to say, necessarily in suffering—another in which, at one extreme, differences are clear and the writer would argue that God has abandoned His earthly charge and, at another extreme, differences are less clear and the writer will act out his most private nightmares, we witness the Holcaust, the same sacrificial humanistic substitiution or scapegoating mechanism by which one's innermost hates or fears or desires may be played out on a global stage and on an infintely more destructive scale. The four themes we have identified in this context become then some of the sites on which these scenes are replayed and thus on which they may continue to be witnessed or observed.

Writing before the Holocaust after it, in other words, Leivick's view acts, in some important way, as if the Holocaust had not taken place. It is not, that is, as if had the Holocaust not come along, he would have been able to say God is alive and well. God was never not dead for him in the manner in which he later speaks of Him. The angel had never not arrived late—from childhood on, he assures us. I think we have to take him quite seriously when he tells us that these childhood experiences—once we have deciphered the dimensions of the confusions they replay—have determined for him everything that he does and is. "These four experiences . . . ," Madison quotes him as saying, "became the susurrus of all my later poems and plays."

Perhaps that is what it means to say—as we did at the outset of this study in echo of Des Pres—that the Holocaust has no end. It has no end because we are still within it. Witnessing the way a writer like Leivick indexes its most intense conflicts we find ourselves still within the presence of those conflicts and "dwell in aftermath." To articulate, as we have tried to do, the non-representational and indexical logic, the diachronic continuity, between the Holocaust and where we are, the way in which the Holocaust continues, survives itself, so to speak, is to articulate a set of parameters by which *l'univers concentrationnaire* "intrudes to occupy our minds," "becomes a demonic anti-world that undermines our own."

Freud offers us a name for such lurid, lugubrious, and obsessive repetition in the wake of trauma. He calls it the work of mourning. Perhaps it is in that sense that Leivick's view constitutes a witness, less to the pastness of the past, than to its presentness and continuation. If we accept Freud's formulation of mourning as "acting out," we may reformulate more precisely the paradigm shift of which we earlier spoke as a move beyond mourning, a move he calls the "working through." In contrast to acting out, working through names the way in which the work of mourning completes itself. The distinctions between the two concepts in Freud are many and complex. But I suggest it may be useful to think of working through much as one thinks of the relationship between interpretation and blindness in literary criticism—as precisely a form of acting out that has begun to take account—and therefore control—of itself. There are in fact only two forms of post-traumatic behaviors, we may say, in this connection: those behaviors that are versions of acting out, and those behaviors that are aware of themselves as acting out, and attempt to give it up. Which is to say, of course, that there is no behavior that is not acting out, only behavior in which acting out proceeds more or less un-self-consciously.

Are we contrasting Leivick with Levinas, acting out with working through? Are we arguing, for example, that Levinas is "better" than Leivick for our purposes, more effective as a commentator on the Holocaust, more comprehensive as a thinker about these matters? We have seen that Leivick also challenges himself in these regards. He stages before us, without ever saying so directly, the child's implication in and responsibility for the violence of the other, an implication that appears by virtue of the trauma of the death of his sister, but that shows up more directly in the text as the recognition in the face to face encounter with the other of the child's own guilt. Behind the more public humanist reading is a series of more private readings: an antisemitic battle that was the progenitor of anger, a battle internal to Judaism between fathers and sons (and between rabbis and their students) that was the progenitor of fear, and a far more personal battle in which the guilty party was Leivick himself as a young child. At these levels of analysis the anecdote reveals to us another dimension in which the limitations of the above position—and responsibility as a theme—appear.

And not only in this text. It appears as well in the poetry (as we have seen) and in dramas Leivick has written. It appears, for example, in a play on the Book of Job, where Job and Isaac have been arguing over who has suffered more and on walks the ram who was caught in the thicket and says to them: you two idiots! I was sacrificed![37]

The difference between Leivick and Levinas that follows from the above examination, I would argue, is not one of substance (or power or comprehensiveness) but one of style. What appears thematically in Levinas appears dramatically in Leivick. One may prefer one style to another. It is probably a bit easier to recognize the theme of responsibility in Levinas than in Leivick (where it has to be deciphered, as Paul de Man would say). Leivick is something like the Rousseau of Yiddish literature in this regard, a writer who acts out the romanticism of his age only to undercut that acting out by the way in which it is staged.

Rather what we *do* assert is the appearance of a difference between them, the distinction between a style that speaks romantically and exposes its own romanticism and another that articulates that opposition thematically where before there was only unanimity. In light of this distinction the paradigm shift of which we spoke earlier may be described more precisely. The shift is not between Leivick and Levinas but from a perspective dominated by the former to one dominated by the distinction between the two. In the terms Ellen Fine invoked, it is a matter of moving from a wound that passes *as* memory (and that enacts itself within and by means of that memory) to the possibility of distinguishing between wound on one hand and memory on the other.

After Auschwitz, in other words, two humanisms remain available to us: a humanism of essential and undying values, and a humanism of personal responsibility; one that depends upon a reservoir of truth and meaning to which one can always appeal (if worse come to worse, we are able to say, we are finally all human), and another that traces diachronically the failure of the first and that, while renouncing all helpful external recourse, assumes upon its own shoulders human responsibility for human behavior. What distinguishes the current way of talking about the Holocaust from previous ways is less a move to give up the first for the second, Leivick's position for Levinas's, than a move to give up the domination of the first and open ourselves to distinguishing wound from memory, remembering the Holocaust from surviving it.[38] If, far from the nemesis of humanism—its monstrous abrogation or violation from the outside—Nazism may be understood as humanism gone wrong, a humanism with a vengeance, so to speak, then Levinas offers us a way of distinguishing a religion of adults from a religion of eternal childhood in which personal responsibility imagined as the difference between Leivick and Levinas comes to the fore and indexes for us—through face-to-face encounters—relation itself, which is to say, human interaction founded upon meeting.

※ ※ ※

After Auschwitz, after the happening of the impossible, everything we are and do has changed, and it is once again to Terrence Des Pres that we are prompted to return. In the passage immediately following the passage with which I began this chapter, Des Pres takes up the question of prognosis and I would like to return now in concluding to that quote. Where does all of this lead? Des Pres asks.

> Where this enterprise will lead I cannot say. Terminal despair is a real possibility. So is nuclear holocaust; what did happen can happen, and historical precedent tends to influence options for the future. The stakes, in other words, are very high. But exactly for these reasons we have turned with new determination to the study of Holocaust matters, hoping thereby to alert understanding, to reveal the enormity of our present predicament, and most of all to transform our expanding awareness of man's capacity for destruction into a kind of consciousness identical with conscience.[39]

"A kind of consciousness identical with conscience," a kind of "French" consciousness, therefore, we are tempted to say, where *conscience* means both. Is not the position Des Pres calls for the one we have tried to articulate, which is to say, an ethical consciousness in which consciousness itself is continuous in the extreme and by extension with suffering, a historical consciousness founded upon our own implication in (and responsibility for) the other individual in which the survivor is understood as the trace or face of the presentness of that past, its "living document"?

It may turn out that we are at the beginning stages in European culture of a process of bereavement which will enlist our energies (and exact extrordinary tolls from us) for some time to come—perhaps for the foreseeable future. To articulate, as I have tried to do, the non-representational, diachronic, symptomatic logic by which the attempts of a writer like Halpern Leivick to write about the Holocaust repeat it, is to suggest some of the ways in which the Holocaust continues, survives itself, so to speak, and therefore something of the means by which we may, in taking account of the nightmares it continues to engender in us, in remaining alert to its organization of our lives, work through its crises and respond ethically to its challaneges.

Along with such "alertness" comes, of course, no guarantees. "Terminal despair," Des Pres warns us, "is a real possibility." That such consciousness seems to have proved fatal for so many in the post-Holocaust era (and we seem to have felt it necessary to invoke this conjunction in the case of Des Pres's own death as well as that of Primo Levi—although there is evidence of accident in both), need not, I suggest, necessarily condemn us.[40] It may even provide us paradoxically with the foundation for hope, one that issues from the very "enormity" of our "predicament" and the peculiar decisiveness of these individual actions. If the trauma of the Holocaust had left us paralyzed, zombies, not unlike the musulmen that Levi, Fackenheim, and others describe, our "predicament" would be considerably worse. At least, in the aftermath of the devastation, if not its vortex, in the witnessing of its endlessness that constitutes that afterward, we retain the possibility of choice, the possibility, we might say, of possibility itself, which is to say, the possibility of history.

The choice available to us in witnessing—and bearing witness to—our own and someone else's devastation is, admittedly, not a great deal upon which to found one's hope. But it does offer us, at least, the prospect, in similar if alternative circumstances, of not doing that, of not taking the actions which lead to that devastation, of recognizing the road we have been traveling and the violence to which it is heading, and giving it up. Witnessing the witnessing of others offers us the prophetic possibility of living on and living through that devastation, of "sur-viving" it.

It is upon such choice, the possibility of such prophetic understanding, such survival, that I would propose our discussion of the memory of the Shoah might helpfully be based.

Conclusion

Reading after Auschwitz

> If thought is not measured by the extremity that eludes the concept, it is from the outset in the nature of the musical accompaniment with which the SS liked to drown out the screams of its victims.
>
> Theodore Adorno

> We come *after*, and that is the nerve of our condition.
>
> George Steiner

"We must first make a distinction," write Wellek and Warren in the opening sentence of their influential book, *Theory of Literature*, "between literature and literary study."¹ Why? Why must we distinguish between these two? What if they are the same? What if literature is a mode of literary study, one that we have chosen, for one reason or another, to pass off as something else? It never occurs to Wellek and Warren that the distinction they regard as self-evident, as one that "goes without saying," in fact, the one from which their entire perspective derives (and for which their volume remained, for so many years, the most famous exemplar), may also be the most problematic of their book.

Nor that it has a history. If the distinction was supportable in the nineteenth century, is it still at the close of the twentieth? Even if we were to grant that the construction of the literary object—the relegation of certain texts to the status of "literature," the development of a technology of close critical reading to engage those texts, etc.—constituted an advance, that the historical-critical method (of which such new critical aesthetics is the heir) offered the promise of a reading that might escape the dogmatic and theocentric presuppositions of earlier models (a promise that is not without complications of its own), does that new critical gesture remain viable once the humanistic foundation upon which it rested has itself collapsed? Is the same reading possible after Auschwitz?

These questions deserve a volume. In the few pages remaining I can do little more than sketch the rudiments of a theory of literary reading that might be built on their basis as we have pursued them in the seven preceding studies: a theory of literature *as* reading, of literature as criticism. At the conclusion of this sketch, I will return to questions posed in the introduction concerning the peculiar appeal of reading for us today.

I. Literature as Reading

> A question is raised by [the Hebrew Bible] which fascinates me: Whether commentary is not always within literature, whether literature itself has not always been a development of commentary. One has still to define why literature is different from commentary on literature.
>
> Geoffrey H. Hartman

> The systematic avoidance of the problem of reading, of the interpretative or hermeneutic moment, is a general symptom shared by all methods of literary analysis whether they be structural or thematic, formalist or referential, American or European, apolitical or socially committed. It is as if an organized conspiracy made it anathema to raise the question, perhaps because the vested interests in literary studies as a respectable intellectual discipline are at stake or perhaps for more ominous reasons.
>
> Paul de Man

". . . among all the narratives [in a society]," Michel Foucault writes, "why is it that a number of them are sacralized, made to function as 'literature'?"[2] Foucault's interests were never primarily in literary study. But as he revitalized so many other fields he touched in passing, so his insights in this domain were trenchant.[3] His question presupposes the fundamental observation that will open for us our entire inquiry: that the question of "literature" and of literary study is a matter of the process of sacralization.[4]

In particular, at least seven distinct observations or sets of observations emerge from the preceding (literary) studies that will help us to locate this disclosure.

1. The first is that literary criticism, far from the arbitrary and "disinterested play of mind upon the best that has been thought or known"—as it has long been understood within the "Arnoldian" tradition—is in fact a considerably more systematic and self-enclosed affair. It is thoroughly mythic in constitution, an entirely self-coherent, patterned, and structured response to the writing to which it directs our attention. And

as a form of academic practice, it constructs its own system of inclusions and exclusions.

Thus, for example, the mainstay of opinion in classical studies for a good part of the nineteenth century (and well into the twentieth) with regard to Sophocles' *Oedipus Tyrannus* was not just any view but in particular the notion of a tragic fate or destiny, of a providential lot or *moira*, in relation to which all of one's relations with the gods were assumed to be conducted. One English-speaking critic could approach the play ritualistically (Bowra, Dodds), another dramatistically (Greene, Waldock, Norwood, Jebb), another historically and humanistically (Whitman), still another in accordance with existentialist philosophy popular in the 1960s (Kott).[5] The same set of primary considerations was observed in each case. If Philip Vellacott and Bernard Knox could come along in the 1950s and 1960s and mount serious challenges to these prevailing views from within theater studies or ancient historical research, it remained exclusively within the context of these ideas about fate and destiny—if only in their repudiation—that such new approaches would have to be articulated.[6]

Similarly, the notion that Shakespeare represents the burgeoning of a certain strain of Renaissance humanist thinking, a figure deemed to be newly liberated from the dark medievalism of his past and looking forward to the enlightened individualism of the two centuries to come, is not just any idea but the governing one.[7] The explosion of interest in Renaissance studies in the 1980s—fueled largely by the new historicists and drawing upon the most sophisticated of contemporary theorists—was still required to speak this same Hegelian language.[8]

Moreover, no one who flouts these unspoken rules can expect to receive a serious hearing. Frank Kermode directs our attention to this rarely acknowledged inclusivity and exclusivity of the critical tradition in the English-speaking world in his discussion of the critical reception afforded Ernest Seisler, whose books were left unreviewed because he deigned to regard A. C. Bradley as an "intellectual pygmy" and "a cerebral castrate," and remarked about Coleridge that he has the "razor-sharpness of melted butter."[9] It is not, Kermode argues, that we need (or need primarily) to read Seisler to better understand Shakespeare but rather to better understand the systematic nature of our own critical and institutional choices, a system that might not otherwise become visible.[10] And other examples within the history of non-conformist response to

Shakespeare's plays which call attention to the constraints with which we customarily proceed—Thomas Rymer on *Othello,* Voltaire on *Hamlet,* Tolstoy on *Lear,* G. B. Shaw on the late comedies—could readily be adduced.[11]

2. The second observation is that this myth or story that criticism characteristically tells with regard to the texts its reads did not spring up overnight or accidentally but is grounded in the texts and traditions that make up the language that it speaks. In the modern context, it has its origins in the critical spirit that, via Matthew Arnold, the English romantic poets, and the German romantic philosophers (especially Hegel, Schiller, the Schlegels, and Schelling) was inaugurated by Kant. And behind Kant, of course, by way of the long European tradition of Aristotelian poetics, stand the Roman rhetoricians, the Alexandrians, the writings of Aristotle'himself (or his students) and finally Plato.[12]

In other words, the critical spirit or "historical-critical method" that operates within philosophy and the criticism of literature are not parallel activities but in significant measure the same activity. "Criticism," "literature," and the distinction between them are demonstrably critico-philosophic concerns that concretize older philosophic concerns that begin with the dawn of philosophy itself, although the contemporary expression of those older concerns shows up as literary criticism in one domain, and philosophy in another.[13]

The view expressed by Bowra, Greene, Whitman, and even Kott that ancient tragedy is to be regarded as a tragedy of destiny or fate may be found already in Hegel's *Aesthetics* (among other places) along with the concomitant notion that the modern drama is to be regarded as a drama of choice or character.[14] The young classicists who attended Hegel's lectures were the same who later taught Nietzsche, Burkhardt, Wilamowitz, Rohde, and others in the German university system and from whom in turn the conceptions with which we currently work—both the aesthetic and the historical conceptions—demonstrably derive.[15]

The view that Coleridge's famous lectures on Shakespeare (upon his return from Germany in the first decade of the nineteenth century) significantly recast the parameters in which Shakespeare's plays and poems were to be discussed, or that A. C. Bradley more than anyone else in the modern arena defined for us the terms in which Shakespearean tragedy was to be read similarly express investments in the philosophic postulates from which that writing derives.[16] The discarding of more mainstream approaches to Shakespeare by Freud's English student Ernest Jones, for example (say, in *Hamlet and Oedipus*) continues to rely upon the views developed by Bradley's Hegelian moralism, views that participate in the oldest of debates within our history.[17]

And both Hegel's views and those of the Schlegels (upon whom Coleridge relied) continue the Platonic-Aristotelian matrix.[18] The tradition of reading literature and of doing criticism participates within the philosophic enterprise par excellence that is their sponsor. It makes little difference whether a particular reader or critic has "read" Kant, Hegel, Aristotle, or Plato since the themes to be expressed and the rules by which critical discourse is conducted are enabled exclusively by the work of these writers. We breathe their air as we attempt to articulate ourselves on these matters.

3. On the other hand, if criticism is mythic, differential, an identifiable part of the tradition of critical philosophy, our third observation must be that great literature, the writing we have deemed to "sacralize" (in Foucault's term) as a special and enigmatic cultural monument, is constitutionally anti-mythic, set up precisely as a radical critique of just those kinds of myths or stories that criticism blithely brings to it. As such, and despite customary claims to the contrary, this literature properly speaking has no tradition. As a critique of the myth, a form of criticism or commentary upon materials out of which it comes, literature assumes the form those materials assume. In some sense, therefore, we may say that the writing of literature is impossible since to write literature would always be to begin with some pattern, some story, even a story of a critique of stories, that served as one's model. The "writerly" as a style, to use a neologism employed to explain Roland Barthes's notion of the *scriptible* a few years ago, is properly speaking impossible.

Thus Sophocles' play, far from an illustration of the myth of parricide and incest and of the importance (ironic or otherwise) of the power of fate or destiny in human affairs, is a fundamental criticism of that idea, a staging of its limitations—its idolatrous origins, its appropriative strategies, its violent and self-destructive consequences.

Shakespeare's representation of the deposition of Richard II, far from dramatizing either the Tudor myth that Henry has usurped the throne from Richard (expounded for example by Tillyard), or more recent critico-poetic accounts of a contest between political and poetic forces (expounded for example by Coleridge), chronicles the collapse or "waning" of such older medieval monarchical conceptions and the inadequacy of more modernist approaches whose memory and structure such critical fictions enact.[19]

4. But fourthly, great literature is not simply anti-mythic. It is not just any old myth whose limits it stages but precisely (and ironically) those of the very myth that criticism would bring to it. In this sense we may legitimately say that great literature is already "about" the criticism that will come along and attempt to displace it.

Thus the tragedy of destiny approach that derives from Hegel is in fact already in some capacity a version or reading of the "reversal of fortune" by which Aristotle understands the play.[20] But the "reversal of fortune" is also the view articulated by the Chorus of Elders at the play's conclusion where Sophocles draws upon the commonplace notion (used in fact by all three tragic poets, expressed by his friend Herodotus, and that the entirety of his play to that point has thrust into some question) that the vicissitudes of fortune alone are constant, and any determination of one's success or fortune before life's conclusion is premature.

In the same way, the view adopted by Bernard Knox in his later writings that Oedipus's search for truth is primary finds its Sophoclean correlative in Oedipus's chiding of the reigning prophetic authorities—Teiresias (the Apollonian enthusiast) and the priest of Zeus—that they failed to solve the riddle of the plague-bearing Sphinx and that "know-nothing Oedipus" had to come along and do so, a view that of course will recur within a hundred years (albeit in a much softened tone) in Plato's Socrates.[21]

The critical notion of the Tudor myth by which so much of Shakespeare's history plays were explained in the 1940s derives of course from the aetiology of the Tudor monarch of their own history, one that is bound up with the notion of the divine right of kings and the legal fiction of the king's two bodies.[22] But the same explanation is also Richard's (as God's "lieutenant"), and he depends upon it when he returns in the central act of the play to the coast of Wales, although (as in the other cases) it is less the efficacy of the use of such ideas that we witness than their critical insufficiency in the present context.

How did literature come to "know" about these myths? Is it not at least curious that literature should criticize the *same* myths that criticism reconstructs? Is literature "psychic"? Or, if we accept the idea that literature is already a certain reading or interpretation of a set of myths (which is not itself an outrageous claim), how does it come about that criticism both reconstructs those myths and fails to recognize that literature has already been deconstructing them? Is criticism (and are critics) simply blind to literature's "transcendent" power, so overwhelmed by literature's "mystical plenitude" in its view, that it is naïvely innocent of literature's more critical activity? Is that why such mythopoetic and anti-mythic activities occur simultaneously? Is criticism, on the other hand (and somewhat more cynically), willfully ignorant regarding literature's intentions, perhaps because it intends to pursue its own more parochial goals?

Thus far we have only spoken of the effects of this literary and critical activity, that criticism turns out to be mythic and to participate in the enterprise of philosophy, and that literature turns out to be anti-mythic and already concerned with the same myths criticism reconstructs. How do these effects come to be generated? What are the strategies operative within criticism and literature that produce them?

5. Thus, fifthly, we are impelled to observe that if great literature is not anti-mythic with regard to just any old myths (but precisely of the myths criticism later brings to it), neither is it in fact anti-mythic in just any old way. Literature has a distinct manner of challenging the myth, a style of mythic encounter that differs decidedly from the style of criticism.

For example, great literature is not simply anarchic with regard to these mythic coordinates or even indecisive (which would in fact be in both cases only negative imitations of those structures). Rather it stages them in accordance with another logic, a diachronic or "historical" or "sequential" logic that we have called here or there "prophetic," and that differs significantly from the synchronic or essentialistic or relational logic by which criticism would erect an isomorphic grid of distinctions in context of which the play comes to be read.

Maurice Bowra and William Chase Greene, although they differ as to whether Sophocles' play should be read as ritual or as drama, share the idea that the play offers us a positive lesson in the power of the gods in human affairs. Cedric Whitman and Jan Kott, although they differ over whether to read the play historically or philosophically, agree that the lesson it offers us is a profoundly negative one. Sophocles, on the other hand, does not view the play as a lesson at all but stages such an explanation as the retrospectively transfigured account by which first Oedipus himself and then (for their own reasons) the Chorus of Elders would contain what has transpired. Far from simply challenging the mythic account with a set of empirical circumstances that either repudiate it or leave it in doubt, Sophocles stages the entirety of its history: its origins in Oedipus's fascination with oracular language, the self-distancing strategies by which Oedipus removes himself from Corinth (which he takes initially to be the seat of his disaster) and from those eyes that have seen what they should not have seen (when he discovers the difficulty closer to home), and the self-destructive violence and blindness into which such strategies issue for both Jocasta and Oedipus.

Tillyard adopts a certain historical understanding of Shakespeare's play. Coleridge, Peter Ure, and Mark Van Doren read it as an opposition between two competing generic styles—the poetic and the political, for example. But Shakespeare refuses either the historical or aesthetic grid and traces instead the progressive transformation of one position into the other in both cases. Far from representing the course of Richard's deposition as the result of either history or aesthetics, Shakespeare follows Richard's progressive transformation from monarchical to theatrical to prophetic roles, Henry's progressive transformation from ambitious to monarchical to theatrical to prophetic roles, and the identicality of both with each other and with the historical, aesthetic, and choral accounts we bring to the play.

Thus literature and criticism have decidedly different strategies with regard to the myth they both treat. Where do these strategies originate? How does it happen to turn out that criticism rebuilds the myth? How does it turn out that literature attacks it? And why the same myth in each case?

6. Our sixth observation is that both literature and criticism are readings of the source material from which literature has come—criticism reading it mythically, and literature anti-mythically. Literature "knows" about these myths at least provisionally because it found them in the same place criticism found them, the source material from which it was itself engendered. Literature did not just happen to stage these myths any more than criticism just happened to reconstruct the myths that literature abrogates. But rather both proceeded from the same origin. Despite appearances, literature "knows" what criticism will do because it reads the same mythic script that criticism does.

Thus, critics of Sophocles direct their attention to the oracular, heroic, funereal structures of the fifth-century *polis* no less than he does. They are perhaps even more knowledgeable about those structures because they have the perspective gained from distance that he lacks, although they in turn treat those structures as patterns to be differentially articulated while he views them as the indices of a crisis.[23] Critical readers of Shakespeare's plays probably know more about the technical concerns of medieval monarchy than Shakespeare, although he is vastly more critical of their deployment in these circumstances than they are.

But if literature and criticism originate in the same mythic sources, why are their responses so different?

7. To answer this question is to venture upon what is clearly our most complicated if final set of observations, and here is where the brilliance of Foucault's observation is so apparent. The critically anti-mythic attitude of literature and the literaturizing mythopoetic attitude of criticism show up as they do because they are both modalities of the sacrificial and it is at this level I would suggest that we must finally investigate them.

For criticism has never not known, it now turns out, that literature has been conducting these anti-mythic experiments, so to speak, upon the body of stories with which it is working. It is not in blindness, naïveté, or ignorance (willful or otherwise) that criticism marches up to great literary texts, trots out the myths that it finds exploded there, and replaces those myths with new ones (or even the same ones) it would prefer to find. It is not in spite of what literature is doing that criticism does what it does but rather *because* of it, as a deliberate and systematic displacement of that central literary critical activity.

How so? Identifying in the explosive display before it not simply a monstrosity but a scandal, a disturbing mirror, a monstrous double of its own critical pretensions, criticism responds as it has learned to respond in the face of any dangerous mimetic contagion: sacrificially. It quarantines or sequesters or cordons off this writing from all but the most trusted and trained cultural hands; it immobilizes or sedates or neutralizes it; it segments or sections it into its fundamental elements; it reconstructs and reconfigures those component elements according to the most approved cultural methods; and it replays its transformed dramas—in teaching it and writing about it—within the anodyne environment of academic literary critical circles. In conclusion, it displays this transformed writing as an object of "scientific" study and trains others to engage it as it does, with asbestos gloves, so to speak, to read it in such a way that at the same time excludes reading it, that its violence is effectively drained from it. In the face of this domesticated monstrosity, it declares itself to be "criticism," and what it reads to be "literature." In short, it "literaturizes" it.[24]

Criticism resembles, in this capacity at least, nothing so much as a antigenic agent sent out by the ruling cultural organism to surround, enclose, and effectively neutralize an intruding foreign body that has entered the system. Its motivation from a modern social point of view is not one of understanding or even mastery of the scandal precisely but of one of combat. But combat as it is always undertaken in a closed cultural community, with the goal, that is to say, less of eradicating or removing the victim than of putting him in a neutralized condition on display for others to observe and "learn" from. Defeated rulers always understand this drama and often take their lives to avoid just this eventuality. The sacralization of violent monstrous writing as literature is something like the capture of King Kong who is placed on display at the margins of the kingdom for all to observe (where he threatens always to break loose and wreak havoc on the city), and who in the final sequence, once he has escaped from those margins and is cornered atop the empire state building, is knocked from it, and in some sense becomes that building. The edifice remains as his monument, the trace of his passing, so to speak.

To suggest, however, that critical activity is "sacrificial," and the function it invariably serves for the surrounding academic environment is sacrificial, points us in turn toward another, older, sacrificial dimension that until now we have overlooked. Here we touch upon what may be the most surprising aspect of criticism of all. For the sources of the literature that criticism reads and appropriates were not just mythic but already sacrificial themselves, and it becomes clear now that in appropriating such readings, criticism was not so much "turning" (or even "returning") to them as much as continuing a tradition it had in effect never abandoned. Criticism never "turns to" those sources at all in this regard, if what we mean by "turn" is give up the path one is traveling to pursue another, since criticism in some real way *is* their modern version, the continuation and renewal of their very mythico-sacrificial constitution in the face of one more cultural impediment. Criticism never "rebuilds" the myth as we said before since it has in fact never not been building it.

Criticism emerges in this understanding as a kind of repetition compulsion to use Freud's language, an incomplete mourning or acting out that never achieves closure upon or effectively works through the trauma that engenders it, and the close association that Maurice Blanchot has long noticed between the experience of literature and the experience of death seems relevant here. Far from a reading of literature (or rather *as* its reading), criticism in fact always already takes place *within* the literature it reads. And as that continuation, obsessive or otherwise, of the sacrificial response to which literature is already a response (and that literature has long ago engaged), criticism may be understood as the subject matter of literature more profoundly than we have thus far allowed.

Criticism, in short, has never been the independent body of critical judgments that we have long declared it to be but the mainstay of the very sacrificial tradition from which literature itself has arisen, a tradition that, in the face of the profound criticism that literature would offer of it, has suddenly been triggered into action.

At this level, criticism turns out to be doubly sacrificial. It is sacrificial with regard to the cultural institutions in which such monstrous writing is to be read (the university, for example) and that it serves by domesticating and safely replaying its distinctions. But it is also sacrificial or protective of the tradition in so far as it repeats the philosophic mechanisms by which Aristotle would already domesticate and safely replay the violence that Plato identifies in the mimetic in general (and tragedy in particular), ancient philosophic mechanisms, that is to say, that we have to assume were themselves already the product of still earlier sacrificial procedures that this Platonic-Aristotelian critical matrix itself continued. The pre-Socratic philosophers and the writers of the Sophistic Enlightenment who were already erecting humanist and naturalist criticisms of Egyptian and Assyrio-Babylonian sacrificial structures are no less important to this discussion than their more familiar philosophic descendants—as Nietzsche and Heidegger knew so well.

The construction of a theory of an ironic tragedy of destiny, therefore, or of a poet of the inherited curse in the case of Aeschylus, is less an effort undertaken in ignorance of what Sophocles is really up to than an effort to contain and subsequently profit from that monstrous activity. Hegel's theories of tragic destiny—with Sophocles' and Aeschylus's plays as their illustration—play their part in the larger economy that constructs a body of knowledge about Greek life and culture (and thereby in the aetiology of our own Indo-European community in the nineteenth century) that has itself yet to be analyzed, although gestures in this direction have begun to be undertaken.[25] The construction of a humanist Shakespeare has as much to do, finally, with the genesis of modern sensibility (in accordance with the Burckardtian thesis) as it does with Shakespeare, a sensibility we now understand that participates in the oldest Platonic and rationalist moves we have.

But once we identify the "sacrificial" origin of criticism in this fashion, and recognize both its contemporary function and the way it continues an older generative process, a new understanding of literature suddenly appears. For if the sources of criticism were already sacrificial, and literature we maintain is a critical reading of those same sources, we come to understand the nature of that literary reading as sacrificial in turn—but this time at another level, sacrificial in this case of sacrifice itself.

As the presentation of those sacrificial sources, as the making overt of the conditions, the strategies, the consequences—in short, the limitations—of the sacrificial structure of the materials from which it has come (limitations whose suppression is required if that sacrificial structure is to be efficacious), literature offers a distinctly anti-sacrificial reading of those origins. If we draw upon the reading of the mechanism of the sacrificial that René Girard has been studying for a number of years, then the making overt of that mechanism—and in particular the arbitrariness of the central substitution—presupposes its inefficaciousness as a structurative device. Sophocles presents Oedipus's mythopoetic transfiguration of his experience in a context that belies it and that presentation itself works against the efficacy of his mythic reading. Shakespeare's presentation of Henry as point for point duplicating Richard undermines any possibility of maintaining a distinction between them, although it is upon such distinction that the mythic grounding effectively depends.

Literature, in other words, is a reading of the same source material from which criticism emerged but whose sacrificiality has itself become visible and questionable, whose sacrificial structure is in crisis, and whose limits it therefore poses overtly in order to gain some distance from them. It is the sacrificial mechanisms of the sources "gone wrong" so to speak, become inefficacious and thereby the source of violence and pestilence themselves rather than their remedy, that literature offers us.

From a perspective from within the "literaturized" writing criticism reads, a new perspective is available. If criticism has never not known that literature is its monstrous double, the most radical critic of its culture-building enterprise, neither it turns out has literature ever not known that this is how criticism would respond to its activity. In treating this mythic violence sacrificially, criticism has in fact only fleshed out what has long been literature's own subject matter.

For it has never been simply the myth—the differential system—that literature has staged. What literature found in the mythic contexts from which it developed was already the entirety of the sacrificial reading—the confrontation with limitlessness or monstrosity, the substitution of the "missing" or displaced mythic pattern for this violence, the engendering of a vocabulary about both this violence and this substitution (that both demystifies and remystifies both)—and it is this entire reading process that literature puts before us. Viewed from within literature, criticism's redoing of these mythic appropriations in its place, its continuation, that is to say, of those source structures, far from reading that literature, reenacts its genesis.

Thus Sophocles has never not known that those around Oedipus would react sacrificially to the surfacing of his history. In fact that sacrificial response is precisely what he stages in the figure of the Chorus members who end by reciting the Oedipus myth. Sophocles "knew" all this so to speak because he found it in the Sophistic Enlightenment of which his play was already a criticism, in the sacrificial mechanism that we must believe suddenly began to unravel in various centers of Greek life in the ancient sixth century—in Miletus, for example—that historians would later interpret as an anticipation of Plato (as "pre-Socratic"), where he could observe, for example, the Pythagorean sacrificial vocabulary, or the Orphic sacrificial mechanism, or other "mystery" cults formed by making explicit and new these generative mechanisms that were invisible prior to that moment. The anti-sacrificial response that finally constitutes Sophocles' play is a response to the crisis that is already fully identified as sacrificial at its origin for him and so philosophy's (and later criticism's) neo-sacrificial strategies are not especially surprising.

And what is the structure of English kingship in its medieval context if not sacrificial from beginning to end? Elias Cannetti, for example, details for us in his famous study of kingship in certain primitive cultures how such monarchical sacrificial mechanisms may operate.[26] We need turn, in Shakespeare, only to *Julius Caesar* to witness, in the successive and increasingly inefficacious substitution of Caesar for Caesar (Pompei, Julius Caesar, Brutus, Mark Antony, Octavius, etc.), the sacrificial process gone explicitly awry.[27] If the sacrificial dimensions of Richard's deposition are not entirely clear in the mid 1590s, they will become painfully so in the explicit references to sacrifice in the great tragedies (*Othello*, for example) and it is not at all certain they are not already apparent in the earlier plays.[28]

❧   ❧   ❧

To what conclusions do these seven observations lead? Suddenly, we are in a position to understand the relation between literature and criticism in a way that until this moment has eluded us. There is no "before" and "after" in this domain, no primary text before a secondary text, no literature, so to speak, before a work of criticism imagined as subsequent to it and independent of it. Literature is both before criticism *and* after it, both the impetus as monstrous writing that triggers the sacrificial critical response and already itself a response to that subsequent critical gesture in the form of the sacrificial source from which it has come. And criticism, similarly, is both subsequent to literature and prior to it, both a differentiating gesture that appears independent of the writing it reads, and already contained by that writing both within the crisis at its center, and within the concluding transfigurative gesture by which that crisis gets "critically" read.

There are in fact, we may say, always only two distinct readings or interpretations in this domain: those that are sacrificial, and those that are aware of their sacrificial dimensions and to which we accordingly give the name "anti-sacrificial." There are no non-sacrificial readings, although some sacrificial readings are more cognizant of the constraints or limitations or repetitions in which they work than others.

Thus the two impulses that have dominated the discussion of Platonic philosophy—the divinely inspired and the analytic, the mimetic or magnetic and the rational or reasonable, the possessed and the possessing—are less two distinct modalities than two moments of the *same* sacrificial modality: a moment of confusion, conflation, violence, and undifferentiating monstrosity in its midst in which the source myth "comes apart," so to speak, is asserted all the more aggressively as it is progressively less and less efficacious, and culminates in a paroxysmic substitution; and a final moment in which such crisis and violence get to be transfiguratively and differentially read.

And the Platonic response to this process (and from which the distinction between criticism and literature will later be derived), the separation of its continuity into two distinct perspectives, one that reads from that differential conclusion and synchronically distinguishes that violence from its truth, and another that reads from within that violent middle and perceives the diachronic continuities between its own mimetic dimensions and the mythopoetic sacrificial gesture that will later come along and substitute its own "true" reading for those dimensions in which it was engendered, is suddenly clear. The distinctions by which we have sequestered one portion of this unholy mixture from another, the rational from the mimetic, the ontological from the divinely inspired, the critical from the literary, and secondly by which we have in historical sequence excluded, rewritten, and then exalted or sacralized the latter in relation to the former, are revealed now to be part of a vast cultural machinery designed to work the way any such sacrificial strategy does: defensively. But defensive in the same way that all mechanisms of sacralization are defensive, which is to say, also protective, generative, promotive exclusively of its own cultural order and vitality by keeping out that which would destroy it—and with the surfacing of that mechanism we may now begin to views matters from another perspective: namely, anti-sacrificially.

Thus the distinction between literature and criticism must be understood, in the first instance, as criticism's distinction, the way criticism (and philosophy before it) identifies both itself and its other. But the real other to which criticism applies this transformative reading is already staging its own account of the relation of criticism to literature. Within the unsettling text criticism reads, what counts as "criticism" (for example, the myth) and what counts as "literature" (for example, the empirical context in which that myth is presented) are not unrelated as they are in analytic discourse but presented in fact as continuous with each other. Within literature, the myth, the synchronic account of the protagonist's experience (Oedipus's, Richard's), is a moment within the very diachronic sequence it is recounting, the retrospective transfiguration of that experience from a moment within it. Only if we repress that empirical context and read via that retrospective mythic view (refusing to "measure new things by old" in *Oedipus,* suppressing Richard's recognition that in one person he "plays many people" and "none contented") are things critically clear for us. Within literature (which is to say, within the crisis of that critical position taken as a whole), we are offered a diachronic account of the relation of the synchronic myth to the diachronic context (namely, that they are continuous) while outside of literature we preserve a synchronic account (that the synchronic and diachronic are clearly opposed).

As a consequence, criticism is scandalized. It confronts in the text before it its monstrous double: both its own distinction (in the figure of the myth) and the undoing of that distinction (in the sequential continuity between the myth and the context in which it is erected and that it reads). In the face of this confusion and conflation, the myth superimposed upon the empirical, the distinction between the diachronic and the synchronic superimposed upon their continuity, criticism gives this monstrous text "special handling," a phrase that translates a German word used by the Nazis to refer to the treatment of Jews.[29] It borrows or appropriates the mythic distinction within the play (the mythic view of Oedipus or of Richard) between the synchronic and the diachronic to name itself and the activity before it, calling the synchronic "criticism" and the diachronic "literature." It orders the relation between the two hierarchically, rendering the text it reads a version of the creative or inventive, and the text it generates a version of the analytic or decisive. And as the final step in this reading process (in which it has moved from a perceived violence, to an exaltation), it teaches others to do the same. It generates a community of students or scholars who repeat this stabilizing reading.

We have always read literature through criticism. But criticism it turns out has always already read through philosophy—Kant and Hegel in the modern world, Aristotle and Plato in the ancient world. And philosophy in turn is already a reading through the Sophistic Enlightenment, which is to say, the source to which "literature" (in the form of Greek tragedy) already responds. Consequently, criticism always simply reads through or repeats the same source material literature already reads.

At the same time, we have always understood literature as distinct from criticism. But it turns out that we obscured the way in which literature constitutes another type of response, a staging or diachronic tracing of its limits rather than the synchronic presentation of its meaning that constitutes criticism; and secondly, that literature is in fact not only a response to the sources from which it has come but, like criticism, always as well a version of those sources, one in particular that has turned back upon itself and is now reflective of its own conditions of possibility, a reflection we have deemed—after the analyses of René Girard—antisacrificial.

How did criticism come to appear synchronic and mythic if it is really also a continuation of the sacrificial (and therefore diachronic) modality of all sacrificial systems? How did literature get to preserve its diachronicity? Moreover, if they are both sacrificial (and therefore both diachronic) in structure, what is the difference between the sacrificial and the anti-sacrificial?

The watershed, of course, is Plato, from whose perspective tragedy assumes one coloring, analytic reasoning another. Plato rejects tragedy's anti-sacrificial position where he finds only a crisis of *mimesis*, runaway "being like another," for which he can ascertain little redeeming value and that he feels mortally threatens the state.

On the other hand, in the mythological modality that grew up as rationalism (as an outgrowth of the criticism of the sacred in the ancient sixth century), he finds an acceptable procedure. Divorcing the rational from the diachronic sequence in which it comes into existence, Plato preserves its purely synchronic terms. *Mimesis* becomes a kind of runaway diachronicity and rationalism a purified synchronicity and the contrast between these two extremes he offers as philosophy. Plato's gesture is quintessentially mythological—the ratio of the synchronic grid of differences by which he would read his history set off against the diachronic sequence in which that historicizing gesture appears—and it remains for Nietzsche to come along, at the other end of the gap that separates us from the ancient world, and play for Plato the playwright, so to speak, to stage Plato's mimetic philosophic mythologizing.

To discover the diachronicity of Platonic rationalism is to discover the sacrificiality of philosophy itself. And once we enter this realm, the difference between the two modalities of the sacrificial becomes clarified: there is the sacrificial that rereads itself from the perspective of its own ending, and there is the sacrificial that is aware of the arbitrariness of that retrospective reading and names it in advance in order that we might give it up.

If we have always read tragedy from the point of view of philosophy, the Platonic-Aristotelian matrix, what we need to begin to do is read philosophy from the point of view of tragedy. This work has begun in part. From a sacrificial point of view, both the style that offers itself as criticism and the style that offers itself as literary may be equally sacrificial or anti-sacrificial. If literary writing emphasizes the mythic grid by which all that has occurred may be reread, it functions sacrificially. If the limitations of that final reading become apparent when placed before their inefficaciousness, then we may speak of the sequence as anti-sacrificial. If the critical perspective that concludes a reading of literature effectively dispels the monstrosity of its original confrontation, then we might designate that criticism sacrificial. On the other hand, if criticism takes account of its own expulsions, we may simply begin to think of it as anti-sacrificial.

In this context both the power and limitation of deconstructive readings become apparent. Shifting ground from a concern with subjects and objects (and consequently an Aristotelian poetics) to a more Platonic concern with language, deconstruction inaugurates what it imagines to be a major advance. Suddenly as never before the mythical nature of the critico-philosophical gesture is evident, and Jacques Derrida's implementation of this strategic shift (as Heidegger's before him and as that of his most brilliant student, Philippe Lacoue-Labarthe, to follow) is legion here.[30] The crisis at the center of philosophy (its *aporia*) suddenly stands before the differential nature of its conclusion. And such diachronic relation is presented not as a collapse of the system but its very condition of possibility.

At the same time, in so far as deconstruction confines this option uniquely to philosophy and continues missing it in the writing to which the distinction literature/criticism has always been applied, it continues the expulsion of this latter monstrous writing just as much as the Aristotelian tradition it rejects once did. If deconstruction constitutes an advance by getting "before" Aristotle's rewriting of the Platonic "being like another" (as representation or imitation) and directs our attention to the Platonic text itself, where a runaway crisis of *mimesis* already begins to be visible, it remains securely within that philosophic drama. It stops short of reading philosophy through tragedy, which is to say, of the Nietzschean criticism that would regard truth as the *mimesis* that wins, that gets to call what it does truth and everything else *mimesis,* or of the Girardian analysis of the sacrificial dimension of that suppression of *mimesis.* Seeing the philosophic as the ground of all textual occurrences even more fully than before (although, to be sure, the philosophic as grounded—or non-grounded—in the aporetic), and borrowing from literature the anti-sacrificial modality by which the structurative mechanism generating that textual rereading becomes visible, and finally condemning the *mimesis* of impersonation or being like another that has enabled that insight, deconstruction in its current avatars expels literature that much more fully. Conceiving of language representationally or imitatively (rather than appropriatively), and detailing that Platonic conception as the metaphorical, the tropological, or the rhetorical, these readers install a sacrificial reading of tragedy—and consequently of literature—more securely than ever before. In the name of a critique of Platonism—rewritten in good Aristotelian fashion as the history of ideas—they insure its perpetuation.

What would a non-Platonic and consequently non-Aristotelian reading of literature look like? Greek tragedy is one example. Shakespeare's plays a second. Biblical Scripture a third. It would look, in short, the way any sacrificial modality looks in which the appearance of a myth or structure of differences is fully embedded at the same time within its symptomatic dimensions. There is even a word in Plato to designate this slippage of the historical sequence that should be suppressed into the moment it gets differentially reread, the recurrence of the past within the present: *anamnesis*. And a number of different vocabularies have begun to find a language for such non-representational strategies. In Holocaust studies, it is the logic of survival, of witness, or of testimony. In critical legal studies, the logic of the evidentiary. In linguistics, the logic of the indexical (Peirce), or of the metonymic (Jakobson), or of the diachronic (Saussure). In historical studies, the logic of the fragment, the archive, or the living monument (Hilberg). In philosophy, the logic of the trace (Levinas), or of repetition (Kierkegaard), or of the legible (Benjamin), or of the anamnetic (Plato). In psychoanalysis, the logic of the symptom (Freud). And throughout our present readings of tragedy and of Hebraic biblical Scripture, it shows up as the logic of the prophetic. There is no key or master concept for these non-representational modalities, in the first place because they appear in each of these disciplines as a way of offsetting more representational conceptions (and therefore in some direct if negative relation to more representational conceptions), but secondly because in fact there is no universal or whole from which such particulars or parts can be seen to derive.

The prophetic, the symptomatic, the tracial, the indexical, the fragmentary, the evidentiary, the legible, the testimonial, the metonymic—these are all names for the logic of the diachronic, for a repetition founded not upon difference but upon sameness or identicality, upon "more of the same," a logic, that is to say, that recognizes in all the above domains the drama in which human beings are engaged and names in advance of the end of those dramas in order that we may gain the option of giving them up if we so choose.

Do these same observations and conclusions apply to Biblical Scripture and writing about the Holocaust? Are the same sacrificial and anti-sacrificial dynamics we have observed in the reading of literature and criticism operative when we read the Hebrew Bible or post-Holocaust writing?

It might appear at first glance, for example, that we could readily treat Biblical Scripture as we treat literature or critical texts. Each of the four biblical passages we have examined have occasioned coherent and familiar interpretive responses, responses that turn out to be in part the same as those already at work within the passages, often the perspective of one or another of the characters themselves.

Thus, for example, two reigning interpretations of the first part of the Joseph story—the reading by the rabbis of Joseph's early dream as prophetic of his Egyptian future, and the humanist reading that this is a piece of wisdom literature, a folksy tale of the jealousy of siblings and the dotage of old age—are both at play within the story. Joseph affirms his own specialness (his father, after all, has given him alone the coat of royalty), and the brothers certainly regard Joseph's behavior as arrogance ("Would you reign over us?" they ask) and respond in kind. And the story at length reveals the limitations of these very positions: that Joseph must learn when and how to interpret dreams, and the brothers must learn both their own implication in the behavior of others and the degree to which the behavior of both Joseph and the brothers (and the violence into which it issues) are the product of the acting out of the desires of their father, Jacob.

Or, in our treatment of the Ten Commandments, we attempted to show, for example, how our customary reading of this text as a "list" rather than a narrative (and therefore as a set of discrete elements or entities rather than the sequential presentation of a univocal conception) reproduces the very idolatrous premises to which the text is already critically responding. The second commandment, for example, is "second" if and only if in fact it is already fully contained within the first. And the logic of both the six hundred and thirteen commandments of the rabbinic tradition and of the idea that the entirety of Torah spells out the name of God find their explication within the same textual understanding.

Similarly, we attempted to show how the two traditional readings of the story of Jonah—the older rabbinical understanding of Jonah's reluctance to prophesy to the Ninevites (for fear of exposing Israel's failure to repent) as positive, and the more modern rabbinical understanding of Jonah's behavior as lacking in compassion—duplicate at once the perspective of Jonah ("Was this not why I fled to Tarshish initially?" he says to God, when Nineveh is saved and he sits upon the mountain to watch) and of God for whom the Ninevitians, who sit in repentance and ashes in prayers to Him, are at the moment more Jewish than Jonah. What the story reveals (through the object lesson of the gourd or *kikayon* plant) is that Nineveh is not the other of Israel but its future or past and, consequently (and ironically), that such reluctance is "Ninevitian" par excellence, an internal duplication that is not unlike the external duplication that occurs when the story of Jonah itself comes to be read liturgically on the afternoon of Yom Kippur, the day of repentance.

Or finally, in our treatment of the Book of Job, we attempted to show how both the modern rejection of God's response to Job's questions and its more traditional endorsement as the glimpse into an incomprehensible, mystified transcendent realm identically reproduce both the formalistic response of his three friends ("you must have done something wrong") and Job's humanist lament ("but I have not done anything wrong; show me where I am guilty"). What the Book of Job teaches is that both groups reject the equation of suffering with the world as it is ("Where were you when I created the universe?" God asks), of the law of anti-idolatry with Judaism as a response to that suffering, and the identification of creation as the name in the divine vocabulary of that anti-idolatrous response—in short, the need to give up responding to the universe as the project of their own egos. Rejecting the absolute alterity of the other man, choosing to live as if suffering were an aberration and not endemic, both reject the diachronic continuity between mythological thinking (the argument of the Satan or adversary), formalistic institutional thinking, humanistic thinking, and the transcendent logic of creation that the Book in fact provides.

And yet having said as much it is immediately necessary to add that the understanding of biblical reading in the first place as "criticism" (in the manner, say, of "classical criticism" or "Shakespeare criticism") that engages the literature before it in the manner of any other literary object is a misnomer in a number of important ways.[31] Where, for example, the subject of aesthetics presumes (in the Kantian model) a fundamental gulf between its own domain and that of the object of its critical attention (an object rendered passive—if inspired—before this appreciative and meaning-oriented gaze), Hebraic biblical reading makes no such assumptions.

In the first place, the individual biblical reader is never independent of the long tradition of exegetical commentary—talmudic, midrashic, kabbalistic, later rabbinic, and so forth—in which Scripture and its reading are embedded.[32] Secondly, the center of critical gravity in biblical interpretation is never the reader at all but the text and the divine encounter whose traces it bears (and before which the individual reader is something like the "site of an instruction").[33] Thirdly, the goal of biblical interpretation is never to identify the "meaning" of Scripture, the fitting or revelatory understandings by which a heterogeneous scriptural presentation may be rendered unified and coherent beyond seeming contradiction or conflict, but rather to show how by virtue of an identifiable Toradic commentary (that is given in advance and available via the above exegetical traditions) what appears outside Torah is in fact within. Finally, the reading or commentary that proceeds in this fashion does so not by the synchronic representational analysis to which we have become accustomed in the West but by a diachronic, "prophetic," or "anti-idolatrous" account consonant with biblical revelation itself.

The clothing of Torah, in other words, within such modern phenomenological garb risks fashioning an object that neither resembles other objects nor reflects anything like the self-understanding of the community from which it comes. Such dangers have not, of course, inhibited readers from aligning this ancient text within a wide variety of alien strategies. The historical-critical method is perhaps the most famous example. And more recent approaches developed in this country that treat Biblical Scripture within the parameters defined for new criticism or poststructuralist theorizing (psychoanalytic, feminist, or Marxist approaches, for example) define for the Hebrew Bible perspectives that differ little if at all from those in which other "literary works" are considered—*The Odyssey, Beowulf, The Inferno,* or *Paradise Lost,* for example. But we should probably be wary of engaging such aesthetic or historical approaches that, while effectively displacing older more dogmatic readings, create as many difficulties with biblical texts as they solve. If we wish to theorize about the ways in which Hebraic Scripture at large stages the sacrificial structures of which it is composed, we will need to pose far more challenging questions about both the assumptions of such modern and post-modern approaches and about the history of response in which they are embedded.

※ ※ ※

In the case of post-Holocaust writing, the obstacles are both similar and different. Once again it would appear on the surface at least that we can read Leivick's texts as we have read the critical tradition that writes about Sophocles or Shakespeare, and as we thought at least we could read traditional and modern approaches to passages from the Hebrew Bible.

Thus, for example, in Leivick's essay we observe a poet, playwright, and critic who, having spent a lifetime articulating the problem of suffering, integrates the most egregious example of that suffering in the public arena within a thoroughly personal account that acts as if to some extent those events never occurred. And as a result we understand or read those events (and their shattering effect), as with the testimony of more direct survivors, less for their direct exposition than for the symptomatic dimension of their exclusions. The Holocaust shows up in Leivick's commentary *as* that commentary.[34] Leivick's subverting of the larger dimensions of the Holocaust within his intensely personal suffering *is* the evidence of the Holocaust. "The witness," Levinas writes, "witnesses to what has been said by (or through or as) [*par*] him. For he has said 'Here I am!' before the other man" ("Le témoin témoigne de ce qui s'est dit par lui. Car il a dit 'Me voici!' devant autrui . . .").[35]

At the same time, as in the case of biblical study, there are unexpected difficulties. In the case of literature, a disproportion already exists between the comprehensiveness of criticism on one hand and the comprehensiveness of literary texts on the other. Literature is able to construct a reading of the critical literature that succeeds and enacts it in ways that criticism is unable to do of literature. In the case of biblical reading, all of the observations we have made regarding literary texts and their relation to critical texts begin to appear important to both Scripture *and* exegesis. Talmud commands as much scriptural authority in some instances as Torah does. The Torah is certainly anti-sacrificial. But so is the rabbinical tradition—Rashi, for example. And so forth.

In the case of literature written after the Holocaust (that addresses itself to the Holocaust specifically), the secondary "critical" text is all there is. We may argue about whether this writing describes the Holocaust in ways that we feel ring true to our sense of it, or whether, as in the case of Leivick, it offers a more personal and testimonial approach (rather than a historical one)—an approach, that is to say, no less powerful for being testimonial or archiving a personal history (and perhaps in some ways even more powerful and more "historical" for being so), but nonetheless less comprehensive as a *theory* of the event. But there appears to be no way of gaging our assessments in the way we did with literature or Scripture. There is no way of examining the "event itself," we feel, the inner reading or commentary (to use Michael Fishbane's phrase), since, given the peculiar dimensions of the occurrence, there *is* no "event itself" of the type to which we customarily refer. "Auschwitz," Lyotard writes, is the name of a "para-experience."[36] If we wish therefore to speak about sacrificial and anti-sacrificial dynamics of texts written in this context it would appear we are limited to talking of these "secondary" texts alone.

This difficulty has occasioned something of a crisis in historical methodology.[37] For the past twenty years or so there have been largely two dominant and disparate approaches to the Holocaust, each of which reflects both solutions to and a compounding of this difficulty. The first, spearheaded by Lucy Dawidowicz in the 1970s, offered a programmatic account of events that derived them from the demonic intentions of the Nazi policy makers (and, in particular, Adolf Hitler), genocidal designs that these leaders announced shortly after the First World War and implemented as the opportunities arose.[38]

The second, developed at roughly the same time out of an interest in the work of Raul Hilberg and others (and given prominence in the 1980s in part by Claude Lanzmann's film, *Shoah*), sought the causes of the events in the movements of a vast and unwieldy bureaucratic machinery (composed of lawyers, doctors, railroad workers, and myriad other middle class and labor class functionaries) by which the German nation slid more gradually (at times almost imperceptibly) and less deliberately into the final solution in conjunction with the success and failure of day-to-day enterprises.[39]

Elaborating the advantages and disadvantages of each of these approaches, some historians have recently begun to seek a third. The "intentionalist" view, it might now be argued, identified the broad contours of the genocidal program—and thus the victimization of the Jews—at the expense of hard detailed historical analysis of the German war machinery that produced it. The "functionalists," on the other hand, rectified this latter deficiency at the expense of proposing any coherent motivational pattern at all. We seem compelled, therefore, one might conclude, to choose between a demonic design that, however attractive as secular theology, is inimicable to history and a historical machinery with only the most arbitrary of relations to causal agency. What remains to be developed is an account that both respects the uniqueness or unprecedented nature of the *Shoah*—its magnitude and categorical quality—and yet that locates it fully within the context of historical forces in which it took place.

To some historians at least, the theory of trauma, as described by psychologists (since Freud, in fact), and increasingly by literary critics and others, appears to fit the bill.[40] In the event of trauma, as in the case of the Holocaust, the secondary effect is all. If by "trauma" we mean the overwhelming of the human registry system by a force too massive to encompass or reify, then apart from the multitude of post-traumatic responses there remains only a "black hole," an inert "traumatic core" that resists (in fact, draws in and prevents from escaping) any attempt to probe or shed light upon its contents.[41]

As before, in other words, the only "text" available for "reading" at all, in this context, is this secondary or subsequent formulation. There is no prior original literature in context of which this critical response may be examined, no Scripture in context of which this exegetical effort may be observed. It is as if the encounter of Moses on Sinai with YHVH is the entirety of Torah, a Torah without the text, so to speak, a burning bush without the ark in which it is to be enclosed.

Moreover, as in the case of post-Holocaust writing, we may wonder whether there is any way of writing about trauma that does not repeat it, any way of shifting within such post-traumatic literature from "acting out" to "working through." But it remains exclusively in context of this subsequent responding text that such questions are able to be posed. The "event itself," so to speak, in some important way, exists only within this retrospective framework—from which vantage point, of course, its "existence" is always first observed and then regarded as necessarily anterior.

In all regards, that is, trauma theory would seem to match the exigencies required—that a theory of the Holocaust respect both uniqueness and history. Is trauma theory an effective way of talking about post-Holocaust writing? Shoshana Felman and Dori Laub seem to think so, and I have examined the efficacy of their claim elsewhere.[42] In the present context, in the chapter on Halpern Leivick, we have certainly emphasized the evidentiary nature of Leivick's responses, the symptomatic logic by which he bears witness to an event he fails to describe (or fails to describe with "historical accuracy").

Moreover, in the case of war shock or the sexual abuse of children (which is where in fact the discussion began in Freud), the distinctions to which we have referred would certainly appear tenable and the psychological literature of these phenomena is pervaded by them.[43] Does the same hold true when we apply this psychological methodology to writing about the Holocaust?

The difficulty that arises when we try to describe the sacrificial dynamics of post-Holocaust writing in these terms inheres ironically in the nature of its success as a psychological tool. Is post-Holocaust writing a literature of witness? Undoubtedly. The symptomatic reading of Leivick, as testimony or witness to the events he is describing, seems powerfully effective—more exclusively so, in fact, than any approach we have encountered in this volume so far. On the other hand, when we ask whether Leivick's writing is "post-traumatic," the issue quickly becomes more complicated.

In the case of war shock or the sexual abuse of children, if we permit ourselves to speak of "trauma," we do so as a way of talking about an interruption that comes from the outside, that arrives out of nowhere, so to speak, that intervenes decisively within an individual's experience and potentially affects that individual in ways that are irrevocable, but that maintains a relation to the events preceding its appearance that is fundamentally arbitrary. It is important to speak this way in context of psychology. Such speech offers the victim of these occurrences the solace that there was nothing he (or she) could do about it, a solace from which recovery may begin (if it is to begin at all). To speak this way about the Holocaust, however, or about texts that follow the Holocaust, is potentially at least to obscure their relation to the past in ways that may create as many difficulties as they dissolve, to obscure the historical relation in favor of a contemporary relation that may, ironically, depend upon that historical relation.

What would it mean to say Leivick's essay is "post-traumatic"? Where's the "trauma"? If the trauma is designated to be the death by fire of his younger sister (of "four" years old), then the text is not about the Holocaust at all, only about that intensely personal tragedy for which the theme of the Holocaust (along with all other scenes of violence) has been substituted. On the other hand, if as we claim, the Holocaust speaks through his text, and moreover does so precisely *as* that substitution, then the "traumatic core," so to speak, is much less easy to identify, not because its contents are resistant to our analysis, but because the locus of those contents is everywhere. The death of his sister was traumatic. But so was the event that afternoon in front of the Polish church, or at the gate of the mad count, or in the Czarist prisons in the intervening years, and so forth. And if they were all "traumatic," it begins to seem less productive to talk of "trauma" than of the proliferation of witness to this substitutive violence.

The same is true for the Holocaust "itself." We may certainly agree, with Fackenheim, that the Holocaust is a "witnessing of the impossible."[44] But to say it is the "impossibility of witness" as Lyotard first suggests (and then Shoshana Felman and Dori Laub echo), a formulation that extends trauma theory to the Holocaust at large, is to suppress the historical dimension entirely.[45] It is one thing to talk about the "impossibility of witness," the collapse of the human registry mechanism, in cases where an event has genuinely intruded—the explosion of a bomb in one's face, the rape of an infant, and so forth. It is quite another to claim as much where such carnage has occurred within a context that is largely without an alternative to which to compare it. To act in this latter more familiar context as if the event has come from without is to do no less than the Holocaust itself: to explode the past, to do away with the developmental nature of the occurrence, and as a result to exculpate the perpetrators and victimize the victims once again.

Trauma theory as applied to the Holocaust in this fashion, in other words, may potentially at least be no less anti-historical (and no less fraught with difficulty as a result) than the intentionalist view was. In fact, in a certain regard, it is another version of that earlier view within the psychological context, a more seductive version to be sure, because it promises an intricacy and intimacy of concrete textual detail that the earlier version lacked, but an intentionalist position nonetheless, in so far as it founds that promise of concrete historical details upon the radical externalization, the veritable exclusion from historical account, of the intervening victimizing agency. The absent intention in trauma theory conceived in this fashion is no less governing (and therefore "intentional") than intention is in intentionalism. In fact in some regards it is its negative imitation. Conceived as trauma, the Holocaust is like the Kyklops in Homer's *Odyssey* once his language ability, his ability to name his victimizers, has been paralyzed: "'Nohbdy,' Nohbdy's tricked me, Nohbdy's ruined me!" Polyphemos tells the other monsters (dropping the "o" or "ought" and adding an "h" or aspirant in the English translation as a symptom or index of that paralysis).[46]

To describe the Holocaust as a trauma, in other words, may be to describe it as unique in a way that is no less problematic in this context than it has been throughout the history of Holocaust discussion over the past fifty years. In the debate over the uniqueness of the Holocaust, a debate that animated the intentionalists and functionalists (the former arguing for the absolute break with the past, the latter for an invention within an old context), trauma theory comes down heavily (and somewhat unexpectedly) on the side of the intentionalists. It is one thing to claim that the Holocaust is unprecedented, a rupture, a caesura, a break with the past in certain regards.[47] All serious researchers in the field have made such a claim. It is another to say that it is unique, unrelated to anything that has gone before. The first view refines the guilt of the perpetrators, specifying its difference in magnitude and quality. They are guilty in this regard and not that. They are guilty to this degree and not that. The second does away with that guilt entirely since in entirely unique circumstances there remains nothing of which the perpetrators can be found culpable. Trauma theory in this regard may even outdo intentionalism since in intentionalism there is at least the context of the demonic—radical evil—with which to contend while in trauma theory there is no intention at all.

To say as much is not to disparage the many advances that trauma theory has made (and is still likely to make) with regard to the Holocaust or writing after the Holocaust. It is, after all, the first diachronic theory of the Holocaust available and that is no doubt a good part of its attractiveness (intentionalism attributing the Holocaust to demonic sources from without, and functionalism to bureaucratic sources from within). It does explain as never before what seems to have taken place since the Holocaust with respect to the silence that envelopes every survivor's account of it (if he or she chooses to talk at all), and with regard to the curious unease on the part of even those who did not have any survivor experience or may even have participated as perpetrators. It seems to explain the other worldly "planet Auschwitz" sense that we have had for a long time about the event that has led some researchers to claim that in some manner we are all survivors of Auschwitz, some simply more close up than others.[48]

If it fails as theory of the Holocaust (and it is not entirely clear to me that it does), it is because it functions so powerfully as testimony. To say that trauma theory fails to describe the Holocaust is not to say that the experience of the Holocaust by its victims is not traumatic. To the contrary. The events of the Holocaust can *only* be experienced as traumatic. But therein lies the difficulty. It is precisely too traumatic—powerful as testimony, poor as theory. If the history of trauma is always the trauma of a history, as one researcher writes, then we are left without a way to differentiate a traumatic event from a non-traumatic one. If all events are traumatic, then effectively no event is traumatic, and we have obscured responsibility for the violence of our current situation no less than the theories that would confine that violence to an external demonic agency. If the approach offers us as never before the intricacies of post-Holocaust reading (as symptomatic of what preceded it), it also occludes more thoroughly than ever before the relation of this catastrophic occurrence to its own past.

In positing a dead stop with the Holocaust, in other words, and Auschwitz as its "traumatic core," in finding a break with the European past more radical even than the intentionalists, it severs the study of the context in which the Holocaust occurred from the present and in doing so detracts from the understanding of where we are after it. Whether the Holocaust is seen to issue from demonic politico-religious designs, monolithic bureaucratic machinery, or a series of traumatic incursions by an arbitrary force from without, the Holocaust as a European development has been abandoned. Trauma theory no more explains the "Holocaust in history" than the views it is erected to outface.

To explain the "Holocaust in history," on the other hand, is not to normalize the Holocaust and here is where the efforts of Ernst Nolte and so many others who participated in the *Historikerstreit* went wrong.[49] It is not to make of the Holocaust an example—of the demonic, the fascistic, the traumatic, or of any other kind of intentionality or lack of intentionality. Rather it is to give up *any* essentialistic approach to this event, any part-to-whole or whole-to-part analysis, and perhaps for the first time to begin to see the diachronic context in which it must be understood, neither, that is to say, as a part of the Europe that produced it nor as different from that Europe but precisely as its extension, its extremity, its monstrous explosion, the good gone wrong, so to speak, where the good is something like the values promoted by Romanticism, the French revolution, and the Enlightenment—humanism, organicism, idealism, everything, in short, that we have for so long in the academy held near and dear and identified, in short, as "culture."[50]

The crisis in historical methodology, in other words, of which the development of trauma theory is a symptom, speaks for itself. Acting out in post-Holocaust writing is no longer an extension—an extremity—of literature alone. It is necessarily now also a matter of psychology and of history, and of the ways in which that writing bears witness to both. To read Halpern Leivick as witness, as witness in spite of himself, as witness in being himself, is to credit the testimonial powers of his narrative as "part 1" of a two-part structure that remains to be completed, as part of an ongoing investigative relation between the Holocaust that speaks through his work and the larger diachronic context in which that work and that Holocaust has appeared. It is to read his text *first* as witness to the history of a trauma, *then* as witness to the trauma of a history.

※ ※ ※

Do the conclusions we have gathered about literature and criticism apply to the Hebrew Bible and post-Holocaust writing? Yes, if we confine our discussion within the fairly narrow parameters we have indicated. Secondary critical readings constructed around the Hebrew Bible certainly act out the issues at stake within those texts—both in traditional and in more modern exegetical writing. And post-Holocaust writing is certainly a literature of witness. No, on the other hand, if we imagine a simple analogy between these domains. The Hebrew Bible projects the discussion of interpretation into the intricacies of scriptural exegesis, where a relation between Scripture and commentary is considerably more fluid. And post-Holocaust writing projects it into the realm of psychology and of historical research where other questions quickly come into play.

And yet, having opened these discussions and probed their limits, we may have glimpsed an answer to a different question. The Hebrew Bible, the Holocaust, and literary reading are not unrelated. They are not independent realms of inquiry. The urgency with which we feel today the necessity of reading may not be unrelated to the Holocaust, which, in turn, may not be unrelated to the contemporary Jewish tradition, or its foundations in the exilic moment after the destruction of the first Temple. And if, as we have observed, the center of gravity of both—that religious tradition and that catastrophe—concerns witness, then we are entitled at least to wonder whether witness is similarly at stake—perhaps even *the* stake—in literary reading.

Is reading our manner of engaging the witness borne around us? Is it possible that rather than read texts, what we always read in fact is witness? Or to put it the other way around (and perhaps more precisely), that what we do when we say we are "reading texts" is witnessing, witnessing the reading or witnessing of others, and that what is "given to be read" (and therefore what constitutes a "text") is simply what bears (or bares) that witnessing?

And if our answer to this question is affirmative, is such witness, we are led to ask—perhaps for the first time since Romanticism—related to the religious witness the scriptural tradition has long claimed for its own?

II. Reading as Witness

All post-Auschwitz culture, including its urgent critique, is garbage. . . .
Whoever pleads for the maintenance of this radically culpable and
shabby culture becomes its accomplice, while the man who says
no to culture is directly furthering the barbarism which
our culture showed itself to be.
Theodore Adorno

Even if "nothing human is alien to us," the burden of the *Shoah* (the
Hebrew word means "annihilation") cannot be overcome because it
cannot be reduced to familiarity. The Holocaust remains human and
alien at the same time. The worst attitude we could take is to persuade
ourselves that it might not happen again *or* that it is something that happened before—that the Holocaust was one catastrophe among others.
It is true that such a perspective divides history by positing a caesura
more divisive than a theophanic event. It makes of the Holocaust
a *novum* (as Emil Fackenheim, among others, has argued); so
that, for the time being, which may last some time, all that
went before and all that presently befalls us must be seen
in the ominous light of that destruction.
Geoffrey H. Hartman

We began this conclusion by asking why commentary need be removed from literature. We then gathered together the conclusions we have been able to reach in the preceding seven studies, noting that it is not necessarily an advance over the older view to regard literature as language where the specificity of literary commentary is excluded no less.

We need now, in order to complete the task we set ourselves in the introduction and bring these reflections to a close, turn to a third matter. We have been concerned with reading throughout this book. It has remained a more or less unexamined presupposition that reading or commentary is important. Is it? What is the nature of its appeal for us? Is its appeal related in some as yet undisclosed way to the historical circumstances in which we live?

To open this question is to embark upon an even more polemical route than we have pursued to this point—although hints that this would be the direction we would need to take are scattered throughout the preceding pages. We are interested in reading today, I would like to suggest, because the condition of our contemporary being is the Holocaust, and post-Holocaustal reading is a form of ethical practice, one that shares certain similarities with the ethical practice exercised for more than two thousand years as the reading of the Hebrew Torah, and one that has as its end or goal witness: the ownership of one's responsibility for the other individual.

The argument of this position demands a volume of its own, no less than our earlier question about literature and literary study. But from what we have said it is already clear what shape such an argument might assume. Consider the following reflections, then, less as a finished exposition than as an approach, one that is subject to change—to refinement or even to fundamental alteration—in context of a fuller treatment yet to come.

"If Auschwitz has no name," Lyotard writes, "is it not because it is the proper name of para-experience, that of the impossibility of forming the we?"[51]

> Is it not the case that in concentration camps there is no plural subject? And is it not further the case that for want of this plural subject, there can remain "after Auschwitz" no subject which could presume to name *itself* by naming this "experience"?

Few commentators today, I suspect, would challenge the assertion that, whatever else it was constructed to achieve, the continental thought that gained ascendancy over the last forty years or so in literature and then other humanities departments in this country—"structuralism/poststructuralism" (as it has come to be called)—attempted a dismembering of the romantic self-consciousness by which European philosophic thinking imagined itself for at least a hundred and fifty years prior to that moment. The disclosure of the death or absence of the subject on the one hand, and of the emptiness or nothingness of the object on the other, remains throughout this critical writing a fundamental and constant project.[52]

But it would hardly be accurate to claim that contemporary thought is discontinuous with the past. The new thinking that has emerged within the past forty years has brought with it significant new readings of all the major thinkers of the past century and a half—Kant, Hegel, Durkheim, Nietzsche, Freud, Heidegger, and others. Suddenly in the place of Kantian moralism we are interested in the Kant of the *Critique of Pure Reason* and the *Critique of Judgment*. Concern with Hegel's *Phenomenology* has replaced concern with his *Logic*. We are less concerned with the Nietzschean dialectic of master-slave morality than we are with his critique of philosophic rhetoric and Platonism. We are less concerned with Freud's biologistic origins for psychoanalytic concepts than in the hints of a social origin of the type found for example in Hegel. We are more concerned with Heidegger's later interest in language and presence than his earlier existential analysis of *dasein*, and care in *Being and Time*. The priority of the social over the individual has attracted our interest in Durkheim and Mauss more than the more local discussions of structures of exchange. And so forth.

In fact, so thoroughly immersed is contemporary thought within the work of these thinkers that we might be encouraged to think it is something of an extension or extremity of their ideas. Derrida's critique of Western metaphysics as a critique of the determination of the history of Being as presence is a version of Heideggerianism. Foucault has openly avowed his filiation with a Nietzschean project that would study the genealogy of the relation between truth and power and the formation of the subject. Lacan has clearly undertaken to "debiologize" Freud by replacing biologistic concepts with the more dialectical analyses of desire and its object that he finds in Hegel. Lévi-Strauss has appropriated a methodology from Saussurean linguistics and an understanding of the primacy of the social (and its nature as a system of exchanges) from Durkheim and Mauss. And so forth.

And yet this continuity may be followed only up to a certain point. For there is one way in which the phenomenological paradigm—the romantic subject of consciousness and object of knowledge—differs absolutely from the thought of the last forty years—and that difference concerns the Holocaust. The Holocaust is the end of humanism (and of the phenomenological subject and object as we know it) and marks a break or "caesura" that cannot be traversed. "After Auschwitz" (the phrase, of course, is Adorno's), nothing is the same.[53] To explore, therefore, the relations between romantic self-consciousness (and its object) and contemporary thought, it would appear we need to say more about this catastrophic event in its historical setting.

※　　※　　※

We have already spoken at length about the two reigning conceptualizations of the Holocaust, those that view this event as the unique product of its demonic purveyors (for whom history serves as little more than the opportunity to deploy such demonic devices), and those that view it as the product of historical forces functioning more or less independently of human agency or intention. We have also noted the recent attempt on the part of others in this domain to deploy a third that would combine elements of both aberrant human intention and aberrant historical development by noting their traumatic effect upon its survivors.

What has not been asked (and what seems necessary to ask if trauma theory is to complete itself and not become just one more superintentionalism) is the relation of the Holocaust to the past. If we read post-Holocaust texts "symptomatically," and we read the Holocaust itself as reflective of a European context that preceded it in which a "good idea" has "gone wrong" and whose explosion it has constituted, what precisely explodes?

What if the Holocaust is an intensification of behavior and attitudes endemic to the history of romantic humanism itself?[54] Thinking specifically of our history in Europe and America within the last two hundred years, we may envision the broad parameters of an argument that would specify the place of the event in something of the following fashion.

The modern world (borrowing Foucault's reading of Nietzsche) begins with the humanism of Kant and Hegel that styles itself as heroically taking up the mantle in a universe from which God has absconded.[55] Constituting himself as an "empirico-transcendental doublet" (as subject and object of his own knowledge), man in this myth displaces God within the great chain of Being (that has also been the history of Metaphysics) and lives—in accordance with familiar Hegelian themes—in the wake of the end of history.

Within the era dominated by this figure, the second stage of the argument might go, Nietzsche erects a nihilist critique. He reads prophetically the origins, the strategies, and the consequences of such a mythic humanistic displacement. Far from arriving in an abandoned universe, Nietzsche argues, "man" has in fact usurped the position of God. But his victory will be short-lived. For the means by which he has achieved that displacement will now insure as well his own demise. What he has done to others will now inevitably reverberate back upon himself as well.

In this context, National Socialism would constitute a third developmental stage. Emerging in Germany and Austria at the conclusion of the "war to end all wars," Nazism may be viewed at once as an extension of a version of this Nietzschean critique and a return to Romanticism in its most elemental expression. Regarding nihilism as negative humanism (the substitution of nothing in the place of man), and drawing upon the resources of social Darwinism to achieve its ends (conceived in the romantic terms of dwelling, purity, and the organic), Nazism renders the distinction between humanism and nihilism non-existent. After Auschwitz, it is no longer possible to conceive of the human without conceiving at the same time of murder. Nazism, we may say, constitutes itself at once as a Romanticism and a nihilism, a romantic humanism founded upon nihilism. Nothing human is alien to it.

In this sense (among others), then, we may speak of the twelve-year Reich (and the perpetration of the Holocaust that sustains it) as a monstrosity.[56] The genocidal demands that the Nazi program makes upon its interlocutors—namely, that they die in order that their captors be gratified—signifies, in the words of Adorno "l'annéatissement de la mort," the annihilation of death, the collapse of the idea that death has any usable meaning. "In the camps," Adorno writes, "death has a novel horror; since Auschwitz, fearing death means fearing worse than death."[57] Romanticism in this process gets "used up." The Holocaust in this sense may be termed its "explosion," Romanticism with a vengeance. Anything that comes after the Holocaust can only refer to it as the marker of a break, a "model" for thought (in Adorno's vocabulary) rather than its illustration.

Within the contours of this argument, contemporary thought may be said to be continuous with the past only up to a certain point. What explodes is Romanticism, the construction of European consciousness as it constituted itself at the beginning of the nineteenth century in England, France, and Germany (among other places) out of the texts of English poetry and German critical philosophy. And the contemporary paradigm may be said to be precisely what remains in the wake of that explosion, which is to say, reading.

Why reading? The movement of thought within which Nietzsche and Heidegger write may already be characterized to some extent as a modality of the diachronic and the prophetic, a criticism of humanism from within, so to speak. But it remains grounded in the human (or humanistic) and the ontological. Nietzsche's analysis of the "death of God" in *The Gay Science* is a staging of the conditions and consequences of Cartesian subjectivity and Hegelian humanism. Heidegger's analysis of temporality in *Being and Time* is a diachronic rendering of the horizon of being in the world that has always been understood synchronically.

But then the Holocaust occurs and explodes the distinction between the human and the murderous. Our mission, Himmler said at Poznán in 1943, is to undertake the glorious action for which the page in history may never be written—to undertake the extermination of the Jews and still to remain decent.[58] Reading, in this instance, is what survives the death of humanism and ontology, the logic that remains once prophetic thought has relinquished all claim to such grounding, a thought that now originates in commentary which transcends being and the human, which is to say, in the infinitely Other. Reading finds in the other man (or woman) not language or time but the trace of the infinite and the infinity of the responsibility to which I am summoned.

There is a second "subtraction" to be identified. The Holocaust poses the limits of the difference between the human and the murderous. But the nuclear explosion by which the war concludes disposes of the difference between ourselves and others. What we do to others now inevitably reverberates back upon ourselves.[59] The explosion (first at Hiroshima, then at Nagasaki) with which the war enveloping the Holocaust ends, allows us to glimpse the nightmarish future of that "reverberation," a future to which some commentators have given the chilling literary rendering of "nuclear sublime."[60] To subtract both of these limits is to live in relation to a system of differences founded otherwise than in the world of "human being" as constructed for us at the beginning of the nineteenth century.

The Holocaust in this context, as monstrosity or explosion, becomes therefore, we may say, a model of reading, and what comes afterward is necessarily the "thought" of that model, a staging of the monstrous limits of romantic humanism, the enacting of the inevitable consequence of the humanist project carried to its ultimate extreme—the foundation of a new human order at the cost of any sacrifice. And it is within that reading that we continue to live. The absolutism developed by the two world wars—the globalization of conflict in the first, the absolutizing of moral and technological strategies and their consequences in the second—bequeaths us no alternative course. In their wake, we remain at once compelled to imitate or repeat this Holocaustal reading of recent European history, and at the same time able to acknowledge that reading specifically as post-Holocaustal.

*   *   *

In place of the paradigm of the subject and the object, in other words, contemporary thought has erected the analysis of difference or textuality—its forms, its conditions of possibility, its strategies, and its consequences. And the particular diachronic logic that this sacrificial analysis engages (minus its sacrificial components) we may designate as reading. This logic is "left over" from the Holocaust that the Nazis imported from nihilist critiques of humanist philosophy undertaken during the latter half of the nineteenth century in Europe, critiques that were themselves borrowed in monstrous translation from the great literary and religious texts of our culture, texts that we have been arguing are in turn already critical reflections of similar crises. Like the logic of the scapegoat itself (or of the "supplement" in Derrida's analysis), reading, that begins as marginal or metaphorical (for example, in Wellek and Warren's book), turns out to be central, foundational, literal—in a way that is generative of these very oppositions.

Reading, in other words, is the logic of the diachronic, the prophetic, anti-idolatrous, anti-sacrificial logic that surfaces from the debris of the explosion of Romanticism. Reading is the sacrificial scapegoat logic of culture itself available to us at once in its most violent manifestations as the Holocaust and its most anti-sacrificial manifestations as the great literary and religious documents of our collective memory. And post-Holocaustal reading in this sense (in the context of structuralism and poststructuralism in which we have been considering it) is the "thought" of this monstrosity.

But Romantic subjectivity was relational as well as cognitive and aesthetic. To remain viable, to complete itself as a project, as a displacement of the Romantic paradigm of subject and object, contemporary reading, in other words, must now begin to assume a new dimension. More than difference (or textuality), even more than the analysis of its constitution, reading finally is ethical. And perhaps it is in this context—as the final stage of the building of this post-Holocaustal thought—that we may understand the battles currently being waged.

In particular, there seem to be largely two dominant attitudes in which all variations we have observed can be largely contained: those that recognize reading independently of ethical practice; and those that embrace reading *as* its practice. The first would engage experience as if the Holocaust had never existed, or having once existed, never touched human subjectivity. This view bears witness to the Holocaust less by virtue of what it says than by virtue of what it fails to say. The second, residing in the shadow of the Holocaust, seeks parallels for the current dilemma in other crises and other religious and literary responses that reflect those crises. If the first perspective reads through Kant, Hegel, the tradition of German idealists—in short, through philosophy—the second reads through the staging of these systems in the great literary, religious, and philosophic texts of our culture.

And between these two styles, between philosophy and literature, Plato and Sophocles, anti-clericalism and anti-idolatry, between, that is to say, two humanisms (one that is nostalgic for the old in either its Romantic or nihilistic posture, and another that is post-Holocaustal, and lives in relation to other absolute discontinuities—diachronic or synchronic), between, in short, an ethics founded upon immanence, and an ethics founded upon transcendence, it would seem all of our discussions take place.

How "true" is the argument we have just outlined? Is the story we have told of the genesis of our concern with reading—the construction of Romantic subjectivity at the beginning of the nineteenth century, its explosion in the Holocaust, the emergence of reading as witness from the debris—any less a "myth" than the accounts it would displace? There are only sacrificial accounts, I have argued. The value of any story resides less in its adequacy or inadequacy to its object, its ability to unveil or obscure a hidden truth, than in its capacity to function as commentary, as a staging of the sacrificial mechanisms of which it is composed.

There is, in short (to return to Lyotard's observation), no "we." Neither is there, if we are to take these writers seriously, a "non-we." Nor is there even (as deconstruction might have it) the impossibility of deciding between a "we" and/or a "non-we." After the Holocaust, by the force of everything we have been arguing about the Holocaust, there is simply no "there is"—in the ontological sense by which for some twenty-four hundred years philosophy has conceived of the ontic. The Holocaust has ushered us into a region in which the very possibility of a "there is" as a reference to the true, which is to say, "that which has being as opposed to that which does not," has dispersed before the "there is" of the "otherwise than being," the *il y a* in Levinas's sense, the trace of the infinitely Other, "illeity," which is also to say, in short, the creaturely "there is" of revelation.

Increasingly, that is to say, we find ourselves thrust not *into* the world, as Heidegger says, and as Job's friends think, but *out of* it, beyond essence, into a "no man's land," where, to borrow the language of Sophocles, "no service of the foot can serve," where Job's question ("why do the evil triumph over the good?") and God's response ("where were you when I created the universe?")—which is to say, the question of the human (or of justice, immanence, the said) and the question of transcendence (or of creation, saying, responsibility)—alone define the parameters in which we continue to meet and speak. In the face of this "there is," our Job-like egos must learn not answers but answerability, not stories (or excuses) like Adam, nor silence and obedience like Noah, but responsibility to the other individual, to speak before this prophetic anti-idolatrous call the Abrahamic *hineiny,* "Here I am." On the one hand, an obligation to the sacred, the holy (or unholy), the ontological à la Heidegger. On the other, a responsibility to the otherwise than being, the other individual or neighbor, the ethical as first philosophy à la Levinas.

It is not a matter of choosing between these alternatives. We cannot but live in relation to some obligation, some sacred or holy, some sacrificial narrative structure. Rather, it is a matter of recognizing the extent to which such living constrains us, endangers us, and at the moment of the gravest threat, turning back. In this place that is "no where," where there are consequently no subjects, no objects, and no choices properly speaking (since responsibility and commandment precede choice, found choice), there are only two possibilities: the possibility of continuing as we are with all that that entails, and the possibility of acknowledging such continuity of sacrifice with violence and at the moment of its inefficaciousness giving it up.

On the one hand, monsters, the good gone wrong, sacrifice and difference become violence (behemoths, leviathans, etc.). On the other, anti-idolatry, prophetic thinking, partnership in the creation of the universe, responsibility. We may continue to enact our losses, our failures, our catastrophes, until death overtakes us. Or, owning our ineluctable responsibility to the other individual (a responsibility we can no more give up, Levinas says, than we can choose another to die in our place), we may acknowledge the acting out we cannot help but continue and work through it, survive on its basis. Collaboration, in other words, ("working with" in the negative sense), or survival ("living through," remaining alive afterwards, but also, doing so by means of the recognition of our collaboration). We may continue the sacrificial distinctions that have led us to this moment of crisis and violence. Or, reading anti-sacrificially the diachronic logic of that structure, its extremity (in the sense both of violence and extension), reading that is to say prophetically, recognizing the sacrificial dramas in which we have always already been engaged, give them up.

It is this final anti-sacrificial reading that we would designate as witness. Reading would then express our capacity to engage—to encounter, to countenance—the witness that others bear (or bare), the diachronic logic that escapes representation (although representation derives from it) and that is constituted by our infinite responsibility to the creative potential of the other individual. If reading has become important for us, it is because the witness that was formerly unbearable (and unbareable) has found voice, and from the inferno of the deathcamps (and its "ominous light"), we have begun again to hear a five-thousand-year-old testimony to the extremity of human destructiveness, a testimony that exceeds the conceptualization of literary commentary and critical literature envisioned for us by Wellek and Warren.

Owning *this* witness—of our moment to the Holocaust and of the Holocaust to centuries of Hebraic, Christian, and Western concern—would of necessity, then, spell an end to literature as we know it, whether as practiced or as constructed. And it would open us instead to the goal for which we have been "saving the text" under the heading of "literature" all along: the preservation of commentary.[61] Engaging this inner reading or witness or commentary (rather than "sacrificing" it), recognizing this commentary to be precisely about the "sacrificing" we would enact, we offer ourselves a way of responding ethically to what is offered by the other individual and thereby constitute, beyond the efforts of Paul de Man, an "ethics of reading."

❦ ❦ ❦

> I am not given to retrospective self-examination, and mercifully forget
> what I have written with the same alacrity I forget bad movies—
> although, as with bad movies, certain scenes return at times
> to embarrass and haunt me like a guilty conscience.... Thus
> seeing a distant segment of one's past resurrected gives
> one a slightly uncanny feeling of repetition.
> Paul de Man

> It would annihilate us all to see
> The huge shape of our being; mercifully
> God offers us issue and oblivion.
> Jorge Luis Borges

It should come as little surprise that I conceive of the present study of the sacrificial dynamics of critical reading within great literature, religious Scripture, and contemporary post-war polemics as a version of the second alternative. Nor that I should relate that project in some fundamental way to the work of Paul de Man, whose writing, probably more than that of anyone else today in literary study, conceives of that study as a lesson in reading.

Perhaps if we suddenly find ourselves today in turmoil over the discovery of a cache of texts that implicate de Man at the outset of his career in a widespread cultural antisemitism, we are in a position now to understand why. Is it not precisely because we have assumed throughout our current engagement—over the last forty years or so—that a theory of reading is a theory of ethics that we are so disturbed when the ethical credentials of the leading philosopher of reading turn out to be questionable?[62]

Yet do we not have available to us, if we are willing to make use of the opportunity (and not either ignore the discovery or denounce the man on the basis of it), in his personal history as it is currently being detailed for us, a convenient allegory for reading the parameters of our current pursuit?

For as far as we can tell, de Man has come to a philosophy of reading from a position as far away from it as possible, from a historical and literary essentialism that regards great literature as the repository of the values of civilized culture, and history as the progressive advance toward an order founded upon those values, in short, from Romantic subjectivity in its most virulent and abject form. To discover de Man to have begun as a Nazi hack is to discover him to have begun as a reactionary in the most heinous way possible in the current context, as a collaborator or accomplice not just with the reigning fascist political regime, nor even just with an ethical practice founded upon murder, but rather (and more precisely) with the most dangerous confusion or conflation of his age: the confusion of humanism with nihilism, the monstrous confusion that we have identified as the Holocaustal explosion of Romantic subjectivity itself and in relation to which, I would suggest, all of contemporary thought would organize itself.

Geoffrey Hartman's most recent indictment of de Man is not easy to dismiss.[63] De Man's glib cultural critique (in his antisemitic essay in *Le Soir*) in which he speaks of the Jews as "cerebral," "cold," and "abstract," and discusses their "Judaizing" effects upon non-Jewish culture (even if de Man considers that effect minimal and even if, as Hartman shrewdly points out, the young journalist embodies those qualities himself), is part of a concrete and familiar antisemitic history in Luther's Germany, the most famous example of which is probably the text by Nietzsche's early mentor, Richard Wagner, on the Jews and music.[64] As such, Hartman says, de Man's essay must be considered a document in the "history of murder."[65]

Moreover, no amount of finessing of his silence about his early Nazi collaboration (excusing it on the basis that it is like Rousseau's refusal to avail himself of the inauthentic mechanism of excuse in *The Confessions,* or, more troublingly, considering it "heroic" and like the "silence" of Walter Benjamin, or most inexcusably, confusing it with the silence of the survivors about which Primo Levi speaks in *The Drowned and the Saved*—all of which strategies de Man's student, Shoshana Felman, employs in her article in *Critical Inquiry* and her collaboration with psychoanalyst and child survivor, Dori Laub) will dispel the difficulty.[66] The problem with Paul de Man's post-Nazi period is not that he does not speak about his collaborationist past but that, by virtue of what we now know, his silence *says only too much*.

For de Man's silence, we are now in a position to understand, is itself the silence of the collaborators, the same silence, that is to say, as his refusal to dissent from participating in the antisemitic issue of *Le Soir* initially, a silence thus that is itself a living remnant, a leftover from another time and place, a *revenant* or visitation, returned to haunt us and bear ghostly witness or testimony to those bygone days. As such, that silence is witnessable by us. To justify that silence, to exonerate that antisemitic article, to propose a theory of the "impossibility of witness" in place of witnessing the impossible as Felman and Laub do, is to continue that unholy and ongoing collaborative alliance.[67]

On the other hand, if de Man's silence was collaborationist, his practice of reading was not. To discover him, at the same time, at the moment of his death to be one of the most thoughtful practitioners of reading we have, suggests that in the entirety of the course of that life we have displayed before us the very movement under discussion in the present essay. Should we really be surprised that de Man seems to have gained insight on his particular blindness precisely from his rejection of his own former position, from his discovery and renunciation in the mid-1960s of the "nihilist allegory" of Nazism (even if in some capacity that renunciation repeats his earlier renunciation of "vulgar antisemitism" within a collaborationist position), and his engagement in its place with the thought issuing from France that he encountered at a conference at Johns Hopkins University the same year where the ideas (and also—except for Lévi-Strauss and Foucault—the presence) of Lévi-Strauss, Barthes, Lacan, Foucault, Derrida, and Girard (among many others) were so much in evidence?[68]

If the study of the problems of critical reading after Auschwitz can only be understood finally as an ethical inquiry (as it has been understood, in fact, for at least twenty-five hundred years within the Hebraic tradition), then do we not have in de Man's personal history—in the most extreme form (and whether de Man would contest that characterization or not)—the baring of the "ineluctable necessity" of that logic?

It would not, of course, be entirely accurate to claim that de Man's position opens the way to an ethics even if, as we do claim, it leads us to the door. To the extent that de Man remained committed to the tropological, to a representational understanding of language (that continued to fascinate him along with so many of his colleagues and students), the diachronic extra-ontological logic of ethics as first philosophy was barred to him. "Ethicity" for him, as Hillis Miller points out, remains a "linguistic" rather than an interpersonal or transcendent matter.[69] "Ethics," de Man writes (commenting upon a passage from Rousseau), "has nothing to do with the will (thwarted or free) of a subject, nor *a fortiori*, with a relationship between subjects. The ethical category is imperative (i.e. a category rather than a value) to the extent that it is linguistic and not subjective."[70] The ethical remains for de Man a "predicament" rather than a predication.[71] The possibility that the ethical exceeds the realm of the law—where for Kant both value and the categorical imperative have their domain—does not seem to have occurred to him.

And yet in his move (now more clear than ever) from essentialism and to a philosophy of reading as demonumentalization, and his foundation of that reading in a language or linguistics conceived as otherwise than "human," he would seem to have cleared the way, ironically, to just such a discussion, one no doubt that René Girard, Martin Buber, and Emmanuel Levinas among others will assist us to pursue. And does not this irony immediately lead us to another—one that would indeed begin to sound like the scenario for a "bad movie" (perhaps a wartime *film noir*), for an "embarrassing" and "uncanny" repetition, perhaps even a "guilty conscience," were its consequences not so devastating—namely, that Paul Adolph de Man should end up as the most powerful expositor of the difficulties of a practice of reading that shares certain fundamental demythologizing features with the texts of the very community his Nazi collaborators would annihilate?

Notes

Preface and Acknowledgments

1. I have not included my essays on Murray Krieger and on Paul de Man in which similar arguments are mounted. See, for example, Goodhart 1986 and 1989.

2. For a bibliography of works by and about René Girard, see Juilland 1986, iii–xxxii. See also my entry on "René Girard" in Groden and Kreiswirth 1993, 355–56.

Introduction

1. De Man 1971.
2. See De Man 1986, 3–20. "The Resistance to Theory" originally appeared in De Man 1982.
3. De Man 1983, viii–ix.
4. De Man 1986, 17. The "conclusion" to which de Man refers concerns the rhetorical "undoing of theory" about which he speaks in the preceding paragraph. He has been talking about the "impossibility" of deciding between two equally adequate readings of the title of Keats's unfinished poem *The Fall of Hyperion*. "Faced with the ineluctable necessity to come to a decision, no grammatical or logical analysis can help us out. Just as Keats had to break off his narrative, the reader has to break off his understanding at the very moment when he is most directly engaged and summoned by the text. One could hardly expect to find solace in this 'fearful symmetry' between the author's and the reader's plight since, at this point, the symmetry is no longer a formal but an actual trap, and the question no longer 'merely' theoretical" (16–17).

This "trap," de Man writes, is in fact "rhetorical" and the resistance to theory is the resistance to this "rhetorical" or "tropological" function of language. "This undoing of theory, this disturbance of the stable cognitive field that extends from grammar to logic to a general science of Man and of the phenomenal world, can in its turn be made into a theoretical project of rhetorical analysis that will reveal the inadequacy of grammatical models of non-reading. Rhetoric, by its actively negative relationship to grammar and to logic, certainly undoes the claims of the *trivium* (and by extension, of language) to be an epistemologically stable construct. The resistance to theory is a resistance to the rhetorical or tropological dimension of language, a dimension which is perhaps more explicitly in the foreground in literature (broadly conceived) than in other verbal manifestations or—to be somewhat less vague—which can be revealed in any verbal event when it is read textually" (17).

5. See, for example, the special memorial issue of *Yale French Studies*, edited by Shoshana Felman in 1985.

6. See Wlad Godzich's introductions to de Man's books in Godzich 1983 and 1986.

7. See, for example, Jonathan Culler's examination of Wayne Booth, M. H. Abrams, and E. D. Hirsch in Culler 1981. For historical accounts of this period, see also Cain 1984, and Leitch 1988.

8. For an example of de Man's observations on the inadequacies of the older critical approaches, see De Man 1983a, translated in the second edition of *Blindness and Insight*, 229–45.

9. De Man 1986, 17.

10. De Man 1986, 12.

11. De Man 1986, 19.

12. De Man aligns his own method of reading with "deconstruction" in the preface of De Man 1979, ix–x. On the differences between De Man's use of this notion and Derrida's, see Gasché 1979 and 1981, Gearhart 1983, and Derrida 1986.

13. De Man 1979, 17. The passage reads as follows: "The reading is not 'our' reading, since it uses only the linguistic elements provided by the text itself; the distinction between author and reader is one of the false distinctions that the reading makes evident. The deconstruction is not something we have added to the text but it constituted the text in the first place. A literary text simultaneously asserts and denies the authority of its own rhetorical mode, and by reading the text as we did we were only trying to come closer to being as rigorous a reader as the author had to be in order to write the sentence in the first place. Poetic writing is the most advanced and refined mode of deconstruction; it may differ from critical or discursive writing in the economy of its articulation, but not in kind."

14. See Hamacher, Hertz, and Keenan 1989. For the writings themselves, see Hamacher, Hertz, and Keenan 1990. For an account of the reorientation that the discovery of these writings occasioned, see Goodhart 1989, 226–45. For a discussion of the differences between de Man's views of literature and those of other literary "apologists," see Goodhart 1986.

15. See Arac, Godzich, and Martin 1983; Hartman 1979; Fish 1980; Suleiman and Crosman 1980; and Tompkins 1980.

Chapter 1: *Lēstas Ephaske*

1. This essay originally appeared in a special issue of *Diacritics* in 1978 devoted to the work of René Girard. See Goodhart 1978. It constitutes the first part of an analysis I undertook at greater length in my doctoral dissertation, completed in 1977 for the State University of New York at Buffalo, under the direction of René Girard. See Goodhart 1977. Aside from correcting technical errors, adding some paragraphs on the critical approaches of Philip Vellacott and Bernard Knox, and amplifying the notes, I have left the text unchanged.

Since its appearance, a number of critics have referred to it in the course of developing their own approaches. See, for example, Girard 1978a, 50; 1978b, 223; 1986, 122; 1987, 40, 169; Culler 1978, 618; 1980, 30, 37; 1981; 1982, 5; Chase 1979,

59–60; 1986, 182–83; Sadoff 1980, 245; McDonald 1980, 75; Farenga 1981, 1; Miller 1981, 36; Felman 1982, 14–16; 1983, 23; Fry 1983, 211; Skulsky 1983, 289; Golsan 1984, 167; 1988, 73; Verhoeff 1984, 261; Huston 1985, 420; Rudnytsky 1986, 338, 350–57; Pucci 1988, 142–43; 1991, 3; Goodkin 1989, 81; Campbell 1989, 199; Ahl 1991, 62, 140; Ferris 1991, 391; and Peradotto 1992, 1. It is perhaps not without significance that while the thesis I argued in 1978 has been so widely cited in some quarters, it has been almost ignored or summarily dismissed in others. See, for example, Segal 1992.

The Greek text of *Oedipus Tyrannus* upon which I have relied throughout this essay is Richard Jebb's (1972). All extended and most shorter English quotations from the play are cited from Philip Vellacott's "literal" translation in Vellacott 1971. On occasion, I have paraphrased Vellacott's rendering or translated the Greek myself.

The secondary literature to the study of the play is vast. For modern approaches in English, see Bowra 1944, Whitman 1951, Greene 1944, Dodds 1963, Opstelten 1952, Waldock 1966, Cameron 1968, Knox 1957 and 1979, and Vellacott 1970 and 1971. The Berkowitz and Brunner Norton critical edition of the play (1970) contains a generous selection of this older criticism. For approaches since 1970 (in addition to those cited above), see also Vernant 1978, Hay 1979, Harshbarger 1979, Tonelli 1983, Goldhill 1984, Brody 1985, Segal 1986, 1986a, 1993, Bushnell 1988, Burkert 1991, and Pucci 1992. For anthologies of critical response, see Mullahy 1955, Cook 1963, Woodard 1966, Kallich 1968, O'Brien 1968, and Bloom 1988. For the epigraph from Nietzsche see 1974, aphorism #1. For the epigraph from Sophocles, see Vellacott 1971, 12.

2. For a sampling of the Homeric and pre-Homeric tradition regarding Oedipus, see Roberts 1915, Jebb 1972, and Berkowitz and Brunner 1970.

3. For translations of the *Poetics,* see McKeon 1941, Hutton 1982, Telford 1968, Else 1970, Butcher 1951, and Fyfe 1965. On the notion of *hamartia,* see Bremer 1969.

4. For a survey of the treatment of the play as a "tragedy of destiny," see below.

5. For a treatment of this play in connection with the genre of mystery, see Grossvogel 1979.

6. Our interest in the paradox of number in Sophocles' play is not new. Both William Chase Greene (1929) and more recently Karl Harshbarger (1965) take up the problem. Moreover, both see the issue as heightening our awareness of Sophocles' "ironies," Harshbarger suggesting in fact that "this [numerical] disparity is at the crux of any interpretation of the play" (121).

But both critics understand that irony in traditional terms. Greene is convinced, finally, that these paradoxes support the myth itself, offering us yet another example of the poet's skill at naturalistic characterization. And for Harshbarger "the fact of who killed Laius is central." If Harshbarger pursues the question, up to a certain point, with unparalleled clarity (the differences between the two versions of the Phocial massacre, he notes, "are not resolved"), and if in the course of his examination he is able to raise some remarkable questions concerning Creon's role in the Theban intrigue and concerning the Chorus's sacrificial substitution of Oedipus for its own complicity in the affair (and, by extension, ours), what concerns him principally about the murder is "whether there is anyone else who might have done it."

I will argue in the present essay that it is the traditional theory of "tragic irony" that is already at stake in the play, and that the play uncovers systematically the arbitrariness of the determination of any unique culprit, that the empirical issue (whether we decide Oedipus killed Laius or not) is less important, finally, than the plague of scapegoat violence for which it comes to substitute.

7. Compare, for example, the Shepherd's words in Jean Cocteau's *The Infernal Machine* (1967): "You are the son of Jocasta, your wife, and of Laius, your father, killed by you at the crossing of three roads. Incest and parricide. May the gods forgive you!" (67).

Many writers have translated and/or rewritten the Oedipus myth. See, for example, the versions of Seneca, Voltaire, Dryden and Lee, Hoffmannsthal, and Gide, among others, collected in Kallich 1968 and Sanderson and Zimmerman 1968. Corneille's version (1657) is also important in this connection.

8. Cf. Jebb 1972, lii–lxii.
9. Norwood 1960, 148–49.
10. Knox 1957, 26.
11. Cf. Knox 1957, 81–90.
12. Knox 1957, 85.
13. Jebb 1972, 104–5.
14. Freud's remarks on the Oedipus myth appear in *The Interpretation of Dreams* (1965, 294–98), and in *A General Introduction to Psychoanalysis* (1952, 339–41).
15. Lévi-Strauss 1969, 491.
16. Peter Rudnytsky (1986) has undertaken to trace this identification, which he feels defines our era as the "age of Oedipus."
17. Cf. Jebb 1972, xi–li.
18. For editions of the *Poetics* in Greek with facing-page translations, see Butcher 1951 and Fyfe 1965.
19. The study of this ironic interpretation has yet to be done. It is not in Aristotle. Nor is it new with Hegel. It is a concept coextant with Kantianism, already fully in place when Hegel writes the *Aesthetics*. On the history of the notion of conflict, see Gellrich 1988.
20. Bowra 1944, 175.
21. Greene 1944, 154.
22. Whitman 1951, 124.
23. Kott 1966, 137.
24. Vellacott, "The Guilt of Oedipus," in Berkowitz and Brunner 1970, 209–10.
25. Vellacott in Berkowitz and Brunner 1970, 210.
26. See, for example, Kirkwood 1958.
27. See Bradley 1965.
28. See Knox 1957.
29. See, especially, Knox 1957, chap. 2. See also Knox's article on *tyrannos* (collected in Knox 1979, 87–95), which contains much of this discussion.

30. Jean-Pierre Vernant is often credited with this insight, although in fact, a similar formulation first appears in Knox, whom Vernant cites though not at this point in the text. "[Oedipus] is the answer to the problem he tried to solve," Knox writes in 1957, 157; 1979, 107. "Oedipus is discovered, at the end of the tragedy, to be identical to the monstrous creature referred to in the riddle which he, in his pride of 'wise man' [sic] believed he had solved," Vernant writes (Vernant and Vidal-Naquet 1981, 109).

31. See, for example, Knox 1982.

32. Nietzsche, of course, also conceived of himself as a philologist in this fashion and also took Plato as one of the primary objects of his analyses.

33. For a bibliographical survey of early modern Sophoclean criticism and scholarship, from which context much of the older approach to Sophocles comes, see Johansen 1962–63, 94–288.

34. Voltaire 1877, 1–58.

35. Voltaire 1877, 20.

36. Voltaire 1877, 20–21. The translation is my own.

37. Cf. Rymer on tragedy in Kermode 1965. For Voltaire's writing on *Hamlet*, see, for example, Hoy 1992. One could easily imagine an anthology that would gather the long history of non-conformist criticism of the classics (which would include Tolstoy and Shaw among others). These are all writers who see both more and less than the mainstream critics. Having less investment in the standard myth, they are in a better position to observe the anti-mythic gestures that writers like Sophocles and Shakespeare make. But having their own mythic investments elsewhere, they regard these challenges as liabilities rather than assets, and fault the classic writers on that basis, either to dismiss the work in question entirely, or, more often, to rewrite it. We need to hear what these critics have to say about the failure of the mythic structures we expect in "great literature," which they observe more clearly than others, but read with the mainstream in crediting "great writers" with being at least as smart as we take ourselves to be.

38. Norwood 1960, 149–50.

39. Norwood 1960, 150.

40. Derrida 1972, 207–20.

41. "The axiom of criticism must be," Northrop Frye remarks (1966, 5), "not that the poet does not know what he is talking about, but that he cannot talk about what he knows." We are moving in this essay toward a reversal of this characterization, toward the suggestion that literature is already a form of criticism (which is why criticism subverts it and takes its name), and criticism already a form of literature (in the way that criticism would like to think of literature as being).

42. Here is why we must reject Karl Harshbarger's argument.

43. "Undecideability" has, of course, become a prominent theme in Derrida's writing and the writing of those who follow his work. See, for example, Hartman 1979. The cultivation of the "pleasure of the text" is a theme of a book by Barthes that bears that title (1975).

44. Cf. Krieger 1960, 1–21.

45. Knox 1955, 21.

46. Cf. Neil Hertz's discussion in "Freud and the Sandman" (1978) of the relations in Freud between the uncanny, the compulsion to repeat, and literature.
47. Freud 1965, 295.
48. Rieff 1963, 288.
49. Cf. Deleuze and Guattari 1972.
50. Cf. Jones 1963, 5–6. Peter Rudnytsky (1986) has attempted to undertake a similar analysis.
51. Cf. Foucault 1961. Curiously, this book has never been translated in full. Roughly two-fifths of it was translated as *Madness and Civilization* (1965).
52. Foucault's anger in his discussion with health care professionals of the institutional status of psychoanalysis and its role in prisons is instructive. See Foucault 1988.
53. "The type of literary study which structuralism helps one to envisage," Jonathan Culler notes (1975, viii), "would not be primarily interpretive: it would not offer a method which, when applied to literary works, produced new and hitherto unexpected meanings. Rather than a criticism which discovers or assigns meanings, it would be a poetics which strives to define the conditions of meaning."
54. See Girard 1968, 1977, 1977a.
55. Girard 1977a, 487–502.
56. The richness of the Second Stasimon as a criticism by the Chorus and behind the Chorus by Sophocles of a plague of oracular idolatry that has exceeded the biological plague and now threatens the possibility of religious belief itself remains to be explored. For an example of how traditional critics deal with these verses, see Winnington-Ingram 1980.

Chapter 2: "Being Nothing"

1. Earlier versions of this chapter were delivered as lectures at the University of Chicago in 1982, the University of Toledo in 1983, the University of Michigan in 1983, and Cornell University in 1985.

The text of *Richard II* from which I will be quoting is that edited by Kenneth Muir 1963. For other important editions, see Wilson 1939, Black 1955, Ure 1969, Baker 1974, Wells 1969 and 1990, and Bevington 1992. One of the most useful research tools currently available for this play is Roberts 1988. For books on the play after 1985 where Roberts stops, see Bloom 1988a, Moseley 1988, and Berger 1989. For a recent collection of important essays in the history of criticism of this play, see Newlin 1984. For other annotated bibliographies of Shakespeare and of *Richard II* in particular, see Berman 1973, and Wells 1990. Black updated his bibliography in 1977 and Bevington's bibliography (1992) is very useful.

2. The older standard work on Renaissance literary criticism is, of course, Spingarn 1963. For more recent account of this tradition, see Godzich 1986 and Bandera 1994.

3. See Tillyard 1962. Schlegel proposed that the history plays were unified. John Dover Wilson's famous Cambridge edition of the play (1939) lays out the case for the notion that Richard is a "royal martyr." Tillyard suggests that Shake-

speare is here following a long-familiar traditional view of Tudor history reflected in a series of older popular Renaissance texts by Edward Hall and others. This discussion shows no signs of letting up. See, for example, Ribner 1952, Law 1953 and 1954, Kantorowicz 1981, Talbert 1962, Kott 1966, Thayer 1967 and 1983, Sanders 1968, Bromley 1971, Ornstein 1972, Manheim 1973, and Battenhouse 1974. Wells 1985 summarizes the discussion.

4. For Elizabeth's remarks, see the famous "Remarks to William Lambarde." Elizabeth is reputed to have said, with regard to certain documents from the reign of Richard II, "I am Richard II. Know ye not that?" and, regarding the Earl of Essex, "He that will forget God, will also forget his benefactors; this tragedy was played forty times in open streets and houses." This report is cited in Chambers 1930, 326–27. For commentary on this anecdote, see Stephen Greenblatt's "Introduction" in Greenblatt 1982.

5. For a discussion of the uneasiness at the end of the 1590s and of the Earl of Essex's appropriation of Shakespeare's play as a tool in his famous rebellion, see Stanley Wells, "John Barton's *Richard II*, 1973–74," in Newlin 1984, 167. For a discussion of the censorship of the deposition scene, see Clare 1990.

6. See, for example, Raysor 1930, Foakes 1971, and Hawkes 1969.

7. Cf. Fletcher 1991. The quote is from Coleridge. See Foakes 1971.

8. See Pater 1889.

9. See Wilson 1939. The Coleridgean tradition is long. Aside from Pater, see Yeats 1903, Swinburne 1909, Chambers 1925, Stirling 1956, and Rossiter 1961.

10. See above, note 3.

11. Cf. *Richard II*, IV.i.137–38: "The blood of English shall manure the ground, / And future ages groan for this foul act."

12. Ure 1969.

13. Ure 1969, lxviii, lxix. See also Van Doren 1953 and Tillyard 1962.

14. See Tillyard 1959. On the notion of Renaissance humanism, see also Lovejoy 1970, Bush 1930, Spencer 1949, Siegel 1957, and Speaight 1955.

15. See Burckhardt 1975, Mazzeo 1967, Huizinga 1959 and 1959a, Panofsky 1939 and 1955, and Ferguson 1956.

16. On the notion of paradigm shift, the important texts are Kuhn 1957 and 1962. In France, see Canguilhem 1978 and Foucault 1966.

17. See, for example, the opening pages of Robertson 1962. "New historicism" may be regarded as a somewhat delayed application to Renaissance studies of the kind of reorientation that swept through medieval studies in this country thirty years earlier—which was similarly conceived as a move away from Hegelianism.

18. See above, notes 15 and 17.

19. Mazzeo 1967.

20. In light of the veritable explosion in recent years of interest in Renaissance studies inaugurated by the work of Stephen Greenblatt and others associated with the "new historicism," many of these older historiographic and aesthetic understandings are in the process of being rethought. See, for example, Greenblatt 1980 and 1988, as well as the numerous treatments of Shakespeare and

other Renaissance concerns by Jonathan Goldberg, Stephen Orgel, Louis Montrose in Goldberg 1986 and 1990, Orgel 1975, Veeser 1989 and 1993. Others who have published in the journal *Representations* have been associated (rightly or wrongly) with their work. See, for example, Joel Fineman 1986 and 1991. For an account of this movement from a humanist perspective, see Meyer Abrams's essay on "the New Historicism" in Abrams 1993. For reflections on this group from a historian of intellectual history whose own work is informed by poststructuralist concerns, see LaCapra 1989a. For a reading of *Richard II* specifically that adopts both new historical and deconstructionist postulates, see Jonathan Goldberg 1988.

21. See, for example, Foucault 1966, Geertz 1973, and Turner 1969.
22. See Greenblatt 1980.
23. Abrams 1971, 1981, 1985, 1985a.
24. Fiedler 1972.
25. It is interesting that the notion of foils, which comes from the art of fencing and suggests the identicality of opposing forces, should come to be the commonplace way in dramatic criticism of referring to contrasts or differences.
26. Jacques Lacan, of course, used the Möbius strip in his famous lecture at Johns Hopkins in 1966 to illustrate a point about psychoanalysis. See Donato and Macksey 1972. For a reading of this play influenced by Lacan, see Lukacher 1989.
27. Nietzsche 1974, aphorism #125.
28. Foucault 1966 and 1970.
29. Foucault 1970, 385.
30. For a powerful discussion of these materials in the ancient fifth-century B.C.E. context, see Knox 1957.
31. The similarities between Richard II and Richard Nixon were not lost on Nixon's critics. See, for example, Myers 1973.
32. Cf. Roman Polanski's production of *Macbeth* in 1986.
33. There are other aspects of Polanski's treatment that are important. The final shot of the head of *Macbeth* impaled upon the sword of Macduff is not unlike that of Charles Manson in a picture widely circulated at the time of his trial for the murder of Sharon Tate (who had starred in a number of horror films). Moreover, heads seem to be at play throughout this production. Early close head shots of Macbeth present him as the bright young star of the Scottish social community, courting a strikingly attractive young wife (played at the time by a young Francisca Annis). And as his relation to the murder of King Duncan changes him, his face begins to alter until the scene in which he surveys his troops. Having developed over the course of the film a beard, he now appears uncannily like Charles Manson. What is interesting is that the final head shot (which continues the visual identification of Macbeth with Manson) also now resembles that of William Shakespeare in the likeness that we have of him from the famous bust. Moreover, it is clear from the way in which Polanski chooses to stage the death of the wife and family of Macduff that the Manson murders cannot be far from his mind (note that this is the first film Polanski distributed after the killings). The point of all this comparison on Polanski's part, I would suggest, is not to make topical references to his most private tragedies, but rather to show that

those tragedies are already at work in Shakespeare's drama, that by a curious process the most prized member of the community may rather quickly become his own worst enemy, and that as Polanski's drama reflects wider patterns, so *Macbeth* already stages the violence of our time.

34. See *King Lear,* I.i.36.
35. Ure 1969, lxviii.
36. Ure 1969, lxviii–lxix.
37. Pater 1889 and Wilson 1939.
38. Kantorowicz 1981. Parenthetical references in the following paragraphs are to pages in this volume. For a contemporary response to this kind of reading, see Siemon 1983.
39. Kantorowicz 1981, 7.
40. Kantorowicz 1981, 9.
41. Kantorowicz 1981, 9–10.
42. Kantorowicz 1981, 13.
43. Kantorowicz 1981, 16.
44. Kantorowicz 1981, 17.
45. Kantorowicz 1981, 17; my translation.
46. Kantorowicz 1981, 18.
47. Kantorowicz 1981, 24–41, vii.
48. Kantorowicz 1981, 36.
49. Zeffirelli's film of this play highlight's just these aspects of it (1980).
50. On the possibility in Shakespeare's English of a pun on *ay, aye, eye, I,* and even *high,* see Booth 1977, 232, 242, 272, 333, 350, 375, 377, 424, 461, 471, 483, 520–21, and 532–33.
51. See, for example, Plato in the *Ion*—in Hamilton 1961. See also M. H. Abrams's discussion of this passage in *The Mirror and the Lamp* (1958), and Culler's discussion of this distinction in 1981a. The distinction between a mirror and a lamp, a reflector and a light source, is itself already a Romantic distinction. For the Renaissance a model, for example, was both.
52. *Hamlet,* III.ii.24. For an entirely different view of mirrors and imitation in *Hamlet* and other plays of Shakespeare, see Girard 1991.
53. Booth 1977, 163. For examples of this idea in Shakespeare sonnets, see Booth 1977, 143, 163, 203–4, 272, 377, and 384–92. See also the dedication to James in the King James version of the Bible in which the same connection is drawn. References also occur in John Donne (for example, in "The Ecstasy," lines 7–8) and in Milton (for example, in "Samson Agonistes," line 163). I thank Graham Storey of Whitman College for these last three references.
54. For a discussion of theories of extramission and intromission in the history of optics, see Lindberg 1976.
55. See, for example, Tillyard's discussion of these matters in 1959.
56. See Schema 1 (p. 298). The most important contemporary discussion of modeling relationships is, of course, René Girard's in 1965. For another Girardian reading of the "crisis of degree" in this play, see Osborne 1985. For an alternative reading of these materials that finds "nothing" in this play similarly important, see McMillin 1984.

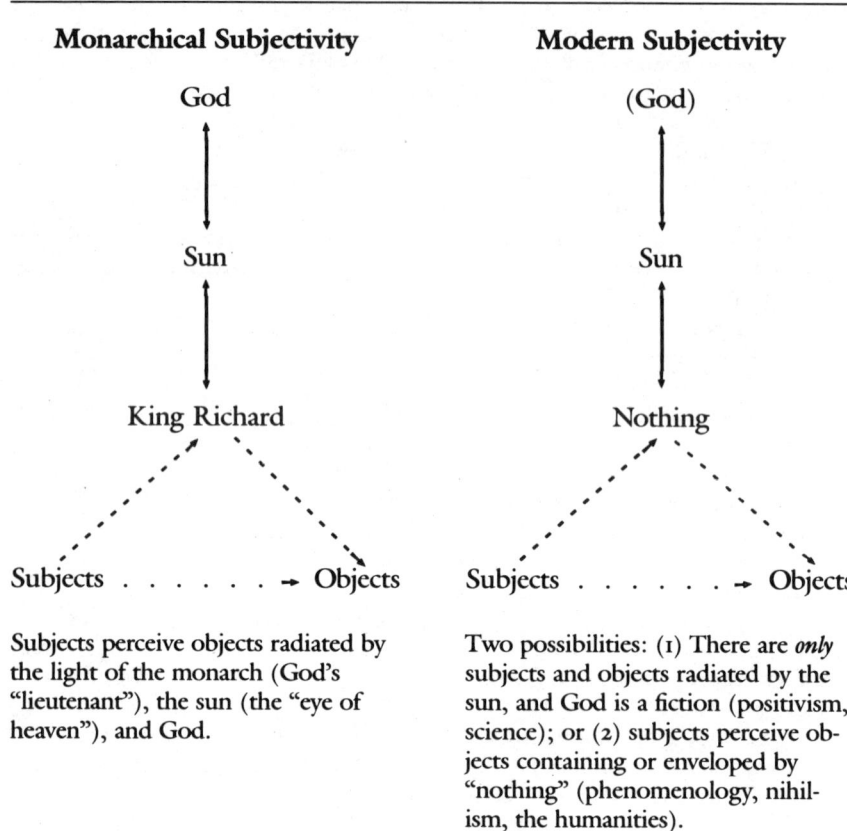

Key: *Solid arrows* indicate real relationships; *dashed arrows* are symbolic relationships; *dotted arrows* are imaginary relationships.

57. See Michel Foucault's brilliant discussion of this strategy at the beginning of *The Order of Things* (1970, 3–18).

58. See Schema 2 (p. 299). The entire action of the play may be mapped onto a grid of three differential registers (or languages or discourses)—heroic or challenger, monarchical or royal, and prophetic or deathbed confessional—and a series of three successive and repeating stages. Richard is monarch in a context in which he is challenged by Henry Bolingbroke, defended by Thomas of Mowbray, and in which John of Gaunt speaks the voice of traditional authority (and issues a deathbed prophecy). Then Richard is in contest for the monarchy with Bolingbroke, his defenders—Bushy, Baggott, and Greene—are in contest with Bolingbroke's defenders—notably Northumberland—and in this context the speech of clerical authority (delivered in the person of the Bishop of Carlisle) contests with the speech of secular authority of the nobility (in the person of the

	Richard II			Henry IV, Henry V
	Acts 1 & 2	Acts 3 & 4	Act 5	
Prophetic language	John of Gaunt	Bishop of Carlisle / Duke of York	Richard	Henry
Monarchical language	King Richard	Richard / Henry	King Henry	King Henry V
Heroic language	Mowbray / Bolingbroke	Bushy, Baggott, and Greene / Northumberland	Exton / Aumerle	Northumberland

aging and ailing Duke of York). Finally, Bolingbroke accedes to the throne (with Exton as his assigned or unassigned defender), Aumerle stages a failed rebellion (and even the Duke of York's wife stages a kind of rebellion in appealing to the new monarch to pardon him), and Richard speaks the truth shortly before he is murdered in Pomfret Castle.

But the trouble is far from over. For Henry will find himself beset by rebellions (led by Northumberland) in the next play, his son will be at first his defender and subsequently his successor, and Henry will recall, on his deathbed, the part he took in the drama of Richard II. And if we regard the murder of the royal personage by Exton (acting on behalf of Henry) to be a duplication of Richard's alleged ordering of the murder of the Duke of Gloucester, then the current drama has only completed that duplication already.

59. Baker 1974.
60. See, for example, Boethius 1962.
61. Boethius 1962, Book 4, Prose 2.
62. Joel Fineman advanced this idea with regard to the sonnets in 1986. See also the collection of his essays on "the subjectivity effect" published by friends on his behalf posthumously in 1991.
63. Borges 1972.

Chapter 3: "I Am Joseph"

1. The following essay was written for a colloquium in honor of René Girard held in 1983 at Cerisy-la-Salle. It still bears the traces of its origin. It was later translated into French by Paul Dumouchel as part of the proceedings of the colloquium. It was followed by a discussion between René Girard, Raymund Schwager, and the author. See Goodhart 1985 and 1985a. The English original was published as Goodhart 1986–88. For the quote from Eric Gans, see Gans 1973, 581.

2. For a bibliography of Girard's writings and the critical response, see Deguy and Dupuy 1982, 315–33, and Juilland 1986, iii–xxxii. The books in which these bibliographies appear are themselves excellent samplings of some of the critical response to Girard's work. For another collection, see Dumouchel 1985. For recent applications of Girard's ideas in psychoanalysis and in psychiatry, see Borch-Jacobsen 1982 and Oughourlian 1982. For recent readings of Girard's work in context of the Christian Bible and theology, see Schwager 1987, Lohfink 1983, and Williams 1991. For a book on the relation of Girard's work to deconstruction, see McKenna 1992. See also Hamerton-Kelley 1987, Livingston 1992. For a short biographical sketch and other books on Girard's work, see Goodhart 1993a.

3. See Dumouchel and Dupuy 1979, Prigogine and Stengers 1979, and Dupuy 1982.

4. The proceedings from the conference at Cerisy were published as Dumouchel 1985. A conference on the work of René Girard, Michel Serres, and Ilya Prigogine was held at the University of Texas at Austin in 1980. Another on "Disorder and Order," centered more focally around the work of Girard and the "mimetic hypothesis," was held at Stanford University in 1981. The proceedings were published as Livingston 1984. A conference on "auto-organization" in the human and natural sciences took place in 1981 and its proceedings appeared as Dumouchel and Dupuy 1983. A conference on "Vengeance" took place at Stanford University in 1988. For the past five years or so there have been yearly meetings of the "colloquium on Violence and Religion" (hereafter COV&R) and an additional meeting at the joint annual convention of the American Academy of Religion and the Society for Biblical Literature. The colloquium produces a newsletter with information about Girard's work. See Niewiadomski, Palaver, and Regensburger 1991. A new journal devoted entirely to Girard's work and research associated with it has appeared, *Contagion. Journal of Violence, Mimesis, and Culture*.

5. Girard 1961.

6. Girard 1972.

7. Girard 1978 and 1982.

8. For further discussion of Girard's views on the Christian Gospel, see Girard 1973 and 1975.

9. "Nouveau prophétisme" was used a few years ago by commentators in France to characterize the work of the "nouveaux philosophes."

10. On the shift away from essentialistic conceptualizations in philosophy and literary criticism, see Levinas 1974, De Man 1971, and Fish 1980.

11. The theme of the "tiers exclu" is persistent in Serres's work. See, for example, his early book on communication (Serres 1968, 41), and a more recent book on the foundations of Rome (Serres 1983, 169). It is interesting that in English we say "excluded middle," whereas in French one says "tiers exclu" ("excluded third"). It is as if in each linguistic context we have domesticated the notion to read either as a middle or as a third, excluding commonly their conjunction—that the "tier exclu" is at once between the communicants (a middle) and outside of them (a third).

12. I know of very little that has been done on this very interesting aspect of Girardian thinking concerning the inefficacy of sacrificial structuration at the

moment of the appearance of Greek humanism, Judaism, and in general, modern cultural forms.

13. On the centrality of the notion of anti-idolatry to Hebraic religion, see Kaufmann 1972. On the centrality of the notion of the prophetic, see also Buber 1982. For a penetrating account of the criticism of idolatry in non-Jewish writing, see Freccero 1975.

14. For a discussion of the way in which the "secondary" or interpretative texts of Jewish tradition extend Torah, see Handelman 1982, 38, and Levinas 1982, 7. The standard authority, in the English-speaking world, for discussions of Jewish spirituality and mysticism, is, of course, Gershom Scholem. See, for example, Scholem 1972 and 1978. On interpretation see also Fishbane 1982, 1985, and 1989.

15. Jewish Publication Society 1917. The specific commandment against idolatry has often been taken to be the second: "Thou shalt not make unto thee a graven image" (Ex. 20:4). The first commandment has been taken, on the other hand, as the statement of Hebraic monotheism. It may be, however, that by virtue of the second commandment we may understand the first as the law of anti-idolatry ("Thou shalt have only an external God, no internal Gods"). The reading, then, of the first as a statement of monotheism would reflect already an exclusion of the second and in general of the diachronic or prophetic context in which the first appears, the only context, in fact, in which such a list of commandments can be read as a text or narrative. For a collection in English of older rabbinic commentaries upon the biblical text, see Feuer and Scherman 1981. On the shift away from viewing the Hebrew Bible as concerned with monotheism as opposed to polytheism and toward viewing it as opposed to paganism, see Lévy 1979a. For a fuller discussion of the interpretive issues raised in counting commandments, see chapter 4.

16. The importance of the work of Emmanuel Levinas to this discussion—and in general to the notion of the exteriority of transcendence—cannot be overestimated. See, for example, Levinas 1961 and 1974. For Levinas's work on Judaism, see his 1968, 1969, 1977, 1982, 1983, 1987a, 1988, 1990, 1990a, 1994a, b. The work of Maurice Blanchot in this connection is also important. See Blanchot 1959 and 1969. For an application of some of these ideas within a political context, see Lévy 1977. For other important accounts of Judaism, see Neher 1962 and Chouraqui 1964.

17. The phrase was used by Foucault to characterize Blanchot's work. See Foucault 1966a. For a profound meditation on the themes of exodus, exile, and the desert in Dante, see Mazzotta 1979.

18. The text of Exodus is from Rabbi J. H. Hertz 1979. See also Everett Fox's edition of Genesis and Exodus (1990). For other important editions of Torah and its commentaries, see Cohen 1979, and Isaiah and Sharfman 1949. On Genesis alone, see also the monumental Artscroll edition of Zlotowitz and Scherman 1977–81.

19. Cf. Ex. 3:10: "Come now therefore, and I will send thee unto Pharaoh, that Thou mayest bring forth My people the children of Israel out of Egypt."

20. Cf. Ex. 3:13: "And Moses said unto God: 'Behold, when I come unto the children of Israel, and shall say unto them: The God of your fathers hath sent

me unto you; and they shall say to me: What is His name? what shall I say unto them'"?

21. Cf. Ex. 3:14–15: "And God said unto Moses: 'I AM THAT I AM'; and He said: 'Thus shalt thou say unto the children of Israel: I AM hath sent me unto you.' And God said moreover unto Moses: 'Thus shalt thou say unto the children of Israel: The LORD, the God of your fathers, the God of Abraham, the God of Isaac, and the God of Jacob, hath sent me unto you; this is My name for ever, and this is My memorial unto all generations."

22. For a similar account of the name of God, see Buber 1982, 80–82. For further commentary, see Levinas 1982, 143–57, and Derrida 1980, 179.

23. See, for example, Scholem 1978, 282–303.

24. Cf. Ex. 3:10–12: "'Come now therefore, and I will send thee unto Pharaoh, that Thou mayest bring forth My people the children of Israel out of Egypt.' And Moses said unto God: 'Who am I, that I should go unto Pharaoh, and that I should bring forth the children of Israel out of Egypt?' And He said: 'Certainly I will be with thee.'"

25. Rashi, the medieval French biblical exegete, and the foremost among commentators of the later rabbinic tradition, draws our attention to this possibility—with the subtlety displayed by so many Toradic commentators. He notes that in the later passage, while the word *'imach* ("with you") does not literally recur, we are entitled to include it. See Isaiah and Sharfman 1949, 23.

26. "Being with" or "being there with" is a better translation than "being." Buber notes that there is no abstract presence in the Hebrew. See Buber 1982, 44–62. For a translation in English of Genesis and Exodus in accord with the principles embodied in the famous translation of Buber and Rosenzweig of Torah into German, see Fox 1990. For a discussion of these translation matters, see Buber and Rosenzweig 1994.

27. Such a notion—that the Torah itself may be understood as a covenant—has led non-Jewish historical scholars of the Bible to see the "Old Testament" as structured around the notion of covenant. See, for example, Eichrodt 1961. For a more personal account of covenant in the "Old Testament" and the Christian Gospel from a Catholic perspective, see Bishop 1982.

28. It is customary within Orthodox synagogues for women to sit segregated from the men.

29. Zlotowitz and Scherman 1977–81, 1613.

30. On the prophetic interpretation of dreams among older commentators, see Zlotowitz and Scherman 1977–81, 1620.

31. E. A. Speiser, for example, in his prestigious edition of Genesis in the Anchor Bible series, summarizes this long and persistent tradition of biblical criticism in which scholars have divided up the text into distinctive compositional sources—a "J" document, an "E" document, and so on—in accordance with the various words employed for the naming of divinity. See Speiser 1964. My own interest—as I hope is clear in this essay—is not to challenge this important work, but to ask a different question: namely, by what principle of coherence can these admittedly diverse and heterogeneous materials be seen as "going together," a principle to whose unifying power the very fervor with which we pursue an in-

terest in heterogeneity in the text may offer ample testimony? On the shift away from traditional historical concerns to a closer reading of narrative and poetic detail, the groundbreaking book, of course, is Robert Alter's *The Art of Biblical Narrative* (1981). It is Alter, for example, who takes Speiser to task over just such issues. Whatever the potential pitfalls of an organicist approach—namely, that it be developed at the expense of historicism—Alter's book is profoundly exciting. He allows us to envision a new biblical criticism as yet in its infancy that would cull the insights of both formalism and historicism (eschewing the limitations of each) into a critical position that is something like that of the Bible itself.

32. Jacob's blessing of the sons of Joseph is itself an interesting moment in context of our presentation. Instead of blessing Manassah (Joseph's first-born) with his right hand, and Ephraim with his left (as tradition would dictate), Jacob crosses his hands and blesses Manassah with his left hand and Ephraim with his right. He does this, he tells Joseph, because Manassah's younger brother "shall be greater than he" (48:19). Is Jacob continuing the sacrificial reading of his earlier days, favoring the younger son, the gesture that set the whole drama into motion (and, perhaps, recalls his own position as second-born)? Or does his gesture here reflect an anti-sacrificial position, one perhaps that he has learned from the events that have transpired? Such a view would recognize at once that Manassah is first-born and that Ephraim must not be slighted, a view that contrasts with the rigid distinction between Cain and Abel at the other end of the first book of Torah. Malbim suggests that Jacob placed his left hand above the right, thereby blessing Manassah with the hand that was on top and Ephraim with the right, refusing to some extent, that is, to distinguish between them. What seems clear, in any event, is that the text of Jacob's blessing of the sons, like the Joseph story proper, and like Jacob's hands within that text (and not to mention the hands or texts of the commentators), superimposes one view upon the other. Jacob has "wisely directed his hands," Rashi tells us in his interpretation of this passage. For all these commentaries, see Zlotowitz and Scherman 1977–81, 2110. I thank Holli Levitsky, of the University of California, Irvine, for drawing my attention to this passage in context of the above argument.

33. Scholem 1972, 141–42.

34. See Serres 1980, 219, from which the epigraph is drawn. A published English translation of this book reads: "He is a Jew, and thus he understands what he must understand in his milieu and his culture, that the sacrifice must be stopped, that there must be a substitute. . . ." See Serres 1982, 164. The differences between "He is a Jew" as a translation of "Il est juif" and "the sacrifice" as a translation of "le sacrifice" in this context are noteworthy.

Chapter 4: Reading the Ten Commandments

1. This essay was written for "Literature, Myth, and the Bible," a conference on the work of René Girard held at Brigham Young University in 1984 and organized by Terry Butler. It was subsequently delivered in modified form at a conference in the Religious Studies Program at Cornell University in 1993.

2. A notable exception to this trend is Herbert Schneidau's book, *Sacred Discontent,* which attempted a reading of the Bible in the 1970s in precisely this vein. See Schneidau 1977.

3. M. H. Abrams has written persuasively about the "covert theology" of Kantian aesthetics both in *Natural Supernaturalism* (1971) and more recent essays on "art-as-such." See Abrams 1981, 1985, 1985a. The standard continental work on the historicity of hermeneutical understanding remains, of course, Gadamer's *Truth and Method* (1975).

4. These questions are germane today, of course, to a multitude of different critical contexts. Russian formalists, Czech and French structuralists, American new critics, phenomenological critics, semiologists, French and American deconstructionists, German and American reader response critics (to name only a few of these contexts) all raise these questions.

5. For an account of modern biblical criticism, see my encyclopedia article, "Biblical Theory and Criticism, 2: Modern Criticism," Goodhart (1993).

6. Culler 1984 and 1986.

7. Foucault 1970, 387.

8. See, for example, Girard 1978, 249.

9. See the *American Heritage Dictionary,* s.v. "Bible."

10. For a useful compendium of Judaic commonplaces on these matters, see Birnbaum 1979.

11. For the discussion of the appearance of Torah-centered Judaism and its relation to the Babylonian exile in the sixth century B.C.E., see Fishbane's essay in Greenspahn 1982. See also Handelman 1982.

12. Robert Alter refers to this distinction at the outset of his groundbreaking study of biblical narrative (1981).

13. For a discussion of the use of terms such as "primitive" or "closed" in contemporary ethnology, see, for example, Lévi-Strauss 1967 and Charbonnier 1969.

14. The perception of this arrangement, of course, was much more common in the Middle Ages. For a summary of medieval views of biblical interpretation, see Mazzotta 1979 and Freccero 1986. For a survey of Catholic and Protestant views of biblical interpretation, see Vawter 1982 and Kelsey 1982.

15. For a discussion of this notion of a "God of wrath and vengeance" in Christian thought, see Schwager 1985.

16. For an account of the typological tradition of interpretation in Christian thought, see Goppelt 1982.

17. The modern work on Hebraic interpretation and biblical hermeneutics is just beginning. For a survey of the field see Fishbane's essay in Greenspahn 1982. For a discussion of biblical interpretation in ancient Israel, see Kugel 1981, 1988, and 1990; Holtz 1984a, 177–211; Fishbane 1985; Rawidowicz 1974; Greer and Kugel 1986, 126–54; and Hartman 1986.

18. The notion that the Christian may be regarded as an episode in the history of the Judaic was developed by Geoffrey Hartman in his introduction to the session on Torah at the English Institute in 1983. The papers that followed—by Herbert Marks, Geoffrey Hartman, Michael Fishbane, and Robert Alter—were

never published as a group, although versions of them appeared elsewhere. See Hartman 1986, Marks 1989, Alter 1985, and Fishbane 1989.

19. My debt to Gershom Scholem on matters relevant to Judaic messianic and mystical ideas, both in this study and elsewhere, is incalculable. If I take issue with one or another of his positions (for example, to oppose his work to Martin Buber's or that of Emmanuel Levinas) it is important to recall, first, that I am only rekindling the debate in which he himself partook, and second, that it is Scholem who almost singlehandedly in the English-speaking world made these discussions possible to begin with. See Scholem 1972, 1973, 1974, 1976, 1978, 1978a, and 1987. On recent revisions to Scholem's positions, see Idel 1986 and 1988.

20. Buber 1982 and Levinas 1990, 1990a.

21. Maimonides 1972, 489.

22. Maimonides 1972, 489. On the notion that followers of Jesus have not always regarded Torah as an "Old Testament" and that Jesus himself may have thought he was teaching Torah rather than replacing it, see Maccoby 1986.

23. See, for example, Goodhart 1985, 1985a, and 1986–88. See also above, chapter 3.

24. The standard Hebrew edition of the *Tanakh* is currently Kittel 1966. Although the Jewish Publication Society's new English translation appeared in 1985, I will be using throughout this book the older 1917 translation (Jewish Publication Society 1950).

25. Cf. Cassuto's interpretation of the Ten Commandments (1967).

26. For Buber's essay, see Buber 1982, 93–117.

27. For a discussion of the traditional Jewish commentary to the first commandment, see Hertz 1979, 294–301, and Feuer and Scherman 1981.

28. Cf. Claude Riveline's reading of this passage in Halpérin 1985, 11–29.

29. Cf. entry "Mitzvah" in Birnbaum 1979, 390.

30. Freedman 1961, 310–11. See also Ginzberg 1906–38.

31. See Kaufmann 1972, 13.

32. See, for example, Levinas 1969, 33.

33. Cf. Scholem 1978, 282–303.

34. The idea that the Torah is the "blueprint of the world" occurs in the opening chapter of *Genesis Rabbah*. See Epstein 1939 and Freedman 1961. The most famous working out of the relation of creation, revelation, and redemption is, of course, Rosenzweig's. See Rosenzweig 1985.

35. Cf. Zlotowitz and Scherman 1977–81, xvi.

36. See Goodhart 1986–88, and chapter 3.

37. See Cohen 1979, 328–38, for a compendium of traditional views on this passage. For Rashi's commentary, see Isaiah and Sharfman 1949, 18–34.

38. On the name of God, see Buber 1982, 80–82.

39. See the tractate *Yoma* 3:8.

40. See, for example, the tractate *Makkot* 23a.

41. Maimonides 1967.

42. For the suggestion that the six hundred thirteen commandments are contained within the ten, see *Numbers Rabbah* on 13:16 and 18:21 in Freedman

and Simon 1983; and the commentaries on the *Sefer Yetzirah* by Sadia Gaon (Lambert 1891, 22), and by Judah Barzillai (Halbershtam 1885, 278). For an English translation of this last book, see Kaplan 1990. See also the *Sefer ha-Bahir*, par. 124, in Scholem 1987. "This tradition was recorded in the Alexandrean exegesis of Philo, but does not appear in rabbinic literature," Elliot Wolfson of New York University notes (personal communication, 1988), "until the Gaonic period, for example, in the writings of Saadia Gaon." I thank Professor Wolfson for his perusal of this essay in manuscript form and for his very helpful suggestions.

43. For the idea that the Law was given in one utterance, see Feuer and Scherman 1981, 23.

44. On this idea, see also Handelman 1982.

45. On the distinction between esoteric and exoteric traditions, see Fishbane 1982, Idel 1986, and Scholem 1974.

46. On this idea, see Scholem 1978.

47. For an example of the use of this kabbalistic idea in narrative fiction, see Borges's short story "The Aleph." In the story, a writer discovers in the basement of a broken down house (which belongs to the writer's rival) an "aleph," which is to say, something that contains within it the entire universe. See Borges 1978.

The following statement, found in a later midrashic text, *ot-yot de-R Akiba* ("the letters of Rabbi Akiba"), reads: "if there is no *aleph*, there is no *bet*; if there is no *bet* there is no *aleph*. If there is no perfect Torah, the entire world could not exist; if the entire world did not exist, the perfect Torah would not exist." See Wertheimer 1950–53, 2:345. "The kabbalists," Elliot Wolfson notes (personal communication, 1988), "exploited the identification of *aleph* and the divine name through a numerical trick: the letters of the tetagrammaton equal 26 (10 + 5 + 6 + 5); the letter *aleph* is א which can be broken down into a *yod* (10), plus a *waw* (6), plus a *yod* (10), which also equals 26." On the idea that the *aleph* contains all the letters, see *Zohar* II 234b.

Have we reached the bottom line by evoking the esoteric suggestion that the whole world may be said to be contained within the *aleph*? Some Kabbalists suggest that the formation of the letter *aleph* from a *yod*, a *vav*, and another *yod* offers a further inquiry, that the whole world may be contained within the first stroke of the *aleph*, which is to say, the *yod*, which is also, of course, the first letter of the tetragrammaton, YHVH, the name of God.

48. Jonathan Bishop, for example, would say (personal communication) that Jesus is the "presencing of the Torah." "The Torah of the Messiah," he says, "is the example of the Messiah. There is no other."

49. Jonathan Bishop (1982) has attempted just such an interpretation from a Christian perspective.

50. See, for example, Scholem's book on Sabbatai Sevi (1973).

51. See Girard 1975 and 1978.

52. Birnbaum 1949, 75.

Chapter 5: "Out of the Fish's Belly"

1. An earlier version of this essay appeared as Goodhart 1985b. The text of the Book of Jonah to which I refer is the older standard translation of the Jewish Publication Society issued in 1917. I have also drawn freely from the commentaries (and occasionally the translations) from other editions: the common Conservative liturgical volume of Hertz 1979, 964–71; the new JPS translation of Orlinsky et al. 1985, 1037–40; and the Artscroll study edition of Zlotowitz (1978).

2. Cf. Is. 11–14 and Jer. 20.

3. Cf. the passage in 2 Kings (14:25): "[Jeroboam] restored the border of Israel from the entrance of Hamath unto the sea of Arabah, according to the word of the LORD, the God of Israel, which He spoke by the hand of His servant Jonah the son of Amittai, the prophet, who was of Gath-hepher."

4. Excerpts from the older exegetical traditions may be found in the commentaries listed above (note 1). Surveys and examples of modern critical approaches to the Book of Jonah may be found in Trible 1994 and 1967, Gunn 1993, Craig 1993, Sasson 1990, Lacocque 1990, Stuart 1989, Bock 1989, Backus 1986, Almbladh 1986, Bickerman 1984, Craigie 1984, Vawter 1983, Magonet 1983, Halpern 1981, Lacocque 1981, Wiesel 1981, Duval 1973, and Aalders 1948.

5. Heschel 1971, 67.

6. Compare the following passages, cited by Scherman, in his introduction to Zlotowitz 1978, xix, xxiii: (1) "Why did Jonah flee? He passed judgment upon himself. He said, I know that this nation [the Ninevites] is close to repentance. Now they will repent and the Holy One, Blessed be He, will dispatch His anger against Israel. And as if it were not enough that Israel calls me a false prophet, even idolators [will do so]" (*Pirkei d'Rabbi Eliezer* chap. 10). (2) "Jonah defended the honor of the child [Israel] rather than the honor of the Father [God]" (*Mechilta, Pesichta Bo*)." (3) Jonah ben Amittai was a true prophet (*Yerushalami Sanhedrin* 11:8).

7. The very words used to describe Jonah's predicament in the water, *mim'eiy hadagah,* can, of course, mean "out of the belly of the great fish" or "from the belly of the great fish," suggesting either Jonah prayed while within the belly or prayed his way out of it, sustaining the same play upon without and within in which interpretation gets caught, as we have been observing.

8. Zlotowitz 1978, 107.
9. Zlotowitz 1978, 118.
10. Zlotowitz 1978, 82.
11. Zlotowitz 1978, 122.
12. Zlotowitz 1978, 123.
13. See above, chapter 3.
14. Zlotowitz 1978, 86, 99.
15. Zlotowitz 1978, 136.
16. Hertz 1979, 964. The author of the "introduction and commentary" to the Book of Jonah is given in Cohen 1979 (from which the Hertz selection is taken) on the title page inserted after page 136 but before page 137 as "Rev. Dr. S. Goldman."

17. Hertz 1979, 964.
18. For an interesting account of the Israelite prophets, see Yehezkel Kaufmann 1960.
19. On these notions of interpretation, see Fishbane 1989.
20. For a discussion of the relation between sacrifice and violence, see Girard 1977.
21. Cf. Lev. 16.
22. For Maimonides, see 1972.
23. Cf. Weissman 1980, 1. For another anthology of midrashic stories, see Ginzberg 1906–38.
24. For these and other meanings for these words, see Brown, Driver, and Briggs 1951.
25. Zlotowitz 1978, xx.
26. Zlotowitz 1978, xix.
27. Zlotowitz 1978, 107.

Chapter 6: "The End from the Beginning"

1. An earlier version of this chapter was delivered as a lecture at Cornell University in 1986 and at Syracuse University in 1989. For recent and modern criticism of the Book of Job, see Zuck 1992, Cotter 1992, Purdue and Gilpin 1992, Zuckerman 1991, Penchansky 1990, Good 1990, Bloom 1988, Leibowitz 1987, Girard 1987, Weiss 1983, Westermann 1981, Tsevat 1980, Gordis 1978, Nemo 1978, Polzin 1977, Levenson 1972, Glatzer 1969, Sanders 1968, Hone 1960, Rowley 1958, and Jung 1954. The standard edition within the university community is Pope 1973.
2. Cf. Pope 1973, 290.
3. Jung 1954.
4. See Pope 1973, xxvii.
5. For an example of the negative response Buber's work has elicited, see Scholem's essays in 1976, 126–71, and 1978, 227–50. See also the essay of Katz (1983, 1–93), who follows Scholem's lead in this matter.
6. Since I wrote these words in the late eighties, Moshe Idel has undertaken a criticism of Scholem in certain important arenas. See, for example, Idel 1988.
7. Buber 1982, 188–98.
8. Buber 1982, 189.
9. It is Levinas, I would like to argue, who restores and extends Buber's importance for us, although Levinas to some extent would argue a problematic relation to Buber and identify an affiliation more directly with Rosenzweig, and although some scholars who study these relations would support that argument. See, for example, Bernasconi 1988, 100–135. Levinas has written many essays on Buber's work which Bernasconi lists.
10. See "Violence and Metaphysics," in Derrida (1978, 79–153), and "At This Very Moment in This Work Here I Am," in Bernasconi and Critchley (1991, 11–48). Bernasconi and Critchley's book (1991) is a compendium of materials on their relation. These editors have taken the lead in promoting the philosophic

reading of Levinas. Others who have followed in this vein are Jill Robbins and Hent de Vries. See Robbins 1991. The leading proponents of "the Jewish Levinas" remain Richard Cohen and Catherine Chalier. See Cohen 1994 and Chalier 1993. At a recent conference on Levinas's work at Loyola University in Chicago in May, 1993, this split was very much in evidence.

11. The requisite ten years it is said to take French books to cross the Atlantic have passed. All of Levinas's Jewish writings have been, or are now in the process of being, translated. See, for example, Levinas 1994, 1994a, and 1994b.

12. Levinas 1961.

13. Levinas 1974.

14. Levinas 1983, 374.

15. The background to this text is exceedingly interesting. See Franz Jozef van Beeck's account in 1989, and the update of this account in Kolitz 1994. Although the story was presented by Mandel as a document, in fact it was a fictional account written by Zvi Kolitz and published in 1947. See Kolitz 1947a.

16. Levinas 1983, 189–93. The piece has been variously translated by Bert Sugarman, Séan Hand, Franz Jozef van Beeck, and others. I translate the passage myself.

17. Here is the French original of the entire passage from Levinas 1983, 189–91: "Nous venons de lire un text beau et vrai, vrai comme seule la fiction peut l'être. Publié dans un journal israélien par un auteur anonyme, traduit sous le titre *Yossel, fils de Yossel Rackover de Tarnopol, parle à Dieu* pour *La Terre retrouvée*—périodique sioniste de Paris—par M. Arnold Mandel, il . . . traduit une expérience de la vie spirituelle profonde et authentique.

Le texte se donne pour un document, écrit pendant les dernières heures de la Résistance du Ghetto de Varsovie. Le narrateur aurait été témoin de toutes les horreurs; il aurait perdu dans des conditions atroces ses jeunes enfants. Dernier survivant de sa famille, et pour quelques instants encore, il nous lègue ses ultimes pensées. Fiction littéraire, certes; mais fiction où chacune de nos vies de survivants se reconnait avec vertige. . . .

Que signifie cette souffrance des innocents? Ne témoigne-t-elle pas d'un monde sans Dieu, d'une terre où l'homme seul mésure le Bien et le Mal? La réaction la plus simple, la plus commune consisterait à conclure à l'athéisme. Réaction la plus saine aussi pour tous ceux à qui jusqu'alors un dieu, un peu primaire, distribuait des prix, infligeait des sanctions ou pardonait des fautes et, dans sa bonté, traitait les hommes en éternels enfants. Mais de quel démon borné, de quel magicien étrange avez-vous donc peuplé votre ciel, vous qui, aujourd'hui, le déclarez désert? Et pourquoi sous un ciel vide cherchez-vous encore un monde sensé et bon?

La certitude de Dieu, Yossel fils de Yossel l'éprouve avec une force nouvelle, sous un ciel vide. Car s'il existe si seul, c'est pour sentir sur ses épaules toutes les responsabilités de Dieu. Il y a sur la voie qui mène au Dieu unique un relais sans Dieu. Le vrai monothéisme se doit de répondre aux exigences légitimes de l'athéisme. Un Dieu d'adulte se manifeste précisément par le vide du ciel enfantin. Moment où Dieu se retire du monde et se voile la face (d'apres Yossel ben Yossel). . . .

Dieu qui se voile la face n'est pas, pensons-nous, une abstraction de théologien ni une image du poète. C'est l'heure où l'individu juste ne trouve aucun recours extérieur, où aucune institution ne le protège, où la consolation de la présence divine dans le sentiment religieux enfantin se refuse elle aussi, où l'individu ne peut triompher que dans sa conscience, c'est-à-dire nécessairement dans la souffrance. Sense spécifiquement juif de la souffrance qui ne prend à aucun moment la valeur d'une expiation mystiques pour les péchés du monde. La position des victimes dans un monde en désordre, c'est-à-dire dans un monde ou le bien n'arrive pas à triompher, est souffrance. Elle révèle un Dieu qui, renonçant à toute manifestation secourable, en appelle à la peine maturité de l'homme responsable intégralement.... La souffrance du juste pour une justice sans triomphe est vécue concrètement comme judaïsme. Israël—historique et charnel—redevient catégorie religieuse."

18. Girard 1961.
19. Girard 1972.
20. Girard 1978 and 1982.
21. Girard 1985.
22. Girard 1985, 207–8. Here is the French text: "Le dieu qui finalement rompt le silence et répond à Job 'du sein de la tempête' ne fait pas la moindre allusion aux questions posées par ces deux passages [16:19–21 and 19:25–27] ou par les protestations d'innocence de Job. Il semble ne pas comprendre que celui-ci est la victime de sa communauté, ou peut-être fait-il semblant. Job, pour lui, est un individu qui fait de la contestation métaphysique sans raison valable. Par ce discours, il court-circuite toute la problématique du bouc émissaire. Ce dieu pose le problème de la façon trompeuse qui a toujours prévalu depuis: il escamote tout ce qui a trait aux rapport de Job à sa communauté—meuilleure façon de neutraliser la force subversive du discours de Job. Les paroles demeurent mais leur sense devient inaccessible ou presque. C'est beaucoup plus efficace que de réduire Job au silence par une violence physique, trop visible.

Pour échapper au redoutable guêpier des rapports humains, ce dieu se réfugie dans la nature.... Un peu s'astronomie, un peu de météorologie, beaucoup de zoologie....

La poésie de ce bestiaire ne doit pas nous dissimuler qu'il constitue l'étalage d'une puissance irrésistible. Ce dieu montre sa force pour ne pas avoir à s'en servir. Ce n'est plus le dieu des amis, certes, qui exerçait sa terreur ouvertment contre les boucs émissaires. Il ne brandit plus les armées célestes contre le rebelle.

Il recourt à la ruse et obtient gain de cause: voici Job enfin docile et silencieux, plein d'admiration terrifiée pour l'autruche et le Leviathan.... Il est difficile de prendre cette farce au sérieux.

23. Girard 1987, 141–42.
24. A more lengthy account of the relation of the fourth song of the "suffering servant" to René Girard's work is forthcoming. I read a paper on this topic, "*'al lo-chamas asah* ('although he had done no violence'): Isaiah 52–53, René Girard, and the Innocent Victim," at an additional session of the annual joint meeting of the American Academy of Religion and the Society for Biblical Literature (hereafter AAR/SBL) in Washington in 1993. An expanded version of the paper

was delivered at the Associated Mennonite Biblical Seminary in Elkhart, Indiana, in June 1994. The publication of the proceedings of the Elkhart conference is in process (edited by Willard M. Swartley). An abstract of the AAR/SBL paper was printed in the COV&R Bulletin for September 1994, with responses from Raymund Schwager and József Niewiadomski. See Goodhart 1994. I replied to Schwager and Niewiadomski in the subsequent issue. See Goodhart 1995.

25. The notion that suffering is a perspective is germane to the Levinas passage. Girard curiously short circuits the anti-sacrificial reading he himself has been developing in order to advocate for an alternative understanding of creation in a manner not unlike the God of chapters 38–42 he chastises for doing the same.

26. See, for example, Pope 1973, xxiv.

27. See chapters 3 and 4.

28. On the failure of the angel to arrive on time, see below, chapter 7.

29. Levinas 1987, 184. This essay is a review of Philippe Nemo's *Job et l'excès du mal* (1978). The French original, which appeared in Levinas 1986, 189–207, reads: "Le 'Où étais-tu lorsque je fondais la terre?' du chapitre 38 verset 4, au début du discours attribué à Dieu et qui rappelle à Job son absence à l'heure de la Création, apostrophe-t-il seulement l'impudence d'une créature qui se permet de juger le Créateur? Expose-t-il seulement une théodicée où l'économie d'un tout harmonieux et savamment agencé ne récèle de mal qu'au regard limité d'une partie de ce tout? Ne peut-on pas entendre dans ce 'Où étais-tu?' un constat de carence lequel ne peut avoir de sens que si l'humanité de l'homme est fraternellement solidaire de la création, c'est-à-dire est responsable de ce qui n'a été ni son moi, ni son oeuvre, et si cette solidarité et cette responsabilité pour tout et pour tous—qui ne se peuvent pas sans douleur—est l'esprit lui-même?" A "constat de carence" is a report or affidavit or declaration of insolvency or deficiency of assets.

30. Levinas 1990a, 49.

31. Levinas 1990a, 48–49.

Chapter 7: "Writing on Fire"

1. The following chapter is a revised and slightly expanded version of an essay that was delivered at an interdisciplinary conference at the University of Minnesota, "The Effects of the Holocaust on the Humanities," 28–30 March 1989. It was also delivered as a lecture (in abbreviated form) at the Bucknell University conference, "Romanticism, 1790–1990," held in 1990, and as a lecture at Whitman College in 1990. An abbreviated version was published as Goodhart 1992. For Ellen Fine's book, see Fine 1982.

2. Fine 1982, xi.

3. See "The Dreaming Back," in Fine et al. 1980, 13–18. The reference to Yeats occurs on p. 15.

4. Habermas is quoted by Saul Friedlander in "Historical Writing and the Memory of the Holocaust." See Lang 1988, 66.

5. The present and following quotes from Friedlander come from Lang 1988, 66–80.

6. On the *Historikerstreit*, see the "Special Issue" of *New German Critique*, no. 44, spring/summer 1988, on the topic. On the "yearning for normalization," see in particular the exchange between Martin Broszat and Saul Friedlander on the "historicization of National Socialism." The issue also contains two essays by Jürgen Habermas in response to Nolte and others. See also Maier 1988.

7. For Foucault, see, for example, 1966. For Fackenheim, see 1982 and 1988. On the notion that the Holocaust is a "caesura," "watershed," or "rupture," see Lacoue-Labarthe 1987, Cohen 1981, and Littell 1975.

8. See Lawrence Langer, "Interpreting Survivor Testimony," in Lang 1988, 26–40. For Victor Frankl, see 1984.

9. "A Plea for the Survivors" is reprinted in Wiesel 1978, 218–47. See also Rosenfeld 1980.

10. Langer's work on survivor testimonies is associated with the Video Archive Project at Yale, which has collected some 3,600 video testimonies to date and has adopted a consciously non-interventionary interview style. For an account of this archive, see Langer 1991.

11. For Hilberg, see 1961.

12. Fine 1988, 41–57.

13. Fine 1988, 41, 43–44.

14. Fine 1988, 44.

15. For the footnote, see Fine 1988, 56n.8.

16. For the interview Fine conducted with Elie Wiesel, see "Dialogue with Elie Wiesel" in Fine et al. 1980, 19–25. The remark Fine quotes in her footnote occurs on p. 25.

17. Fine 1988, 44.

18. Fresco 1984, 417.

19. Lyotard borrows the word "modèle" from his text of Adorno to express the incommensurability of the Holocaust with any system of meaning in which we would try to situate it. It cannot be an example, Lyotard argues. It is the model itself from which examples will be drawn.

20. See Lanzmann 1985.

21. Hartman 1988, 31. André P. Colombat delivered a brilliant talk examining *Nuit et brouillard* and *Shoah* in these terms at a meeting of the Modern Language Association in New Orleans in December 1988. See Colombat 1988.

22. "'The Alarming Nature of Darkness': Witnessing *Shoah*" (unpublished manuscript).

23. See Furet 1989 for a sampling of current historians' opinions on these matters. Furet's volume contains essays by Bauer, Friedlander, Hilberg, Marrus, Vidal-Naquet, and others.

24. On a notion that historical methodology is changing from a history of documents, images, and statistics to one of the voices and faces of those who were there, see Vidal-Naquet 1981. For Levinas's notion of the "trace," see, for example, Levinas 1963. This essay has been translated as "On the Trail of the Other," by Hoy (1966, 34–46), and retranslated by Lingis as "The Trace of the Other" in Taylor (1986, 345–59). For a brilliant reading of the differences between

Levinas's use of this term and its appropriation by Jacques Derrida, see Bernasconi 1988a.

25. I thank Anita Norich (Professor of English, University of Michigan) who introduced me to the complexities of modern Yiddish literature. Her encouragement, generosity, and boundless knowledge of the field have been a constant source of inspiration for me. Her own work in the field promises to change the way we think about Yiddish fiction. See Norich 1991. Very little of Leivick's large corpus has been translated into English. Benjamin and Barbara Harshav's bilingual anthology (1988) is a start for American Yiddish writers. See also Leftwich 1974, which contains a bibliography of materials that have been translated (340–46), and Howe and Greenberg 1976 and 1956. For the history of Yiddish literature, see Liptzin 1985, which contains useful bibliographical information, and Madison 1971. A good deal of information about Yiddish writers is to be found in Zalman Reisen's as yet untranslated biographical dictionary and compendium (1928), and the more recent *Lexikon fun der Nayer Yiddisher Literatur* of which all eight volumes have now appeared. The YIVO, the Institute for Jewish Research, in New York City, and especially its librarian emeritus, Dina Abramovitch, has long been an invaluable source of information. The speech from which I will be quoting remains untranslated although portions of it appeared in Leftwich 1974, 132–37. Landis published an anthology of Yiddish drama in 1980 that includes, in his introduction to Leivick's play, *The Golem,* the portion of the speech reproduced below. See Landis 1980, 217–20.

26. For information about the end of Leivick's life, see Madison 1971, 379.

27. The Yiddish word *yichud* is related etymologically to the Hebrew *ychidcha* ("unique" or "only"), which occurs significantly in the *akeidah* to describe Isaac, and derives from *echad* ("one").

28. The rebelliousness and iconoclasm of a generation of Yiddish writers (against the perceived sternness of their fathers), and the anti-Orthodox and sometimes anti-Jewish images it produced, merit more extended study. For recent studies of the relation of Yiddish literature to the communities from which it came, see the work of Anita Norich, Sidra Ezrachi, David Roskies, Janet Hadda, and others close to the journal *Prooftexts*.

29. Howe cites a comment of Yiddish writer Schlomo Bickel: "In Leivick's commentary on Job, the complaint of the innocent man of suffering remains a central motif, but Leivick brought into play another revealing motif. Job says: 'Blessed be the man of suffering / Who calls God himself to judgment'" (1976, 38). "But what of Job himself," Howe asks, "he who demands judgment? As soon as his sorrows are quieted, his complaints are stilled."

30. Madison 1971, 349–50. Reisen's information is slightly different. Here is what Reisen writes: "When Leivick was six years old, a terrible misfortune happened in the household that left a deep impression on his soul throughout his entire life. On a winter night, when their mother went out of their house for a little bit, a younger sister of his who was four years old, fell in her nightgown on the burning stove and from a spark became entirely engulfed in flames and spent months afterwards lying in bed in terrible pain until she died" (translated by Anita Norich for the author).

Whatever the historical details of the event—whether it occurred on the same day or over a period of months—what is important here is Leivick's continuing association of the death with incidents of antisemitism, relations between rabbis and their Torah students, and relations between fathers and sons.

31. The text Joseph Landis translated contained a number of ellipses. It occurred to me that perhaps in the portions of the text he chose not to translate, something of importance to the current discussion was lodged. Since the original text was not at that time available to me, I phoned him at the journal *Yiddish*. It turned out later (when I did in fact look at the original) that the ellipses masked only a few incidental remarks more relative to the particular occasion of the talk and the larger matters in context of which this anecdote was introduced. But in the course of speaking with Professor Landis, I explained my interest in these anomalies and their importance in my view and received shortly after the conversation the following words in the form of a short note: "Here's my report. The four incidents about which you inquired are all mentioned in the English text of the essay: (1) The gentile who cuffed him crying 'take off your hat!' (2) His peering into the madman's cell, (3) His pressing his tongue against the frozen iron pipe, (4) the fever." Landis's response, of course, only compounds the issue.

32. I thank Alena Clej (English Department, University of Michigan), who heard a version of this paper delivered at the Bucknell Conference on Romanticism and noted, in discussion with me afterwards, that this branding occurred in this scene as a repetition of the death by fire.

33. Harshav and Harshav 1988, 749. The poem first appeared in 1955 in *A Leaf on an Apple Tree*. See Leivick 1983.

34. Levinas 1983, 190–91.

35. For the French original, see chapter 6, note 17.

36. Fackenheim 1988, 402.

37. See Howe and Greenberg 1976, 126–45.

38. See, for example, Wiesel's comments in "Why I Write," in Rosenfeld and Greenberg 1978, 200–206: "Wherever one starts one reaches darkness. God? He remains the God of darkness. Man? Source of darkness. The killers' sneers, their victims' tears, the onlooker's indifference, their complicity and complacency, the divine role in all that: I do not understand. A million children massacred: I shall never understand . . .

People tend to think that a murderer weakens when facing a child. The child reawakens the killer's lost humanity. The killer can no longer kill the child before him, the child inside him.

Not this time. With us it happened differently. Our Jewish children had no effect upon the killers. Nor upon the world. Nor upon God" (202–3).

Later in the essay, Wiesel uses the same biblical image that Leivick uses: ". . . I have not forgotten the dead. . . . Even in my Biblical and Midrashic tales, I pursue their presence, mute and motionless. The presence of the dead then beckons in such tangible ways that it affects even the most removed characters. Thus they appear on Mount Moriah, where Abraham is about to sacrifice his son, a holocaust offering to their common God. . . . They appear in Hasidic and Talmudic legends in which victims forever need defending against forces that would crush them. . . . They die with Isaac, lament with Jeremiah, they sing with the *Besht,* and, like him, they wait for miracles—but alas, they will not come to pass" (204).

39. Des Pres, in Fine 1982, xi.

40. In the case of Primo Levi, the common assumption has been that his death was a suicide. Cynthia Ozick argues, for example, in 1991, that the event can be meaningfully linked to a change in attitude reflected for example in *The Drowned and the Saved.* See Levi 1988. At a conference on his work held at Cornell University in May 1989, Ruth Feldman challenged this assertion. See Tarrow 1990. What strikes me as interesting in both discussions is the odd appeal of some component of auto-destruction, whatever the factual status of these deaths.

Reading after Auschwitz

1. Wellek and Warren 1956, 15.
2. Foucault 1988, 308.
3. Cf. Foucault's remarks on *Don Quixote* (1966, 46–50), on Velázquez's "Las Meninas" (1966, 3–18), on Magritte's "Ceci n'est pas une pipe" (1983), and on the *Odyssey* (1977). Bouchard has collected some of Foucault's literary analyses in Foucault 1977.
4. For a recent engagement of literature and the question of the sacred, see Bandera 1994.
5. See above, chapter 1, note 1.
6. Vellacott 1971 and Knox 1957.
7. See above, chapter 2, note 15.
8. See above, chapter 2, note 20.
9. Zeisler 1954 and Kermode 1983, 160–61.
10. Kermode 1983, 161.
11. See above, chapter 1, note 37.
12. For a useful collection of these older texts, see Adams 1992.
13. See Lacoue-Labarthe and Nancy on the German Romantics (1988).
14. Hegel 1962.
15. For an analysis of this cultural context, see Silk and Stern's book on Nietzsche (1990).
16. See above, chapter 2, notes 6–9. See also Arthur M. Eastman's chapter on A. C. Bradley (1968).
17. Jones 1954.
18. See Goodson 1988 and von Helmholtz-Phelan 1907 on the Coleridge/Schlegel connection.
19. See discussion of these matters above, in chapter 2.
20. See above, chapter 1, note 3.
21. Cf. Knox 1982.
22. Cf. Kantorowicz 1981.
23. See Fontenrose 1978, Knox 1964, and Loraux 1986.
24. Very little work has been done on the technological side of the institution of literary critical activity.

25. See Bernal 1987.
26. See Canetti 1963.
27. Cf. René Girard's essay on *Julius Caesar* (1991).
28. Cf. *Othello*, V.ii.65: "Thou dost stone my heart, / And makest me call what I intend to do / A murder, which I thought a sacrifice."
29. *Sonderbehandlung*.
30. It is interesting to note Derrida's assertion that he began his studies with the intention of examining literature. See Derrida 1983. For Lacoue-Labarthe, see 1987, 1989, 1990; Lacoue-Labarthe and Nancy 1988.
31. I have attempted to outline some of these ways in Goodhart 1993.
32. Cf. Levinas on talmudic study in 1990a, 1994a, b.
33. On these issues of hermeneutics see Scholem's essay on revelation (1978) and Fishbane 1989.
34. Cf. Finkelstein 1992.
35. Levinas 1982, 105 (my translation).
36. Lyotard 1989, 373.
37. See Friedlander's discussion in Hartman 1994, 252–63.
38. Thus Lucy Davidowicz understands Hitler's program as fully in place in 1922 when *Mein Kampf* is published. See Dawidowicz 1976. For an example of how bitter the opposition can get, see Dawidowicz 1989. For a summary of the intentionalist/functionalist controversy, see Browning 1992, 86–121.
39. Thus, for example, in *Fateful Months* (1991) Christopher Browning attempts to pinpoint the decision to kill the Jews to the spring of 1941. For other references to the functionalist approach, see the work of Hilberg 1961, Bauer 1989, Browning 1992, Marrus 1987, and Kershaw 1993, but also the book on Lanzmann's *Shoah* (Cuau et al. 1990) and Furet 1989.
40. See Felman and Laub 1992, Caruth 1990, 1991, 1991a.
41. See Fresco 1984.
42. Goodhart 1992a.
43. See Freud on trauma (1967) and Caruth on these materials in *American Imago* (1990, 1991).
44. Fackenheim 1988.
45. Cf. Lyotard 1988 and Felman and Laub 1992.
46. Fitzgerald 1963, 157.
47. See Cohen 1981, Rubenstein 1992, and Lacoue-Labarthe 1990 on the notion of a break or "caesura."
48. See Fackenheim 1988 for "planet Auschwitz."
49. Maier 1988.
50. A powerful debate on these issues almost got started in the public argument that took place in the *New York Review of Books* between Jacques Derrida, Richard Wolin, and Thomas Sheehan around the first publication of Richard Wolin's *Heidegger Controversy*. See Derrida 1993, 1993a, Sheehan 1993, 1993a, and Wolin 1991, 1993.
51. Lyotard 1989, 373.
52. Given the familiarity of this bibliography, I will not make citations except where necessary.

53. For two very different accounts of this phrase, see Richard Rubenstein's *After Auschwitz* (1992) and Lyotard's "Discussions, or Phrasing 'after Auschwitz'" (1989).

54. Fasching 1992, 1993; Lifton 1967, 1986, 1990.

55. Foucault 1966.

56. The notion that in many ways the Nazis pursued the Holocaust even to the detriment of the war effort in other arenas has become increasingly accepted.

57. Adorno 1987, 371.

58. For Himmler's Poznán speech on 4 October 1943, see Dawidowicz 1976, 130–40. For a discussion of this speech, see Friedlander's essay in Hayes 1991, 23–35.

59. See Fasching 1992, 1993, Siebers 1993, Hales 1991, and Ruthven 1993.

60. See, for example, the *Diacritics* issue on "Nuclear Criticism."

61. The phrase "saving the text" is of course the title of a book by Geoffrey Hartman. See Hartman 1981.

62. See Goodhart 1989; Hamacher, Hertz, and Keenan 1989, 1990.

63. Hartman 1991. Hartman's essay first appeared in the Tel Aviv journal *History and Memory,* edited by Saul Friedlander.

64. For Luther's texts on Jews, see Edwards 1983 and Luther 1543. Geoffrey Hartman reminds us just how widespread this antisemitic attitude was in Europe, citing, for example, Richard Wagner's essay on "The Jews and Their Music" as one of the primary texts. See Hartman 1991 and Wagner 1869.

65. Hartman 1988.

66. Felman and Laub 1992.

67. See Goodhart 1989. The extremities to which individuals may go excuses neither those individuals nor those extremities. But it does suggest that at any given moment, at one extreme, we need not press their worst qualities. We can continue to read Heidegger, de Man, Eliade, not in spite of their past associations, but in an interesting way because of them, with renewed awareness on that basis, to gain an insight on both the resonance of that language within their own life, and of the way in which the Other speaks through them, and thus a renewed appreciation for both the representational and tracial or symptomatic aspects.

68. Donato and Macksey 1972.

69. Miller 1987, 41–59.

70. De Man 1979, 206.

71. *The Post-Romantic Predicament* was actually listed at one point on the jacket of the Norton critical edition of Flaubert's *Madame Bovary* as a book of which de Man was the "author." See Flaubert 1965.

Works Cited

Aalders, G. Charles. 1948. *The Problem of the Book of Jonah*. London: Tyndale.
Abrams, Meyer H., ed. 1958. *Literature and Belief*. New York: Columbia University Press.
Abrams, Meyer H. 1958a. *The Mirror and the Lamp: Romantic Theory and the Critical Tradition*. New York: W. W. Norton.
Abrams, Meyer H. 1971. *Natural Supernaturalism*. New York: W. W. Norton.
Abrams, Meyer H. 1981. "Kant and the Theology of Art." *Notre Dame English Journal* 13: 75–106.
Abrams, Meyer H. 1985. "Art-as-Such: The Sociology of Modern Aesthetics." *Bulletin of the American Academy of Arts and Sciences* 38/6: 8–33.
Abrams, Meyer H. 1985a. "From Addison to Kant: Modern Aesthetics and the Exemplary Art." In Ralph Cohen, ed., *Studies in Eighteenth-Century British Art and Aesthetics*, 16–48. Berkeley: University of California Press.
Abrams, Meyer H. 1989. *Doing Things with Texts: Essays in Criticism and Critical Theory*. New York: W. W. Norton.
Abrams, Meyer H. 1993. *Glossary of Literary Terms*. 6th ed. New York: Harcourt Brace Jovanovich.
Adams, Hazard, ed. 1992. *Critical Theory since Plato*. Rev. ed. Fort Worth, Tex.: Harcourt Brace Jovanovich.
Adams, Hazard, and Leroy Searles, eds. 1986. *Critical Theory since 1965*. Tallahassee: Florida State University Press.
Adorno, Theodor W. 1967. *Prisms*. London: N. Spearman.
Adorno, Theodor W. 1987. *Negative Dialectics*. Translated by E. B. Ashton. New York: Continuum Books.
Ahl, Fred. 1991. *Sophocles' Oedipus: Evidence and Self-Conviction*. Ithaca: Cornell University Press.
Almbladh, Karin. 1986. *Studies in the Book of Jonah*. Stockholm: distributed by Almqvist and Wiksell International.
Alter, Robert. 1981. *The Art of Biblical Narrative*. New York: Basic Books.
Alter, Robert. 1985. *The Art of Biblical Poetry*. New York: Basic Books.
Arac, Jonathan, Wlad Godzich, and Wallace Martin, eds. 1983. *The Yale Critics: Deconstruction in America*. Minneapolis: University of Minnesota Press.
Backus, William D. 1986. *The Paranoid Prophet*. Minneapolis: Bethany House.
Baker, Herschel, ed. 1974. *The Riverside Shakespeare: The Second Part of Henry the Fourth*. Boston: Houghton Mifflin.
Bandera, Cesáreo. 1994. *The Sacred Game: The Role of the Sacred in the Genesis of Modern Literary Fiction*. University Park: Pennsylvania State University Press.

Barthes, Roland. 1975. *The Pleasure of the Text*. Translated by Richard Miller. New York: Hill and Wang.
Battenhouse, Roy. 1974. "Tudor Doctrine and the Tragedy of *Richard II*." *Rice University Studies* 60/2: 31–53.
Bauer, Yehuda. 1978. *The Holocaust in Historical Perspective*. Seattle: University of Washington Press.
Bauer, Yehuda. 1982. *The History of the Holocaust*. New York: F. Watts.
Bauer, Yehuda, ed. 1989. *Remembering for the Future: Working Papers and Addenda*. New York: Pergamon.
Beeck, Franz Jozef van, S.J. 1989. *Loving the Torah More than God? Towards a Catholic Appreciation of Judaism*. Chicago: Loyola University Press.
Benjamin, Andrew, ed. 1989. *The Lyotard Reader*. Cambridge, Mass.: Basil Blackwell.
Benjamin, Walter. 1969. *Illuminations*. New York: Schocken.
Benjamin, Walter. 1978. *Reflections: Essays, Aphorisms, Autobiographical Writings*. New York: Harcourt Brace Jovanovich.
Benoist, Jean-Marie. 1975. *La révolution structurale*. Paris: Grasset. See Benoist 1978.
Benoist, Jean-Marie. 1978. *The Structural Revolution*. New York: St. Martin's.
Berger, Harry, Jr. 1989. *Imaginary Audition: Shakespeare on Stage and Page*. Berkeley: University of California Press.
Berkowitz, Luci, and Theodore Brunner, eds. 1970. *Oedipus Tyrannus*. New York: W. W. Norton.
Berman, Ronald. 1973. *A Reader's Guide to Shakespeare's Plays: A Discursive Bibliography*. Glenview, Ill.: Scott, Foresman.
Bernal, Martin. 1987. *Black Athena: The Afroasiatic Roots of Classical Civilization*. New Brunswick, N.J.: Rutgers University Press.
Bernasconi, Robert. 1988. "'Failure of Communication' as a Surplus: Dialogue and Lack of Dialogue between Buber and Levinas." In Bernasconi and Wood 1988a.
Bernasconi, Robert. 1988a. "The Trace of Levinas in Derrida." In Bernasconi and Wood 1988, 13–29.
Bernasconi, Robert, and Simon Critchley, eds. 1991. *Re-Reading Levinas*. Bloomington: Indiana University Press.
Bernasconi, Robert, and David Wood, eds. 1988. *Derrida and "Différance."* Evanston: Northwestern University Press.
Bernasconi, Robert, and David Wood, eds. 1988a. *The Provocation of Levinas: Rethinking the Other*. New York: Routledge.
Bevington, David, ed. 1992. *The Complete Works of Shakespeare*. 4th ed. New York: Harper Collins.
Bickerman, Elias J. 1984. *Four Strange Books of the Bible*. New York: Schocken.
Birnbaum, Philip. 1949. *Daily Prayer Book*. New York: Hebrew Publishing.
Birnbaum, Philip. 1979. *Encyclopedia of Jewish Concepts*. New York: Hebrew Publishing.
Bishop, Jonathan. 1982. *The Covenant: A Reading*. Springfield, Ill.: Templegate.

Black, Matthew W., ed. 1955. *A New Variorum Edition of Shakespeare: The Life and Death of King Richard the Second.* Philadelphia: J. B. Lippincott.
Black, Matthew W. 1977. *The Life and Death of King Richard II: A Bibliography to Supplement the New Variorum Edition of 1955.* New York: Modern Language Association of America.
Blanchot, Maurice. 1959. *Le livre à venir.* Paris: Gallimard.
Blanchot, Maurice. 1969. *L'entretien infini.* Paris: Gallimard. See Blanchot 1992.
Blanchot, Maurice. 1992. *The Infinite Conversation.* Translated by Susan Hanson. Minneapolis: University of Minnesota Press.
Bloch, R. 1978. "Midrash." In Green 1978, 32–33.
Bloom, Harold, ed. 1988. *Sophocles' Oedipus Rex.* New York: Chelsea House.
Bloom, Harold, ed. 1988a. *William Shakespeare's Richard II.* New York: Chelsea House.
Bloom, Harold, ed. 1988b. *The Book of Job.* New York: Chelsea House.
Bloomfield, Morton. 1972. *In Search of Literary Theory.* Ithaca: Cornell University Press.
Bock, Emil. 1989. *Kings and Prophets.* Edinburgh: Floris Books.
Boethius. 1962. *The Consolation of Philosophy.* Translated by Richard Green. Indianapolis: Bobbs-Merrill.
Booth, Stephen. 1977. *Shakespeare's Sonnets.* New Haven: Yale University Press.
Borch-Jacobsen, Mikkel. 1982. *Le sujet freudien.* Paris: Flammarion. See Borch-Jacobsen 1988.
Borch-Jacobsen, Mikkel. 1988. *The Freudian Subject.* Translated by Catherine Porter. Stanford: Stanford University Press.
Borges, Jorge Luis. 1972. "Oedipus and the Riddle." In *Selected Poems, 1923–1967,* 190–91. New York: Dell.
Borges, Jorge Luis. 1974. *In Praise of Darkness.* Translated by Norman Thomas di Giovanni. New York: E. P. Dutton.
Borges, Jorge Luis. 1978. *The Aleph and Other Stories, 1933–1969.* Translated by Norman Thomas di Gionanni. New York: E. P. Dutton.
Bowra, C. Maurice. 1944. *Sophoclean Tragedy.* Oxford: Oxford University Press.
Bradley, A. C. 1965. *Shakespearean Tragedy.* New York: Fawcett.
Bremer, J. M. 1969. *Hamartia: Tragic Error in the Poetics of Aristotle and in Greek Tragedy.* Amsterdam: Adolf M. Hakkert.
Brody, Jules. 1985. *"Fate" in "Oedipus Tyrannus": A Textual Approach.* Buffalo: Department of Classics, State University of New York at Buffalo.
Bromley, John. 1971. "The Allegory of the Garden: *King John* and *Richard II.*" In *The Shakespearean Kings: A Study in Political Drama,* 41–60. Boulder: Colorado Associated University Presses.
Brooks, Cleanth, ed. 1955. *Tragic Themes in Western Literature.* New Haven: Yale University Press.
Brown, Francis, S. R. Driver, and Charles A. Briggs, eds. 1951. *A Hebrew and English Lexicon of the Old Testament.* Oxford: Clarendon.

Browning, Christopher R. 1991. *Fateful Months: Essays on the Emergence of the Final Solution.* New York: Holmes and Meier.
Browning, Christopher R. 1992. *The Path to Genocide, Essays on Launching the Final Solution.* New York: Cambridge University Press.
Buber, Martin. 1958. *I and Thou.* 2nd ed. New York: Charles Scribner's Sons.
Buber, Martin. 1967. *On Judaism.* New York: Schocken.
Buber, Martin. 1982. *On the Bible: Eighteen Studies.* Introduction by Harold Bloom. New York: Schocken.
Buber, Martin, and Franz Rosenzweig. 1994. *Scripture and Translation.* Translated by Lawrence Rosenwald and Everett Fox. Bloomington: Indiana University Press.
Budick, Sanford, and Geoffrey Hartman. 1986. *Midrash and Literature.* New Haven: Yale University Press.
Burckhardt, Jakob. 1975. *The Civilization of the Renaissance in Italy.* 2 vols. New York: Harper and Row.
Burckhardt, Sigurd. 1968. *Shakespearean Meanings.* Princeton: Princeton University Press.
Burkert, Walter. 1991. *Oedipus, Oracles, and Meaning: From Sophocles to Umberto Eco.* Toronto: University of Toronto Press.
Bush, Douglas. 1930. *The Renaissance and English Humanism.* Toronto: University of Toronto Press.
Bushnell, Rebecca. 1988. *Prophesying Tragedy: Sign and Voice in Sophocles' Theban Plays.* Ithaca: Cornell University Press.
Butcher, S. H. 1951. *Aristotle's Theory of Poetry and Fine Art.* New York: Dover.
Cain, William E. 1984. *The Crisis in Criticism: Theory, Literature, and Reform in English Studies.* Baltimore: Johns Hopkins University Press.
Cameron, Alister. 1968. *The Identity of Oedipus the King: Five Essays on the "Oedipus Tyrannus."* New York: New York University Press.
Campbell, S. 1989. "The Land and Language of Desire—Where Deep Ecology and Post-Structuralism Meet." *Western American Literature* 24/3: 199–211.
Canetti, Elias. 1963. *Crowds and Power.* Translated by Carol Stewart. New York: Viking.
Canguilhem, Georges. 1978. *On the Normal and the Pathological.* Translated by Carolyn Fawcett. Introduction by Michel Foucault. Boston: D. Reidel.
Caruth, Cathy. 1990. "Introduction." *American Imago* 48/1: 1. Special issue: "Psychoanalysis, Culture, and Trauma: I."
Caruth, Cathy. 1991. "Introduction." *American Imago* 48/4: 417–23. Special issue: "Psychoanalysis, Culture, and Trauma: II."
Caruth, Cathy. 1991a. "Unclaimed Experience: Trauma and the Possibility of History." *Yale French Studies* 79: 181–92.
Cassuto, Umberto. 1967. *A Commentary on the Book of Exodus.* Translated by Israel Abrahams. Jerusalem: Magnes Press, Hebrew University.
Chalier, Catherine. 1993. *Levinas: L'utopie de l'humain.* Paris: Albin Michel.
Chambers, E. K. 1925. "Richard the Second." In *Shakespeare: A Survey,* 88–96. London: Sidgwick and Jackson.

Chambers, E. K. 1930. *William Shakespeare: A Study of Facts and Problems.* 2 vols. Oxford: Oxford University Press.
Chambers, Ross, ed. 1982. *Discours et pouvoir.* Ann Arbor: Department of Romance Languages, University of Michigan.
Charbonnier, G. 1969. *Conversations with Claude Lévi-Strauss.* Translated by John Weightman and Doreen Weightman. London: Jonathan Cape.
Chase, Cynthia. 1979. "Oedipal Textuality: Reading Freud's Reading of Oedipus." *Diacritics* 9/1: 54–78. Reprinted in Chase 1986, 175–95.
Chase, Cynthia. 1986. *Decomposing Figures: Rhetorical Readings in the Romantic Tradition.* Baltimore: Johns Hopkins University Press.
Chouraqui, André. 1964. *A History of Judaism.* New York: Walker.
Clare, Janet. 1990. "The Censorship of the Deposition Scene in *Richard II.*" *Review of English Studies* 41: 81–94.
Cocteau, Jean. 1967. *The Infernal Machine.* Translated by Albert Bermel. New York: New Directions.
Cohen, Arthur, ed. 1969. *The Soncino Books of the Bible: The Twelve Prophets.* London: Soncino.
Cohen, Arthur. 1979. *The Soncino Chumash.* London: Soncino.
Cohen, Arthur. 1981. *The Tremendum.* New York: Crossroad.
Cohen, Arthur, and Paul Mendes-Flohr, eds. 1988. *Contemporary Jewish Religious Thought.* New York: Free Press.
Cohen, Richard A. 1994. *Elevations: The Height of the Good in Rosenzweig and Levinas.* Chicago: University of Chicago Press.
Colombat, André P. 1988. "Auschwitz in Film: *Nuit et brouillard* (1956) and *Shoah* (1985)." Paper delivered at the annual meeting of the Modern Language Association in New Orleans, 1988.
Cook, Albert, ed. 1963. *Oedipus Rex: A Mirror for Greek Drama.* Belmont, Calif.: Wadsworth.
Cotter, David W. 1992. *A Study of Job 4–5 in the Light of Contemporary Literary Theory.* Atlanta: Scholars Press.
Craig, Kenneth M. 1993. *A Poetics of Jonah: Art in the Service of Ideology.* Columbia: University of South Carolina Press.
Craigie, Peter. C. 1984. *Twelve Prophets.* Philadelphia: Westminster.
Cuau, Bernard, et al., eds. 1990. *Au sujet de "Shoah": le film de Claude Lanzmann.* Paris: Belin.
Culler, Jonathan. 1975. *Structuralist Poetics.* Ithaca: Cornell University Press.
Culler, Jonathan. 1978. "On Trope and Persuasion." *New Literary History* 9/3: 607–18.
Culler, Jonathan. 1980. "*Fabula* and *Sjuzhet* in the Analysis of Narrative: Some American Discussions." *Poetics Today* 1/3: 27–37. Revised and reprinted in Culler 1981a, 169–87.
Culler, Jonathan. 1981. "Issues in Contemporary American Critical Debate." In Konigsberg 1981, 1–18.
Culler, Jonathan. 1981a. *The Pursuit of Signs.* Ithaca: Cornell University Press.
Culler, Jonathan. 1982. "Semiotic Consequences." *Studies in Twentieth Century Literature* 6/1–2: 5–15.

Culler, Jonathan. 1984. "A Critic against the Christians." *Times Literary Supplement* (November 23): 1327–28.
Culler, Jonathan. 1986. "Comparative Literature and the Pieties." *Profession 1986* 30–32.
Dawidowicz, Lucy S. 1976. *The War against the Jews, 1933–1945*. New York: Bantam.
Dawidowicz, Lucy S. 1989. "Perversions of the Holocaust." *Commentary* (October): 56–60.
DeGuy, Michel, and Jean-Pierre Dupuy, eds. 1982. *René Girard et le problème du mal*. Paris: Grasset.
Deleuze, Gilles, and Félix Guattari. 1972. *Anti-Oedipe*. Paris: Minuit. See Deleuze and Guattari 1977.
Deleuze, Gilles, and Félix Guattari. 1977. *Anti-Oedipus: Capitalism and Schizophrenia*. Translated by Robert Hurley, Mark Seem, and Helen R. Lane. New York: Viking.
De Man, Paul. 1971. *Blindness and Insight: Essays in the Rhetoric of Contemporary Criticism*. New York: Oxford University Press.
De Man, Paul. 1979. *Allegories of Reading: Figural Language in Rousseau, Nietzsche, Rilke, and Proust*. New Haven: Yale University Press.
De Man, Paul. 1982. "The Resistance to Theory." *Yale French Studies* 63: 3–20.
De Man, Paul. 1983. *Blindness and Insight: Essays in the Rhetoric of Contemporary Criticism*. 2nd ed., revised. Minneapolis: University of Minnesota Press.
De Man, Paul. 1983a. "The Dead-End of Formalist Criticism." In De Man 1983, 229–45.
De Man, Paul. 1984. *The Rhetoric of Romanticism*. New York: Columbia University Press.
De Man, Paul. 1986. *The Resistance to Theory*. Minneapolis: University of Minnesota Press.
Derrida, Jacques. 1967. *L'écriture et la différence*. Paris: Seuil. See Derrida 1978.
Derrida, Jacques. 1972. *La dissémination*. Paris: Seuil. See Derrida 1981.
Derrida, Jacques. 1972a. "La double séance." In Derrida 1972, 207–20.
Derrida, Jacques. 1978. *Writing and Difference*. Translated by Alan Bass. Chicago: University of Chicago Press.
Derrida, Jacques. 1980. *La carte postale*. Paris: Flammarion. See Derrida 1987.
Derrida, Jacques. 1981. *Dissemination*. Translated by Barbara Johnson. Chicago: University of Chicago Press.
Derrida, Jacques. 1983. "The Time of a Thesis: Punctuations." In Montefiore 1983, 34–50.
Derrida, Jacques. 1986. *Memoires: for Paul de Man*. Translated by Cecile Lindsay, Jonathan Culler, and Eduardo Cadava. New York: Columbia University Press.
Derrida, Jacques. 1987. *The Post Card: From Socrates to Freud and Beyond*. Chicago: University of Chicago Press.
Derrida, Jacques. 1993. Letter to the editor. *New York Review of Books* (February 11): 44.

Derrida, Jacques. 1993a. Letter to the editor. *New York Review of Books* (March 25): 65.
Descombes, Vincent. 1980. *Modern French Philosophy*. New York: Cambridge University Press.
Des Pres, Terrence. 1977. *The Survivor: An Anatomy of Life in the Death Camps*. New York: Washington Square Press.
Des Pres, Terrence. 1980. "The Dreaming Back." In Fine et al. 1980, 13–18.
Dodds, E. R. 1963. *The Greeks and the Irrational*. Berkeley: University of California Press.
Donato, Eugenio, and Richard Macksey, eds. 1972. *The Structuralist Controversy: The Languages of Criticism and the Sciences of Man*. Baltimore: Johns Hopkins University Press.
Dreyfus, Hubert. 1983. *Michel Foucault: Beyond Structuralism and Hermeneutics*. 2nd ed. Chicago: University of Chicago Press.
Dumouchel, Paul, ed. 1985. *Violence et vérité*. Colloque de Cerisy autour de René Girard. Paris: Grasset. See Dumouchel 1987–88.
Dumouchel, Paul, ed. 1987–88. *Violence and Truth*. London: Athlone Press (1987) and Stanford: Stanford University Press (1988).
Dumouchel, Paul, and Jean-Pierre Dupuy. 1979. *L'enfer des choses*. Paris: Seuil.
Dumouchel, Paul, and Jean-Pierre Dupuy, eds. 1983. *L'auto-organisation*. Colloque de Cerisy. Paris: Seuil.
Dupuy, Jean-Pierre. 1982. *Ordres et désordres*. Paris: Seuil.
Duval, Yves-Marie. 1973. *Le livre de Jonas dans la littérature chrétienne grecque et latine*. Paris: Etudes augustiniennes.
Eastman, Arthur M. 1968. *A Short History of Shakespearean Criticism*. New York: W. W. Norton.
Edwards, Mark U. 1983. *Luther's Last Battles: Politics and Polemics, 1531–46*. Ithaca: Cornell University Press.
Ehrenberg, Victor. 1954. *Sophocles and Pericles*. Oxford: Basil Blackwell.
Eichrodt, Walther. 1961. *Theology of the Old Testament*. 2 vols. Translated by J. A. Baker. Philadelphia: Westminster.
Else, Gerald. 1970. *Aristotle, "Poetics."* Ann Arbor: University of Michigan Press.
Epstein, I., ed. 1939. *Midrash Rabbah*. London: Soncino.
Fackenheim, Emil. 1982. *To Mend the World: Foundations of Future Jewish Thought*. New York: Schocken.
Fackenheim, Emil. 1988. "Holocaust." In Cohen and Mendes-Flohr 1988.
Farenga, Vincent. 1981. "The Paradigmatic Tyrant: Greek Tyranny and the Ideology of the Proper." *Helios* 8/1: 1–31.
Fasching, Darrell J. 1992. *Narrative Theology After Auschwitz: From Alienation to Ethics*. Minneapolis: Fortress.
Fasching, Darrell J. 1993. *The Ethical Challenge of Auschwitz and Hiroshima: Apocalypse or Utopia*. Albany: State University of New York Press.
Felman, Shoshana. 1982. "Le scandale de la vérité." In Chambers 1982, 1–28.

Felman, Shoshana. 1983. "From Sophocles to Japrisot (via Freud)." *Littérature* 49, 23–42.

Felman, Shoshana, ed. 1985. "The Lesson of Paul de Man." *Yale French Studies* (Special memorial issue) 69.

Felman, Shoshana, and Dori Laub. 1992. *Testimony: Crises of Witnessing in Literature, Psychoanalysis, and History.* New York: Routledge.

Ferguson, Wallace K. 1956. *The Renaissance.* New York: Henry Holt.

Ferris, D. 1991. "Where Three Paths Meet: History, Wordsworth, and the Simplon-Pass." *Studies in Romanticism* 30/3: 391–438.

Feuer, Avrohom Chaim, and N. Scherman. 1981. *Aseres Hadibros/The Ten Commandments.* Brooklyn, N.Y.: Mesorah.

Fiedler, Leslie. 1972. *The Stranger in Shakespeare.* New York: Stein and Day.

Fine, Ellen S. 1982. *Legacy of Night: The Literary Universe of Elie Wiesel.* Albany: State University of New York Press.

Fine, Ellen S. 1988. "The Absent Memory: The Act of Writing in Post-Holocaust French Literature." In Lang 1988, 41–57.

Fine, Ellen S., Jane Gerber, Lea Hamaoui, and Rosette C. Lamont, eds. 1980. "The Holocaust." *Centerpoint: A Journal of International Studies,* 4/1 (fall).

Fineman, Joel. 1986. *Shakespeare's Perjur'd Eye: The Invention of Poetic Subjectivity in the Sonnets.* Berkeley: University of California Press.

Fineman, Joel. 1991. *The Subjectivity Effect in Western Literature Tradition: Essays toward the Release of Shakespeare's Will.* Cambridge, Mass.: MIT Press.

Finkelstein, Norman. 1992. *The Ritual of New Creation: Jewish Tradition and Contemporary Literature.* Albany: State University of New York Press.

Fish, Stanley. 1980. *Is There a Text in This Class? The Authority of Interpretative Communities.* Cambridge: Harvard University Press.

Fishbane, Michael. 1982. "Jewish Biblical Exegesis: Presuppositions and Principles." In Greenspahn 1982, 91–110.

Fishbane, Michael. 1985. *Biblical Interpretation in Ancient Israel.* Oxford: Clarendon.

Fishbane, Michael. 1989. *The Garments of Torah: Essays in Biblical Hermeneutics.* Bloomington: Indiana University Press.

Fitzgerald, Robert, ed. 1963. *Homer: The "Odyssey."* Translated by Robert Fitzgerald. Garden City, N.Y.: Anchor.

Flaubert, Gustave. 1965. *Madame Bovary.* Translated by Paul de Man. New York: W. W. Norton.

Fletcher, Angus. 1991. *Colors of the Mind: Conjectures on Thinking in Literature.* Cambridge: Harvard University Press.

Foakes, R. A., ed. 1971. *Coleridge on Shakespeare.* Charlottesville: University Press of Virginia.

Fontenrose, Joseph. 1978. *The Delphic Oracle.* Berkeley: University of California Press.

Foucault, Michel. 1961. *Histoire de la folie à l'âge classique.* Paris: Plon. See Foucault 1965.

Foucault, Michel. 1965. *Madness and Civilization: A History of Insanity in the Age of Reason.* Translated by Richard Howard. New York: Pantheon.

Foucault, Michel. 1966. *Les mots et les choses*. Paris: Gallimard. See Foucault 1970.
Foucault, Michel. 1966a. "La pensée du dehors." *Critique* 229: 523–46. See Foucault 1987.
Foucault, Michel. 1970. *The Order of Things*. Translated by Alan Sheridan. New York: Random House.
Foucault, Michel. 1977. *Language, Counter-memory, Practice: Selected Essays and Interviews*. Edited by Donald Bouchard. Ithaca: Cornell University Press.
Foucault, Michel. 1983. *This Is Not a Pipe*. Berkeley: University of California Press.
Foucault, Michel. 1987. "Maurice Blanchot: The Thought from Outside." Translated by Brian Massumi. In Foucault and Blanchot 1987.
Foucault, Michel. 1988. *Politics, Philosophy, Culture: Interviews and Other Writings, 1977–1984*. New York: Routledge.
Foucault, Michel, and Maurice Blanchot. 1987. *Foucault/Blanchot*. New York: Zone Books and Cambridge, Mass.: MIT Press.
Fox, Everett, ed. 1990. *Genesis and Exodus*. New York: Schocken.
Frankl, Victor. 1984. *Man's Search for Meaning*. New York: Pocket Books.
Freccero, John. 1975. "The Fig Tree and the Laurel: Petrarch's Poetics." *Diacritics* 5: 34–40.
Freccero, John. 1986. *Dante: Poetics of Conversion*. Cambridge: Harvard University Press.
Freedman, H., ed. 1961. *Midrash Rabbah: Genesis I*. London: Soncino.
Freedman, H., and Maurice Simon, eds. 1983. *Midrash Rabbah*. London: Soncino.
Fresco, Nadine. 1984. "Remembering the Unknown." *International Review of Psycho-Analysis* 11/4: 417–27.
Freud, Sigmund. 1952. *A General Introduction to Psychoanalysis*. Translated by Joan Rivière. New York: Washington Square Press.
Freud, Sigmund. 1965. *The Interpretation of Dreams*. Translated by James Strachey. New York: Avon.
Freud, Sigmund. 1967. *Beyond the Pleasure Principle*. Translated by James Strachey. New York: Bantam.
Friedlander, Saul. 1994. "Trauma, Memory, and Transference." In Hartman 1994, 252–63.
Fry, Paul H. 1983. *The Reach of Criticism: Method and Perception in Literary Criticism*. New Haven: Yale University Press.
Frye, Northrop. 1966. *Anatomy of Criticism*. Princeton: Princeton University Press.
Furet, François, ed. 1989. *Unanswered Questions. Nazi Germany and the Genocide of the Jews*. New York: Schocken.
Fyfe, W. Hamilton. 1965. *Aristotle: The "Poetics."* Cambridge: Harvard University Press.
Gadamer, Hans Georg. 1975. *Truth and Method*. New York: Seabury.
Gans, Eric. 1973. "Pour une esthétique triangulaire." *Esprit* 429: 564–81.
Gasché, Rodolphe. 1979. "Deconstruction as Criticism." *Glyph* 6: 177–215.

Gasché, Rodolphe. 1981. "Setzung and Ubersetzung: Notes on Paul de Man." *Diacritics* 11/4: 36–57.
Gearhart, Suzanne. 1983. "Philosophy *before* Literature: Deconstruction, Historicity, and the Work of Paul de Man." *Diacritics* 12/4: 63–81.
Geertz, Clifford. 1973. *The Interpretation of Cultures*. New York: Basic Books.
Gellrich, Michelle. 1988. *Tragedy and Theory: The Problem of Conflict since Aristotle*. Princeton: Princeton University Press.
Gentili, Bruno, and Roberto Pretagistini, eds. 1986. *Edipo: Il teatro greco e la cultura europea*. Roma: Edizioni dell'Ateneo.
Gibbs, Robert. 1992. *Correlations in Rosenzweig and Levinas*. Princeton: Princeton University Press.
Gide, André. 1950. *Two Legends: Oedipus and Theseus*. Translated by John Russell. New York: Random House.
Ginzberg, Louis. 1906–38. *The Legends of the Jews*. Philadelphia: Jewish Publication Society.
Girard, René. 1961. *Mensonge romantique et vérité romanesque*. Paris: Grasset. See Girard 1965.
Girard, René. 1965. *Deceit, Desire, and the Novel*. Translated by Yvonne Freccero. Baltimore: Johns Hopkins Press.
Girard, René. 1968. "Symétrie et dissymétrie dans le mythe d'Oedipe." *Critique* 249: 99–135.
Girard, René. 1972. *La violence et la sacré*. Paris: Grasset. See Girard 1977.
Girard, René. 1973. "Discussion avec René Girard." *Esprit* 429: 528–63.
Girard, René. 1975. "Les malédictions contre les pharisiens et la révélation évangélique." *Bulletin du Centre Protestant d'Etudes* 3: 5–29.
Girard, René. 1977. *Violence and the Sacred*. Translated by Patrick Gregory. Baltimore: Johns Hopkins University Press.
Girard, René. 1977a. "Dionysus and the Violent Genesis of the Sacred." Translated by Sandor Goodhart. *boundary 2* 5/2: 487–505.
Girard, René. 1978. *Des choses cachées depuis la fondation du monde*. Paris: Grasset. See Girard 1987a.
Girard, René. 1978a. "An Interview with René Girard." *Diacritics* 7/1: 31–54. Reprinted in Girard 1978b, 199–229.
Girard, René. 1978b. *"To Double Business Bound."* Baltimore: Johns Hopkins University Press.
Girard, René. 1982. *Le bouc émissaire*. Paris: Grasset. See Girard 1986.
Girard, René. 1985. *La route antique des hommes pervers*. Paris: Grasset. See Girard 1987.
Girard, René. 1986. *The Scapegoat*. Baltimore: Johns Hopkins University Press.
Girard, René. 1987. *Job, the Victim of His People*. Translated by Yvonne Freccero. Stanford: Stanford University Press.
Girard, René. 1987a. *Things Hidden since the Foundation of the World*. Translated by Stephen Bann and Michael Metteer. Stanford: Stanford University Press.
Girard, René. 1991. *A Theater of Envy: William Shakespeare*. New York: Oxford University Press.

Glatzer, Nahum N. 1969. *The Dimensions of Job: A Study and Selected Readings*. New York: Schocken.
Glatzer, Nahum N., ed. 1972. *The Judaic Tradition*. Boston: Beacon.
Godzich, Wlad. 1983. "Introduction: Caution! Reader at Work!" In De Man 1983, xv–xxx.
Godzich, Wlad. 1986. "Foreword: The Tiger on the Paper Mat." In De Man 1986, ix–xviii.
Godzich, Wlad, and Nicholas Spadaccini, eds. 1986. *Literature among Discourses*. Minneapolis: University of Minnesota Press.
Goldberg, Jonathan. 1986. *Voice Terminal Echo: Postmodernism and English Renaissance Texts*. New York: Methuen.
Goldberg, Jonathan. 1988. "Rebel Letters: Postal Effects from *Richard II* to *Henry IV*." *Renaissance Drama* 19: 3–27.
Goldberg, Jonathan. 1990. *Writing Matter: From the Hands of the English Renaissance*. Stanford: Stanford University Press.
Goldhill, Simon. 1984. "Exegesis: *Oedipus Rex*." *Arethusa* 17: 177–200.
Golsan, Richard J. 1984. "Sacrificial Violence and Evangelical Message: René Girard's *Bouc émissaire*." *Helios* 11/2: 167–78.
Golsan, Richard J. 1988. "Combatting the Persecutory Text: René Girard's *La route antique des hommes pervers*." *Helios* 15/1: 73–81.
Good, Edwin M. 1990. *In Turns of Tempest: A Reading of Job*. Stanford: Stanford University Press.
Goodhart, Sandor. 1977. *Who Killed Laius? Sophocles' Mythic Arithmetic*. Ann Arbor: University Microfilms.
Goodhart, Sandor. 1978. "*Lēstas Ephaske:* Oedipus and Laius's Many Murderers." *Diacritics* 8/1: 55–71.
Goodhart, Sandor. 1985. "'Je suis Joseph': René Girard et la loi prophétique." Translated by Paul Dumouchel. In Dumouchel 1987–88, 69–83.
Goodhart, Sandor. 1985a. "Débat: Sandor Goodhart et Raymund Schwager." In Dumouchel 1985, 83–89.
Goodhart, Sandor. 1985b. "Prophecy, Sacrifice, and Repentance in the Story of Jonah." In McKenna 1985, 43–63.
Goodhart, Sandor. 1986. "After the *Tragic Vision:* Krieger and Lentricchia, Criticism and Crisis." In Hendricksen 1986, 179–97.
Goodhart, Sandor. 1986–88. "'I am Joseph': René Girard and the Prophetic Law." In Juilland 1986, 85–111. Reprinted in Dumouchel 1987–88, 53–74.
Goodhart, Sandor. 1989. "Disfiguring de Man: Literature, History, and Collaboration." In Hamacher, Hertz, and Keenan 1989, 226–45.
Goodhart, Sandor. 1992. "'One Isaac Waiting to Be Slaughtered': Halpern Leivick, the Holocaust, and Responsibility." *Philosophy and Literature* 16/1: 88–105.
Goodhart, Sandor. 1992a. "The Witness of Trauma." *Modern Judaism* 12: 203–17.
Goodhart, Sandor. 1993. "Biblical Theory and Criticism, 2: Modern Criticism." In Groden and Kreiswirth 1993, 84–89.

Goodhart, Sandor. 1993a. "René Girard." In Groden and Kreiswirth 1993, 355–56.
Goodhart, Sandor. 1993b. "Reading the Ram: Abraham, Isaac, and the Text of Sacrifice." *Bulletin of the Colloquium on Violence and Religion* 5 (October): 8–9.
Goodhart, Sandor. 1994. "Isaiah 52–53, René Girard, and the Innocent Victim." *Bulletin of the Colloquium on Violence and Religion* 7 (October): 11.
Goodhart, Sandor. 1995. "Reply to Father Schwager and Józef Niewiadomski." *Bulletin of the Colloquium on Violence and Religion* 8 (March): 12–13.
Goodkin, R. E. 1989. "'Killing Order(s)': Iphigenia and the Detection of Tragic Intertextuality." *Yale French Studies* 76: 81–107.
Goodson, Alfred C. 1988. *Verbal Imagination: Coleridge and the Language of Modern Criticism*. New York: Oxford University Press.
Goppelt, Leonhard. 1982. *Typos: The Typological Interpretation of the Old Testament in the New*. Translated by Donald H. Madvig. Grand Rapids, Mich.: W. B. Eerdsmans.
Gordis, Robert. 1978. *The Book of Job: Commentary, New Translation, and Special Studies*. New York: Jewish Theological Seminary of America.
Green, William Scott, ed. 1978. *Approaches to Ancient Judaism*. Missoula, Mo.: Scholars Press.
Greenblatt, Stephen. 1980. *Renaissance Self-fashioning: From More to Shakespeare*. Chicago: University of Chicago Press.
Greenblatt, Stephen. 1982. "Introduction." In Greenblatt, ed., *The Power of Forms in the English Renaissance*, 3–6. Norman, Okla.: Pilgrim Books.
Greenblatt, Stephen. 1988. *Representing the English Renaissance*. Berkeley: University of California Press.
Greene, William Chase. 1929. "The Murderers of Laius." *Transactions of the American Philological Association* 60: 76–86.
Greene, William Chase. 1944. *Moira: Fate, Good, and Evil in Greek Thought*. Cambridge: Harvard University Press.
Greenspahn, Frederick, ed. 1982. *Scripture in the Jewish and Christian Traditions: Authority, Interpretation, Relevance*. Nashville, Tenn.: Parthenon.
Greer, Rowan A., and James L. Kugel, eds. 1986. *Early Biblical Interpretation*. Philadelphia: Westminster.
Groden, Michael, and Martin Kreiswirth, eds. 1993. *The Johns Hopkins Guide to Literary Theory and Criticism*. Baltimore: Johns Hopkins University Press.
Grossvogel, David. 1979. *Mystery and Its Fictions*. Baltimore: Johns Hopkins University Press.
Gunn, D. M. 1993. *Narrative in the Hebrew Bible*. New York: Oxford University Press.
Gurr, Andrew, ed. 1984. *William Shakespeare: "King Richard II."* New York: Cambridge University Press.
Halbershtam, Hayim, ed. 1885. *Perush Sefer Yetzirah le-ha-rav . . . Yehudah Barzilai ha-Bartseloni zal*. Berlin: Bi-defus Ts. H. Ittskovski.
Hales, Peter B. 1991. "The Atomic Sublime." *American Studies* 32: 5–31.
Halpérin, Jean, ed. 1985. *Idoles*. Paris: Denoël.

Halpern, Baruch, ed. 1981. *Traditions in Transformation: Turning Points in Biblical Faith*. Winoa Lake, Ind.: Eisenbrauns.
Hamacher, Werner, Neil Hertz, and Tom Keenan, eds. 1989. *Responses: On Paul de Man's Wartime Journalism*. Lincoln: University of Nebraska Press.
Hamacher, Werner, Neil Hertz, and Tom Keenan, eds. 1990. *Paul de Man: Wartime Journalism, 1939–1943*. Lincoln: University of Nebraska Press.
Hamerton-Kelley, Robert, ed. 1987. *Violent Origins: Walter Burkert, René Girard, and Jonathan Z. Smith on Ritual Killing and Cultural Formation*. Stanford: Stanford University Press.
Hamilton, Edith, ed. 1961. *The Collected Dialogues of Plato*. Princeton: Princeton University Press.
Handelman, Susan. 1982. *The Slayers of Moses: The Emergence of Rabbinic Interpretation in Modern Literary Theory*. Albany: State University of New York Press.
Harari, Josué, ed. 1979. *Textual Strategies: Perspectives in Post-Structuralist Criticism*. Ithaca: Cornell University Press.
Harshav, Benjamin, and Barbara Harshav. 1988. *American Yiddish Poetry*. New Haven: Yale University Press.
Harshbarger, Karl. 1965. "Who Killed Laius?" *Tulane Drama Review* 9: 120–31.
Harshbarger, Karl. 1979. *Sophocles' "Oedipus."* Washington, D.C.: University Press of America.
Hartman, Geoffrey H., ed. 1979. *Deconstruction and Criticism*. New York: Seabury.
Hartman, Geoffrey H. 1981. *Saving the Text: Literature/Derrida/Philosophy*. Baltimore: Johns Hopkins University Press.
Hartman, Geoffrey H. 1986. "The Struggle for the Text." In Budick and Hartman 1986, 3–18.
Hartman, Geoffrey H., ed. 1986a. *Bitburg in Moral and Political Perspective*. Bloomington: Indiana University Press.
Hartman, Geoffrey H. 1988. "Blindness and Insight: Paul de Man, Fascism, and Deconstruction." *The New Republic* 198/3 (March 7): 26, 28–31.
Hartman, Geoffrey H. 1991. *Minor Prophecies: The Literary Essay in the Culture Wars*. Cambridge: Harvard University Press.
Hartman, Geoffrey H., ed. 1994. *Holocaust Remembrance: The Shapes of Memory*. New York: Basil Blackwell.
Hawkes, Terence. 1969. *Coleridge on Shakespeare*. London: Penguin.
Hay, John. 1979. *Oedipus Tyrannus: Lame Knowledge and the Homosporic Womb*. Washington, D.C.: University Press of America.
Hayes, Peter, ed. 1991. *Lessons and Legacies: The Meaning of the Holocaust in a Changing World*. Evanston: Northwestern University Press.
Hendricksen, Bruce, ed. 1986. *Murray Krieger and Contemporary Critical Theory*. New York: Columbia University Press.
Hertz, J. H., ed. 1979. *The Pentateuch and the Haftorahs*. 2nd ed. London: Soncino.
Hertz, Neil. 1978. "Freud and the Sandman." In Harari 1979, 296–321.
Hertz, Neil. 1985. *The End of the Line*. New York: Columbia University Press.

Heschel, Abraham Joshua. 1971. *The Prophets, Volume II*. New York: Harper and Row.
Hilberg, Raul. 1961. *The Destruction of the European Jews*. New York: Harper and Row.
Holtz, Barry, ed. 1984. *Back to the Sources: Reading the Classic Jewish Texts*. New York: Summit.
Holtz, Barry. 1984a. "Midrash." In Holtz 1984, 177–211.
Hone, Ralph E., ed. 1960. *A Voice out of the Whirlwind: The Book of Job*. San Francisco: Chandler.
Howe, Irving, and Eliezer Greenberg. 1956. *A Treasury of Yiddish Stories*. New York: Holt, Rinehart, and Winston.
Howe, Irving, and Eliezer Greenberg. 1976. *A Treasury of Yiddish Poetry*. New York: Schocken.
Hoy, Cyrus, ed. 1992. *"Hamlet": An Authoritative Text, Intellectual Backgrounds, Extracts from the Sources, Essays in Criticism/William Shakespeare*. New York: W. W. Norton.
Hoy, Daniel J. 1966. "On the Trail of the Other." *Philosophy Today* 10/1: 34–46.
Huizinga, Johan. 1959. *Men and Ideas: History, the Middle Ages, the Renaissance: Essays*. Translated by James S. Holmes and Hans van Marle. New York: Meridian.
Huizinga, Johan. 1959a. *The Waning of the Middle Ages: A Study of the Forms of Life, Thought and Art in France and the Netherlands in the XIVth and XVth Centuries*. New York: Doubleday.
Huston, J. D. 1985. "A Message from Corinth: The Importance of the Off-Stage World in 'Oedipus the King.'" *Centennial Review* 29/4: 420–37.
Hutton, James. 1982. *Aristotle's "Poetics."* New York: W. W. Norton.
Idel, Moshe. 1986. "Infinities of the *Torah*." In Budick and Hartman 1986, 141–57.
Idel, Moshe. 1988. *Kabbalah: New Perspectives*. New Haven: Yale University Press.
Isaiah, A. B., and B. Sharfman. 1949. *The Pentateuch and Rashi's Commentary*. Brooklyn: S. S. and R.
Jebb, Richard. 1972. *Sophocles: The Plays and Fragments, Part 1: The "Oedipus Tyrannus."* New York: Scholarly Press.
Jewish Publication Society of America, ed. 1950. *The Holy Scriptures*. Philadelphia: Jewish Publication Society of America. 1917 translation.
Johansen, Holger Friis. 1962–63. "Sophocles 1939–1959." *Lustrum* 7: 94–288.
Jones, Ernest. 1954. *Hamlet and Oedipus*. Garden City, N.Y.: Doubleday Anchor.
Jones, Ernest. 1963. *The Life and Work of Sigmund Freud*. New York: Anchor.
Juilland, Alphonse, ed. 1986. "To Honor René Girard." *Stanford French Review* 10/1–3 (10th anniversary volume).
Jung, C. G. 1954. *Answer to Job*. London: Routledge.
Kallich, Martin. 1968. *Oedipus: Myth and Drama*. New York: Odyssey.
Kamerbeek, J. C. 1967. *The Plays of Sophocles, Part 4*. Leiden, The Netherlands: E. J. Brill.

Kantorowicz, Ernst H. 1981. *The King's Two Bodies: A Study in Medieval Political Theology*. Princeton: Princeton University Press.
Kaplan, Aryeh, ed. 1990. *Sefer Yetzirah: The Book of Creation*. York Beach, Maine: S. Weiser.
Katz, Steven T. 1983. *Post-Holocaust Dialogues: Critical Studies in Modern Jewish Thought*. New York: New York University Press.
Kaufmann, Yehezkel. 1960. *The Religion of Israel, from Its Beginnings to the Babylonian Exile*. Translated by Moshe Greenberg. Chicago: University of Chicago Press.
Kaufmann, Yehezkel. 1972. *The Religion of Israel*. New York: Schocken. Abridged version of Kaufmann 1960.
Kelsey, David. 1982. "Protestant Attitudes regarding Methods of Biblical Interpretation." In Greenspahn 1982, 133–61.
Kermode, Frank. 1965. *Four Centuries of Shakespearean Criticism*. New York: Avon.
Kermode, Frank. 1983. *The Art of Telling: Essays on Fiction*. Cambridge: Harvard University Press 1983.
Kershaw, Ian. 1993. *The Nazi Dictatorship: Problems and Perspectives of Interpretation*. 3rd ed. New York: Routledge.
Kirkwood, Gordon M. 1958. *A Study of Sophoclean Drama*. Ithaca: Cornell University Press.
Kittel, Rudolf, ed. 1966. *Biblia Hebraica*. Stuttgart: Württembergische Bibelanstalt.
Kitto, H.D.F. 1954. *Greek Tragedy*. New York: Doubleday Anchor.
Klein, Richard, ed. 1984. "Nuclear Criticism." *Diacritics* 14/2 (summer).
Knapp, Peggy A., ed. 1983. *Assays: Critical Approaches to Medieval and Renaissance Texts*. Vol. 2. Pittsburgh: University of Pittsburgh Press.
Knox, Bernard. 1955. "Sophocles' 'Oedipus.'" In Knox 1979, 96–111.
Knox, Bernard. 1957. *Oedipus at Thebes*. New York: W. W. Norton.
Knox, Bernard. 1964. *The Heroic Temper: Studies in Sophoclean Tragedy*. Berkeley: University of California Press.
Knox, Bernard. 1979. *Word and Action: Essays on the Ancient Theater*. Baltimore: Johns Hopkins University Press.
Knox, Bernard. 1982. "The Freedom of Oedipus: A Reading of Sophocles' Tragedy." *The New Republic* (August 30): 28–34.
Kolitz, Zvi. 1947. *The Tiger Beneath the Skin: Stories and Parables of the Years of Death*. New York: Creative Age Press.
Kolitz, Zvi. 1947a. "Yossel Rakover's Appeal to God." In Kolitz 1947, 81–95.
Kolitz, Zvi. 1994. "Yossel Rakover's Appeal to God." Newly translated with an afterword by Jeffrey V. Mallow and Franz Jozef van Beeck. *Cross Currents* 44/3 (fall): 362–77.
Konigsberg, Ira, ed. 1981. *American Criticism in the Poststructuralist Age*. Michigan Studies in the Humanities 4. Ann Arbor: University of Michigan Press.
Kott, Jan. 1966. *Shakespeare Our Contemporary*. Translated by Boleslaw Taborski. New York: Anchor.

Krieger, Murray. 1960. *The Tragic Vision*. Chicago: University of Chicago Press.
Kugel, James. 1981. *The Idea of Biblical Poetry: Parallelism and Its History*. New Haven: Yale University Press.
Kugel, James. 1988. "Torah." In Cohen and Mendes-Flohr 1988, 995–1005.
Kugel, James. 1990. *In Potiphar's House: The Interpretative Life of Biblical Texts*. San Francisco: Harper and Row.
Kuhn, Thomas. 1957. *The Copernican Revolution: Planetary Astronomy in the Development of Western Thought*. Cambridge: Harvard University Press.
Kuhn, Thomas. 1962. *The Structure of Scientific Revolutions*. Chicago: University of Chicago Press.
LaCapra, Dominick. 1989. *Soundings in Critical Theory*. Ithaca: Cornell University Press.
LaCapra, Dominick. 1989a. "Intellectual History and Critical Theory." In LaCapra 1989, 182–209.
Lacocque, André. 1981. *The Jonah Complex*. Atlanta: John Knox Press.
Lacocque, André. 1990. *Jonah: A Psycho-religious Approach to the Prophet*. Columbia: University of South Carolina Press.
Lacoue-Labarthe, Philippe. 1987. *La fiction du politique: Heidegger, l'art, et la politique*. Paris: Christian Bourgeois. See Lacoue-Labarthe 1990.
Lacoue-Labarthe, Philippe. 1989. *Typography: Mimesis, Philosophy, Politics*. Edited by Christopher Fynsk with introduction by Jacques Derrida. Cambridge: Harvard University Press.
Lacoue-Labarthe, Philippe. 1990. *Heidegger, Art, and Politics: The Fiction of the Political*. Translated by Chris Turner. Cambridge, Mass.: Basil Blackwell.
Lacoue-Labarthe, Philippe. 1993. *The Subject of Philosophy*. Translated by Thomas Trezise et al. Minneapolis: University of Minnesota Press.
Lacoue-Labarthe, Philippe, and Jean Luc Nancy. 1988. *The Literary Absolute: The Theory of Literature in German Romanticism*. Translated by Philip Barnard and Cheryl Lester. Albany: State University of New York Press.
Lambert, Mayer, ed. 1891. *Commentaire sur Sefer Yesirah, ou Livre de la création par le gaon Saadya de Fayyoum*. Paris: E. Bouillon.
Landis, Joseph C. 1980. *The Great Jewish Plays*. New York: Avon.
Lang, Berel, ed. 1988. *Writing and the Holocaust*. New York: Holmes and Meier.
Langer, Lawrence. 1991. *Holocaust Testimonies: The Ruins of Memory*. New Haven: Yale University Press.
Lanzmann, Claude. 1985. *"Shoah": An Oral History of the Holocaust. The Complete Text of the Film*. New York: Random House.
Law, Robert. 1953. "Links between Shakespeare's History Plays." *Studies in Philology* 50: 168–87.
Law, Robert. 1954. "Shakespeare's Historical Cycle: Rejoinder." *Studies in Philology* 51: 40–41.
Leftwich, Joseph. 1974. *An Anthology of Modern Yiddish Literature*. The Hague: Mouton.

Leibowitz, Joseph H. 1987. "The Image of Job as Reflected in Rabbinic Writings." M.A. thesis, University of California, Berkeley.
Leitch, Vincent B. 1988. *American Literary Criticism from the Thirties to the Eighties*. New York: Columbia University Press.
Leivick, Halpern. 1983. *A Leaf on an Apple Tree*. 33. Paris: Editions Albin Michel.
Levenson, Jon Douglas. 1972. *The Book of Job in Its Time and in the Twentieth Century*. Cambridge: Harvard University Press.
Levi, Primo. 1986. *Sommersi e i salvati*. Torin: Einaudi. See Levi 1988.
Levi, Primo. 1988. *The Drowned and the Saved*. New York: Random House.
Levinas, Emmanuel. 1961. *Totalité et infini*. The Hague: Martinus Nijhoff. See Levinas 1969.
Levinas, Emmanuel. 1963. "La trace de l'autre." In Levinas 1982a, 187–202.
Levinas, Emmanuel. 1968. *Quatre lectures talmudiques*. Paris: Minuit. See Levinas 1990a.
Levinas, Emmanuel. 1969. *Totality and Infinity: An Essay on Exteriority*. Translated by Alphonso Lingis. Pittsburgh: Duquesne University Press.
Levinas, Emmanuel. 1974. *Autrement qu'être, ou au-delà de l'essence*. The Hague: Martinus Nijhoff. See Levinas 1981.
Levinas, Emmanuel. 1977. *Du sacré au saint: cinq nouvelles lectures talmudiques*. Paris: Minuit. See Levinas 1990a.
Levinas, Emmanuel. 1981. *Otherwise than Being: Or, Beyond Essence*. Translated by Alphonso Lingis. The Hague: Martinus Nijhoff.
Levinas, Emmanuel. 1982. *L'au-delà du verset*. Paris: Minuit. See Levinas 1994a.
Levinas, Emmanuel. 1982a. *En découvrant l'existence avec Husserl et Heidegger*. Paris: Vrin.
Levinas, Emmanuel. 1982b. *Ethique et infini*. Paris: Fayard. See Levinas 1985.
Levinas, Emmanuel. 1983. *Difficile liberté*. Paris: Editions Albin Michel. See Levinas 1990.
Levinas, Emmanuel. 1985. *Ethics and Infinity*. Pittsburgh: Duquesne University Press.
Levinas, Emmanuel. 1986. *De Dieu qui vient à l'idée*. Paris: Vrin.
Levinas, Emmanuel. 1986a. "The Trace of the Other." Translated by Alphonso Lingis. In Taylor 1986, 345–59.
Levinas, Emmanuel. 1987. *Collected Philosophic Papers*. Translated by Alphonso Lingis. Dordrecht: Martinus Nijhof.
Levinas, Emmanuel. 1987a. *Hors sujet*. Paris: Fata Morgana. See Levinas 1994.
Levinas, Emmanuel. 1988. *A l'heure des nations*. Paris: Minuit. See Levinas 1994b.
Levinas, Emmanuel. 1990. *Difficult Freedom*. Translated by Sean Hand. Baltimore: Johns Hopkins University Press.
Levinas, Emmanuel. 1990a. *Nine Talmudic Studies*. Translated by Annette Aronowicz. Bloomington: Indiana University Press.
Levinas, Emmanuel. 1994. *Outside the Subject*. Translated by Michael Smith. Stanford: Stanford University Press.

Levinas, Emmanuel. 1994a. *Beyond the Verse*. Translated by Gary D. Mole. Bloomington: Indiana University Press.
Levinas, Emmanuel. 1994b. *In the Time of the Nations*. Translated by Michael Smith. Bloomington: Indiana University Press.
Lévi-Strauss, Claude. 1967. *Structural Anthropology*. New York: Anchor.
Lévi-Strauss, Claude. 1969. *The Elementary Structures of Kinship*. Translated by Rodney Needham et al. Boston: Beacon.
Lévy, Bernard-Henri. 1977. *La barbarie à visage humain*. Paris: Grasset. See Lévy 1979.
Lévy, Bernard-Henri. 1979. *Barbarism with a Human Face*. New York: Harper and Row.
Lévy, Bernard-Henri. 1979a. *Le testament de Dieu*. Paris: Grasset. See Lévy 1985.
Lévy, Bernard-Henri. 1985. *The Testament of God*. Translated by George Holoch. Baltimore: Johns Hopkins University Press.
LeWinter, Oswald, ed. 1963. *Shakespeare in Europe*. Cleveland: World Publishing.
Lifton, Robert Jay. 1967. *Death in Life: Survivors of Hiroshima*. New York: Simon and Schuster.
Lifton, Robert Jay. 1986. *The Nazi Doctors: Medical Killing and the Psychology of Genocide*. New York: Basic Books.
Lifton, Robert Jay. 1990. *The Genocidal Mentality: Nazi Holocaust and Nuclear Threat*. New York: Basic Books.
Lindberg, David C. 1976. *Theories of Vision from Al-Kindi to Kepler*. Chicago: University of Chicago Press.
Liptzin, Sol. 1985. *A History of Yiddish Literature*. New York: Jonathan David.
Littell, Franklin H. 1975. *The Crucifixion of the Jews*. New York: Harper and Row.
Livingston, Paisley, ed. 1984. *Disorder/Order*. Stanford Literature Studies 1. Saratoga, Calif.: Anma Libri.
Livingston, Paisley, ed. 1992. *Models of Desire: René Girard and the Psychology of Mimesis*. Baltimore: Johns Hopkins University Press.
Lohfink, Norbert. 1968. *The Christian Meaning of the Old Testament*. Milwaukee: Bruce Publishing.
Lohfink, Norbert. 1983. *Gewalt und Gewaltlosigkeit im Alten Testament*. Freiburg, Germany: Herder.
Loraux, Nicole. 1986. *The Invention of Athens: The Funeral Oration in the Classical City*. Translated by Alan Sheridan. Cambridge: Harvard University Press.
Lovejoy, Arthur O. 1970. *The Great Chain of Being: A Study of the History of an Idea*. Cambridge: Harvard University Press.
Lukacher, Ned. 1989. "Anamorphic Stuff: Shakespeare, Catharsis, and Lacan." *South Atlantic Quarterly* 88: 863–98.
Luther, Martin. 1543. "On the Jews and Their Lies." Translated by Martin H. Bertram. In Sherman 1971, 121–306.
Lyotard, Jean-François. 1988. *The Differend*. Minneapolis: University of Minnesota Press.

Lyotard, Jean-François. 1989. "Discussions, or Phrasing 'after Auschwitz.'" In Benjamin 1989.
Maccoby, Hyam. 1986. *The Mythmaker: Paul and the Invention of Christianity*. New York: Harper and Row.
Madison, Charles A. 1971. *Yiddish Literature: Its Scope and Major Writers*. New York: Schocken.
Magonet, Jonathan. 1983. *Form and Meaning: Studies in Literary Technique in the Book of Jonah*. Sheffield, England: Almond Press.
Maier, Charles S. 1988. *The Unmasterable Past: History, Holocaust, and German National Identity*. Cambridge: Harvard University Press.
Maimonides, Moses. 1967. *The Commandments*. Translated by Charles B. Chavel. London: Soncino.
Maimonides, Moses. 1972. *Mishneh Torah: Hilkhot Teshuvah VII*. Reprinted in Glatzer 1972.
Manheim, Michael. 1973. *The Weak King Dilemma in the Shakespearean History Play*. Syracuse: Syracuse University Press.
Marks, Herbert. 1989. "Prophetic Stammering." *Yale Journal of Criticism* 1/1: 1–20.
Marrus, Michael. 1987. *The Holocaust in History*. Hanover, N.H.: University Press of New England.
Mazzeo, Joseph Anthony. 1967. *Renaissance and Revolution*. New York: Random House.
Mazzotta, Giuseppe. 1979. *Dante, Poet of the Desert*. Princeton: Princeton University Press.
McDonald, David. 1980. "Forms of Absence: Derrida and the Trace of Tragedy." *Helios* 7/2: 75–95.
McKenna, Andrew J., ed. 1985. "René Girard and Biblical Studies." *Semeia: An Experimental Journal for Biblical Criticism* 33.
McKenna, Andrew J. 1992. *Violence and Difference: Girard, Derrida, and Deconstruction*. Stanford: Stanford University Press.
McKeon, Richard, ed. 1941. *Aristotle*. New York: Random House.
McMillin, Scott. 1984. "Shakespeare's *Richard II*: Eyes of Sorrow, Eyes of Desire." *Shakespeare Quarterly* 15: 40–52.
Miller, J. Hillis. 1981. "The Ethics of Reading." In Konigsberg 1981, 19–41.
Miller, J. Hillis. 1987. *The Ethics of Reading*. New York: Columbia University Press.
Montefiore, Alan, ed. 1983. *Philosophy in France Today*. Translated by Kathleen McLaughlin. Cambridge: Cambridge University Press.
Moseley, C.W.R.D. 1988. *Shakespeare's History Plays: "Richard II" to "Henry V," the Making of a King*. New York: Penguin.
Muir, Kenneth, ed. 1963. *William Shakespeare: "The Tragedy of King Richard the Second."* New York: New American Library.
Mullahy, Patrick. 1955. *Oedipus: Myth and Complex: A Review of Psychoanalytic Theory*. New York: Grove.
Myers, Robert John. 1973. *The Tragedy of King Richard, the Second; the life and Times of Richard II (1367–1400), King of England (1377–1399) compared to those

of Richard of America in his second administration. Washington, D.C.: Acropolis Books.
Neher, André. 1962. *L'existence juive.* Paris: Seuil.
Neher, André. 1970. *Exil de la Parole, du silence biblique au silence d'Auschwitz.* Paris: Seuil. See Neher 1981.
Neher, André. 1981. *The Exile of the Word: From the Silence of the Bible to the Silence of Auschwitz.* Translated by David Maisel. Philadelphia: Jewish Publication Society.
Nemo, Philippe. 1978. *Job et l'excès du mal.* Paris: Grasset.
Neusner, Jacob. 1990. *Tractate Yoma.* Chicago: University of Chicago Press.
Neusner, Jacob. 1991. *Tractate Makkot.* Atlanta: Scholars Press.
Newlin, Jeanne T. 1984. *"Richard II": Critical Essays.* New York: Garland.
Nietzsche, Friedrich. 1966. *Beyond Good and Evil, Prelude to a Philosophy of the Future.* Translated by Walter Kaufmann. New York: Vintage.
Nietzsche, F. W. 1974. *The Gay Science.* Edited by Walter Kaufmann. New York: Random House.
Niewiadomski, Józef, Wolfgang Palaver, and Dietmar Regensburger, eds. 1991. *Bulletin of the Colloquium on Violence and Religion.*
Norich, Anita. 1991. *The Homeless Imagination in the Fiction of Israel Joshua Singer.* Bloomington: Indiana University Press.
Norwood, Gilbert. 1960. *Greek Tragedy.* New York: Hill and Wang.
O'Brien, Michael, ed. 1968. *Twentieth-Century Interpretations of "Oedipus Rex."* Englewood Cliffs, N.J.: Prentice-Hall.
Opstelten, J. C. 1952. *Sophocles and Greek Pessimism.* Translated by J. A. Ross. Amsterdam.
Orgel, Stephen. 1975. *The Illusion of Power: Political Theater in the English Renaissance.* Berkeley: University of California Press.
Orlinsky, Harry, et al., eds. 1985. *Tanakh.* Philadelphia: Jewish Publication Society.
Ornstein Robert. 1972. "Richard II." In *A Kingdom for a Stage: The Achievement of Shakespeare's History Plays,* 102–24. Cambridge: Harvard University Press.
Osborne, Laurie E. 1985. "'Crisis of Degree' in Shakespeare's *Henriad.*" *Studies in English Literature* 25: 337–59.
Oughourlian, Jean-Michel. 1982. *Un mime nommé désir.* Paris: Grasset. See Oughourlian 1991.
Oughourlian, Jean-Michel. 1991. *The Puppet of Desire: The Psychology of Hysteria, Possession, and Hypnosis.* Translated by Eugene Webb. Stanford: Stanford University Press.
Ozick, Cynthia. 1991. *Metaphor and Memory: Essays.* New York: Vintage International.
Panofsky, Erwin. 1939. *Studies in Iconology: Humanistic Themes in the Art of the Renaissance.* New York: Oxford University Press.
Panofsky, Erwin. 1955. *Meaning in the Visual Arts.* Garden City, N.Y.: Doubleday.
Paolucci, Anne, and Henry Paolucci, eds. 1962. *Hegel on Tragedy.* Garden City, N.Y.: Anchor.

Pater, Walter. 1889. *Appreciations*. Excerpted in Muir 1963, 191–98. See also Buckler 1986, 391–550.

Penchansky, David. 1990. *The Betrayal of God: Ideological Conflict in Job*. Louisville, Ky.: Westminster/John Knox.

Peradotto, John. 1992. "Disauthorizing Prophecy: The Ideological Mapping of 'Oedipus Tyrannus.'" *Transactions of the American Philological Association* 122: 1–15.

Polanski, Roman, dir. 1986. *Macbeth*. Videorecording. Burbank: RCA/Columbia Pictures Home Video. 139 minutes. Originally released as a motion picture in 1971.

Polzin, Robert M. 1977. *Biblical Structuralism: Method and Subjectivity in the Study of Ancient Texts*. Philadelphia: Fortress.

Pope, Marvin H., ed. 1973. *Job: Introduction, Translation, and Notes*. Garden City, N.Y.: Doubleday.

Prigogine, Ilya, and Isabel Stengers. 1979. *La Nouvelle alliance*. Paris: Gallimard.

Pucci, Pietro. 1988. "Reading the Riddles of *Oedipus Rex*." In Pucci 1988a, 131–54.

Pucci, Pietro, ed. 1988a. *Language and the Tragic Hero: Essays in Honor of Gordon M. Kirkwood*. Atlanta: Scholars Press.

Pucci, Pietro. 1991. "The Endless End of the 'Oedipus Rex' (Sophocles)." *Ramus: Critical Studies in Greek and Roman Literature* 20/1: 3–15.

Pucci, Pietro. 1992. *Oedipus and the Fabrication of the Father: "Oedipus Tyrannus" in Modern Criticism and Philosophy*. Baltimore: Johns Hopkins University Press.

Purdue, Leo G., and W. Clark Gilpin. 1992. *A Voice from the Whirlwind: Interpreting the Book of Job*. Nashville, Tenn.: Abingdon.

Rawidowicz, Simon. 1974. "On Interpretation." In Rawidowicz 1974a.

Rawidowicz, Simon. 1974a. *Studies in Jewish Thought*. Philadelphia: Jewish Publication Society.

Raysor, T. M. 1930. *Coleridge's Shakespeare Criticism*. Cambridge: Harvard University Press.

Reisen, Zalman. 1928. *Lexikon fun der Yiddisher Literatur*. 4 vols. 3rd ed. Vilna.

Ribner, Irving. 1952. "The Political Problem in Shakespeare's Lancastrian Tetralogy." *Studies in Philology* 49: 171–84.

Rieff, Philip, ed. 1963. *Character and Culture*. New York: Collier.

Riveline, Claude. 1985. "Les différentes formes de l'idolâtrie dans la Bible et aujourd'hui." In Halpérin 1985, 11–29.

Robbins, Jill. 1991. *Prodigal Son/Elder Brother: Interpretation and Alterity in Augustine, Petrarch, Kafka, Levinas*. Chicago: University of Chicago Press.

Roberts, Carl. 1915. *Oidipus: Geschichtes eines poetischen Stoffes in Altertum, I*. Berlin.

Roberts, Josephine A., ed. 1988. *"Richard II": An Annotated Bibliography*. 2 vols. New York: Garland.

Robertson, D. W. 1962. *Preface to Chaucer: Studies in Medieval Perspectives*. Princeton: Princeton University Press.

Rosenfeld, Alvin H. 1980. *A Double Dying: Reflections on Holocaust Literature*. Bloomington: Indiana University Press.

Rosenfeld, Alvin H., and Irving Greenberg, eds. 1978. *Confronting the Holocaust: The Impact of Elie Wiesel*. Bloomington: Indiana University Press.

Rosenzweig, Franz. 1985. *The Star of Redemption*. Notre Dame, Ind.: University of Notre Dame Press.

Rossiter, A. P. 1961. *Angel with Horns and Other Shakespeare Lectures*. New York: Theater Arts Books.

Rowley, H. H. 1958. *The Book of Job and Its Meaning*. Manchester, England: Manchester University Press.

Rubenstein, Richard. 1992. *After Auschwitz: History, Theology, and Contemporary Judaism*. Baltimore: Johns Hopkins University Press.

Rudnytsky, Peter. 1986. *Freud and Oedipus*. New York: Columbia University Press.

Ruthven, Ken. 1993. *Nuclear Criticism*. Carlton, Victoria, Australia: Melbourne University Press.

Rymer, Thomas. 1965. "A Short View of Tragedy." Excerpted in Kermode 1965, 461–69.

Sadoff, Dianne. 1980. "Story and the Figure of the Father in *Little Dorrit*." *PMLA* 95/2: 245.

Sanders, Paul S., ed. 1968. *Twentieth-Century Interpretations of the Book of Job: A Collection of Critical Essays*. Englewood Cliffs, N.J.: Prentice-Hall.

Sanderson, James L., and Everett Zimmerman. 1968. *Oedipus: Myth and Dramatic Form*. Boston: Houghton Mifflin.

Sasson, Jack M. 1990. *Jonah: A New Translation with Introduction, Commentary, and Interpretation*. Anchor Bible. New York: Doubleday.

Saunders, Wilbur. 1968. *Shakespeare's Political Agnosticism: "Richard II." The Dramatist and the Received Idea: Studies in the Plays of Marlowe and Shakespeare*. Cambridge: Cambridge University Press.

Scherman, Nosson. 1978. "Introduction." In Zlotowitz 1978, xix–lxxv.

Schneidau, Herbert N. 1977. *Sacred Discontent: The Bible and Western Tradition*. Berkeley: University of California Press.

Scholem, Gershom. 1972. *Major Trends in Jewish Mysticism*. New York: Schocken.

Scholem, Gershom. 1973. *Sabbatai Sevi*. Princeton: Princeton University Press.

Scholem, Gershom. 1974. *On the Kabbalah and Its Symbolism*. Translated by Ralph Manheim. New York: Schocken.

Scholem, Gershom. 1976. *On Jews and Judaism in Crisis: Selected Essays*. New York: Schocken.

Scholem, Gershom. 1978. *The Messianic Idea in Judaism and Other Essays on Jewish Spirituality*. New York: Schocken.

Scholem, Gershom. 1978a. *Kabbalah*. New York: New American Library.

Scholem, Gershom. 1985. *Reshit ha-Kabalah ve-Sefer ha-Bahir*. Jerusalem: Akademon. See Scholem 1987.

Scholem, Gershom. 1987. *Origins of the Kabbalah*. Princeton: Princeton University Press.

Schwager, Raymund, S.J. 1985. "Pour une théologie de la colère de Dieu." In Dumouchel 1985, 59–68.
Schwager, Raymund, S.J. 1987. *Brauchen wir einen Sündenbock?* Munich: Kösel. See Schwager 1989.
Schwager, Raymund, S.J. 1989. *Must There Be Scapegoats? Violence and Redemption in the Bible.* Translated by Maria L. Assad. New York: Harper and Row.
Schwartz, Murray. 1983. "Anger, Wounds, and the Forms of Theater in *King Richard II:* Notes for a Psychoanalytic Interpretation." In Knapp 1983, 115–29.
Segal, Charles. 1986. "Time, Theater, and Knowledge in the Tragedy of Oedipus." In Gentili and Pretagistini 1986, 459–84.
Segal, Charles. 1986a. *Tragedy and Civilization: An Interpretation of Sophocles.* Cambridge: Harvard University Press.
Segal, Charles. 1992. "A Review of Frederick Ahl's *Sophocles' Oedipus: Evidence and Self-Conviction.*" *Classical World* 86/92: 155.
Segal, Charles. 1993. *"Oedipus Tyrannus": Tragic Heroism and the Limits of Knowledge.* New York: Twayne.
Serres, Michel. 1968. *Hermès ou la communication.* Paris: Minuit.
Serres, Michel. 1980. *Le parasite.* Paris: Grasset. See Serres 1982.
Serres, Michel. 1982. *The Parasite.* Baltimore: Johns Hopkins University Press.
Serres, Michel. 1983. *Rome, le livre des fondations.* Paris: Grasset.
Shaw, G. B. 1961. *Shaw on Shakespeare.* Edited by Edwin Wilson. New York: E. P. Dutton.
Sheehan, Thomas. 1993. Letter to the editor. *New York Review of Books* (March 25): 66–67.
Sheehan, Thomas. 1993a. "A Normal Nazi." *New York Review of Books* (January 14): 29–35.
Sheppard, J. T. 1920. *The "Oedipus Tyrannus" of Sophocles.* Cambridge.
Sherman, Franklin, ed. 1971. *Luther's Works.* Vol. 47. Philadelphia: Fortress.
Siebers, Tobin. 1993. *Cold War Criticism and the Politics of Skepticism.* New York: Oxford University Press.
Siegel, Paul. 1957. *Shakespearean Tragedy and the Elizabethan Compromise.* New York: New York University Press.
Siemon, James. 1983. "The King's Other Body." *Shakespeare Newsletter* 33/3: 32.
Silk, M. S., and J. P. Stern. 1990. *Nietzsche on Tragedy.* New York: Cambridge University Press.
Skulsky, Harold. 1983. "On *The Pursuit of Signs.*" *Journal of Aesthetics and Art Criticism* 41/3: 289–99.
Speaight, Robert. 1955. *Nature in Shakespearean Tragedy.* London: Hollis and Carter.
Speiser, E. 1964. *Genesis: The Anchor Bible.* New York: Doubleday.
Spencer, Theodore. 1949. *Shakespeare and the Nature of Man.* Lowell Lectures. 2nd ed. New York: Macmillan.
Spingarn, Joel. 1963. *A History of Literary Criticism in the Renaissance.* New York: Harcourt, Brace, and World.

Steiner, George. 1967. *Language and Silence: Essays on Language, Literature and the Inhuman.* New York: Atheneum.
Stirling, Brents. 1956. *Unity in Shakespearean Tragedy.* New York: Columbia University Press.
Stuart, Douglas K. 1989. *Hosea-Jonah.* Dallas: Word Publishing.
Suleiman, Susan, and Inge Crosman. 1980. *The Reader in the Text: Essays on Audience and Interpretation.* Princeton: Princeton University Press.
Swinburne, A. C. 1909. *Three Plays of Shakespeare.* New York: Harper and Brothers.
Talbert, Ernest William. 1962. *The Problem of Order: Elizabethan Political Commonplaces and an Example of Shakespeáre's Art.* Chapel Hill: University of North Carolina Press.
Taplin, Oliver. 1978. *Tragedy in Action.* Cambridge: Cambridge University Press.
Tarrow, Susan, ed. 1990. *Reason and Light: Essays on Primo Levi.* Ithaca, N.Y.: Center for International Studies.
Taylor, Mark, ed. 1986. *Deconstruction in Context.* Chicago: University of Chicago Press.
Telford, Kenneth A. 1968. *Aristotle's "Poetics": Translation and Analysis.* Chicago: Henry Regnery.
Thayer, Calvin G. 1967. "Shakespeare's Second Tetralogy: An Underground Report." *Ohio University Review* 9: 5–15.
Thayer, Calvin G. 1983. *The Death of Divine Kingship: "Richard II." Shakespearean Politics: Government and Misgovernment in the Great Histories.* Athens: Ohio University Press.
Tillyard, E.M.W. 1959. *Elizabethan World Picture.* New York: Random House.
Tillyard, E.M.W. 1962. *Shakespeare's History Plays.* New York: Collier.
Tolstoy, Leo. 1906. *Tolstoy on Shakespeare.* Translated by V. Tchertkoff. New York: Funk and Wagnalls.
Tompkins, Jane P. 1980. *Reader-Response Criticism: From Formalism to Poststructuralism.* Baltimore: Johns Hopkins University Press.
Tonelli, Franco. 1983. *Sophocles' Oedipus and the Tale of the Theater.* Ravenna, Italy: Longo.
Trible, Phyllis Lou. 1967. *Studies in the Book of Jonah.* Ann Arbor: University Microfilms.
Trible, Phyllis Lou. 1994. *Rhetorical Criticism: Context, Method, and the Book of Jonah.* Minneapolis: Fortress.
Tsevat, Matitiahu. 1980. *The Meaning of the Book of Job and Other Biblical Studies.* New York: Ktav.
Turner, Victor. 1969. *The Ritual Process: Structure and Anti-structure.* Chicago: Aldine.
Ure, Peter, ed. 1969. *William Shakespeare: "King Richard II."* The New Arden Shakespeare. London: Methuen.
Van Doren, Mark. 1953. *Shakespeare.* Garden City, N.Y.: Doubleday.
Vawter, Bruce. 1982. "The Bible in the Roman Catholic Church." In Greenspahn 1982, 111–32.

Vawter, Bruce. 1983. *Job and Jonah: Questioning the Hidden God.* New York: Paulist Press.
Veeser, H. Aram, ed. 1989. *The New Historicism.* New York: Routledge.
Veeser, H. Aram, ed. 1993. *The New Historicism Reader.* New York: Routledge.
Vellacott, Philip. 1970. "The Guilt of Oedipus." In Berkowitz and Brunner 1970, 209–10.
Vellacott, Philip. 1971. *Sophocles and Oedipus.* Ann Arbor: University of Michigan Press.
Verhoeff, H. 1984. "Does Oedipus Have His Complex? The Interpretation of 'Hamlet.'" *Style* 18/3: 261–83.
Vernant, Jean-Pierre. 1978. "Ambiguity and Reversal: On the Enigmatic Structure of *Oedipus the King.*" *New Literary History* 9/3: 475–501.
Vernant, Jean-Pierre, and Pierre Vidal-Naquet. 1972. *Mythe et tragédie en Grèce ancienne.* Paris: Maspero. See Vernant and Pierre Vidal-Naquet 1981.
Vernant, Jean-Pierre, and Pierre Vidal-Naquet. 1981. *Tragedy and Myth in Ancient Greece.* Translated by Janet Lloyd. Atlantic Highlands, N.J.: Humanities Press.
Vidal-Naquet, Pierre. 1981. *Les Juifs, la mémoire et le présent.* Paris: Maspero.
Voltaire (François-Marie Arouet). 1877. "Lettres sur Oedipe." *Oeuvres complètes.* Edited by A. Beuchot. Vol. 2: 1–58. Paris.
von Helmholtz-Phelan, Anna Augusta. 1907. *The Indebtedness of Samuel Taylor Coleridge to August Wilhelm von Schlegel.* Bulletin of the University of Wisconsin Philology and Literature Series 3–4. Madison: University of Wisconsin.
Wagner, Richard. 1869. *Das Judentum in der Musik.* Leipzig.
Waldock, A.J.A. 1966. *Sophocles the Dramatist.* Cambridge: Cambridge University Press.
Weiskel, Thomas. 1976. *The Romantic Sublime: Studies in the Structure and Psychology of Transcendence.* Baltimore: Johns Hopkins University Press.
Weiss, Meir. 1983. *The Story of Job's Beginning: Job 1–2, a Literary Analysis.* Jerusalem: Magnes Press, Hebrew University.
Weissman, M. 1980. *The Midrash Says.* Brooklyn: Benei Yakov.
Wellek, René, and Austin Warren. 1956. *Theory of Literature.* 3rd ed. New York: Harcourt, Brace, and World.
Wells, Robin Headlam. 1985. "The Fortunes of Tillyard: Twentieth-Century Critical Debate on Shakespeare's History Plays." *English Studies* 66: 391–403.
Wells, Stanley, ed. 1969. *King Richard the Second.* New York: Penguin.
Wells, Stanley. 1984. "John Barton's *Richard II*, 1973–74." In Newlin 1984.
Wells, Stanley, ed. 1986. *William Shakespeare, The Complete Works.* Oxford: Clarendon.
Wells, Stanley. 1990. *Shakespeare, A Bibliographical Guide.* Oxford: Clarendon.
Wertheimer, Solomon Aaron. 1950–53. *Bate midrashot.* 2 Vols. Jerusalem: Mosad ha-Rav Kuk.
Westermann, Claus. 1981. *The Structure of the Book of Job: A Form-Critical Analysis.* Philadelphia: Fortress.

Whitman, Cedric. 1951. *Sophocles: A Study of Heroic Humanism*. Cambridge: Harvard University Press.
Wiesel, Elie. 1978. *A Jew Today*. New York: Random House.
Wiesel, Elie. 1978a. "A Plea for the Survivors." In Wiesel 1978, 218–47.
Wiesel, Elie. 1981. *Five Biblical Portraits*. Notre Dame, Ind.: University of Notre Dame Press.
Williams, James G. 1991. *The Bible, Violence, and the Sacred*. San Francisco: Harper Collins.
Williams, Raymond. 1976. *Keywords: A Vocabulary of Culture and Society*. Revised ed. New York: Oxford University Press.
Wilson, John Dover, ed. 1939. *The Works of Shakespeare: "King Richard II."* Cambridge: Cambridge University Press.
Winnington-Ingram, R. P. 1980. *Sophocles: An Interpretation*. New York: Cambridge University Press.
Wolin, Richard. 1991. *The Heidegger Controversy: A Critical Reader*. New York: Columbia University Press.
Wolin, Richard. 1993. Letter to the editor. *New York Review of Books* (March 25): 66.
Woodard, Thomas, ed. 1966. *Sophocles: A Collection of Critical Essays*. Englewood Cliffs, N.J.: Prentice-Hall.
Yeats, W. B. 1903. *Ideas of Good and Evil*. New York: Macmillan.
Young, James. 1988. *Writing and Rewriting the Holocaust: Narrative and the Consequences of Interpretation*. Bloomington: Indiana University Press.
Young, James. 1993. *The Texture of Memory: Holocaust Memorials and Meaning*. New Haven: Yale University Press.
Zeffirelli, Franco, dir. 1980. *Romeo and Juliet*. Videorecording. Hollywood: Paramount Home Video.
Zeisler, Ernest Bloomfield. 1954. *Othello: Time Enigma and Color Problem*. Chicago: A. J. Isaacs.
Zeitlin, Froma. 1986. "Thebes: Theater of Self and Society." In Gentili and Pretagistini 1986, 343–78.
Zlotowitz, Meir. 1978. *The Twelve Prophets: Yonah*. Brooklyn, N.Y.: Mesorah.
Zlotowitz, Meir, and Nosson Scherman. 1977–81. *Bereishis/Genesis*. 6 vols. Artscroll Tanach Series. New York: Mesorah.
Zuck, Roy. 1992. *Sitting with Job: Selected Studies on the Book of Job*. Grand Rapids, Mich.: Baker Book House.
Zuckerman, Bruce. 1991. *Job the Silent: A Study in Historical Counterpoint*. New York: Oxford University Press.

Index

abdication: of Richard II, 42, 47, 69, 80–81, 90–91; scene in *Richard II*, 47
Abel, 83, 102, 303n. 32. *See also* sacrificing
Abraham: and *akeidah* (*see akeidah*); compared with Jonah, 141, 152; covenant with God, 106; father of Judaism, 129; God of, 127, 302n. 21; grandfather of Jacob, xiii; *hineiniy*, 283; Job and, 177, 191; Joseph story and, 106, 117; in Leivick's talk, 223, 225–27, 229–31; Micah and, 149; midrash about, 128–29; son of Terah, 128–29; themes of life of, 129; tribes of, 204
Abrams, M. H., 46, 290n. 7, 296nn. 20 and 23, 297n. 51, 304n. 3
absence, 123, 173; of *alah* in Joseph story, 111; of father in *Hamlet*, 94; of God in Book of Job, 176; of God in Holocaust, 179–81, 238; of God in Nietzsche, 48; of Job at Creation, 168, 210, 311n. 29; king as presence of, in *Richard II* and *Hamlet*, 77; of memory in post-World War II French Jews, 220; object as presence of, 77; of reference to Phocis by Herdsman in *Oedipus Tyrannus*, 17; in Richard II's prison speech, 89; of subject in poststructuralism, 277. *See also* death
Abulafia, Abraham, 120. *See also* mysticism
academic study: Book of Job and, 198; Buber and, 175; literary criticism and, xi, xii, 247, 253; as sacrificial activity, 254
accusation: in Book of Job, 168, 193, 203, 208–10, 212; in Joseph story, 118–19; in *Oedipus Tyrannus* (*see Oedipus Tyrannus*); the Satan and, 206–7, 211; as truth of "problem of evil," 209; violence and, 101. *See also* Girard

acting out: criticism as, 254; Freud on mourning and, 240; in Joseph story, 114, 264; Leivick and, 241; in post-Holocaust writing, 274; in post-traumatic literature, 269; as response to Holocaust, 284. *See also* working through
Adam, xiii, 106, 210, 283
adonai ("Lord"), 132, 134. *See also* name of God
Aeschylean morality, 27
Aeschylus, 255
aesthetics, xi, 27, 122; as critical approach, 266; "fatal aestheticizing," 220; Hegel and, 248, 292n. 19; of Holocaust, 220; and interpretation, of *Hamlet*, 95; and interpretation, of *Richard II*, 7, 44, 252; Kantian, 4, 265; mirrors in, 75; new critical, 245; new historicism and, 295n. 20; in nineteenth-century German criticism, 248; Romantic subjectivity and, 281. *See also* Benjamin, Walter
akeidah ("binding" of Isaac): comparison to Book of Job, 207; counterpart to Joseph story, 148; Elie Wiesel on, 314n. 38; in Leivick's anecdote, 223, 225–27, 229–31; monumentalism of, 106; use of *olah* in, 111
Akiba, Rabbi, 125, 306n. 47. *See also* Maimonides; Messiah
alah ("sacrifice"), 111. *See also* Joseph; *olah*; sacrifice
aleph, 137, 306n. 47. *See also* Borges
Allegories of Reading. See de Man
Alter, Robert, 14, 123, 303n. 31, 304nn. 12 and 18, 305n. 19. *See also* biblical
alterity, in Levinas: of divinity, 9, 130, 134, 178, 180, 196, 200, 210, 238; of other individual, 265

anagn risis ("recognition"), 22. *See also* Aristotle

anarithmos ("numberless"), 37, 41. *See also* Oedipus Tyrannus

annihilation, 93, 95, 285, 288; in Adorno, 279; killing of Jews, 217; as meaning of Hebrew word *shoah*, 275; in *Richard II*, 72. *See also* Holocaust; shoah

anti-idolatry: 283; Abrahamic *hineiniy* and, 283; anti-clericalism and, 282; Book of Job and, 188; consonant with revelation, 266; creation and, 196, 198, 201, 204, 265; God of, 104, 197–98; Hebraic religion and, 301n. 13; interpretation as practice of, 130–31, 161; Isaiah and, 189; Jonah and, 156, 159; Joseph story and, 99–121; as learning when to stop, 106; life of, 191, 201; in Messianic times, 138; as monotheism, 131; reading as, 131, 137, 281; as trap, 159. *See also* law of anti-idolatry; prophetic; Torah

anti-sacrificial: xiii–xiv; *alah* as, 111; criticism and, 259, 262; diachronic and, 284; Girard's reading as, 106, 311n. 25; Holocaust and, 267; interpretation as, 161; Jacob and, 303n. 32; Jonah and, 145, 162–63; Joseph story and, 107, 111, 115; 117; literature as, 256, 260, 262; New Testament and, 109; as position, 40; reading as, 8, 281; sacrificial and, 258, 261, 264, 268; Sophocles and, 257; Torah as, 106, 264; tragedy and, 261. *See also* sacrificial

antisemitism, 227, 231, 233, 314n. 30; de Man and, 285, 287

appropriation, 6, 24, 83, 249; of Benjamin, 119; critical, 33, 122, 254; of desire of another, 182; Essex's, 295n. 5; Exton's, 84; Freud's, 37; of God's role, 158; Henry IV's, 69, 85; Herdsman's, 35; humanistic, 239; interpretive, 160, 174, 194; Job's, 207; of knowledge, 192; of language, 132; mimetic, 84, 112–14, 182; mythic, 6, 15–16, 36, 257; Nazis', 155; of notion of trace, 313n. 24; oracular, 7; of power, 25; Richard II's, 73; by subjects, 100; theories of language, 262

arbitrariness: in Book of Job, 184; of casting of lots, 145, 147; of differences, 101; in functionalist views of Holocaust, 269; literary criticism and, 246; of myth, 40; of Oedipus's guilt, 29, 31–32, 34–38, 292n. 6; of retrospective reading, 261; of substitution in Girard's view of sacrifice, 256; in trauma theory, 270, 273; of victim, 101, 102; of violence in Leivick, 226

Aristotle: cathartic views of tragedy in, 30, 36; on *hamartia*, 14; in Norwood's criticism of Sophocles, 16; in history of criticism, 248–49, 260, 262; irony and tragedy in, 292n. 19; prizing *Oedipus Tyrannus*, 6; on "recognition," 22; on "reversal of fortune," 22, 250; sacrificial approach to tragedy of, 255

arithmos ("number"), 39, 127. *See also* difference; number; plague; Sophocles

Arnold, Matthew, xi, 3, 8, 246, 248. *See also* tradition

aseret hadibrot ("ten words"), 104, 126, 197. *See also* Ten Commandments

Athanasian Creed, 63. *See also* Kantorowicz

atheism, 179–81, 237. *See also* death; Holocaust

Athens, 20, 25–26, 33. *See also* Knox

Auschwitz: Adorno and, 275, 278; Book of Job and, 212; compared to post-exilic moment in ancient Israel, 205; as conflation of humanism and murder, 279; critical reading after, 287; culture after, 276; death and, 279; Des Pres on, 215; Fackenheim on, 239; Friedlander on, 216; as happening of the impossible, 239, 242; Holocaust and, 273; humanism after, 241; in Leivick, 224; Levinas on, 238; Lyotard on, 317n. 53; as name of para-experience, 268, 276, 279; planet, 272, 316n. 48; reading after, xiv, 245; Rubenstein on, 317n. 53; survivors of, 272. *See also* deathcamps

autocriticism, 36, 100

avoidance, xi, 5, 9, 246

basileus ("king"), 25. *See also Oedipus Tyrannus*
being: "being with," 302n. 26; great chain of, 87, 278; Heidegger and, 277, 280; Holocaust and, 276; identified: —with death, 92; —with desire, 88; —with evil, 87; —with love, 87; —with opening, 88; Judaic law and, 200; Judaism and, 178; medieval hierarchies of, 53; nothing, 42–95; otherwise than, 134, 182, 200, 202, 283; Platonic, 161, 261–62, 283; playing at, 91; supreme, 85–86, 93, 197; Western metaphysics and, 277; in the world, 196. *See also* Levinas
Benjamin, son of Jacob, 107, 109–10, 119
Benjamin, Walter, 220, 263, 286
Benveniste, Emile, 4. *See also* structuralism
Bible, 122–24, 143, 155, 173, 297n. 53; as anti-paganism, 301n. 15; Christian, 103, 183, 300n. 2; commentary and, 246; critical reading of, 126, 131, 137; in Girard's thought, 102, 300n. 2; Hebrew, 6–7, 85, 100, 103, 106, 120; Judeo-Christian, 183; literary readings of, 266–67, 303n. 31, 304n. 2; non-Jewish readings of, 302n. 27; prophetic spirit and, 159; root of word, 304n. 9; sacrificial dynamics and, 264, 274. *See also* biblical; Torah
biblical: canon, 107, 204; Girard and, 186; Hebrew text, 118, 301; Joseph story as, 120; Leivick and, 221–33; Levinas on, 178, 236; Rashi and, 302n. 25; reading, 8, 122–38, 265–66; Scripture, 104, 263–66; theme of Messiah, 145; Wiesel and, 314n. 38. *See also* Alter; Bible; criticism; Hartman
Bishop, Jonathan, 12, 105, 132, 134, 306nn. 48 and 49. *See also* Messiah
Blanchôt, Maurice, 104, 219, 254, 301nn. 16 and 17. *See also* death
blessing, xiii, 208, 303n. 32
blindness: of criticism, xii, 240, 251–53; de Man on, 287, 290n. 8; in interpretation of Shakespeare, 53; in *King Lear*, 87; obedience and, 124; of Oedipus, 28, 34–38, 252; in *Oedipus Tyrannus*, 18; in *Richard II*, 78–79

Blindness and Insight, 1, 290n. 8. *See also* de Man
blood, 53–95, 115–20, 223–35, 295n. 11
Bloom, Harold, 9, 291n. 1, 294n. 1, 308n. 1
body natural (body politic), 62–66, 74, 82, 88. *See* Kantorowicz
Boethius, 86–87, 89, 92, 299n. 60
Book of Common Prayer, 63–64
Book of the Consolation of Israel, 188–90
Book of Job, 168–212; Book of Jonah and, 145, 160; Buber and, 174–77; Girard and, 182–88; God and, 191–203; interpretations of, 265, 308n. 1; Leivick on, 241; Levinas and, 177–82, 236; Pope and, 173–74; as questioning of evil, 7, 168; the Satan and, 203–12; as wisdom literature, 139, 160. *See also* Job
Booth, Stephen, 76, 297n. 50
Borges, Jorge Luis, 93, 95, 285, 299n. 63, 306n. 47
Bowra, Maurice, 22–23, 247–48, 251, 291n. 1, 292n. 20
Bradley, A. C., 24, 247–49, 292n. 27, 315n. 16
Brinkley, Tony, 220, 312n. 22
Brothers Karamazov, The, 38. *See also* Dostoyevsky
Broszat, Martin, 312. *See also Historikerstreit*
Browning, Christopher, 218, 316nn. 38 and 39
Buber, Martin, 9, 288; on Deutero-Isaiah, 188; on Job, 173, 175–78, 194, 197, 201–6, 308n. 5; Levinas and, 308n. 9; on Messiah, 125; on name of God, 302nn. 22 and 26, 305n. 38; on Psalm 73, 197; relation to Scholem, 174, 305n. 19; on the prophetic, 301n. 13; *The Prophetic Faith*, 176, 305n. 26; on Ten Commandments, 126
Burckhardt, Jacob, 44–45, 295

Cain, 83, 102, 303n. 32
catharsis ("purgation"), 30, 36. *See also* Aristotle
cheirodeikta ("pointed at by the hand"), 41
choreuein ("to make the Chorus"), 40–41. *See also* Sophocles

Christian, 76, 306n. 49; Augustinian, 45; being, 87; Bible, 183, 300n. 2; Book of Jonah and, 166; coming of Messiah, 125; covenant, 302n. 27; Girard's view of, 100–102, 123, 186, 300nn. 2 and 8; God of wrath, 304n. 15; interpretation of Hebrew Bible, 108–9, 123–25, 172, 186, 300n. 2; Kantorowicz and, 63; love, 87, 138; Old Testament, 125; Passion, 62, 183; relation to Judaism, 125–26, 137–38, 166, 183–88, 304n. 18; typology, 304n. 17; view: —of creation, 188; —of Holocaust, 284; —of name of God, 133; —of Ten Commandments, 127, 131. *See also* Jesus

Cocteau, Jean, 292n. 7. *See also* Sophocles

Cohen, Arthur, 217, 312n. 7, 316n. 47

Coleridge, Samuel Taylor: relation to Schlegel, 315n. 18; Seisler on, 247; on Shakespeare, 43–44, 51, 61, 94, 248–49, 252, 295nn. 7 and 9

commandment, 7, 190–91; Levinas on, 210; responsibility and, 283

commentary: biblical, 122, 266, 274; on danger of humanism, 49; on Exodus 3, 134; Foucault's, on Nietzsche, 48; of Hebrew teacher in Leivick's anecdote, 226; on Holocaust, 239, 267–68; inner literary criticism as, xi, 7–9, 137–38; interpretive, 136–38; ironic, in *Richard II*, 70; in J. H. Hertz, 155, 307n. 16; Leivick's, 239; literature as, 249; moral, 140; of Pirkei d'Rabbi Eliezer, 166; of Pope, 173; rabbinical, 107, 115, 148; Rashi's, 305n. 37; and the sacrificial, 282; traditional, 305n. 27; within literature, 246, 275–76, 284; witness and, 284

confession: of Claudius in *Hamlet*, 83; demanded by Lear, 87; in Jewish liturgy, 166; of Oedipus, 15, 19, 21, 38; in psychoanalysis, 38–39; in *Richard II*, 298n. 58; Rousseau's, 286

conscience: Bolingbroke's "guilt of," 51, 83–84; de Man's "guilty," 285, 288; Oedipus's moral, 23; Richard II's, 82. *See also* conscience

conscience: consciousness of suffering in Levinas, 180, 237, 310n. 19; conscious conscience, 242. *See also* conscience; Des Pres

Consolation of Philosophy. *See* Boethius

conspiratorial, 20, 28, 95

contemporary theory, 2

contented, 47, 67, 70, 77, 88–92, 259

covenant, xiii, 106, 129, 189, 302n. 27

creation: alterity of God and, 210; anti-idolatry and, 265; Book of Job and, 8, 173; completion of, 201; Deutero-Isaiah and, 189; expulsion of Oedipus and, 40; in Genesis, 106; Girard and, 311n. 25; Holocaust and, 212; Job's absence at, 168; justice and, 201; Levinas on, 168, 196, 210–11; literary, 44; order to, 177, 187; participation with God in, 191, 201, 283; reading Book of Job and, 212; repentance and, 164–65; responsibility and, 203, 210, 283; revelation of, 7, 176–77, 201; Rosenzweig and, 305n. 34; the Satan and, 207; as separation, 198; speech of God on, 191, 202; as synchronic gesture, 200; suffering and, 187–89, 191, 203; Torah and, 198. *See also* anti-idolatry; Book of Job; Girard; suffering

crisis: of degree, 297n. 56; of historical methodology, 268, 274; imitative rivalry, 36; Judaism and, 182, 188, 205; literature, criticism, and, 258–59; Norwood's, 32; Oedipus's, 33; oracular, 39; Plato and, 261–62; the prophetic and, 200; representational, 30, 34–35, 253; sacrificial crisis, 9, 101, 103, 118, 162, 199, 204, 256–57, 284; Shakespeare and, 94; Theban, 18; tragic, 40

critical reading, xi, 1–5, 10, 126, 131, 172; development of, 245; of Hebrew Bible, 285; literature as, 256; sacrificial dynamics of, 287

criticism: anti-essentialist, 300n. 10; biblical, 122, 156, 172–73, 264–67, 274, 301n. 13, 302n. 31, 304nn. 5, 12, 14, and 17; 308nn. 1 and 6; Bolingbroke's, 79; classical, 22–23, 26, 30, 33–34, 37, 291n. 1, 293n. 33; Culler's, 294n. 53; dramatic, 296n. 25; Frye's, 293n. 41; of humanism, 280; human-

ist, 5, 93; literary study and, xi–xii, 1, 8, 22, 29, 33, 39, 173, 240; literature as, 246–63; new, 3; non-conformist, 293n. 37; Norwood's, 22, 30, 34; nuclear, 317n. 60; prophetic, 176; Renaissance, 294n. 2; rhetorical, 1; of self, 211; Shakespeare's, 43–44, 51–53, 67, 74–75, 79, 85–86, 94, 95, 294n. 1; Sophocles', 294n. 56. *See also* autocriticism; critical reading; critics
critics: classical, 16, 22–24, 27–28, 30, 39, 290n. 1, 291n. 6, 294n. 56; de Man on, 1; deconstructive, 2; formalist, 60; literary, 251, 269; new, 304n. 4; non-conformist, 293n. 37; older versus younger, 3–4; phenomenological, 304n. 4; psychoanalytic, 60; reader response, 304n. 4; of Nixon, 296n. 31; scene of instruction, 209; of Shakespeare, 44, 61, 68, 74, 94; of Sophocles, 252; Yale, 9. *See also under individual names*
Culler, Jonathan, 290nn. 1 and 7, 294n. 53, 297n. 1, 304n. 6
culture: aesthetics and, 122; bereavement and, 243; Christian, 87; civilized, 285; criticism and, 256; demystification of, 106; Enlightenment, 274; European, 88; fundamental questions about, 10; Girard's view of, 182–83, 194; great texts of, 281–82; Greek, 255; Holocaust and, 219, 274–75; Jewish, 121, 128, 151; non-Jewish, 286; origins of, 101; Platonic, 103, 114; prophetic logic of, 102–3, 106; sacrifice in primitive, 39, 257; sacrificial, 108, 114, 199; sacrificial crisis and, 163, 203; scapegoat logic of, 281

David (in Torah), 85, 141, 152, 177
de Man, Paul, 1–6, 9, 241; *Allegories of Reading*, 6; antisemitism and, 285–86; avoidance of reading and, 246; on blindness and insight, 287; *Blindness and Insight*, 1, 290n. 8; collaboration and, 285; deconstruction and, 290nn. 12 and 13; demythologizing and, 288; essentialism and, 285, 300n. 10; ethics of reading and, 284, 287; extremity and, 317n. 67; forgetting and, 285; Goodhart on, 289n. 1, 290n. 14; Hartman on, 286; new criticism and, 290n. 8; reading lesson of, 285; "The Resistance to Theory," 1–6, 289nn. 2–4; silence about early writing, 286–87; tropological and, 287. *See also* conscience; critical reading; death; literary study
death, 284; annihilation of, 279; in Book of Job, 191–92, 210; in Book of Jonah, 144, 152–54, 157; of de Man, 1, 287; of Des Pres, 243; of God in atheism, 237; of Jacob, 138; of Jesus, 108; of Joseph, 115, 117; of Leivick's sister, 231–32, 234, 240, 270–71, 314n. 32; literature, Blanchot, and, 254; in *Macbeth*, 296; mourning after, in Judaism, 164; as movement toward the other in Levinas, 211; in *Oedipus Tyrannus*, 14, 17–18, 28–29, 32; of Primo Levi, 315n. 40; in Psalm 73, 197; of Queen Elizabeth, 43; reading as survivor of, 280; relation to symbolic systems, 201; responsibility for, in Levinas, 201; as scarring in Leivick's anecdote, 235; of subject in structuralism, 277; as theme in Leivick, 314
deathbed confessions, in *Richard II*, 298n. 58, 299n. 58; as freedom from prison of world, 86, 89; of Gloucester, 54–55, 59, 81, 83; of God in Nietzsche and, 48–49, 280; of John of Gaunt, 57–58, 79, 90; of kings, 47, 66–67; the king's two bodies and, 63; relation to being, 87–88, 92–93; of Richard II, 86; Shakespeare and, 93; stillness and, 89
deathcamps, 215, 218, 284. *See also* Auschwitz; Des Pres; Holocaust; shoah
decalogue, 104. *See also* Ten Commandments
deconstruction: Bible and, 183; Book of Jonah and, 152, 158, 160, 167; critics and, 2; de Man and, 6, 9, 290nn. 12 and 13; Derrida and, 262; Job and, 187, 194; Joseph story and, 107, 114, 118; Lacoue-Labarthe and, 217; literary criticism and, 262, 282, 300n. 2, 304n. 4; literature and, xi, 6, 34, 37, 251; Norwood and, 33; *Richard II*

deconstruction *(continued)*
    and, 296n. 20; *Sacrificing Commentary* and, 10
Delphic oracle, 13, 23–25, 33, 35, 71
deposition: double, 42–53; kings and, 65–66; in *Richard II*, 7, 42–43, 47, 50, 53, 58, 68, 74, 249, 252, 257, 295n. 5; self-, 64, 67, 69–70, 77
Derrida, Jacques: conference at Johns Hopkins University, 287; deconstruction and, 6, 9, 262, 277, 281, 290n. 12, 293nn. 40 and 43; on Holocaust, 316n. 50; on Levinas, 178, 308n. 10, 313n. 24; literature and, 316n. 30; on name of God, 302n. 12; on presence, 93. *See also* de Man
Des Pres, Terrence, 215–17, 240, 242–43, 315n. 39. *See also* Holocaust
desire, 238; being and, 88; Bolingbroke's, 82, 84; emulous, 36; Girard's views on, 100, 182, 194; Hegel and, 277; Job and, 183; in Joseph story, 110, 112–13, 117, 264; Leivick and, 224, 233; Nietzschean, 49; Oedipal, 22, 36, 38–39; as philosophic problem, 93; Platonism and, 103; post-Holocaust, 219; prophetic and, 103, 159; unconscious, 39, 60, 103, 159. *See also* mimesis; unconscious
destiny: responsibility and, 180; in Sophocles, 6–7, 14, 22–26, 247–50, 255, 291n. 4; subjectivity and, 93. *See also* fate
Deutero-Isaiah, 176, 188, 191, 197, 205. *See also* Buber; creation
Deuteronomy, 122, 127, 138
diachronic: anti-idolatrous, 266; contemporary thought, 281; continuity, 143, 147, 158, 165, 196, 240–41, 258, 260, 265; creation and, 165; extra-ontological, 287; extremity, 284; Heidegger's being and, 280; historical, 251; Holocaust and, 272, 274; identicality, 82, 263; Job and, 196, 200; Jonah and, 161; literature and, 259–60; mimesis and, 261; Möbius strip and, 156; non-essentialist, 273; non-representational, 9; non-synchronic, 48, 51–52, 259–60, 282; philosophy and, 262; Platonic rationalism and, 261; prophetic and, 200, 206, 301n.

15; reading, 280–81; sacrificial and, 260; Saussurean, 263; sequence, 261; suffering and, 200; symptomatic, 243; witness, 284
difference: analogy, 239; arbitrary, 101; creation and suffering, 187; de Man and literary apologists, 290n. 14; Derrida and de Man, 290n. 12; in dramatic criticism, 296n. 25; Holocaust and, 272, 277; human and murderous, 280; idolatry and divinity, 158; inside and outside, 161; interpretation of Phocial massacre, 291n. 6; Israelites and Ninevites, 155–56, 159, 166; Job and the Satan, 207–9; Judaism and Christianity, 138; king's two bodies, 64; kings and subjects, 67; Latin and Hebrew, 167; Leivick and Levinas, 241–42; in Leivick's anecdote, 225, 227, 239; Levinas and Derrida, 313n. 24; literature and criticism, xi; number and, 41; Old Testament and *tanakh*, 124; Platonic, 103; in psychoanalysis, 38; rational and irrational, 175; repetition, 263; *Richard II*, 44, 49, 51, 67, 84; Richard II and Henry IV, 46, 52, 79; sacred and profane, 162; sacrifice, 199; sacrificial and anti-sacrificial, 261; stage and world, 94; structure of, 29, 263; symbolic exchange, 100; synchronic, 261; textuality, 281; translation, 303n. 34; Tudor myth, 51; violence, 81, 101, 200, 283
Difficult Freedom, 178, 236. *See also* Levinas
divinity: ancient Israelite religion, 127; in Athanasian Creed, 63–64; contrasted with idolatry, 158; in interpretations of Book of Job, 210; *kikayon* as, 154, 163; as king, 76–77, 92; name of, 302n. 31; radical alterity of, 9, 130, 178, 196; the Satan and, 206; tests Job, 171; as violence, 101
doctrine of the two natures, 63
Doren, Mark Van, 44, 252, 295n. 13
Dostoyevsky, Fyodor, 38, 182
"Dostoyevsky and Parricide" (Freud), 38
doubles: in Book of Jonah, 147, 162; Buber, 174; Deutero-Isaiah, 191; "double dying," 217; Girard's views

of, 101, 182; Job's reward, 206; Joseph story, 107, 120; king's two bodies, 62; literature as monstrous double, 253, 256, 259; Macbeth, 53; man and God, 278; of Oedipus in criticism, 35; Richard as "double-fatal," 74, 82; *Richard II*, 43, 47–50, 66, 72, 76, 80

drama: Hebraic biblical narrative, 117, 303n. 32; of humanism, 49; of kingship, 42–43; philosophic, 262; prophetic, 102–4, 118, 159, 174, 200, 263; psychoanalysis, 29, 37–38; sacrificial, 284; Shakespeare's, 52; of sufferer, 67

dramatic irony, 59. *See also* irony

dreams: Holocaust as bad dream, 215–16; *Interpretation of Dreams*, 37, 292n. 14; Joseph's, 107, 110–15, 264; knowledge and, 103; parable of the *kikayon*, 156; parricide and incest, 22; prophetic interpretation, 302n. 30

Durkheim, Emile, 10, 277

ehyeh, 105, 132–34. *See also* name of God

enemy twins, 40, 101

Ephraim, 13, 303

esoteric, 7, 104, 130, 136, 306

Essex, 43, 295

ethics: de Man and, 286–87; Holocaust and, 242–43, 276; Job and, 195; Judaism and, xiv; Judaism and Christianity on, 138; law of anti-idolatry and, 199–200; Levinas and, 134, 168, 211, 283; literature and, 9; reading as, 209, 282, 284, 285, 287; Ten Commandments and, 126–27; witness and, 211. *See also* face; Miller

evil: Boethius on, 87; Book of Job and, 7, 168–212, 283; Jonah and, 143, 149–50, 153, 164; Joseph story and, 109, 112, 115, 117; Levinas on, 168, 237; "lot of man," 23; nothing and, 88, 93; trauma theory and, 272

existential, 88, 175, 200, 207–8, 247, 277

Exodus, 302n. 18; Judaism as thought of, 104; name of God, 104; relation to Joseph story, 114; commandments, 126–27, 132–35; in Dante, 301n. 17

expulsion: in Book of Jonah, 142, 144–45, 147, 162; criticism and, 8, 30, 262; deconstruction and, 262; from Eden, 106; in Girard's thought, 40, 101, 182, 186; in Joseph story, 111, 113, 116; of Oedipus, 37; of scapegoats, 40; theories of sacrifice and, 162; in Torah, 108. *See also* sacrifice

eye, 298; in Leivick, 223–34; light and, 76–77; as pun, 70, 73, 297n. 50

face: ethics and, 134; "face of God," xiii; face to face, xiii, 134, 192, 205–6, 211, 228–29, 240, 242; God's concealing of His, 179–80, 237, 309n. 17, 310n. 17; Macbeth's in Polanski's film, 296; Pole's fist across Leivick's, 223, 225, 228, 233; in *Richard II*, 72, 75, 78; as trace, 242. *See also* Levinas

Fackenheim, Emil, 217, 238–39, 243, 271, 316n. 48

failed mediation, 78, 88, 93. *See also* subjectivity

fate, 6, 22–24, 247–49. *See also* destiny; *moira*

Felman, Shoshana: on *Oedipus Tyrannus*, 291n. 1; on trauma theory and Holocaust, 269, 271, 286–87, 290n. 5. *See also* Laub

Ferguson, Wallace, 45

fiction: Borges and, 306n. 47; criticism and, 250; de Man and, 5; Freud and, 37–38; Girard and, 100; Hamlet and, 94; Hebrew Bible and, 7; Jonah and, 167; Joseph story and, 108, 118; knowledge and, 103, 298; Kolitz and, 309n. 15; Levinas on, 236–37; midrash and, 120; mythogenesis and, 35; Yiddish, 313n. 25

figure: Foucault on, 123; ghost in *Hamlet*, 77; in Leivick, 230–31

Fine, Ellen, 215, 218–19, 241, 312n. 16

Fineman, Joel, 45, 296n. 20, 299n. 62

Fishbane, Michael: biblical criticism, 123, 304nn. 17 and 18, 306n. 45, 308n. 19, 316n. 33; inner commentary, 268, 301n. 14; Torah-centered Judaism, 301n. 11

formalism, 10, 74, 143, 303n. 31

Fletcher, Angus, 43, 295n. 7

Foucault, Michel: Blanchot and, 301n. 17; discontinuity in, 217, 312n. 7; on *Don Quixote*, 315n. 3; on Homer, 315n. 3;

Foucault, Michel *(continued)*
humanism and, 123, 304n. 7; on literature, 246, 249, 253, 315n. 3; on madness, 294n. 51; on Magritte, 315n. 3; new historicism and, 45, 296n. 21; Nietzsche and, 48–49, 277–78, 296nn. 28 and 29; paradigm shift and, 295n. 16; on psychoanalysis, 294n. 52; on Velázquez, 298n. 57. *See also* sacralization

Frankl, Victor, 217, 312n. 8

Fresco, Naomi, 219

Freud, Sigmund: appropriation of Sophocles, 37–39; on biology, 277; contemporary theory and, 277; Dostoyevsky and, 38; on dream as rebus, 112; on *Hamlet*, 249; *Interpretation of Dreams*, 37, 292n. 14, 294n. 47, 302; Lacan and, 277; language and, 172; mourning and, 240; on Oedipal desires, 22; on Oedipus, 37–38; parricide and incest, 36; Platonism and, 103; repetition compulsion, 254, 294n. 46; symptom, 263; trauma, 269, 270, 316n. 48. *See also* acting out; *Oedipus Tyrannus*; psychoanalysis; working through

Friedlander, Saul, 216, 311nn. 4–6, 312n. 23, 316nn. 37 and 38, 317nn. 58 and 63

Frye, Northrop, 293n. 417

galut, 221. *See also golus*

Gans, Eric, 99, 299

Geertz, Clifford, 45

Genesis, 129, 135, 198; creation and, 198; Joseph story, 100, 106–8, 114, 117; Speiser on, 302n. 31, 305n. 34; translations of, 301n. 18, 302n. 26

Gern, Walter, 111

ghost, 66, 69, 77, 94

Girard, René, xiii, 9, 99; absence of discussion of Bible, 123, 303n. 1, 304n. 8; on anti-sacrificial, 260; bibliography of, 289n. 2, 300n. 2; Cerisy colloquium, 299n. 1; on Christianity, 300nn. 4, 7, and 8; on contemporary theory, 287; *Diacritics*, 290n. 1; ethical reading and, 288; Goodhart and, 290n. 1; Hebrew Bible and, 299n. 1; influence of, 99; intellectual biography, 289n. 2; Isaiah 52–53, 189, 310n. 24; Jewish reading of Gospel, 138, 306n. 51; Job, 173, 183–88, 194, 308n. 1, 310nn. 21–23, 311n. 25; journal on, 300n. 4; mimesis, desire, and violence, 100–103, 182–83, 300nn. 5 and 6, 310nn. 18–20; on Oedipus, 290n. 1, 294n. 55; and prophetic, 106, 121; sacrificial dynamics, 199, 256, 262, 300n. 12; science and, 300n. 4; on Shakespeare, 297nn. 52 and 56, 316n. 27; theories of sacrifice, 308n. 20; and tragedy, myth, and violence, 39, 294n. 54. *See also* doubles; enemy twins

globe, 88, 90

God's anointed, 49, 76

Goethe, Johann Wolfgang von, 10, 94

Goldberg, Jonathan, 45, 296n. 20

golus, 234. *See also galut*

Goodhart, Sandor: on biblical criticism, 304n. 5; on de Man, 289n. 1; discussion with Girard and Schwager, 299n. 1; on Girard, 300n. 2; on Isaiah, 310n. 24; on Krieger, 289n. 1; responses to essay on Oedipus, 290n. 1; on trauma theory and witness, 316n. 42

great chain of being, 87, 278. *See also* being

great literature, xi, 2, 88, 249–51, 285, 293

Greek tragedy, 22, 24, 260; the prophetic and, 103–4, 263. *See also* tragedy

Greenblatt, Stephen, 45, 295nn. 4 and 20, 296n. 22

Greene, William Chase, 23, 247–48, 251, 291nn. 1 and 6

Habermas, Jürgen, 216, 311n. 4

hamartia ("missing of the mark"), 14, 23, 33, 291

Hamlet: as meditation on art and nature, 75; being nothing, 94–95; as figure of Richard II's mind, 89; Claudius's confession in, 83; Freud on, 249; mirrors in, 297n. 52; kingship in, 69, 77; remembering in, 94–95; Richard II's language as, 69; Voltaire on, 248, 293n. 37; world as stage, 94–95. *See also* Shakespeare

harmosei ("fit"), 40

Index

Hartman, Geoffrey, xii; on biblical reading, 123, 304nn. 17 and 18; on de Man, 286; on Derrida, 293n. 43; on Holocaust, 275, 312n. 21, 316n. 37; on literature and commentary, 246, 317n. 61; as theorist of reading, 9, 290n. 15; on Walter Benjamin, 220

Hasidism, 104–5, 108, 132, 175, 314n. 38

Hebrew Bible, 6–7; as anti-pagan, 301n. 15; as demystification of sacrifice, 106, 120; Hartman on, 246; prophetic thinking and, 100, 106; reading and, 264, 266–67, 274. *See also* Torah

Hegel, Georg Friedrich Wilhelm, 10, 30; being, 88, 93; as critical philosopher, 45, 52, 248–50, 260, 277, 282; humanism of, 10, 45, 48, 278, 280, 295n. 17; irony, 292n. 19, 315; subjectivity and, 77; on tragedy, 6, 24, 26–27, 248–50, 255

Heidegger, Martin, 10, 255; being, 77, 88, 178, 277, 283; controversy and, 316n. 50; de Man and, 9; deconstruction and, 6, 262; diachronic and, 280; existentialism and, 175; past associations of, 317n. 67; temporality and, 280

hermeneutics, 126, 246, 304nn. 3 and 17; 316n. 33

Herodotean morality, 15

Hertz, Neil, 290n. 14, 294n. 46, 317n. 62

Hertz, Rabbi J. H., 155, 301n. 18, 305n. 27, 307nn. 1 and 16, 308n. 17

Heschel, Abraham, 141, 307n. 5

Hilberg, Raul, 132nn. 11 and 23, 316n. 39; archive, 263; bureaucratic support, 220; functionalism, 268; progressive revelation of Holocaust, 218

Himmler, Heinrich, 280, 317n. 58

Historikerstreit ("historian's controversy"), 216, 273, 312n. 6

Hitler, Adolf, 10, 268, 316n. 38

Holocaust, 215–43; Buber on, 194; as caesura, 312nn. 7 and 19; contemporary being and, 275–76; Des Pres on, 242–43; endless, 240; ethics and, 282; as explosion, 239, 279–80; history and, 273–74; as humanism gone wrong, 238–39, 242; and humanities, 9; intentionalism versus functionalism, 268, 272; Leivick on, 224–29, 231, 234, 238–39, 267; Levinas on, 178–79, 236–38; Nazi war effort and, 317n. 56; reading and, 274, 281; Romanticism and, 277–78; as sacrificial, 264; trauma theory and, 269–73; Wiesel on, 314n. 39; witness and, 263, 270, 284

Huizinga, Johan, 45, 295

humanism: after Auschwitz, 241–42; Boethius and, 86; conflated with nihilism, 238; culture and, 273; de Man and, 286; ethics and, 282; Foucault on, 48–49, 123; God in Book of Job on, 204; Greek, 301n. 12; Holocaust as end of, 277–80; of Job, 186, 225; stake of *Oedipus Tyrannus*, 37; Renaissance, 295n. 14; *Richard II* as, 44; in Shakespeare criticism, 53. *See also* man

Husserl, Edmund, 10

hybris ("arrogance" or "rashness"), 24–26

Idel, Moshe, 305n. 19, 306n. 45, 308n. 6

idolatry: 301n. 13; commandment against, 128–29, 131–32, 301n. 15; Israel and, 139; Job and, 199–201, 206, 209, 211; Jonah and, 154, 156, 158–59, 165; in Oedipus, 30, 34–35, 294n. 56; of Platonism, 99; reading, 200. *See also* anti-idolatry

imaginary, 47, 72, 88–91, 100, 201, 298

infinitely Other, 14, 280, 283

interpretation, 306n. 49; biblical, 266, 274, 301n. 14, 304nn. 14 and 17, 308n. 19; blindness and, 240; of Book of Job, 172, 203; Buber's, of Hasidism, 175; de Man on, 1–6; Girard on, 40; humanist, 7; of Jonah, 140, 145, 160–62, 307n. 7; of Joseph story, 110, 264; literature as, 250; of *Oedipus Tyrannus*, 22, 291n. 6, 292n. 19; prophetic, 302n. 30; Rashi's, of Jacob, 303n. 32; of *Richard II*, 61; sacrificial, 258; Talmudic, in Leivick, 224; of Ten Commandments, 122–38, 305n. 25; of Torah, 124–25, 127–28, 130–31, 136–38; typological, 304n. 16. *See also* criticism; midrash

Interpretation of Dreams, The, 37, 292n. 14. See also Freud

irony: criticism and, 51, 59–60; de Man and, 2; of de Man's antisemitism, 292; in Jonah story, 152; in *Oedipus Tyrannus,* 16, 22; of Leivick's technique, 227; literature's, 250; Richard II's, 70; Shakespearean, 50, 84; Sophocles', 23, 31, 249; tragic, 39, 255

Isaac, 313n. 27; binding of, 106, 111, 117, 148, 207, 221–34; God of, 127, 302n. 21; Leivick, on Job and Isaac, 241; six million Isaacs, 221–27, 231; Wiesel on, 315n. 38. See also Abraham; *akeidah*

Israel: as light of nations, 201; biblical interpretation in ancient, 304n. 17; Book of the Consolation of, 188–91; denounced by prophets, 139; —Deuteronomy 6.4, 122; —Exodus 3.10, 301n. 19; —Exodus 3.10–12, 302n. 24; —Exodus 3.13, 301n. 20; —Exodus 3.14–15, 302n. 21; famine in, 118; *golus* and, 232, 234; Jacob's name, xiii, 106–7, 138; Jonah and, 139–67, 265; Joseph's brothers and, 119; 2 Kings 14.25, 307n. 3; Leivick in, 221–22, 227; Levinas on, 180, 237, 310n. 17; Mechilta, Pesichta Bo and, 307n. 6; one who struggles with God, xiii; Pirkei d'Rabbi Eliezer and, 307n. 6; Psalm 73, 197

Jacob: blessing sons of Joseph, 303n. 32; desires enacted, 264; Esau and, xiii, 102; God of, 127, 302n. 21; in Joseph story, 108–19; Micah 7.20, 150; prayer of, 138; redeemed, 191; *temimut,* 168, 211; wrestling with angel, 106

Jakobson, Roman, 4, 263

Jebb, Richard, 16, 21–22, 247, 291n. 1, 292n. 8

Jerusalem: Book of Jonah and, 163; Deutero-Isaiah and, 190; Henry IV's pilgrimage to, 80, 83; Leivick in, 221, 227, 232, 234–35; Temple in, 163

Jesus: as Messiah, 125, 306n. 48; Girard's view of, 102, 138, 183, 186; Torah and, 138, 305n. 22; typology of, 108

Job: friends of, 283; Girard on, 310n. 22; humanism of, 225, 265; Isaac and, 241; Levinas on, 311n. 29; question of, 283; trials of, 221; Yiddish literature and, 313n. 29. See also Book of Job

Jonah: Book of, 139–67, 307nn. 1–7 and 16; idolatry and, 7; interpretations of, 264–65, 307nn. 6–7 and 16; reluctance of, 7

Joseph: and brothers, 7; children of, xiii, 303n. 32; interpretation and, 264; Jacob and, 303n. 32; story of, 99–121

Julius Caesar, 52, 257, 316n. 27. See also Shakespeare

Jung, Carl, 172, 308n. 1

justice: in Book of Job, 169, 172–212; God of, 127, 149; Heschel on, 141; the human and, 283; Leivick on, 225–26, 229, 237; Levinas on, 134, 237, 310n. 17

kabbalah, 104–5, 137, 266, 306n. 47

kalos ("beautiful"), 22. See also Aristotle

Kant, Immanuel, 10, 52, 77, 248–49, 260, 277–82; aesthetics and, 7, 265, 292n. 19, 304n. 3; critical formalism and, 10; ethical and, 288

Kantorowicz, Ernst, 62–64, 74, 295n. 3, 297nn. 38–48, 315n. 22

Kierkegaard, Søren, 10, 263

kikayon ("gourd"), 140, 153–54, 156–63, 165–67, 265

king: also a man, 61; breath of, 56; deposition of, 7, 42–43; divine right of, 250; dramatization of English, 42; Job and, 183; Jonah and, 144, 149; light of, 297n. 53; *Macbeth* and, 296n. 33; medieval, 257; in *Oedipus Tyrannus,* 16, 29, 31–32; Richard II as, 42–95, 299; as sacrificial, 257. See also absence; death; divinity; doubles; king's two bodies; nothing; Shakespeare; subjects

king's two bodies, 60–66, 85, 250. See also Kantorowicz

Knox, Bernard: challenge to prevailing interpretations, 247; "Gods are deathless," 296n. 30; historical interpretation of Oedipus, 25–27; Oedipus as answer to riddle, 36, 292nn. 29 and 30; Oedipus's search

for truth, 250; Oedipus's suspicions, 20; *Oedipus at Thebes,* 27; Teiresias's response to Oedipus, 20
Kott, Jan, 23, 42–43, 247–48, 251, 292n. 23, 295n. 3

Lacan, Jacques, 178, 277, 287, 296n. 26
Lacoue-Labarthe, Philippe, 217, 262, 312n. 7, 315n. 13, 316nn. 30 and 47
Landis, Joseph, 313n. 25, 314n. 31
Langer, Lawrence, 217, 312nn. 8 and 10
language: de Man on, 1–6, 287–88, 289n. 4; death of God and, 48; deconstructive, 262–63; Freudian, 254; God's, 132–33, 193; Greek prophetic, 30, 35–36; Hegelian, 247–48; Heidegger on, 277; idolatry and, 132; indexical, 218, 220; Job's, 198; Jonah's, 144, 156–57, 161, 167; Joseph's, 111, 114, 115; Judaic prophetic, 103; Kantorowicz on, 62–63; Knox on, 26; Lear's, 61; literary, 123; literature as, 275; monstrous, 271; nature of, 10; non-representational, 263; Norwood on, 16; oracular, 252; prohibition of name of God in, 132; reading and, 280; Richard II's, 54, 56, 59–61, 68–70, 298n. 58, 299; Sophoclean, 283; symbolic, 201; Torah's, 198; of the West, 36, 172
Lanzmann, Claude, 220, 268, 312n. 20, 316n. 39
Laub, Dori, 269, 271, 286–87, 316nn. 40 and 45, 317n. 66. *See also* Felman
law: anti-kikayonic, 159; anti-representational, 132; Covenant and, 106; Decalogue, 133–35, 197, 306n. 43; English Common, 62; ethics and, 288; Job and, 169, 193, 207; Jonah and, 149; Judaism and, 99–121; monotheistic, 132; of Moses, 104–6, 124, 136; old versus new, 109, 124–25; oral, 205; prophetic, 99–121, 207; sacrificial, 125; suffering, creation, and, 196–205; Torah as, 120–21, 160, 196–205, 207. *See also* anti-idolatry; law of anti-idolatry
law of anti-idolatry: anti-paganism, 130; centrality of, 129; Covenant, 106; creation and, 9; as first commandment, 135, 301n. 15; idolatry of, 155–57, 159–60, 208; interpretation of commandments and, 130; Jonah and, 9; Judaism as, 191–98, 203, 265; learning when to stop, 106, 199, 201; monotheism and, 132; prophetic and, 104, 121, 200, 207; radical alterity and, 178, 180; reading and, 200; revelation of, 7; as second commandment, 128; suffering, creation, and, 187–89, 198–205; unpronounceability of name of God and, 134. *See also* law
legein phobous ("speak of fears"), 36
Leivick, Halpern, 8, 221–36, 238–43; biography, 313nn. 26 and 30; evidentiary and, 267–68, 270, 274; Landis and, 314n. 31; oeuvre, 313n. 25; poetry and, 314n. 33; repetition and, 314n. 32; suffering and, 313n. 29; Wiesel and, 314n. 38
Levi, Primo, 243, 286, 315n. 40. *See also* Holocaust
Lévi-Strauss, Claude, 22, 100, 277, 287, 292n. 15, 304n. 13
Levinas, Emmanuel, 8–9, 104, 125, 134, 173; anti-essentialist, 300n. 10; Derrida and, 313n. 24; and ethics, 288; on Holocaust, 221, 236–38, 240–42, 309nn. 16 and 17, 314n. 34; Jewish exegesis, 301nn. 14 and 16; Jewish studies, 305nn. 19, 20, and 32, 308n. 9, 309nn. 10–14, 316nn. 32 and 35; on Job, 168, 178–82, 184–201, 209–11, 311nn. 29–31; and name of God, 302n. 22; otherwise than being, 283–84; on the trace, 263, 312n. 24; on witness, 267
lieutenant, 76, 250, 298
light: at Creation, 165, 198; Job and, 191; mirrors and, 76–77, 297n. 51, 298; of nations, 138, 189, 201; ominous, 275, 284. *See also* king; model
literary: language, 1, 2, 5, 123; theory, 4–5
literary study, xi, xii, 10; Culler and, 294n. 53; de Man and, 285; Foucault and, 246; literature and, xii, 245, 276; sacralization and, 246
literature, 95; anti-mythic, 249; biblical, 168, 171; Christian, 125; commentary and, 246; as criticism, 246, 249–50, 293n. 41; criticism and, 248, 250; de Man on, 290n. 14; as deconstruction,

literature *(continued)*
251–70; departments of, 122; Derrida and, 316n. 30; Freud and, 294n. 46; great, 88, 293n. 37; "historical-critical method" and, 248; humanistic, 93; literary study and, 245; midrashic, 198; philosophy and, 249; rabbinic, 135, 306n. 42; as reading, 246, 250; relation to criticism, xi–xiii, 1–6, 8–10, 34, 37; Renaissance, 42–45; as sacralized narrative, 246; and the sacred, 315n. 4; scriptural, 206; Shakespeare's, 52; of Solomon, 107, 139; study of Sophocles', 26–29; theory of, 246; tradition and, 249; Wellek and Warren on, 245; wisdom, 160, 207; witness, 270, 274–76, 282, 284–85, 289n. 4; writing of, 249; Yiddish, 221, 224, 241, 313nn. 25 and 28. *See also* commentary; criticism; literary study

Maimonides, Moses: on Akiba's view of Messiah, 125; on commandments, 135; as interpreter, 161; on messianic times, 138; on *teshuvah,* 143, 163
man: absence at Creation, 210; alone, 179; also king, 44, 61–62, 93; capacity for destruction, 242; end of, 48–49; expulsion from Eden, 106; exteriority of God to, 180, 182; Foucault on, 278; humanity of, 168, 238; Jonah story and, 155; nothing in place of, 279; Oedipus becomes, 36–37; other, 265, 267, 280; part in Covenant, 106; relations of, with God in Book of Job, 176–77, 191, 198, 202, 206, 208, 210; responsibilities of, 180, 194, 237; science of, 289n. 4; suffering of, 313n. 29; usurps God, 49, 279; Wiesel on, 314n. 38. *See also* humanism
mantic, 20, 26, 28, 33–34, 103. *See also* blindness
Marx, Karl, 10
masterpiece, 16, 37, 39
Marrus, Michael, 312n. 23, 316n. 39
Mauss, Marcel, 100, 277
Mazzeo, Joseph, 45, 295nn. 15 and 19
Mehlman, Geoffrey, 10
memory: collective, 281; enacted in criticism, 250; Holocaust and, 215–20, 311n. 4; Job and, 208; Leivick and, 231–32; Oedipus and, 34; wound as, 241–43
Messiah: coming of, xiv, 125, 145, 167–68, 201; Jesus as, 125, 138
metaphysics, 46, 167; Derrida on, 277, 308n. 10; Foucault on, 278; founding distinction of, 49; Girard on, 92, 185; Kott on, 42
Micah, 149–50
midrash, 108, 120, 128–29, 136, 164
Miller, J. Hillis, 9, 317n. 69
mimesis: criticism and, 253; desire and, 100, 182, 194; hypothesis of Girard, 99, 300n. 4; in Joseph story, 112–14; plague, 30; Plato and, 255, 258–59, 261–62, 300; in *Richard II,* 72, 83–84, 88; rivalries, 138; sacrificial and, 7; substitution and, 117. *See also* violence
mirrors: criticism and, 95, 253, 297n. 52; Renaissance notions of, 75–77, 297n. 51; Richard II and, 71–75, 77–79, 83–84, 93; in *Richard II,* 42–95
Möbius strip, 48, 118, 156, 196, 296n. 26
model: aesthetic, 265; Bolingbroke as, 50; childhood as, 224; collapse of, 77; criticism and, 84, 245; of criticism, 2, 4, 22; Girard's thought and, 99, 297n. 56; grammatical, 289n. 4; Holocaust as, 220, 279, 312n. 19; Job as, 183, 187; Joseph story, part 2, as, 107, 118; king as, 76; literary, 249; mirror(s) and, 76, 93, 297n. 51; of Oedipus, 36; *paradeigma,* 37, 39, 41; of psychoanalysis, 38; of reading, 280; subjects and, 79; Torah as, 198; of tragedy, 16; violence and, 84. *See also* subjectivity
moira ("fate" or "destiny"), 7, 22, 247
monarchical subjectivity, 51, 65, 75–78, 85, 88, 298; as theater, 67
monstrous: being, 93, 95; Holocaust, 238, 273, 280, 286; literature, 253–56, 258–60, 262; Nazism, 242, 286; nothing and evil, 87, 93; Oedipus, 26, 293n. 30; reading, 281; Richard II, 74; subjectivity, 85; thought, 89; writing, 95
Moses: Exodus 3, 104–5, 132–34, 301n. 20, 302nn. 21 and 24; as Job, 177, 211; as

Jonah, 141, 152; at Sinai, 7, 136, 138, 206, 209, 269; Torah of, 104, 124
mysticism: Abulafia, 120; Buber and Scholem, 175, 301n. 14, 305n. 19; criticism and, 251; esoteric traditions of, 104, 125, 175; Job and, 172; Kantorowicz, 62–63; Levinas on, 180–81, 237
myth: Book of Job and, 176, 187, 203, 205–7, 209, 212; criticism, literature, and, xi, 6–8, 44, 46, 51–52, 68, 246, 248–54, 256–63, 282, 293n. 37; de Man and, 288; humanism and, 278–79; of Oedipus, 13–17, 19–22, 24–25, 27–40, 146, 291n. 6, 292nn. 7 and 14; religion and, 123; Richard II and, 89; Tudor, 42–44, 51, 53, 249–50

name of God, 122–38; Exodus 3, 104–5, 132–33, 302n. 22, 305n. 38; kabbalah and, 105, 306n. 47; prohibition regarding, 132–34; Torah and, 137, 264
new historicism, 45, 295n. 17, 20
Nietzsche, Friedrich: critical theory and, 10, 277; death of God, 48–49, 280; Foucault on, 48–49, 277–78; Hegel and, 248; Nazism and, 279; nihilism and, 279; Plato and, 261, 293n. 32; pre-Socratic philosophy and, 255; the prophetic and, 279; Shakespeare and, 95; tragedy and, 262, 315n. 15; Wagner and, 286
Nineveh, 140–45, 147–51, 153–59, 161–63, 165–67, 265
Nolte, Ernst, 216, 273, 312n. 6
Norwood, Gilbert, 16–17, 22, 29–34, 37, 247, 292n. 9, 293nn. 38 and 39
nothing: being nothing, 42–95; Cordelia and, 87; as evil, 87; Henry IV and, 85; the human and, 279; king in *Hamlet*, 69; McMillin and, 297n. 56; memory and, 219; mimesis, violence, and, 84; objects and, 277; Oedipus and, 26, 37, 250; in place of king, 298; Richard II, 47, 50–51, 53–54, 69–71, 74, 77, 91–95; Sartrean, 175; subjectivity, 78, 85, 87–88
number: commandments and, 135–36, 138; in Leivick's anecdote, 234–35; logic of, 39, 41; murderers of Laius, 17–20, 28, 291n. 6; plague and, 13, 35, 37, 41

Oedipus, 6, 13–41; Borges on, 93; dramatic renditions of the play, 292n. 7; Freud on, 292n. 14; Harshbarger on, 292n. 6; compared with Jonah, 146; Jones on, 249; Knox on, 250; like Richard II, 71; myth and, 259–60, 291n. 2; play, 291n. 1; Rudnytsky on, 292n. 16; Sophocles and, 247, 251–52, 256–57; Vellacott on, 292n. 24; Vernant on, 293n. 30
Oedipus Tyrannus, accusation in: of Oedipus, 20; of Oedipus and Creon, 21, 29; of Teiresias, 15, 18, 21
olah ("sacrifice"), 111. *See also* sacrifice
Old Testament, 8, 108–9, 124–25, 171–72, 302n. 27, 305n. 22
ontological, 9–10, 93, 178, 182, 259, 280, 283, 287
oracle: appropriation of, 7, 35; crisis of, 39; at Delphi, 13, 17–19, 23–24, 71; idolatry of, 35, 294n. 56; language, 26, 35, 252; model, 41; riddles and, 37
Orgel, Stephen, 45, 296n. 20

Panofsky, Erwin, 45, 295n. 15
paradeigma ("model" or "example"), 15, 37, 39, 41
parricide and incest: arbitrariness of, 32; Cocteau on, 292n. 7; guilt of Oedipus for, 7, 13, 15, 24, 32, 35, 39, 249; Lévi-Strauss on, 22; Norwood on, 31–32; Teiresias's reference to, 19
Pater, Walter, 43, 61, 64, 295nn. 8 and 9, 297n. 37
Pentateuch, 104, 222
peripeteia ("reversal"), 22
philology, 27, 212
philosophy: as critical spirit, 248–49, 259–60, 279, 282; de Man and, 285, 288, 300n. 10; deconstruction and, 262; the ethical and, 283, 287; humanism and, 281; Levinas and, 283; literature and, 282; logic of the trace, 263; mythic, 251; neo-sacrificial, 257, 261; as the ontic, 283; Platonism, 258, 261; tragedy and, 261–62
Phocis, 17, 21, 30, 32
Pirkei d'Rabbi Eliezar, 166, 307n. 6
plague: *hybris* as, 26; mimetic, 30; numberless, 35, 37, 41; Oedipus as culprit

plague *(continued)*
    for, 36; as oracular idolatry, 294n. 56; as scapegoat violence, 292n. 6; Sphinx and, 250; Theban, 14, 18, 32
Platonism: being like another, 262–63; Christianity and, 87; contrasted with Judaism, 161; criticism and, 248–50, 255, 258, 260–61; essentialism and, 102, 175; Knox on, 27; literature and, 282; mirrors in, 75, 297n. 51; Nietzsche on, 277, 293n. 32; as philosophy, 52; pre-Socratics and, 257; the prophetic and, 103, 159, 175; rationalism and, 26, 102; repudiation of mimetic, 30, 36, 258; responsibility and, 178; synchronic logic, 9; tragedy and, 261
plot: Aumerle's, 80–81; of earth, 57; funereal, 71; Gloucester's death, 55–57, 83; Hamlet's, 94–95; *King Lear,* 87; Oedipus's suspicions, 71; Richard II and, 74–75, 90
Poetics, 14, 16, 291n. 3, 292n. 18, 294. *See also* Aristotle
Polanski, Roman, 52–53, 296nn. 32 and 33
polyzēlos ("emulous rivalry"), 36
Pope, Marvin, 173–74, 308nn. 1, 2, and 4; 311n. 26
post-sacrificial, 40
poststructuralism, 3, 10, 276, 281
power: of art, 16; Book of Job and, 171, 177, 185–87, 189, 191–93, 198; commandment and, 135; of fantasy, 79; of Freud, 22; of gods, 7, 14, 249, 251; of kingship, 50; Lear's, 72; literature's, 251; modalities of, 90; new questions about, 10; of Oedipus, 25; of Joseph story, part 2, 109; relations of, 45; Richard II's, 55–58, 61, 65–69, 73, 92; texts and, 100; of truth, 35; of Tudors, 43; unifying, 302n. 31
presence: of an absence, 77; absence of God's, 176; being as, 277; of dead, 314n. 381; divine, 140, 180, 237; of ghost in *Hamlet,* 94; lacking in Hebrew, 302n. 26; of other in mirror, 93; problem of, 93; as theme in Heidegger, 277; Torah as, 122
prophecy, 139–67; John of Gaunt, 57, 298n. 58; Jonah, 139, 141–42, 145, 149, 164; language, 9; rebus, 167; riddle of Sphinx, 25; suppressing, 144, 152
prophetic, 99–121; anti-idolatrous, 283; biblical reading, 7, 137; Buber, 176, 301n. 13; Buber and Scholem, 175; Carlisle, 90; Chorus, 21; Creation, 198, 204; definition, 102, 159, 200, 284; diachronic, 9, 200, 251, 263, 266, 280–81, 301n. 15; dreams, 103, 302n. 30; ecstatic, 120; excluded middle, 103; explanatory, 102; Freud, 38; Girard, 100, 102, 106, 138, 183, 186–87; God, 104, 106; Hebraic, 106; Henry IV, 85; Job, 174, 195, 204–6; John of Gaunt, 58, 74, 90; Jonah, 139–41, 143, 146–47, 151, 156–59, 166–67; in Joseph story, 107, 110–12, 114–15, 117, 264; language, 30, 35–36, 298n. 58, 299; law, 121, 207; Möbian strip, 118; mode of thinking, 8, 10; Nietzsche, 49, 279; origins, 102; Platonism and, 102; Richard II, 7, 68, 79–80, 90–91, 252; ritual and, 103; sacrificial crisis, 103; Shakespeare, 79; Sphinx, 93; spirit, 159; Teiresias, 250; witnessing, 243
psychoanalysis, 172, 286; criticism of *Richard II,* 60; Foucault on, 294n. 52; Girard on, 99, 3003n. 2; Lacan on, 296n. 26; language, 9; logic of symptom, 263; poststructuralism, 266. *See also* Freud

Queen Elizabeth, 42–44, 46, 59, 62, 68, 295n. 4

rabbinic interpretation: anthologies, 301n. 15; on commandments, 135–36, 264, 306n. 42; exegesis, 7, 104, 266–67; of Job, 171, 177; of Jonah, 141, 146, 148, 154, 265; of Joseph story, 107, 109, 113; in Leivick, 222, 227; of name of God, 302n. 25; prophetic, 115
Rashi: on Creation, 198; as exegete, 161, 267; on Exodus, 305n. 37; on Jacob's blessing of Joseph's sons, 303n. 34; on Jonah, 154, 161; on Joseph story, 109–10; on name of God, 133, 302n. 25
real, 8, 39, 201, 239, 259, 298

redemption, 201, 215, 305n. 34
reluctance: Jonah's, 7, 141, 146, 151–52, 154–55, 161, 265; Satan's, 207
Renaissance, 295n. 3; historiography, 45; humanism, 44, 247, 295n. 14; literary criticism, 294n. 2; literature, 42; mirrors, 75, 297n. 51; new historicism, 45, 247, 295n. 17, 296n. 20; notion, 44–46, 295n. 16; theories of vision, 76
repentance, 139–67; Job, 206, 208, 212; Jonah, 140, 142–46, 148–50, 152–53, 155, 162–67, 265; Pirkei d'Rabbi Eliezer, 307n. 6; *teshuvah,* 198; Yom Kippur, 265
repetition: biblical narrative, 117; Bolingbroke's, 50, 80; compulsion, 254; de Man, 285; Jonah, 146–47, 153; in Joseph story, 113; Kierkegaard, 263; Leivick, 226, 314n. 32; in *Richard II,* 79; sacrificial reading, 258; sameness and, 239, 263; Shakespeare and, 52; traumatic, 240; uncanny, 288
representation: being like another, 262; crisis, 30; diachronic and, 284; domestication, 8; duplication, 112; figuration, 112; imitation, 32, 262; literal, 78; mythic, 51; non-representational forms, 220, 240, 243, 263; prohibition of, 128, 132; synchronic logic, 143, 266; trope, 9
resistance: "The Resistance to Theory," 1–6, 289nn. 2 and 4; theorist of, 9; Warsaw Ghetto, 179, 236
Resnais, Alain, 220
responsibility: accusation, 208; commandment, 283; creation, 210, 284; for death of the other, 201; for European thought, 10; Holocaust and, 215–43; for human behavior, 180, 238, 241; infinite, 280; Job's, 195, 203, 211; Levinas on, 168; for one's own existence, 180; for other individual, 178, 201, 242, 276, 283; personal, 242; for plague, 32; prophetic living, 198; reading, 211; religious existentialism, 175; for sacrificial behavior, 120; for suffering, 181, 210; transcendence, 283; for violence, 240–41, 273; witness, 211

revelation: in Book of Job, 176–77, 181, 187, 196, 201, 206, 211; Christian, 124; of death of Leivick's sister, 234; Girard's view of, 100–106, 186; in Jonah story, 158–60; of law of anti-idolatry, 156, 159; Levinas on, 134, 283; messianic, 201; Mosaic, xiii, 138; progressive disclosure of Holocaust, 218, 230; Rosenzweig on, 305; Scholem on, 316n. 33; scripture and, 7, 266
reversal, 22, 149, 226, 250
rhetorical: de Man on, 2–4, 6, 9, 289n. 4, 290n. 13; deconstruction on, 262: —Isaiah 40, 190; —Job, 192; Nietzsche, 277; Oedipus, 20; *Richard II,* 53, 66; Roman, 248; scriptural, 153; Voltaire, 29
Richard II, 42–95, 298, 299; conception of authority, 7; Elizabeth on, 295n. 4; as monarch, 298n. 58; Schlegel on, 294n. 3; Shakespeare's treatment of, 249–50, 252, 256–57, 259–60; similarities of reign to Nixon's, 296n. 31; speaks the truth, 299n. 58
Robertson, D. W., 45, 295n. 17
Rousseau, Jean Jacques, 241, 286–87

sabbath, 164–65, 201. *See also shabbat*
sacralization, 113, 162, 246, 254, 259
sacred: blood, 59; "first prize," 37; fundamental, 10; Girard on, 100–102, 182; Holocaust, 219; holy, 283; kingship, 61; Levinas on, 104; literature and, 315n. 4; rationalism and, 261; Shakespeare and, 43; theories of, 162
sacrifice (*alah*), 111; burnt offering, 113; difference, 41; expel, 9; Girard on, 39–40, 103–4, 182; Isaac, 221, 223–24, 226, 232, 314n. 38; in Jonah story, 139–67; in Joseph story, 111, 114, 117–20; literary reading, 256; of ram, 241; in Shakespeare, 257, 316n. 28; Serres on, 99, 303n. 34; theories of, 100; violence, 199, 283, 308n. 20
sacrificial: *alah,* 111; in Book of Job, 195, 202–4; Chorus, 7; discussion of Bible, 123; Girard on, xiii, 101–4, 138, 182–87, 194, 199, 311n. 25; Isaiah 52–53, 189; and Jacob, 303n. 32; in Jonah story, 142, 145, 147, 155–56, 159–64,

sacrificial *(continued)*
166–67; in Joseph story, 7, 107–8, 114–21; laws, 125, 300n. 12; Leivick and, 221, 224, 234; literature and, xi, 8; literature, criticism, and, 253–64; Oedipus, 39; Old Testament, 109; post-Holocaust writing, 267–68, 270; Scripture and, 266–67; substitution, 239; Torah and, 106; theory of post-Holocaust writing, 281–85; tragedy and, 36; victimage, xiv; violence, 40
sacrificing, xiv, 8, 83, 101, 284
Sartre, Jean Paul, 77, 88, 175, 178
Satan, the, 171, 182, 203, 206–9, 211, 265
Saussure, Ferdinand de, 4, 10, 263
scapegoat, 36, 101, 163, 184–85, 187, 281, 292n. 6
Scholem, Gershom: on Abulafia, 120; Buber and, 175, 308n. 5; on Messiah, 125; mysticism, 301n. 14, 305n. 19, 308n. 6; revelation and, 316n. 33
scriptural: canonization, 188, 204; excisions, 53; exegesis, 266–67, 274; two-part structure and, 126, 206; use in Yiddish literature, 224; witness and, 275
Scripture: Book of Jonah and, 140, 142–43, 151, 159–60, 165, 167; commentary and, 274; as document, 122; Hebrew, 186, 188; Job and, 211; *kal vachomer* in, 153; law of anti-idolatry and, 104; lots in, 145; as non-Platonic reading, 263; reading and, 264, 266–69, 285; revelation of sacrificial, xiii; Shakespeare as, 43; as *ta biblia*, 140
Serres, Michel, 99, 103, 121, 300nn. 4 and 11, 303n. 34
shabbat ("sabbath"), vii, 164
Shakespeare, William: Essex's rebellion and, 295n. 5; exemplar, 6; humanist reading of, 7, 247, 255; literature, criticism, and, 247–50, 252–53, 255–57, 265, 267; new historical readings of, 295n. 20; non-conformist reading of, 293n. 37; non-Platonic reading, 263; pun on "I," 297n. 50
Shakespeare, William, characters: Banquo, 52–53; Bishop of Carlisle, 44, 65–66, 68–69, 79, 82, 90–91, 298n. 58, 299; Bolingbroke, 7, 42–95, 298n. 58, 299n. 58; Cordelia, 72–74, 87, 95; Exton, 50, 82–84, 299; Hamlet (*see* Hamlet); Macbeth, 52–53, 83, 296n. 33; Prince Hal, 51, 85; Richard II (*see* Richard II); Thomas Mowbray, 47–49, 54–56, 59–60, 72–74, 79–83, 91, 298n. 58, 299
shoah ("annihilation"), 217–18, 221, 243, 268–69, 275, 312nn. 21 and 22, 316n. 39
sin, 23–24, 143, 163–64, 169, 198, 209
Socratic, 27, 103, 159, 255, 257
Sophistic enlightenment, 25, 27, 255, 257, 260
Sophocles: bibliography, 293n. 33; exemplar, 6; literature, criticism, and, 247, 249–52, 255–57, 267, 282–83; non-conformist criticism of, 293n. 37; *Oedipus Tyrannus*, 13–41, 247, 291n. 1; paradox of number, 291n. 6; second stasimon, 294n. 56; text and critical response, 291n. 1
Sophocles, characters: Chorus, 7, 14–41, 250–51, 257, 291n. 6, 294n. 56; Creon, 13, 17–21, 40, 71, 291n. 6; Jocasta, 13–14, 18–21, 35, 37, 252; Cocteau on Jocasta, 292n. 7; Laius, 13–22, 24, 28–31, 35–37, 40, 292nn. 6 and 7; Oedipus (*see* Oedipus); Teiresias, 13–15, 17–21, 29, 35, 38, 40
Sphinx, 13, 25–26, 39, 93, 250
structural linguistics, 4, 100
structuralism, 3, 100, 276, 281, 294n. 53. *See also* poststructuralism
subject: absence of, 277; aesthetic, 265; Bolingbroke as, 51, 80; Carlisle on, 69; contemporary thought and, 281, 283; in deathcamps, 276; deconstruction and, 262; ethics and, 287; Exton as, 82; Fineman on, 299n. 62; Foucault on, 277–78; John of Gaunt on, 73; Girard on, 100; Kantorowicz on, 62; mirrors and, 75–77; Mowbray as, 56; Richard II and, 57, 65–67, 71, 77, 79, 85, 91–92; in *Richard II*, 42–95, 298
subjectivity: Cartesian, 280; Elizabethan, 62, 67, 299n. 62; modern, 77–78, 93, 298; monarchical, 51, 53, 77, 85, 88, 298; phenomenological, 278; Romantic, 277, 281–82, 285–86

suffering: Book of Job and, 7, 172, 184, 193, 201, 208–12, 265; creation and, 188–89, 191, 200, 203–5; Des Pres on, 242; human, 14, 23, 171–72, 176–77, 183–87, 194–95; Jonah and, 150; Judaism and, 191, 195–96; Leivick and, 221, 223, 229, 267, 313n. 29; Levinas on, 179–82, 184, 194, 196, 200, 237–39, 311n. 25; servant of YHVH, 177, 188–89, 310n. 24; Yiddish literature and, 221

symbolic: Girard on, 100; Judaic law and, 201; real and, 39; real, imaginary, 298; Richard II and, 47, 72, 88–89; suffering and, 238

synchronic: Book of Jonah and, 143, 159; diachronic and, 9, 48, 51, 156, 200, 259–60; Heidegger and, 282; Job and, 196, 202, 210; literature and, 251, 259; Plato and, 258, 261; suffering and, 187; Torah and, 266

ta biblia, 123

Talmud: Abulafia and, 120; Akiba and, 125; authority of, 267; Jewish exegesis, 7, 104, 136, 141, 171, 178, 266; legends in, 314n. 38; Leivick on, 224–25, 228; Levinas on, 316n. 32; oral law, 205; on suppressing prophecy, 144, 152

Tanakh, 124, 305n. 24

teimimut ("uprightness"), 168, 211

Ten Commandments, 7, 104–5, 126–38, 197, 264, 301n. 15, 305n. 25

Terah, 128–29

teshuvah ("repentance"), 143, 162–64, 167, 198, 206

testimony: de Man's silence as, 286; of Herdsman, 16, 19, 21, 32; to human destructiveness, 284; Leivick's talk as, 270; logic of witness and, 263; of Oedipus, 19; survivor, 267, 312n. 8; trauma theory and, 273

tetragrammaton, 132–33, 306n. 47

theater, 42, 67, 91, 94, 247

theology: Abrams on, 46, 304n. 3; apocalyptic, 10; Book of Job and, 171–72, 176–77, 225; Bowra on, 23, 27; Christian, 300n. 2; false, 102; Holocaust and, 269; Kantorowicz on, 63–64; Kott on, 42; Levinas on, 180, 237; medieval, 86; onto-theology, 86–87

theory: of biblical reading, 304n. 5; contemporary critical, 48; de Man on, 1–6, 289n. 4; Girard's, of human community, 100–101, 189; of literature, 245; of literature as reading, 246–75; of reading, 8–9; of reading as witness, 275–88; of tragic irony, 39, 292n. 6; of vision, 76

thing: divine, 90; idolatrous, 154; of nothing, 69, 70, 77; uplifted, 111, 113–14

thoughts: of Holocaust victim, 179, 237; of Jonah, 151–52; of Oedipus, 23, 25; of Richard II, 56–57, 70, 73, 86, 88–90

Tillyard, E., 42–44, 249, 252, 294n. 2, 295nn. 13 and 14, 297n. 55

Torah: Covenant and, 302n. 27; creation, suffering and, 191; editions of, 301n. 18; ethics and, 276; exegesis and, 7, 301n. 14; Exodus and, 135; Girard and, 106; interpretation and, 130–31, 266–67; Jacob and, xiii; Jesus and, 305n. 22, 306n. 48; Jonah and, 159; Joseph story and, 108–16, 120; Judaism and, 104–6, 304n. 11; law of, 196, 199; Leivick and, 224–26, 314n. 30; Levinas on, 179, 236; life of, 191, 201; Messiah and, 125; in midrash, 198, 305n. 34, 306n. 47; name of God and, 133; Old Testament and, 124–25; sacrificial cultures and, 108; *tanakh* and, 124; as teaching, xiv; Ten Commandments and, 135–38, 264; translation of, 302n. 26; Yom Kippur and, 164–65

trace: after Auschwitz, 241–42; of divine encounter, 266; of infinite, 280, 283; Levinas on, 221, 238–39, 263, 312n. 24; Torah as, xiv

tradition: Aristotelian, 248, 262; Arnoldian, xi, 246; biblical, 186; of biblical criticism, 116, 302n. 31; Christian, 124, 127, 133, 304n. 16; classical, 22, 35, 37; Coleridgean, 295n. 9; critical, 29, 33, 247, 267; esoteric, 136, 306n. 45; exegetical, 109–10, 140–41, 172, 266, 307n. 4; Hasidic, 105, 132; idealist, 282; Jewish, xiii, 7, 124, 127, 136, 144, 274, 287, 301n. 14;

tradition *(continued)*
  kabbalistic, 105; literary, 172, 294n. 2; medieval humanist, 86; messianic, 125; mystical, 104; philosophic, 172; pre-Homeric, 291n. 2; prophetic, 103; rabbinic, 154, 264, 267, 302n. 25; religious, 274; ritual, 103; sacrificial, 255; scriptural, 275; of Shakespearean criticism, 44; Western, 39
tragedy: Aristotle on, 16, 30, 36; classical views of Sophocles, 22–28, 248; Girard on, 40; Leivick and, 222, 224, 235, 270; Norwood on, 16; of destiny, 14, 250, 291n. 4; Plato on, 30, 36, 255, 261–63; prophetic and, 103–4; Rymer, 293n. 37; Shakespearean, 248; Ure on, 61; Vernant on, 293n. 30; Voltaire on, 28–29
trauma: acting out, 240; Fresco on, 219–20; Freud on, 240, 316n. 43; Holocaust and, 243, 269, 272–74, 278; Leivick, 231, 240, 270–71; price of romanticism, 10; violence as, 8; working through, 254
tropological, 3, 6, 9, 262, 287, 289n. 4
Turner, Victor, 45, 296n. 21
tyrannos ("one who seizes power illegitimately"), 25, 37, 292n. 29

unconscious, 20, 39, 60, 103, 159
"until the conversion of the Jews," 166
Ure, Peter, 44, 51, 61, 67, 74, 86, 252, 294n. 1, 295nn. 12 and 13, 297nn. 35 and 36
usurpation, 44, 46, 49, 53, 80, 82, 160

Velázquez, Diego Rodriguez de Silva y, 78, 315n. 3
Vellacott, Philip, 23–24, 26, 247, 290n. 1, 292nn. 24 and 25, 315n. 6
violence: criticism and, 30; Derrida and Levinas and, 308n. 10; Girard on, xiii, 39–41, 100–102, 138, 182–83, 185–86, 310n. 21; Hamlet and, 94; idolatry and, 199–200; Isaiah 52–53, 189, 310n. 24; Jonah story and, 149, 162; Joseph story and, 117–20, 264; *Julius Caesar* and, 52–53; Leivick and, 225–26, 228–31, 240, 270–71; limitlessness, 37; literature, criticism, and, 253–60; mimesis, nothing and, 87; Polanski's *Macbeth* and, 297n. 33; post-Holocaust and, 283–84; Psalm 73 and, 197; questions about, 10; Richard II and, 84; sacrifice and, 113, 308n. 20; scapegoat, 292n. 6; Sophocles and, 33–36, 252; tragedy and, 39; tragic-prophetic crisis, 104; trauma theory and, 273; witness and, 243
Voltaire, 28–30, 248, 292n. 7, 293n. 34; on *Julius Caesar*, 257; on *King Lear*, 59, 61, 70, 72–74, 87, 95, 248, 297n. 34; on *Macbeth*, 296nn. 32–33; on *Richard II*, vii, ix, 7, 42–95, 249, 294n. 1, 299n. 63; on *Romeo and Juliet*, 68, 297n. 49; on *Sonnets*, 297n. 53

Whitman, Cedric, 23, 247–48, 251, 291n. 1, 292n. 22
Wiesel, Elie, 215–17, 219, 307n. 4, 312nn. 9 and 16, 314n. 38
Wilson, John Dover, 43, 61, 64, 294nn. 1 and 3, 295n. 9, 297n. 37
witness, 215–43; creation and, 210; to the Holocaust, 179, 236–37, 239–40, 243, 263, 271, 311n. 22; Job as God's, 177; Leivick as, 270–71, 274; Levinas on, 267; of Phocial massacre, 13–14, 17–19, 28, 31; reading as, 211, 275–76, 282, 284, 286–87
working through, 240, 269. *See also* acting out

Yeats, 215, 295n. 9, 311n. 3
Yiddish, 8, 221–22, 224, 226, 241, 313n. 25, 314n. 41
Yom Kippur, 7, 134, 143–45, 149–50, 162–65, 265
Youra, Steven, 220, 312n. 22

Zeus, 13, 23–24, 194, 250

Library of Congress Cataloging-in-Publication Data

Goodhart, Sandor.
    Sacrificing commentary : reading the end of literature / by Sandor Goodhart.
      p. cm.
    Includes bibliographical references and index.
    ISBN 0-8018-5084-3 (h : alk. paper)
    1. Criticism.   I. Title.
PN81.G628   1996
801'.95—dc20   95-35210